HOW TO MAKE IT IN THE
NEW MUSIC
BUSINESS

■

HOW TO MAKE IT IN THE
NEW MUSIC
BUSINESS

THIRD EDITION

Practical Tips on Building a
Loyal Following and
Making a Living as a Musician

ARI HERSTAND

Liveright Publishing Corporation

A Division of W. W. Norton & Company
Celebrating a Century of Independent Publishing

For information about permission to reproduce selections from this book, write to Permissions,
Liveright Publishing Corporation, a division of W. W. Norton & Company, Inc.,
500 Fifth Avenue, New York, NY 10110

For information about special discounts for bulk purchases, please contact
W. W. Norton Special Sales at specialsales@wwnorton.com or 800-233-4830

Manufacturing by Sheridan
Book design by Ellen Cipriano
Production manager: Anna Oler

ISBN 978-1-324-09186-8

Liveright Publishing Corporation
500 Fifth Avenue, New York, N.Y. 10110
www.wwnorton.com

W. W. Norton & Company Ltd.
15 Carlisle Street, London W1D 3BS

1 2 3 4 5 6 7 8 9 0

FOR SARAH

CONTENTS

■

PREFACE TO THE THIRD EDITION

■

So, what has changed since the second edition of *How to Make It in the New Music Business?*

Uh, Covid.

But more specifically, what has shifted in the music industry over the past three years? And what have I added to this new edition? Well, for one, TikTok launched global superstars such as Lil Nas X, Megan Thee Stallion, Doja Cat, and Olivia Rodrigo—not to mention the countless other independent artists who saw massive success from the short-form video social network. I will go deep into all things TikTok: how you can be successful on the platform, how others have been successful, how TikTok has altered the global music industry, and where this is all heading.

Independent artists and labels continue to grab a bigger piece of the recorded music revenue pie. And because the majors are losing so much of their market share, they are now offering artists record deals that were unthinkable just three years ago. I will discuss many of these deals, how they went down, and how you can prepare to receive them yourself.

Of course, with the entire live music industry shut down for most of 2020 and much of 2021, artists had to get creative. And to make up for this lost revenue from performance fees and ticket and merch sales—

which of course drives the majority of most performing artists' income streams—most took to livestreaming. New platforms popped up left and right, offering both ticketed and free livestreamed events with lots of monetization possibilities. Since March 2020 there have been over 100,000 livestream concerts across all platforms. So get ready for an entire new section that addresses how to livestream effectively on any platform and breaks down the exact strategies used by the most successful livestreamers in the world.

Whereas in the past I've focused mainly on the American music industry, this edition goes global. The book has been translated into multiple languages, and has been kindly adopted by universities worldwide. So, no matter where you live, I'll explain how best to collect all of your royalties, tour your region, and build a worldwide fanbase.

And in case it wasn't clear in previous editions, I know there are many jobs in the music industry other than recording artist. And this book can be useful for you no matter what career you'd like to pursue in music. But to give some more practical direction to the nonmusicians (and music business students—I heard you, professor!), I've added an extensive chapter on the many other careers that exist in the industry.

Of course, now that NFTs, crypto, and the blockchain have dominated the conversation (and injected millions into the music ecosystem), I spend quite a bit of ink discussing all things crypto. (And if this sentence just made your head spin and you have no idea what I'm talking about, I got you. Keep reading.)

What else? Release strategies have evolved. Email, DMing and text message etiquette have all evolved. Social media advertising and influencer marketing have exploded. TikTokers became a thing. Instagrammers became less of a thing. Success on Twitch became a thing. Twitter and Snapchat became more niche. And Facebook, I mean Meta, I mean Facebook, I mean, whatever, Zuck.

Press isn't what it once was. There is now an entirely new strategy on how (and why) to approach media and press.

The Music Modernization Act (in the US) finally got implemented and the Mechanical Licensing Collective (MLC) began collecting and distributing hundreds of millions of dollars in mechanical royalties to publishers and songwriters. I discuss what all the new revenue streams are and how to make sure you're grabbing all of the money out there that's owed to you.

This third edition is far more extensively updated than the previous one, with new amendments in every chapter. Over the past year, I conducted over 100 interviews with the movers and shakers of the industry (many you can hear as part of my new podcast, the *New Music Business*). I've continued to keep up with the goings on in the industry (so you don't have to!), and have tried to stay ahead of the curve. I've added newer, smarter, more efficient techniques that others have utilized successfully, and am thrilled to share a bunch of recent examples of independent artists kicking butt on their own (and how they're doing it). So even if you've devoured the first two editions ten times over, I encourage you to spend some time with this new edition.

As for me, I launched a 1970s funk/soul immersive concert experience with my project Brassroots District, released my first solo album in seven years and ran the UnCancelled Music Festival, which raised over $100,000 in ten days for hundreds of musicians and venues in the weeks directly following the live music shutdown. I got a crash course in politics when I helped change (and rewrite!) California's gig worker law, AB5, by lobbying politicians, negotiating with unions and lawyers, and appearing on news programs across the country. I ran the three-day, four-night songwriting camp and conference, SongCon, in NYC, hosting songwriters from all over the world. I developed and launched a handful of new courses for Ari's Take Academy, which now has over 5,000 students. Crossed 100 episodes on the *New Music Business* podcast. And I got married.

I'm staying active in music so I don't lose touch (and because, well, it's my entire life and my soul won't allow me to do anything else). And I am keeping up with the ever-evolving landscape so that I can help guide today's musicians. Wherever you are at on your journey, you now have a partner along the way.

We're all in this together!

—Ari Herstand, August 2022

AUTHOR'S NOTE

■

Before you dig in, I need to point out that everything in this book is based on my own experiences or what I've learned from others in the biz. And even though things worked out a certain way for me and others I reference in this book, uh, *results may vary*. Also, I'm a musician, not a lawyer. Please don't use this book as a guide to drafting contracts or navigating legal matters. It's not meant for that. Definitely consult an attorney for all legal issues you may have, and be sure to check out "Some Words of Caution (and Other Stuff You Really Need to Read)" on pages 580–83.

Also, without fail, things in the music industry will have changed by the time you're reading this. Companies may get acquired, laws may get passed, revelations may be made.

HOW TO MAKE IT IN THE
NEW MUSIC
BUSINESS

■

INTRODUCTION

■

JANUARY 15, 2008, WAS THE GREATEST DAY OF MY LIFE. IT WAS THE DAY I walked into the Minneapolis City Center Starbucks, shook my manager's hand, handed him my green apron and made my final triple tall, nonfat, with whip-caramel macchiato.

It wasn't dramatic. I didn't tell my shift supervisor off or chuck an iced pomegranate green tea in his face—like I had dreamed of many a time. There wasn't a big send-off. No parade down 1st Avenue. My manager asked me what I was going to do. I told him that I was a musician and that I was going to make it.

He thanked me for my work and told me that there would always be an apron with my name on it if I needed it.

Luckily, I never did. Well, actually, luck had nothing to do with it.

People always ask successful musicians what their lucky break was. And most don't have an answer. They mention a few instances here and there that, in retrospect, were turning points or little victories. But very seldom do you hear, "We were playing the Fine Line and after the show a bald man in a suit came up to us, handed us a record contract and told us it was our lucky day."

That is what everyone outside the music industry expects. No one really understands the music business. The songwriting process eludes people. But, even more so, the business confuses the hell out of everyone—musicians included.

I had been fortunate enough to take to the business early on.

I went to the University of Minnesota as a music education and classical trumpet major. Since eighth-grade band class, I thought I wanted to be a high school band director—like Mr. Saltzman (whom I wrote a song about on my first record). But my freshman year of college, that all changed.

I had been in a ska/funk/rock/jam/pop band (we had an identity crisis—more on that later) all four years of high school. I mostly played trumpet and sang backups. All six of us went to different colleges around the country. I was the only one who ended up in Minnesota. The first week of school in my dorm when everyone's door was closed, I planted myself in the floor's lounge with my acoustic guitar and started riffing. Someone walked by, poked her head in and said, "That's cool." Then walked off. (That song turned into one of the first I ever wrote, "Rose Stained Red.")

I wrote a bunch of songs those first few weeks on piano and guitar. I spent more time in the practice space of the music building writing songs than practicing my trumpet.

When a group of friends and I stopped into the European Grind coffee shop on campus where a singer/songwriter happened to be performing, I asked the barista if I could get a gig. He opened up the calendar book and said, "How about October 12? You get all the coffee you can drink."

My roommate (who was also a music major—we lived in the arts dorm) had a superfancy digital camera. He took a photo of me playing guitar, and I printed up a bunch of 8.5 × 11 black-and-white flyers and put them all over the music building and my dorm. My very first concert as a singer/songwriter, at the European Grind, was packed (with about 35 people).

My roommate, a cellist, performed the show with me and recorded it on his MiniDisc recorder. For those of you who have no idea what that is, it was like the Talkboy in *Home Alone 2,* except it ran on a digital Mini-Disc instead of a cassette and was much better quality. These were hot for about twenty-seven months.

Listening back to the show, I realized that I didn't suck too bad. Everyone there seemed to enjoy themselves and the manager of the European Grind asked me back!

A few months later, I found myself in the music section of a Barnes & Noble staring at the bright yellow *All You Need to Know About the Music Business* book by Donald Passman. I bought it and finished it that week.

I had found my calling.

I sat my parents down that spring and told them that I was not going to be a band director and I was not going to finish at the University of Minnesota. I had found a contemporary music industry school in St. Paul and told my parents I was going to transfer there. With credits transferring, I got in and out in three consecutive semesters, one science credit away from an associate degree in music business (from a school which has since gone under).

While at the music industry school I worked my a$$ off. I never skipped a class. I was never late (even to the 9 A.M., three-hour music economics class). I went to office hours of all my teachers (they were all musicians or ex-industry heads—not sure if I can call them professors). Contrast that with my music education studies at the University of Minnesota, where I skipped half my classes, rolled into my 8 A.M. (classical) music history lecture well into the Baroque era hung over, and cheated off of my roommate on virtually every test.

When I graduated in August of 2005, I got to work on my first solo album. In December of that year, I released it to 250 people at the Varsity Theater in Minneapolis.

I became a force on the University of Minnesota campus. From sometime around that CD release show to when I left Minneapolis for L.A. in 2010, I was one of the most popular musicians on campus (and in the Twin Cities). The U had about 40,000 undergraduate students, so it wasn't a bad market to start with. However, the music editor for the *Minnesota Daily* wasn't feeling what I was putting out. He wrote three hate pieces on me in one semester. He despised my presence so much that in the fall of 2008 he listed me in the top three worst bands of Minneapolis (I was #1). Ironically, the top three "best" bands broke up shortly thereafter, and the "worst" three bands all went on to have successful careers. He then wrote a scathing album review of my 2008 release, which garnered some of the most comments of any *Minnesota Daily* article on the website and finally, I made the cover of the December Joke edition next to Lindsay Lohan and the president of the University of Minnesota. My headline? "Surgeons' Attempt to Reattach Local Musician's Balls Fails."

As these articles were pouring out from the desk of a writer who will go unnamed, I was filling the 800-seat Varsity Theater, had just opened for Ben Folds in front of 3,200 people and had begun a massive college tour that paid incredibly well. I had received about thirty other positive reviews that year in papers around the country, but, of course, I can pretty much recite the *Minnesota Daily*'s hate pieces word for word.

Managing my career all on my own from the beginning, booking 100 percent of my noncollege shows and tours (we'll get to college agents in Chapter 9), getting songs placed on multiple TV shows and starting an artist development company where I helped manage another Minneapolis band, I became the go-to person in the Minneapolis music scene for music business advice.

I moved from Minneapolis to L.A. in the summer of 2010. I had done all I could in Minneapolis. The scene was imploding on itself and some of my favorite bands were breaking up. I needed a change. I didn't choose L.A. because of the industry (however, it didn't hurt); I chose it because of the winters.

Many of you are reading this book because you've read some Ari's Take articles. I started Ari's Take for the same reason I wrote this book—to help musicians succeed in the music industry.

And regardless of whether you want to be a musician or not, everyone working in the New Music Business needs to put themselves in the modern musician's shoes. Artists and songwriters are at the heart of the music industry. If you don't understand what we go through, you won't be effective no matter what lane you choose to pursue in the industry. Chapter 16 is wholly devoted to the various professions one can pursue in the music industry other than recording artist (there are over 100!). But for the majority of this book, whenever I say "you," pretend you're an artist or manager, or need to assist one. Because at some point, on some level, everyone working in music does.

Over the course of my career I've had to learn everything the hard way. My education at the music industry school was great. I learned how things used to work in the music business. I got some great history. But I realized very quickly that the old tactics and ways of the biz don't work in today's industry.

We're in a very exciting time. In 2021, DIY, self-released artists earned more than $1.5 billion just from recorded music alone. And Spotify reported that in 2021, over 16,500 artists made over $50,000 just from Spotify revenue. These numbers showcase that it's not just a few anomalies, but a global trend. Never before in the history of the modern music industry have independent musicians been able to sustain healthy, long-term careers on their own—without the help of a record label.

Every day, the path to success is being realized on roads not yet paved.

Ingrid Michaelson cracked the *Billboard* Hot 100, has been certified Platinum and consistently performs for thousands a night around the world. She has self-released every digital song/album since day one. Ron Pope also self-releases his music and has over a billion streams from over 2 million monthly listeners and plays sold-out venues around the world. Amanda Palmer broke a Kickstarter record when she made $1.2 million on her campaign. She has since made over $1.6 million directly from her fans via Patreon and currently receives $50K+ a month from her fans on the platform. Chance the Rapper's music has been streamed over 5 billion times. He was #7 on the *Forbes* 30 Under 30 music list for 2015. And he made history as the first artist without a label to play *Saturday Night Live* and win the Grammy for Best New Artist. Lauv also has over 5 billion streams, cracked the *Billboard* 200 and the *Billboard* Hot 100, has been certified Platinum and headlined arenas all across Asia and has performed on *The Tonight Show*. Brent Faiyaz has over 10 million monthly listeners, has made it on the *Billboard* Hot 100 and has been certified multi-Platinum. Tom Misch has gotten over 500 million streams with 4 million monthly listeners and performed at Coachella music festival in 2018. R3HAB has over 18 million monthly listeners and performed at the Electric Daisy Carnival (EDC) festival.

3Lau made over $11 million on his NFT drops in early 2021. RAC made more money from his fans via Twitch and Patreon in 2020 than he had projected to make from his full nationwide tour (canceled because of COVID-19) and has made $1 million to date on his NFT drops. Lucidious has over 200 million streams and 500,000 monthly listeners without any of his songs on official Spotify playlists.

Lil Pump made over $500,000 in two hours from 859 investors from his new single, "Mona Lisa" (feat. Soulja Boy) via a blockchain-powered crypto investment (and NFT) platform. The investors not only own an NFT, but will receive royalties from the single.

Zoë Keating's music has been featured in countless commercials, TV shows, video games and films. She reached #1 on the *Billboard* classical charts. Peter Hollens built a video empire, amassing over 2.7 million YouTube subscribers, 1 million Facebook followers, 3 million TikTok likes and over a billion total views—without ever leaving home. He now runs his own record label. Scott Bradlee, with his musical collective, Postmodern Jukebox (PMJ), has over 5.5 million YouTube subscribers and 2 billion views. PMJ tours the theaters of the world with multiple rotating casts (sometimes performing in different cities on the same night!). UK-based singer/songwriter dodie created a massive following on YouTube with her quirky songs and personality. She cracked the *Billboard* 200 (and ten other *Billboard* charts), and now has over 2 million YouTube subscribers, 500,000 TikTok followers, 1 million Twitter followers, and 1 million Instagram followers, with half a billion collective views, and sells out headlining shows around the world. Justin Vibes consistently goes viral on TikTok playing the vibraphone. He now has over 8.5 million followers, 105 million Likes and a healthy revenue stream from sponsorship and brand deals. The Puerto Rican hip-hop artist Bad Bunny initially gained popularity on SoundCloud, but quickly found mainstream success collaborating with Cardi B and Drake. He performed at the 2020 Super Bowl halftime show and has gone Platinum multiple times, topped the *Billboard* 200 and Hot 100, and has billions of streams from around 50 million monthly listeners. Joey Bada$$ initially went viral on YouTube with a freestyle rap. He has collaborated with Mac Miller, Action Bronson and Kendrick Lamar, hit the *Billboard* R&B/Hip-Hop Albums chart and has 7 million monthly listeners and over half a billion streams.

Mothica built up a dedicated following on TikTok, releasing regular, candid videos. One of those videos featuring a new song went viral, with thousands of people using the song in their own TikTok videos. She now has over 2 million monthly listeners and runs her own record label. Clare Means reached #1 on the iTunes Singer/Songwriter charts, was once the most popular musician on (the now-defunct livestreaming app) Periscope, and currently makes a good living livestreaming. Vo Williams has over 1,500 placements of his original music in film, TV and video games, and had his music used as the season theme songs for both the Milwaukee Bucks and Tampa Bay Lightning the years they won championships. He now runs his own sync licensing company. Vulfpeck has millions of streams, performed on *The Late Show with Stephen Colbert* and sells out headlining shows all over the world—including Madison Square Garden.

The husband-and-wife duo aeseaes play to 40,000 people every month on the livestreaming platform Twitch and have become one of the most successful music channels on the platform. They earn more now from their livestream community than their previous full-time, 9-to-5 jobs combined. They raised nearly $50,000 on Kickstarter for their 2021 album and have hundreds of Patreon supporters who pay them a flat amount every month on top of their 2,000 "subs" on Twitch.

The thing that all of these artists have in common is that they created their own musical career path and refused to follow the traditional method of signing to a major label—surrendering their fate to the powers that be. These artists aren't household names, but they are making it work. And making it work well.

Your uncle Joe will continue to ask you when are you going to try out for the latest singing-contest TV show. Your seatmate on the plane will ask you when they're going to hear you on the radio. Your parents will ask when are you going to grow up and get a "real job." Because they don't understand this new world.

Making it in the New Music Business is not about lucky breaks. It's about hard work. If you want to succeed in music, you have to work harder than everyone else. You have to want it more than everyone else.

If you want to make a living in music, you're going to need to be comfortable doing multiple kinds of jobs that may not fall rigidly in line with your vision (as it is now). When musicians tell me "But I just want to write songs and play music, I don't want to do any of this business stuff," I want to scream *"Yeah, me too!"*

I didn't get good at the business because I love it. I got good at the business side of my music career because I believe in my art so much that I knew if I didn't I wouldn't succeed.

No one is going to handle your business for you. At least not yet. And even when managers, labels, attorneys, agents and sponsors do start knocking, you should know what to expect of them. You should know where they all fit into your business. Never hand off part of your business to someone just because they ask. Hand off part of your career when you have to. When it's more than you can handle. When you know exactly what needs to get done, how it needs to get done, but you just don't have the time (or resources) to do it yourself.

Eventually, you will be at a point where people are pounding down your door begging to work with you. By that point, you will know where you could use some help and what to pass off. But you'll also have a strong handle on how to run your business on your own. You will always be the one in control. You make all the decisions. Never forget that your team works for you. Without you, they have nothing.

But you're a long way from a team.

You have to build up the demand first. The days of the "big break" are pretty much over. A music career is now a slow, progressive upward slope. If you persevere, you will eventually be able to sustain a comfortable lifestyle, earning your income from doing something you love. If you're looking for quick fame and instant success, you're in the wrong field. There are a lot easier ways to get famous. Go make a sex tape or something.

This book is intended to give you the concrete steps you should take to rise to a level of success where you are making a good living doing what you love. You can get there. It won't be easy, but if you love it enough, and work hard enough, it will happen. I will show you how.

1.

WHY MUSIC?

For Love or Money (or Sex)

It was never about fame back then.
We just thought about what gave us goosebumps.
—QUINCY JONES

Music is not different from life. I think that's probably the
greatest attraction to those of us who play music.
—HERBIE HANCOCK

If you're a songwriter, you're always writing songs. It's not a choice
you have. It's an affliction.
—CHRIS STAPLETON

If you don't love the process and you're only looking for the
success of it, then I guarantee that the success will never come.
Because you gotta aim at what's in front of you in the moment.
—DAVID HODGES, 60 MILLION ALBUMS SOLD

BEFORE YOU INVEST EVERY LAST PENNY OF YOUR SAVINGS, DESTROY
your relationships and hop in a van with four other smelly dudes or
dudettes for two months, step back and ask yourself why you want to be
a musician. This may seem like a dumb question at first glance. But it's

the most important one you will ever ask yourself. And it will define the course of your life.

"Because I love music" is not the answer you're looking for. I love Thai food. But I don't want to eat it every day for the rest of my life. A music career, unlike most other careers in the world, requires more than just a passing enjoyment. A music career requires a passion like no other. A drive that will sustain you through the months of eating PB&J and begging your landlord for a break on this month's rent.

After seeing the 2001 Cameron Crowe film *Almost Famous*, I thought a music career was all parties, tour buses, "band-aids" who looked like Kate Hudson, and sold-out arena shows. Who *wouldn't* want to be a musician if that was the life? The reality is, a music career *can* have these perks, but most of the time it entails working sixteen-hour days, skipping the parties to book a tour or practice your instrument, trekking through blizzards to put up posters for your shows, convincing your friends to pay $10 for an 11:30 P.M., 25-minute set at a dingy bar on a Tuesday, soliciting playlisters and influencers on Instagram and TikTok, and spending hours tweaking your social media ads to lower your cost per click. But it will all be worth it when you step out on stage to a packed house for 25 minutes of bliss.

Those who enter music to become famous fail. Not to say that those who have the vision of world domination fail. You need lofty goals and unwavering confidence to succeed in such a difficult field. But fame, in and of itself, will not sustain your drive. Fame should be looked at as an occupational hazard to a music career.

Many guitarists picked up the guitar to impress a guy or girl. I know I did. It worked. I got the girl. But she didn't last. The guitar stuck, though. And I quickly realized that my love of the guitar (and music in general) kept me going long after the thrill of impressing a girl faded.

Hobbyists play the guitar to impress people. Musicians master their instruments to feed their soul.

You must decide early on what kind of artist you want to be. You should please yourself first and always. Don't write music you think people want to hear. Don't play songs you think people want to hear. Yes, it's important to create entertaining shows, but if you bend every which way to attempt to please every single person, you'll forget which way is up and tumble over. Do you want to be in a cover band and play to hordes of drunk people singing along? Then, yes, you do need to play the songs people want to hear. And you could make a decent living doing this. But this book isn't about how to succeed as a cover band. And I presume you have loftier goals than the local cover circuit. To succeed as an original artist you have to pave your own path.

Following musical trends to adjust your production is not the same as writing songs you think people want to hear. If you're true to your art, the fans will come.

The most important thing you should remember is to be authentic. If you're a goofball, be a goofball. If you're an angry introvert, be an angry introvert. The reason fans connect to artists on a deep, spiritual level is because artists bring truth. Artists have a unique way of telling a story that's both relatable and personal. From the beginning of time, artists have looked at the world differently and revealed their compelling visions through their creations. And from the beginning of time, audiences have enjoyed experiencing these special creations.

Before you embark on this crazy journey that is a music career, you must understand that you may not receive much support from your family. Maybe you know that and it's *why* you've chosen this field. Maybe music is your family. Maybe music is the only love in your life. Great. But if you seek your family's approval, you won't get it with music, most likely. Your family will not understand your career. Most of the world doesn't understand the music industry. Everyone you meet will ask you "So are you trying to be a musician?" without actually understanding how truly insulting (albeit innocently naïve) a question that is. There's a great scene in the 2014 film *Whiplash*. If you haven't seen it yet, go watch it immediately. It's one of my favorites. The protagonist, Andrew Neiman, is a nineteen-year-old jazz drummer in the top music school in the country. At the dinner table with his father, aunt, uncle and cousins, his aunt and uncle brag about their sons' success. One is the star football quarterback for his (Division III) university and the other is in the model UN. They ask Andrew, "How's the drumming going," and he tries to explain that he is doing really well, but no one at the table understands what that means. "Will the studio find you a job," his uncle barks. Eventually, Andrew gets fed up defending his career choice and takes jabs at his cousins' seemingly trivial little victories of touchdowns and school records and chides that the NFL is never going to call his quarterback cousin. His uncle asks, "Got any friends, Andy?" Andrew replies, "No . . . I never really saw the use."

The uncle continues, "Lennon and McCartney, they were school buddies." Andy bites back: "Charlie Parker didn't know anybody until Joe Jones threw a cymbal at his head."

"So that's your idea of success?"

"I think being the greatest musician of the 20th century is anyone's idea of success."

Andrew's father chimes in: "Dying broke, drunk and full of heroin at 34 is not exactly my idea of success."

Andrew protests, "I'd rather die drunk, broke at 34 and have people at a dinner table talk about me than live to be rich and sober at 90 and nobody remember who I was."

Even though Andrew is a jazz drummer, this brilliantly sums up every conversation every musician has with their family at some point in their lives. Even Andrew's father tries to be supportive, but he just can't understand why Andrew wants to pursue a career that's so emotionally taxing, with no clear path to sustained success.

It's one of the first big hurdles we all need to get over. Even though I've been a professional musician for fifteen years, my parents still hope (secretly) that I'll become a lawyer or a doctor.

WHAT DOES MAKING IT MEAN?

Making it is survival. If you can survive, you are succeeding.
—BRUCE FLOHR, ARTIST MANAGER/A&R, SWITCHFOOT,
ALLEN STONE, THE BAND PERRY, DAVE MATTHEWS BAND

The idea that someone just has "it" is a myth that we put on those that we think are great. It's almost an excuse, to ourselves, to not try hard.
—ANDY GRAMMER

The only difference between success and failure is whether or not you stop.
—OAK FELDER

That's the subtle sickness of material success. There is no enough.
—WILL SMITH

A lot of people to whom I mentioned the title of this book asked me how I could write a book called *How to Make It in the New Music Business* when I haven't made it. The gall! But, I see their point. I've never reached the level of Super Bowl halftime performance fame that penetrates the world they live in. Maybe I will, maybe I won't. But that doesn't matter. "Making it" is defined differently by everyone. To those outside the industry, "making it" means superstardom. If you want to be a superstar, you need a boatload of money, provided by either a label or an investor. And even then, it's no guarantee. But to make it as a full-time musician just takes lots of hard work. By the time you're finished with this book, you will have a clear idea of how you can make it as a full-time musician. Some of you will go on to be world-conquering superstars, and some of you will make solid livings as regional musicians. Neither is "better."

I love coffee. There's this great boutique coffee and doughnut shop in New Orleans where I have been spending most of my time writing this book. It's not a big chain. But the owners are super cool, the employees all seem to enjoy themselves and they seem to be doing solid business. They have been in this same spot for the past ten years. But because they're not Dunkin' Donuts, have they not made it? I would say they have.

What about the local bookstore with eight employees that's been around since the seventies and is well respected in the community? Since they're not Amazon, have they not made it?

Or what about the online boutique clothing line that nets $1 million a year? Because they're not in Nordstrom or Macy's, have they not made it?

For some reason, music seems to be one of the only professions where the sole definition of "making it" is superstardom. If your uncle Joe's coworker hasn't heard of you, then you haven't made it in his eyes. Well, your uncle Joe's coworker hasn't actually heard of hundreds of bands you would probably deem to have made it. It's all relative.

Your goal should be to sustain as a full-time musician. The "big break" you're waiting for will never come—if you just wait for it. If you want to succeed you must put in the work. I know you're saying to yourself right now, "But, Ari, I'm different! I'm better than everyone else. I *am* a superstar and 'they' will find me!"

First, though, you need to define who "they" are. Do you even know? A label? Which label? Specifically. And why that label? Or is it a manager you're waiting for? Will any do?

The thing is, too many musicians are waiting for those with the answers to come a-knockin', without actually knowing why. If the reason you're waiting is because you don't want to put in any work for yourself, then you should just throw in the towel right now. Because even if Capitol Records somehow stumbled on you singing in a bar and said to themselves "This is the next big thing," you would *still* need to put in a hell of a lot of work. But the thing is, Capitol Records doesn't seek out talent in bars anymore. And even if they did, you'd have to virtually sign away your entire life to work with them because you have absolutely no clout. And no negotiating power.

I won't deny that a label, at the right time, can help. But not any label. And not too soon.

I'm going to reveal a startling statistic. Over 98 percent of all acts who sign to a major label will fail. Meaning, 98 out of 100 acts major labels sign this year will not recoup their advance and will be dropped. So even if you somehow get a major record deal, the odds are against you that you will be in the 2 percent. Major labels promise the world to *every* act they sign. And, for the most part, they have good intentions when they sign each act. However, people move in and out of labels all the time. So even if the head of A&R at Columbia Records signs you tomorrow and promises you the full weight of the label, she might be replaced next week, and the new CEO may not give two sh*ts about you and drop you—not without refusing to release your masters (or rights) back to you unless you pay them every penny they had invested in you at the start, of course.

But, "getting discovered" is a fantasy of our parents' generation. It doesn't happen like that anymore. Well, sure, Rihanna was "discovered." But that's the one in a million. You're better off buying a lottery ticket and funding your career that way. If you actually want a career in music and don't just want to be famous, you have to work for it. Labels typically don't want to sign unknown artists. They're too much work (and money) to develop. Labels mostly want acts that are proven, have a fan base and are making things happen on their own. Of course we can point to the exceptions, but again, they are the exception. Not the rule.

You don't want a record deal. At least not yet. You want to build your career to the point where every label is pounding down your door begging to work with you. And then, at that point, you can decide if you're better off continuing to go at it on your own, or signing.

You have officially "made it" when you're using your creative talents to pay all of your bills. Not when you perform the Super Bowl halftime show.

THE PURPOSE OF THE DAY JOB

> If you're a songwriter, you want a job that takes your body
> but not your mind, because you want your mind for writing
> songs. And if you work in an office, it takes your mind.
> —DR. DON CUSIC, PROFESSOR OF MUSIC BUSINESS,
> BELMONT UNIVERSITY

I'm going to be asking you "why" a lot in this book because so many people just get caught up in a routine of "how it is" or "how it's supposed to be" that they rarely question why it is they're actually doing something. And if it's truly the best course of action. There's not a single musician on the planet that I know of who has never worked a "day job." I've had quite a few. Every single musician currently working a day job dreams of the day they can quit. Every time I got a drink sent back for not being hot enough or too sweet or not sweet enough, I was another inch further out the door.

Why do you have the day job you have? The answer should be to make enough money to live on while you're building your music career. It should not be to grow in the company. Or to be able to have money to go clubbing on the weekends. Those are the normal person's reasons. We're not normal people! As Zig Ziglar said, "The chief cause of failure and unhappiness is trading what you want most for what you want right now." Print out this quote and tape it up in your bedroom.

Treat yourself to luxuries when you've quit your day job and are bringing in enough money with your music to afford them. If you raise your standard of living to match the fat paycheck that you're getting from your day job, it will be that much more difficult to strip it back down when you actually quit and have to live conservatively on your music income. You're not going to jump from a day job into a million-dollar record label advance. Get rid of that fantasy. You're going to quit your day job when you are making enough money with your music to pay your bills and eat.

Yes, there are some jobs that actually can assist in your music career. If you can land one of those, that's of course ideal. I've seen musicians get in on the ground level of video game companies and eventually get promoted to full-time composer. Their dream job. But I wouldn't consider this a day job. This is an opportunity. A day job, by definition, is a way to make the money to fund your passion. Ideally, you'll find opportunities, which pay well, are enjoyable and keep you inspired.

In 2021, once the shock of the COVID-19 lockdown subsided, people began reevaluating their lives and having "pandemic epiphanies." And the Great Resignation took hold. More people quit their jobs than ever before on record.

You don't need to take a day job that will make you unhappy, uninspired and disrespected anymore. Either take a day job that pays well, has flexible hours and leaves you open and inspired to kick your music career into gear or, better yet (for some), freelance. Now more than ever it is easier to find freelance work—no matter what your skill set. Lyft, Uber, Postmates, DoorDash, TaskRabbit and the rest busted open the gig economy. But more specialized platforms enable high-skill workers to find gig opportunities. SoundBetter, Fiverr, Thumbtack, Upwork and Freelancer are all great places to start when looking to market your unique skill set.

Here's a radical idea. Don't have a day job. Now, I understand food, rent, insurance, er, life, costs money. And until music is paying the bills, you gotta eat. Yeah, I hear you. But don't call it a *day job*. That immediately puts you in the mindset that every minute of your shift is a wasted minute. It will turn into an infuriating drudge. So, just don't get a *day job*. If you want a full-time job that's not in line with your creative and professional goals, make sure it inspires you. Or at least keeps your mind free. If you're going to be spending the majority of your life (for the time being) here, it better not make you miserable. And if it does, you better write a damn good album about it.

Stop calling it a *day job*. By doing that, you're admitting that you have bought into the twentieth-century concept of a J.O.B. *Blech.*

Find ways to pay your bills. Whether it's a well-paying 9-to-5 that motivates you, or a string of freelancer gigs, work smart.

But don't get stuck. Trapped.

I've seen it happen far too often. A musician takes a soul-sucking job which pays incredibly well (thank you, bachelor's degree), and they get used to the lifestyle.

Do Not Accept the Promotion

I see so many of my musician friends justify a big promotion at work with how much more money they're making that they can now invest in their music. Bull. It never works out that way. They celebrate the promotion by blowing $300 on drinks and a fancy dinner. Which then turns into $300 drinking Fridays and fancy dinner Wednesdays, Thursdays and Saturdays.

If you accept a promotion at work, it means that you are excited to move up in the company. Which you're not. Or, at least, shouldn't be if making it as a musician is your ultimate goal.

Find a job with the flexibility to be able to take off a week to go on a quick regional tour. Find a job that allows you to find someone to cover your shift when you get a last-minute opportunity. Find a job that doesn't make you work five (or six, or seven!) days a week. Find a job that doesn't emotionally, mentally or spiritually drain you, so when you return home from work you don't just want to zombie out in front of the TV.

Yes, try to have a good time at work. It will make you a happier person. But don't get too comfortable there. Because then you'll never quit.

To build a successful music career (like any small business or startup) requires a sh*t ton of time, effort, money and work. Building a music career requires working at it for twelve hours a day. Every single day. Of course, not many humans can actually do that. But that's what it takes. Are you willing to put in the time?

That's why you have to quit your day job as soon as possible. So you can put in the necessary time.

Giving music lessons is a fantastic "day job" because you can ease out of it when your music income starts to bring in more of the total pot of money you need to live. (Or pick up more students when a few months are a bit light.) Driving for Lyft, Uber or a food delivery app is also great because you can pick your hours and work more when you need and less when you don't. Playing cover, wedding and corporate gigs is a fantastic way to earn enough to get by. But again, like any day job, don't get too comfortable with this, and make sure it leaves you enough time for performing original shows, writing songs and working on your (original) music business. Cover gigs are a day job. And you should try to get out of them as soon as possible. And like any day job, they can be a trap if you're not careful.

Do not use your degree to get a full-time, corporate job. As happy as it makes your parents, you will be miserable, or worse, content!

One exception to this rule. And I've only seen it done by *the* most disciplined. Set up a one-year plan. Get the highest-paying job you can find. Live extremely conservatively. Come home and work your craft. Master your DAW. Practice your instrument. Write as much as you can. Go out and see as much live music as you can (but never buy more than one drink at the venue). And save every cent you get from your cushy paycheck above the cost of living and seeing live music. This is your research year.

Most musicians don't have this amount of discipline because they want everything *now*. But, if you're reading this book, there's a good chance you may be one of the select few who are disciplined enough to succeed with this plan. Because if you do, one year later, you can quit your day job (with enough saved to sustain you for at least 6 months) and you'll be able to rededicate all that time solely to your music career. If you were working 8 hours a day at your day job and 4 hours when you got home practicing, now you can devote 6 hours a day working at your art and 6 hours a day working at the business.

THE BACKUP PLAN

I never had one. If you have a backup plan, you will fall back on it. A music career is just too hard. Do not have a backup plan. If you're currently enrolled in a university getting a degree to make your parents happy for an education that they are paying for, fine. But you make damn sure that this degree is not for you to find a career-job. A one-year, high-paying job as described above? Sure. But if you ever say to yourself "I can always find a job as an architect if this music thing doesn't work out," you will, without fail, in five years find yourself staring at a blueprint.

THE 26-YEAR MARATHON (THE GOALS)

If you're achieving what you wanted to achieve with
your musical dreams then you've made it.
—LYNN GROSSMAN, SECRET ROAD,
INGRID MICHAELSON'S MANAGER

I always tell people when we get involved, you have to be prepared
for a marathon. I always ask artists "how do you define success?"
Because success is defined in the eye of the beholder. So what's
your goal line look like?
—JONATHAN AZU, CULTURE COLLECTIVE

A dream written down with a date becomes a goal. A goal broken
down into steps becomes a plan. A plan backed by action makes
your dreams come true.
—GREG REID

A music career is not a sprint. It's a marathon. So many young musicians think that they will "make it" within the first few years of dropping their first single. I know I did. You need to be realistic about your goals and pursuits. Sure, there is a bit of luck that determines the speed of your success, but there's no luck in determining whether you will succeed. The harder you work, the quicker you will reach your goals.

But what are your goals? Do you even know? "Becoming a rock star" is too ambiguous. What does that mean? Selling out arenas? Hits on the radio? Making a million dollars? These can be some of the metrics you use to define milestones in your career, but you need obtainable, concrete goals that you spend every day working toward. Goals can shift. Mine sure have. But goals help keep you focused at every stage of your career.

But you need SMART goals:

Specific
Measurable
Achievable
Realistic
Timebound

This acronym was first written down by George Doran in a 1981 article, but is now a ubiquitous goal-setting technique used across various industries.

"I want to make a living with music" is not a SMART goal. Sure, we all do. But that kind of "goal" gives you no guidance. An example of a SMART goal is more pinpointed: "I want to play a sold-out show at the Echo in 6 months." Here's a breakdown:

Specific: Concretely defines what you're aiming for: sell out a venue.
Measurable: That's 350 tickets.
Achievable: Very possible.
Realistic: If you've never played a show in L.A. before, have no online following or traction, selling 350 tickets in 6 months is not realistic. If you've played L.A. a bunch and your previous show sold 100 tickets and you're starting to gain some traction online, then sure, 350 tickets is not that far-fetched.
Timebound: 6 months.

Once you know what you are aiming for, then you can reverse engineer it. Here's how you'd do so using our Echo example: Find out who books the Echo. See what kinds of shows are on their calendar. Do you know any of those bands? If so, can you hop on any of those bills? Do you want to do a headline show or a co-bill? Do you have any connections to the talent buyer? If not, track down their email. Use Ari's perfect cold email approach from Chapter 7 to reach out and get some holds. Once the date is locked, plan out your promotional calendar so every day you are working on selling 350 tickets.

Reverse engineer. March confidently in that direction.

Create a Word document and title it "My Music Marathon." Then make four sections:

6 Months
1 Year
3 Years
26 Years

Under each section, write down where you see yourself in 6 months, 1 year, 3 years and 26 years. You can have lofty goals, but be realistic. These need to be SMART goals. There are many different paths to sustained success, so I can't define your goals for you. If the live show is your bag and you want to build your live game, then your 6-month plan could be to sell out a well-respected club in town, be the local opener for 3 national touring acts, and expand into 5 new cities. Your 1-year plan could be to sell out an even bigger respected club in town, be the opener on a national tour, and expand into 5 regional markets. Your 3-year plan could be to headline in 10 regional markets with at least 100 tickets sold in each and work with a respected booking agent. And your 26-year plan could include international tours twice a year, being a well respected act in your genre, a collection of records you are extremely proud of, playing with a handful of your idols, and supporting a family on both active (touring) and passive (royalties) income. Very possible.

If you're a studio rat and want to just work the writing, recording and licensing angle, then your 6-month goal could be to secure five clients and one paid sync placement. Your 1-year goal could be to have 5 sync placements earning collectively five figures, begin working with a respected sync agent, and have three records released by artists you care about. Also, quite feasible. Your 3-year plan could be to have at least one client whose record you produced and/or wrote on reach Gold status, land a publishing deal and make six figures. And your 26-year plan could be to have been nominated for multiple Grammys, reached Platinum status on records you produced and/ or wrote, and own a publishing company with staff producers and writers.

If humans scare you and you want to create from your basement, your best bet is to work the internet. Your 6-month plan could be to release monthly songs, garner 1 million combined streams, collab with other artists and gain 50,000 new followers. Your 1-year plan could be to have over 5 million combined streams, 150,000 monthly listeners and a monthly income of $3,000. Your 3-year plan could be to have 100 million combined streams, 1 million total followers, making $25,000/month. And your 26-year plan could be to run a production music company grossing $5 million annually.

Or if you're a player, your 6-month plan could be to get fifteen paid freelance gigs. In 3 years, you're the go-to musician on your instrument in your local scene, making enough money from just your freelance gigs to live a comfortable life. And for your 26-year plan you are backing up the stars and are one of the most respected players on your instrument.

These examples just scratch the surface. Have fun with this list. If it turns into a mini novel, great! Really put some thought into it and allow it to be a constant work in progress.

Print out this goal sheet and stick it to the wall of your rehearsal space. It's good to glance at every once in a while to keep you on track. Get a highlighter and color the goals you reach. Hopefully, in six months, section one will be fully colored. Whenever you have updates or slight shifts to your trajectory, make a new goal sheet. Print it out and put it up. Don't just make it a doc on your computer. Hanging this tangible sheet of paper in the physical world gives it life and demands respect.

Have everyone in your band make a goal sheet like this. Then discuss it in a band meeting. Make sure everyone's visions align and make one master Music Marathon sheet for the band. Because if all of you want to be spending the majority of your year on the road except your bassist, who just wants to record, play occasional local shows and raise his family, then you want to address this sooner than later. It may be time to find another bassist. You don't want this to come up a week before you're leaving for your first big tour. Sound absurd? I've seen it happen. "Yo, guys, I don't know about this tour. I mean, we're not going to make any money and I need to be looking out for my family. I really don't think it's a good idea. And I don't want to be away for this long." "Really dude? You couldn't have told us this, like, *a year ago* when we were planning this thing?" Commence epic band fight in which you admit you slept with the mother of his children when they first started dating. Don't let it come to that. For the sake of his children. So have the goals discussion early on.

Remember, these have to be SMART goals. Make sure this list is extremely specific so you can reverse engineer it. Don't worry, throughout the course of this book, we will discuss the steps you need to take to achieve your goals. This 26-year marathon list is just to get you thinking.

Your goals and plans can always shift over time. But this will at least give you some focus and direction. Oftentimes, musicians aren't sure where they should be devoting their efforts, but with a goal sheet, you can always make sure you're still on track.

Every six months, reevaluate your list. Right now, open your calendar and set a recurring block of time for every six months to sit down and rewrite your 26-year marathon.

Making a SMART goals sheet is the single most important thing you can do in your music career no matter what stage you're at. If you're just starting off, make a goals sheet. If you're five decades into your music career, make a goals sheet. No one's above setting goals. And it's never too late to get your career on track.

HOW TO FORM YOUR BAND

For those of you reading this who are not solo artists and do not yet have a band, there are many great tools these days to help you team up with other like-minded musicians. Having read this book is the most important prerequisite to officially teaming up, obviously. Aside from Craigslist, some platforms you should know about are Jammcard and BandMix. But honestly, the most tried-and-true method of meeting other like-minded musicians is by going to local shows and open mics. You'll start to see the same faces. You'll be able to pick out the musicians. Get to know the other musicians currently performing out.

And, of course, attending a music school is a great way to find a network. Many bands form in college. Attending a music school throws you into a supportive environment with like-minded individuals. And even after you graduate, the network you built up will always remain. Yes, music school is expensive and yes, it may not be for everyone, but it can be an investment in your career like studio time and new gear.

WHY NO ONE CARES ABOUT YOUR MUSIC

People will like the music, but they will love you.
You want to be able to tell your story in a way that people can
connect with you on a personal level.
—HUNTER SCOTT, TREND PR

The most frustrating thing is to put out an album that you spent the past two years of your life working on (and sunk way more money than you have into the production) and have it just bounce around your local scene a bit and lose traction before it was ever gained. This is the story of every local band on the planet. Some are putting out truly brilliant records with A-list players and top-notch songwriting. Why does no one seem to care about it when it's so undeniably great? It's because there's no story.

Everyone has a great story, but most just don't realize it yet. People love to be in the know and to be able to educate their friends about their favorite new band's backstory. Radio stations love to be able to give the ten-second explanation of why you stand out. Jimmy Fallon needs a two-line introduction that will get people to stick around. And journalists, especially, need a story to write about.

When was the last time you read a review about a band in your local newspaper (or *Pitchfork*) that discussed the music: the song structure, guitar tones, harmonic and melodic choices, drum tones, the pocket, innovative syncopation, varied time signatures, sonic flourishes, unusual studio techniques that they *heard* in the recording and were not spelled out in the press release? The things that musicians get off to, reviewers and average listeners couldn't give two sh*ts about.

And that, my friends, is the disconnect and the reason publicists and managers exist. These talented folks will help you craft the most interesting story that nonmusicians will actually care to read about.

But for the time being, you are your own publicist and your own manager. You need to find the most interesting storyline for your project and run with it. Everywhere. This should be in your band bio, listed in your press release, told in interviews, written up everywhere about you. It's the "he was discovered while busking on the streets of L.A. and now has chart-topping radio hits" story. Adele's breakup album. The White Stripes' brother/sister/husband/wife/ex-husband/ex-wife confusion. Bruno Mars and Meghan Trainor's behind-the-scenes songwriting careers. Bon Iver's northern-woods-of-Wisconsin-cabin recording. Marshmello's bucket head and secret identity. Cardi B's history on a reality TV show. Lil Nas X's black queer identity as a country-rap crossover. Lizzo's marching band past and body positivity.

You need something that every journalist wants to write about. Every influencer can scream about. The story that bumps every other album release off the cover. The story every diehard fan tells their friends when showing them your videos. Some bands decide to go the gimmick route: performing in costume or focusing on their weird instruments. And that's fine. As long as there is a tangible story that people can talk about.

A great song is one thing, but a great song with an amazing backstory is what really sells the project and makes you memorable.

So, what is your story? Everyone has one. Actually, everyone has a million different little stories that have led to where you are right now. Your band bio should not be each member's entire backstory on how they started taking piano lessons at a young age and then you all came together in high school to form "the greatest rock band the world has ever known!" This is so bland it's actually annoying. This doesn't set you apart. Have you overcome personal obstacles? What do you do outside music? Are you an avid reader of fantasy novels? Do you play arena football on the weekends? Is your great-uncle John Coltrane?

Your story must align with your entire project. When people hear your story, see your live show, browse your Instagram, listen to your record, watch your TikTok videos, it all lines up. So, home in on this story early on. Sprinkle it throughout your bio and reinforce it (seamlessly) in everything you do. Authentically.

Whether you like it or not, your story is just as important as your music. That cuts deep, I know. I can sense your blood pressure rising. Breathe. In. And. Out. You want to succeed as a musician? You're going to have to accept some of these truths. Musicians used to be able to rely on marketing departments and PR firms to craft their stories and reinforce them through album and tour promo. This is now your job to master.

The Disconnect Between Musician and Blogger

One of the first concerts I ever saw was the Dave Matthews Band at Alpine Valley. I was mesmerized by all the intricate elements they effortlessly incorporated into a jam rock format. In high school, I admit, I became somewhat fanatical. I appreciated (and studied) the astounding musicianship. There are few drummers on the planet who play like Carter or acoustic guitarists who play like Dave. I sang along to LeRoi's sax solos, transcribed Butch's keyboard solos, funked out to Stefan's bass lines and, of course, geeked when Boyd ripped into his screaming fiddle solos that lifted "Tripping Billies" to spiritual heights.

I lived in a Dave bubble in high school, surrounded by my musician buddies who "got it." I went to countless DMB shows alongside 40,000 other Daveheads. So I was quite startled when I got to college and realized that it wasn't actually "cool" to like "Dave." I was chastised by the hipsters of Minneapolis and started seeing DMB top countless Worst Bands Ever lists. But every blog article I read never actually discussed the music. What these bloggers hated were the fans. Not really the music. DMB fans were typically classified as suburban, bro-y frat boys sporting cargo shorts, popped collars and flip-flops packed into SUVs who pound Bud Light. As someone who was never in a frat, didn't own a collared shirt to pop, grew up in the city, drove a run-down old Ford Taurus wagon and drank craft beer, I was always so confused by these takedown articles. Why was my favorite band so universally despised? I started questioning my entire taste in music. But how was it that I could love The Beatles, Bob Dylan, Paul Simon, Miles Davis, Stevie Wonder, Bill Withers, Marvin Gaye, Aretha Franklin, James Taylor, Atmosphere, Eminem, Ani DiFranco, Death Cab for Cutie, Ben Folds, Béla Fleck, Jeff Buckley, Radiohead and Prince (all acts universally "acceptable" to like by bloggers), but also love DMB (universally hated by these same people)?

I finally got it. (Most) music bloggers don't actually know anything about music. They don't know how to write about music. They only know how to write about the *culture* of music. And a band's culture is defined by who their perceived fans are. These bloggers have never actually been to shows of these bands they claim to hate. They've never studied music. They've never written a song. They exist in a world surrounded by other hipsters who bond over their mutual hatred of popular music('s fans). They claim to "love" music, but they don't. Not like you or I love music. They love the culture of music.

The Dave Matthews Band's perceived image has overshadowed their music. Regardless of whether you care for their music or not, it doesn't matter. All music is subjective. Some people hate Dylan. Some love him. Some hate The Beatles. Some love them. No artist gets a pass. There are plenty of people out there who don't enjoy music the same way you do. Because they're not musicians. You enjoy "great" music. But your definition of "great" is different from theirs. You study music; they study the culture of music.

So, keep this in the back of your mind when crafting press releases, your bio and your entire promotional campaign. Unfortunately, it is *not* (all) about your music. You can't fight this. You must accept it if you have any hope of controlling your own PR and gaining any sort of traction.

DOES AGE MATTER?

The question I get asked frequently by older musicians is "does age matter." There's no simple answer because it all depends on what your goals are. But I'll tell you one thing—age has absolutely no correlation with success (or talent). Uncle Joe will tell you, "If you haven't made it by thirty, give up." Stop listening to Uncle Joe! Joshua Radin *started* his musical career at 30, two years after he picked up the guitar for the first time. Matt Nathanson put out seven albums (and one major-label album) before releasing his chart-topping (indie-label) hit "Come On Get Higher" at 35. Lizzo was 30 when she got her first hit with "Juice." Bill Withers released his debut album at 32. Sheryl Crow released her debut album at 31 (after working as a music teacher, jingle writer and backup vocalist). Daniel Powter's hit "Bad Day" came out when he was 34. Khruangbin's Mark Speer was 35 when the band released their debut album and 39 when they first charted. Willie Nelson was 40 when *Shotgun Willie* came out. Bonnie Raitt didn't see commercial success until she was 40. Sharon Jones released her debut record at 40 and it wasn't until she was 58 that she got a Grammy nomination. Leonard Cohen was 50 when he released "Hallelujah." 2 Chainz didn't get a #1 album until a month before his 36th birthday. John Ondrasik of Five for Fighting was 35 when their smash hit "Superman (It's Not Easy)" took over the airwaves. James Murphy was also 35 when LCD Soundsystem released its debut album. Andrea Bocelli was 34 when he released his debut album. Rachel Platten was 34 when "Fight Song" reached #1. Butch Vig was 36 when he produced Nirvana's *Nevermind,* and it wasn't until he was 40 that his own band, Garbage, released their debut chart-topping album. Dan Wilson was 37 when his first hit, "Closing Time," was released with his band Semisonic (and he was 46 when he won his first Grammy for cowriting six songs on the Dixie Chicks' Album of the Year *Taking the Long Way*). Sia had her first #1 single at 41. Neil Young was 44 when he released "Rockin' in the Free World." Chris Stapleton was 37 when his debut, award-winning solo album was released. Debbie Harry was 31 when Blondie released their first album, and not until a few years later did they see worldwide success. Joe Satriani didn't release his first album until he was 30. Christine McVie of Fleetwood Mac was 34 when *Rumours* was released. Michael Fitzpatrick was 40 when Fitz and the Tantrums released their debut album. Thelonious Monk released his best-selling album, *Monk's Dream*, at 46. Louis Armstrong, although a renowned trumpeter-performer for decades, was 64 when his best-selling album *Hello, Dolly!* was released. Charles Bradley was 63 when he released his debut album. And although a lifelong musician and producer, Seasick Steve was 67 when he released his first multinational charting (major-label debut) album.

But these are artists you've most likely heard of. And this is when they "made it big." If you take away one thing from this book, it's that you don't need to "make it big" to "make it." Don't let age scare you. There are 16-year-olds writing better songs than I could ever dream of writing. And there are 50-year-olds dusting off their guitar, reconnecting with their soul and deciding to finally pursue a career they can believe in. Age means nothing. If you work hard enough, you *will* make it, regardless of your age.

That being said, life happens. And I'd be lying if I told you it was easy to start a rock career with a spouse and kids at home. Once kids enter the picture, all bets are off. There's this bit in Alex Blumberg's podcast *StartUp* where he jokes with an investor about how parents fool themselves into thinking it's possible to work just as hard at their entrepreneurial pursuits with kids, exclaiming "you just get better at managing your time." They eventually concede that, in fact, parents can't devote as much time to their passions and careers as nonparents.

If a music career is more important to you than a family, you have nothing to worry about. If you're 23, want to start a family by 27 and you just formed a rock band to take over the world, you're going to come to a crossroads very soon. You're going to have to decide whether you want to be an absent parent on the road with your band or at home raising your kids working a 9-to-5. There's a balance, sure, and there are many successful musicians with children. But most of these successful musicians didn't have kids until their music career was coasting a bit and they had enough passive income that they didn't need to spend their entire life on the road.

But again, pull out your goals sheet and ask yourself, "Can this be achieved with a family?" Everyone's situation is different. Maybe your partner has an income to support your family while you devote all of your time (and money) to your musical pursuits. Maybe you just want to play locally and not tour. Maybe you want to be a local hired gun or a producer-engineer. Maybe you want to be a YouTuber, Instagrammer or livestreamer. Maybe you want to live in the college or Performing Arts Center (PAC) circuit and fly out to one-off gigs every once in a while (more on this in Chapter 9). Not every career in music requires incessant touring. But it's hard to be a successful indie band, singer/songwriter, DJ or hip-hop act and not tour.

It also all depends on what your idea of success is. And no one can define what success is but you. Remember that.

If you're an indie act making five figures staying at home licensing your music to film and television, that's success. Could you make six or seven figures if you toured? Maybe. But you don't have to if you don't want to. There's no right or wrong. You should do what's going to make you the happiest.

Happiness needs to be built into every career decision. There are more important things in life than money. Actually, once you have enough money to support the lifestyle you want, you shouldn't make any decision based solely on money ever again.

2.

THE NEW INDUSTRY

Self-promotion. If you don't want anything to do with it,
stay in your f*&king basement.
—BEN FOLDS

There's so much more to the business than just the money.
—DEREK SIVERS

We play in a game with no rules. Just because it worked one way
for someone doesn't mean it's going to work that way for you.
Figure out what's going to work for you.
—AMY MADRIGALI, TALENT BUYER, THE TROUBADOUR

I have seen the artists change for the better. They have a much
better idea of who they are because they can talk directly to their
audience. They have a much better work ethic because they're
realizing they can create their own business before the manager
or the lawyer or the label comes in. But, the downside is, it's
taking away from what the band used to be able to focus on: The
creativity. All they had to do was write songs, tour and play
live. Now, you're a business. Has it affected the art?
I'm sure it has. How could it not?
—BRUCE FLOHR, RED LIGHT MANAGEMENT

YOU THOUGHT YOU WERE A MUSICIAN

And now, for the most disappointing realization that every modern musician eventually comes to terms with: You will never be able to *just* make music for a living.

The sooner you accept this, the sooner you can get your music career on track.

Sounds simple, but it's astounding how many musicians I meet who think they can succeed by just writing great songs, making great recordings and putting on great shows. Yes, making great music is *of course* important. It's the foundation of the entire operation. Having great music is the baseline. And it's assumed that you have great music before following any other tips in this book. But, it is not (and, actually, has never been) all that musicians have to worry about.

How are you going to play live if you don't know how to book a show? How are you going to get people to those shows if you don't know how to promote? How are you going to grow your fanbase if you don't know how (where, or, *gasp*, why) to put your songs online? How are you going to generate passive revenue if you don't know how to collect all of your royalties? How are you going to get noticed if you don't know how to approach gatekeepers, influencers and tastemakers?

There are way too many musicians who believe that all it takes is to create one great song, throw it up on Spotify and wait for it to take over the world and get "discovered" by "someone."

Believe me, I wish we lived in a world where the greatest music in the world was instantly and universally recognized, cherished and (financially) rewarded. But, the reality is, that's far from the truth. So! What are you going to do about it? Are you going to live in the majority and do nothing but b*&ch about how "people are stupid" for liking the music they like (while your music disappears into oblivion), or are you going to work your a$$ off to get your music the recognition it deserves? Your choice.

The harder you work, the luckier you get.

—TED LASSO

THE 50/50 RULE

If I only had two dollars left, I would spend one on PR.

—BILL GATES

You must split your time equally between the music and the business. Early on, of course, most of your time will be spent solely on the music because you don't have a business yet. This period doesn't count. This is the incubation stage. The developmental stage. But once you have decided that music is going to be your business, that's when the 50/50 rule comes into play.

When you're writing and recording your album, 80% of your time will be spent on the music. And this is balanced by the period after you release the album, when 80% of your time will be spent on promoting the album (the business).

When you're not working on specific projects, you should be splitting every week between business and music equally. Maybe Sunday through Tuesday is spent on songwriting, practicing and rehearsing. Then Wednesday through Friday is spent on booking, promotion, social media, networking and research. If you're ever bored as a musician, you aren't doing it right. I haven't been bored since *Friends* was still on the air.

But the 50/50 rule doesn't just have to do with your time. It has to do with your money as well. Fifty percent of your money should be spent on your art and fifty percent of your money should be spent on the promotion of that art. Sounds simple enough, but I can't tell you how many artists run a crowdfunding campaign for $10,000, then spend $12,000 actually creating their album and devote $27 to promote the thing. If your album is going to cost $12,000 to create, then you should run your crowdfunding campaign for $24,000. If you don't think you can raise that much, then either create an EP or find a way to cut your costs. There is no sense in spending a boatload of money on a masterpiece if no one is going to hear it. And if you spend no money on marketing and promotion, no one will hear it. Period.

EMBRACE THE HYPHEN

For a long time I made 100% of my income on my original music. I thought that was the singular marker of success: making ALL of my money on music. However, ignoring other revenue streams and creative opportunities denied me personal (and professional) growth. There are few musicians on the planet, big or small, who *only* make money on music. And there's nothing wrong with that. Dr. Dre has Beats. Beyoncé, Rihanna, and Adam Levine have clothing lines. Justin Bieber, Lady Gaga and Taylor Swift have fragrances. Thirty Seconds to Mars frontman Jared Leto is an Academy Award–winning actor.

Musician-actors are not a new thing. And musician-entrepreneurs are becoming more commonplace (if we remove the fact that all musicians are truly entrepreneurs anyway). I'm currently a musician-CEO-author-podcaster-blogger-educator-consultant. But I was once a musician-barista, a musician-actor-Lyft driver, a musician–sub shop delivery driver. Musician-teacher, musician–camp counselor. "Musician" will always begin your title, but don't be ashamed of your other titles. Embrace them! Initially your titles won't be so glamorous (Musician-Barista), but eventually you'll be able to drop the job titles you don't want and add ones that you do.

The goal is to be making 100% of your income from your creative talents.

WHAT'S RIGHT AND WHAT'S WRONG IN MUSIC

There's one thing I've learned down here in Colombia.
Good and bad are relative concepts.
—STEVE MURPHY FROM *NARCOS*

Forget everything you've ever thought about ownership; right and wrong; good and bad. These are all subjective terms. And we've been brought up to believe that there are absolute truths when it comes to right and wrong. Sure, murder is wrong. That we can all agree on. But is murder for justice, like in the death penalty, also wrong? That is one of the biggest debates in our society today. We could agree that stealing is wrong. But the line that distinguishes stealing from sharing is quite blurry.

If you get stuck in dogmatic ideologies, you can never grow as an artist or businessperson. Allow yourself to evolve in your beliefs. Only when we allow our beliefs to be challenged can we grow. Only when we question the status quo do we realize that what we thought to be absolute truths may, in fact, not be so.

The music industry has evolved tremendously in the last ten years, and every day we are being asked to challenge our beliefs on what constitutes right and wrong. Is file-sharing just like stealing a microwave from an appliance store? Well, no, it's not. But that was the argument by the labels when Napster first popped up over twenty years ago.

The record labels stood by their perceived absolute truths about what was right and wrong and thought it was a good idea to "defend" their rights by suing music's biggest fans. The Recording Industry Association of America (RIAA), the organization that represents the major labels, sued over 35,000 individuals for illegally downloading music in the mid-2000s. We heard of 12-year-olds being sued for hundreds of thousands of dollars. A recently deceased 83-year-old who hadn't even owned a computer before her passing got sent notices. A grandfather actually died while in litigation, and the RIAA told his family they had sixty days to grieve and then the RIAA would start to depose his children.

Was this right or wrong? Well, at the time, the RIAA clearly thought this was the right course of action. History shows that it was not. Suing grandmas, children, and, in general, music's biggest fans, was in fact wrong. Even if they did actually download music "illegally."

The music industry is not black and white. Just because you have a legal right to stop people from doing something doesn't mean it's smart to try to enforce that right. Like when Taylor Swift sent cease-and-desist letters to moms selling mugs on Etsy that used a T-swift lyric. Sure, Ms. Swift had trademarked a three-word phrase ("shake it off") and technically had the right to "defend the mark," but is it the smartest move to send cease-and-desist letters threatening to sue fans because they used a song lyric on mugs in an Etsy store? I'm not so certain.

Spotify has drawn a line in the sand, saying that they don't allow playlisters to charge for inclusion. That's apparently wrong. But paying for *consideration* to be included on a playlist seems to be A-OK. And TikTok is perfectly peachy having their creators get paid to include songs in their videos. That's apparently just fine.

ARE YOU NEARSIGHTED OR FARSIGHTED?

When you make business decisions, don't merely think about how they are going to affect your bottom line this year. Think about how many life-long fans it will bring you and how these fans will support your bottom line over the course of your entire career. The major record labels' vision became shorter and shorter over the years to the point where if the first song they put out by an artist wasn't a smash-it-out-of-the-park hit, then that artist was typically dropped. Bruce Springsteen's first two albums flopped. But Columbia stuck it out with him because they believed in him as an artist. And because of that belief, allowing him to grow as an artist and entertainer, the third record he delivered was *Born to Run*. How many artists have labels dropped because their first album (or single!) flopped, depriving us of the next Springsteen?

The labels have had it all wrong for sometime now. They have ignored the reason they exist: the fans. They look at fans as numbers on a spread-sheet. The labels have been clinging to the Drakes, Adeles, Weeknds, Biebers, Swifts, Beyoncés and Billie Eilishes, knowing that if they can just get a couple hits this year, their books will work out and they'll get their Christmas bonuses. Record-label execs turn over these days more than IHOP pancakes. As long as record labels treat fans as one-dimensional customers, they will continue to fail. They have lost touch with what sus-tains a music career. It's not about the hit of the moment. It's about the connection the fan has with the artist.

Building loyal fans is the most important aspect of a music career. The money will follow.

For every business decision you make for the rest of your career, ask yourself this question: Is this the best decision for my fans?

If you can answer yes every time, then you can never fail.

THE NEW TEAM

Historically, a musician's team was comprised of a personal manager, an entertainment attorney, a booking agent, a record label, a business manager, a publisher and a publicist. And this team hasn't ever been questioned or improved upon. Until now.

Yes, these team members are important when you've reached a level that demands this sort of personnel. But it is no longer enough to just have these members of the team. And what about before you obtain these team members?

The modern music fan demands a constant stream of content to stay engaged: songs, videos, photos and tweets. It's no longer acceptable to just release content once every three years that a traditional team would help develop, promote and rally behind. Musicians today are expected to put out high-quality content every day.

So how do you do this? By surrounding yourself with talented team members who can help this process—because no one can do it all on their own. Bands have a leg up on solo artists because they can allocate some of these duties among the members. The bands who succeed the quickest are the ones where every member has business duties in addition to their musical duties. That's a lot of duty. I'm 12.

Graphic Designer

Fifteen years ago you could get away with creating one 11 x 17 poster for every local show and one poster per tour. Now, if you're not pumping out multiple images on your socials for every career milestone (local show, tour, TV placement, opening gig, festival slot, music video, album release and single release), you're neglecting your career. Graphic design artist is now a required position every band must employ. It's no longer a job you should outsource for every design need you have. It's best if someone in your band (or you) learns basic graphic design. You don't need to be a Photoshop pro, but at least become capable enough to touch up photos, resize images, create jpegs and PDFs, add text to images and create good-looking posters. Canva has become the go-to graphics creation site. Learn it. Love it. Master it. Until your design skills rival the pros, keep your designs simple. The simpler the better. Keep it classy. There's nothing that screams amateur more than a messy-looking poster with five different fonts in 6 different colors, pixelated photos haphazardly sliced together. If you suck at design, hire a professional photographer and just put some text on the photos and crop or resize the image depending on the use.

If you need a brand-identifying design (like an album cover, band logo or T-shirt), then yes, outsource to a professional. 99designs.com, Upwork and Guru.com are great places to find an inexpensive, yet talented, graphic design artist. They will host a design contest for you: You submit all of the information for the item you need, and how much you're willing to pay, and then dozens of graphic design artists submit designs. You pick the one you like and *boom*, you found the best graphic design artist for your project. Fiverr.com is also a good option for finding inexpensive graphic design artists.

The vertical 11 × 17 poster design is outdated. Unless you're printing physical posters to hang in coffee shops or record stores, why are you designing to these standards? Graphic designers now work mostly in pixels, not inches.

Luckily, there are very simple photo-editing, text-adding and graphic design phone apps you can download to help you create good-looking posters/photos for Instagram. As to not list apps that may be defunct by the time you're reading this, just google "adding text to photo app" or "beginning graphic design app." Many great ones are free (but they'll add a logo or watermark) and most cost just a few bucks to remove the logo—

definitely worth it. Having a text-adding app on your phone is crucial for promoting on the go. Keep an arsenal of promo and live photos saved on your phone, add text and *bam,* you have a good-looking show poster for all your socials. If you want to get creative and have an eye for design, then go in deep with some design apps.

However, not everything can be done on the phone. It's definitely important to learn basic image editing on your laptop. Photoshop is the industry standard and is what I've been using for years to create all my T-shirt, poster, album and logo designs along with Facebook, Twitter and website cover photos. You need to be able to adjust the size and dimensions of your images without having to contact a graphic design artist every time you need a slight change. So, the person in your band (or you if you don't have a band) with the best design eye should learn a graphic design/photo editing program. Again, Canva has become the go-to for most small business and bands. You can host all design templates in the cloud and anyone on the team can create a new one quickly, easily and cheaply.

Find a program and master it. At the end of the day it doesn't matter what you use as long as you can do what you need with it.

Recording Engineer

It's no longer acceptable to just put out music every three years. Sure, you can still spend time creating an expensive masterpiece in the form of an album every few years, but you also need to be releasing high-quality recordings very often (like once a month). Get Logic or Pro Tools (if your budget is tight you can start with GarageBand—it comes preinstalled on MacBooks), or if you work primarily "in the box," Ableton, Cubase, Bitwig and FL Studio are all solid options used by the pros. Master your software enough to record demos, rehearsals, live shows and (potentially) "radio-ready" songs and albums. With the onslaught of inexpensive recording programs that have come out over the past fifteen years, there's no excuse to not learn one. You can still hire a producer and engineer and go into "the studio" for your album if you have a budget, but someone on your team needs to be your on-call recording engineer.

These regular releases can be your covers, demos and band rehearsals. Put these on Bandcamp, TikTok, YouTube, Instagram and Patreon. You can officially release the best songs on Spotify, Apple Music and the rest if you want.

And how do you build up a home studio to do this? We'll dig into this in Chapter 3.

Videographer

If you haven't noticed, video is kind of a big deal. And it's not just about the official music video anymore. With TikTok taking over the entire industry, short, snappy, vertical videos are oftentimes more important at fan acquisition than official music videos. Fight this all you want, but if you don't have video, you're missing out on serious engagement. Every video needs to be high-quality. It's no longer acceptable to record cover songs in front of your MacBook camera and throw them up on YouTube. Sure, in 2007 this was cutting-edge. Not anymore. You're now competing with every influencer and label act. Every video you put on Instagram, TikTok and YouTube needs to be on brand. Communicating the message you're looking to get across. I can't tell you what your video needs to look like without knowing what your project is all about, but your videos need a vibe and cohesive look. It's not as difficult to achieve as it sounds. As with your graphic design program, learn video editing. The top video-editing software available right now is Final Cut Pro and Adobe Premiere; iMovie is pretty good as well (and is free). Great, free video editing software is not hard to come by nowadays. Choose one and get good at it. It's not hard. Just do it. You don't want to have to outsource this to a pro video editor every time you want to release footage from your latest show or rehearsal.

Smartphone cameras are getting better and better. They're still not as good as DSLR cameras, but they will do for the time being until you can afford to purchase a good camera. When using your phone as a camera, it's all about the lighting. Shooting outside during the day is ideal because there's no better light source than the sun. Experiment with locations. Shade is best (so the sun doesn't wash your face out). You may have heard the term "magic hour," which is sunrise or sunset. Everything looks gorgeous around then.

If you're making TikTok or Instagram videos, shooting on your phone is standard. If you're putting together a longer-form, long-lasting video (like cover video, behind the scenes in studio or music video), you're going to want to spend time editing this on your laptop, using a professional video-editing program.

Sure, as often as you can, work with a professional team and put out high-quality music videos (shot, edited and directed by professionals). But not many indie musicians have the budget to put out expensive videos like that every month. So, get good at video editing on your own (like so many successful influencers have) and just start releasing quality content. And, to be honest, some of the most successful videos of the past ten years weren't the most professional-looking, they just had a vibe that matched the project.

Above all, you need to be putting out regular videos, of all types, across multiple platforms. And there's different etiquette for each platform (TikTok vs. Instagram vs. YouTube vs. Facebook vs. Twitch). We'll get deeper into this in Chapter 11.

Photographer

You need lots of high-quality photos. It's worth it to hire a professional photographer for band promo photos at least once a year. Also, hire a pro to shoot your biggest shows. But you can't just put out promo photos all the time. Instagram demands frequent high-quality photos. There are some inexpensive photo-editing apps (for like $3). Edit every photo you post. Notice how the Likes pour in when you post well-edited photos.

Digital Specialist

If you have a family member who loves you (and your music) and is willing to join your team, keep them close, thank them profusely, shower them with green room beer and get them laid frequently. Hopefully they will stick with you when they're offered jobs paying ten times (or more realistically a hundred times) what you can pay. The most in-demand professionals are web/app developers and digital marketers. So, if a band member can get good at this, that's ideal, but somewhat unrealistic. Unlike video editing or graphic design, web development and digital marketing (like social media advertising) takes *way* more time to master. At the very least, learn some basic HTML code and how to run basic Facebook ads.

This may be one of the boldest concepts of this entire book, but I'm putting it out there. The musicians who achieve this will zoom past their peers: *Add a creative digital specialist to your team.* First. Before a manager, booking agent, label or anyone else. Offer them an equal cut of your income. Sure, it may be next to nothing now, but if they believe in your music enough, they might be crazy enough to join you on this journey.

You want to be able to track and analyze everything you have online. At the very least, add Google Analytics to your website.

Of course you can quickly and easily create a website with no coding knowledge with Bandzoogle or Squarespace, but going way above and beyond what every other band out there is doing can be extremely beneficial.

Companies like Facebook, Airbnb, Twitter and Dropbox succeeded without spending a penny on traditional marketing. As cool as it is to get a billboard of your band on Sunset Boulevard or hearing fifteen seconds of your song on your favorite radio station (from the ad you bought), some developers have tried to improve their odds. Ryan Holiday, author of *Growth Hacker Marketing*, discussed how contractors for Airbnb, through creative engineering, got all of their initial postings listed on Craigslist. He writes, "because Craigslist does not technically allow this, it was a fairly ingenious work-around. As a result, Airbnb—a tiny site— suddenly had free distribution on one of the most popular websites in the world." (Airbnb has since come out strongly against the practice, however, which it claims was carried on without its knowledge.) Scott Bradlee of Postmodern Jukebox mastered the clickbait-headline writing style of Reddit and was able to get many of their YouTube videos to go viral on Reddit initially. For free.

You want to find creative marketing techniques that are trackable. And digital specialists understand how tracking works and can conceive of ideas that typical musicians cannot.

I realize that not every musician can convince a talented digital person to join the team for little to no pay, but it's worth putting in the back of your mind for when you get an investment or start pulling in some decent dough.

For the time being, you can create a great-looking website with Bandzoogle or Squarespace. They charge a low monthly hosting fee and offer tons of good looking templates to choose from with "drag and drop" functionality for adding a music player, show calendar, photos, store, videos, social integration, blog and anything else you need on your website. I've found Bandzoogle and Squarespace offer the easiest way for musicians to create good looking websites with no coding knowledge.

How to Learn All This Stuff

I, like so many other musicians, am completely self-taught at most of this. How did we learn it all? Well, you can learn pretty much anything you need from YouTube tutorials. Or by simple googling. Working in Final Cut Pro and can't figure out how to slice the video? It's a five-second Google search: "How to slice video in Final Cut Pro." Or want to make an animated GIF? Tons of simple tutorials on YouTube. Or if you learn better in a formal education environment, there are tons of online courses you can enroll in from anywhere in the world to learn all of this stuff.

TO SIGN OR NOT TO SIGN

There's music and then there's the music business. Make sure
everything is in writing and always protect yourself.
Don't expect others to protect you.
—RYAN PRESS, VICE PRESIDENT, A&R,
WARNER/CHAPPELL MUSIC

Even with the 50/50 rule, there isn't enough time in the day for you to cover all of the business duties required to run a full-time music career successfully. Of course you *want* professionals to handle most of the business, but it's not most musicians' realities at first. The most important thing you need to remember is: *Do not hand off your career to someone just because they show some interest.* That's the quickest way to seal your demise. Sure, the right label or manager could help you become a superstar. But the wrong one could make sure you work at Starbucks for the rest of your life. So, choose wisely. If you ever get a contract, get your own lawyer (not one referred by the person giving you the contract—duh) to review it. And, when the time is right, make sure you know the reasons to sign or not to sign with the pros.

MANAGER

Ingrid knows everything going on at all times.
I feel like we are business partners.
—LYNN GROSSMAN, INGRID MICHAELSON'S MANAGER

The relationship between manager and artist is a marriage of the
minds. It can't all be on just one of us to have the vision.
—NICK BOBETSKY, MANAGER, STATE OF THE ART

The most successful and enjoyable experiences in my career have
been artists who are right there with you in terms of how hard
they work.
—JUSTIN LITTLE, MANAGER, BAILEY BLUES

The relationship between artist and manager is the most
important relationship you have on your team. It's somebody
you're hopefully going to be with for the rest of your career—the
rest of your life, if you're lucky—so take it seriously.
—ROB ABELOW, MANAGER, ROLL CALL

Before, people used to get signed because of their talent. And
then you had the labels come in and do their marketing, put
money behind it and things happened. Now, it's a different world.
We don't really take risks. And when we take risks, it's because we
see something is already reacting.
—ANNA SAVAGE, MANAGER, FULL STOP MANAGEMENT

The manager is the most important person in your operation. Your manager is your teammate. Your partner. Your friend. The two of you (or six,
depending on how many are in your band) are in it together. Us versus

the world. The manager is the liaison between the artist and everybody else. The manager oversees everything from the recording process to the album release campaign to the tour routing, booking and performing to the social media management to the lead singer's divorce. The manager handles the business, first and foremost. The best managers handle the business with creative finesse. To navigate the constantly evolving musical landscape, managers need truly creative minds. You don't want a manager who is operating the same way this year as she was last year. Every day is new. Every day is different.

The two extremes of artist managers are the Well-Connected Manager and the Best-Friend Manager. Every manager exists somewhere on this spectrum.

The Well-Connected Manager (WCM)

Everyone understands the concept of the Well-Connected Manager. She has multiple clients, usually works at a management company, and one of her phone calls is more effective than 30 emails and calls from a Best-Friend Manager. Well-Connected Managers typically have Day-to-Day Managers who work under them and do just that: manage the day-to-day responsibilities of the band and report back to the Well-Connected Manager.

The Well-Connected Manager gets her band in-studio performances at radio and TV stations. Gets the band a record deal. Obtains a publishing deal. Gets songs placed on TV, in movies and on playlists. Finds sponsorships, endorsements and influencer partnerships. Hires the booking agent, accountant, marketing agency and publicist. And obtains write-ups in major blogs, magazines and newspapers (if a publicist isn't involved).

These people have the clout to make these things happen with a phone call.

But what this Well-Connected Manager typically doesn't do is live and breathe the band she's working for (she just has too many clients or is burnt out from all the years of climbing the ladder and busting a$$). That's why a Best-Friend Manager is nice to have. At least at first.

The Best-Friend Manager (BFM)

The Best-Friend Manager starts with zero connections and has to make them all on his own. But, he lives and breathes the band. He and the band work together on a vision and lofty goals. He screams at the top of every rooftop about how his band is going to take over the world and works tirelessly to make it happen.

He's the tour manager when the band is on the road. He imports mailing list addresses after the show, runs the SMS texting system, adds tour dates to the proper outlets and calendars, goes Live from the road, brainstorms and encourages the artist to keep up with TikTok and Instagram (or runs it himself). Sets up OBS behind the scenes for the livestreams, runs the merch table (or finds people to do it). Manages the website and works with the graphic designer and web developer to keep the site up to date and truly representative of the band. Writes the press release and bio (or finds a writer to do it). Finds the best distribution company (if a label isn't involved) and distributes the music appropriately. Becomes a master at all of the necessary social media sites (and apps) and trains the band on how to use them. Manages all of the finances (before a business manager is involved). Contacts the street team in every city and arranges flyering, postering and social media promo in advance of the band's shows. Hires interns to handle all of the above duties that he doesn't have time for. And he is the band's therapist.

But this stuff not only needs to get done, it all has to be up to professional standards. Everything needs to be representative of the band. If the band is unstoppable on stage or has an album that defines a new genre but the website is a WordPress template from 2002 and the Instagram has broken links, outdated Highlights and an unread inbox, then your band's fan retention is suffering.

Some BFMs see their band to the top and become WCMs. Some get fired and replaced by a WCM when they start to see some success. Some become Day-to-Day Managers or Tour Managers.

WCMs typically make 15%–20% (gross) commission on your entire career. BFMs take what they can get. Which is typically nothing for a while.

If you have a BFM, it's best to just split up everything that's coming in equally with them for the time being. Make your BFM an equal member of the band. If you have 4 members, then your BFM is the 5th member and you split the money equally. If it's just you, it might make sense to give him 30% of the gross income and you keep 70% until you reach a certain threshold. Like, 30% until you make at least $10,000 monthly gross and then the manager's cut drops to 25%. Once you surpass $25,000 a month, the manager's cut drops to 20%. And then once you surpass $100,000 a month, the cut drops to 15%. It may seem counterintuitive to cut the percentage once you're making more. Shouldn't your manager get rewarded for working your income up to this level? Actually, it will still work out to be more money even if it's a smaller percentage: 30% of $8,000 = $2,400; 25% of $20,000 = $5,000; 20% of $50,000 = $10,000; 15% of $150,000 = $22,500.

And managers need to be making more money initially when you're not making much to make it worthwhile for them to work on your project as hard as they are. You get the glory of being on stage every night. They don't. So, show them that you appreciate what they're doing and split your earnings with them. And an occasional "thank you" never hurt anyone.

If you're not bringing in much of anything for any kind of commission to make sense (and you have savings or a day job), you can pay your manager a flat monthly fee until a certain point. Like, $500 a month until you're making $5,000 a month. Then, after $5,000 a month, the 30%, 25%, 20%, 15% model falls into place.

Remember, the manager's commission is typically taken from the gross earnings (all earnings before expenses). There are some expenses that are exempt in some management contracts like label advances, tour support, marketing support and touring expenses.

This sliding scale commission model can work equally for bands and solo artists. Have these possible breakdowns in your arsenal when you're negotiating pay with your potential BFM. There will be much less negotiating with WCMs because they're pretty set in their ways.

Music industry traditionalists will chastise the $500 per month flat and sliding scale models because "that's not how it works." But, you know what, *there are no absolutes in the NEW music industry.* Most BFMs aren't doing it for the money anyway, but if you want them to be able to work on your band as their full-time job, they need to be making enough money to actually live on. No matter how much they love your music, if they can't pay their rent or buy food, they're not going to stick around very long.

I know what you're thinking, "But Ari, we don't have a BFM *or* a WCM. How do we find *either*?"

Finding a manager is about timing, being in the right place at the right time and, really, making it seem like you don't need a manager. No one wants to work with a band that seems to be struggling, but everyone wants to hop on a speeding train. That being said, music is magic. Managers believe this. It's why they chose such an unstable career path. If a manager happens to hear something so special that it moves him on a deep, spiritual level, he may decide to take you on no matter what the stage of your career. Even if this is your first demo on SoundCloud and you don't even have an Instagram yet.

But this is rare. Most managers want to see you kicking butt on your own before they will even give you a second glance. They want to know that if they decide to work with you that you will put in the effort needed to maintain a modern music career. Managers know that it's not just about the music. They want bands who will work hard, just like them. So, you should have all of your social media sites up to industry standards. You need high-quality video. You need professional promo photos. You need your live show to be better than bands that are selling out arenas. You need to look like a band ready to take over the world.

Whatever you do, don't sign with a manager who is neither a Best-Friend Manager or a Well-Connected Manager just to have a manager. I meet too many artists who love talking about their "manager." "Oh yeah my *manager* is handling this. My *manager* is handling that." Blah-blah. Unimpressive. I don't care. If your manager really was handling this and that, you wouldn't need to tell me about it and I'd see it. And your manager should never be handling stuff you don't know about. The moment your manager makes deals that you have no idea about is the moment your career becomes their career and you lose all control. Do not wear your ignorance as a badge of honor and proudly exclaim, "Oh I don't know, my manager deals with that." No! You're the boss. You're in charge. You should know everything that goes on. Your manager works for you. Stay in the loop. Stay hands-on.

The Family Manager (FM)

There have been some pretty successful family managers (Joe Jackson for Michael, Joe Simpson for Jessica and Ashley, Sharon Osbourne for Ozzy, Jay Z for Beyoncé, Mac Reynolds for Imagine Dragons (brother of lead singer Dan) and Jonetta Patton for her son Usher. This is definitely an option *if* you have a great relationship with this family member already and they are willing to devote the time and energy it takes to build an indie music career. But, make sure this family member does their homework, learns the industry and will let you move on to a Well-Connected Manager if that's the best move for your career. FMs are essentially BFMs—with more guilt trips.

The Band Member Manager (BMM)

Bands (as opposed to solo artists) have the luxury of splitting up all the required business duties it takes to run a successful indie music career. One member should fill the role of acting manager, until you find someone who will take over this role. This member should be the most organized, levelheaded, personable and friendly member of the group. The BMM will lead band meetings, book most of the initial shows, allocate duties among the rest of the group and do all of the outreach.

I recommend getting a BMM agreement drawn up by an entertainment attorney. Make sure it includes these points:

- BMM will be the acting manager and booking agent until other qualified professionals fill these duties.
- BMM responsibilities include:
    1. scheduling band meetings,
    2. negotiating all deals with talent buyers,
    3. maintaining all outreach via email, phone and social media,
    4. routing tours,
    5. pitching music supervisors, licensing companies, influencers and playlisters,
    6. networking online and off (with music industry professionals, musicians and fans),
    7. keeping up with best music industry practices,
    8. allocating necessary business duties to other band members,
    9. finding other qualified professionals to assist with these duties.
- Each band member agrees to take on business duties assigned to him/her by BMM and will work at these duties diligently.
- BMM will have the flexibility to make minor decisions on behalf of the band (booking, publicity, social media, etc.), but

will bring every major decision (hiring/firing of team members, touring prospects, label/agent/management deals) to the band for a vote.

■ If the BMM will keep the accounting records on behalf of the band or if this will be assigned to someone else.

■ How and when the band gets paid.

Being the acting manager for your project, you're going to have to work out tough negotiations so that they are favorable to your career. To not get stepped on or screwed, you will have to look out for your best interests, but by doing this you will upset people in the process. This is inevitable. This is inherently more difficult for artists to deal with than for cold-hearted business people. It's not how artists are wired. It's a blessing and a curse. To effectively manage your career you need to be strong, but sensitive, smart and ethical. If you're true to yourself, make certain that your decisions and interactions remain honest, and you fill yourself with empathy, you'll be able to shield off the daggers thrown your way.

Band Agreement

Remove any confusion. Create a band agreement. If you can't afford to hire a lawyer, write out guidelines that everyone agrees to. Use the list below as a guide.

THE BRIDGE

11 Things Every Band Agreement Needs to Include

1) **Songwriting Credit and Copyright** Coldplay splits every song equally 4 ways no matter who actually wrote the song. The Beatles didn't. How will you split songwriting credit?

2) **Compensation** It's best to split all (non-songwriting) income equally. But make sure you designate what percentage of the net income (after all expenses) you're going to keep in the bank account each month and what percentage you will pay the members. Make a point to revisit this breakdown every six months.

3) **Responsibilities and Expectations** Include that everyone will follow reasonable instructions from the manager or BMM and carry out agreed-upon duties diligently. You should outline some general expectations every member will follow. Show up on time. No vomiting on stage. Those kinds of things.

4) **Termination** If a member quits, (s)he loses all rights to future earnings of any kind (except songwriting royalties paid out by his/her own admin publishing company and PRO—more on what a PRO is in Chapter 13) and this member is void of having to cover any expenses or current debt. If a member is voted out, give the member his/her percentage of the value of all band gear and current cash on hand. If the band breaks up, split up everything equally.

5) **Who Covers Expenses** Initially, you may have family members helping cover expenses. Will they get paid back? If so, how? Will every member cover expenses out of pocket or only from the band bank account?

6) **Band Gear Costs** I recommend every member covers 100% of the expenses for their personal equipment (strings, drum heads, amps, etc.) and every member splits group gear expenses equally (PA, lights, van, trailer).

7) **Power of Authority** You should designate one person who has the authority to sign contracts on behalf of the band (the BMM), but require that nothing can be signed without group consent.

8) **Decision-Making** Every group decision must be voted on by the entire group. If there is an even number, give the manager the tie-breaking vote. Or give the BMM two votes.

9) **Side Projects** Are members allowed to participate in side or solo projects?

10) **Hiring New Members** Bring all new members in by unanimous decision. Make clear that all new members are entitled to all new revenue (including all future royalties of past albums), but not ownership/compensation for songs they didn't write.

11) Rights to the Name If (when) the band breaks up or a member leaves, who gets the right to use the band name? You should have a stipulation that if a member leaves (or is voted out), that member loses all rights to the band name.

Manager: To Sign or Not to Sign

If you have been approached by a manager and are wondering if you should sign with her, weigh the options. Make a "Pro" and "Con" sheet and write down all of the qualities, good and bad, this manager brings to the table. Do not sign with a manager just because one asks. Working with the wrong manager could absolutely destroy your career. There are countless stories of managers stealing hundreds of thousands of dollars, intentionally blocking deals, keeping secrets and using the artists to make as much possible money for themselves, while keeping the artists in the poorhouse.

And *always* ask around about this manager. Has he burned bridges? Do his former clients despise him? Google the sh*t out of him. Do not sign until you're certain this is the person for you.

Here are a few general guidelines on whether to sign or not to sign with a manager:

Reasons to Sign

- She has connections you don't.
- You are one of his only clients (if not his only one).
- She loves your music and has been to a bunch of your shows.
- He has been sharing your music relentlessly (without being paid to do it).
- She is a full-time manager.

- He has a plethora of experience in the music industry.
- Her other clients are hot acts of today (not legacy acts).
- He keeps up with the music industry and current trends.
- You respect her.
- You trust him.
- Your career vision and goals align.
- The manager is not you.

Reasons Not to Sign

- She has no more connections than you do.
- He has never seen a show of yours.
- You are one of many clients.
- She acts like she is doing you a favor by working with you.
- He has a day job other than music management.
- You don't trust her.
- She doesn't know the difference between artist and songwriter royalties.
- He doesn't have other clients from who you can get referrals (or his references don't check out).
- He doesn't know how to hunt down every royalty stream that exists for your digital music.
- She has never booked a tour (or worked with an agent to book one) and has no concept of how club or theater booking works.
- All of his "claims to fame" happened over ten years ago.
- She doesn't understand the intricacies of the music industry.
- He doesn't keep up with what's happening in the music industry.
- Your gut says not to.

Trust Your Manager

Your manager is your teammate and there needs to be trust, otherwise the plays can't be made and the game falls apart. Once you decide to work with a manager, you will have to trust that they are doing what they think is best for your career. They are always looking out for your best interests. They want you to succeed. They want you to win. Remember, the only way they get paid is when you get paid.

Audit Your Manager

But that being said, no matter who your manager is, you must always maintain control of your business. You should know the deals going on. You should know how much you're getting paid for every deal. You should have your own attorney (not one referred by your manager) look over your management contract before signing. And throughout your career, you should be able to take a look at every deal made by your manager if you want to. Don't let your manager manipulate you into giving up control. It's your music and your career. They're just along for the ride. Did your manager say you only made $1,200 on the show last night (even though 400 people came)? Ask to see the performance agreement and settlement sheet from the venue (or from the agent). If your manager ever makes excuses as to why you can't see the contracts or doesn't give you full transparency, it's a serious red flag. Legitimate managers will happily show you any documents concerning your career. Only the shady ones will want to keep stuff from you. Maintain control. Always. And forever. Or find a new manager.

THE BRIDGE
7 Ways to Find a Manager

There are a few concrete steps you can take, when you're ready, to get your music in front of managers.

1) **Get Included on Spotify Playlists** Spotify has become the new discovery mechanism for music industry professionals. Ten years ago it was Hype Machine and blogs. There are many playlist plugging strategies out there you can master to get on user-generated playlists, and your distributor may be able to help you get into official editorial playlists. You should also submit all of your new releases directly to Spotify via the submission portal in Spotify for Artists. The more playlists you get added to, the better chance your music will show up on managers' Discover Weekly. More on how to do this in Chapter 5.

2) **Social Media** OK, you have to be somewhat sneaky about this so as to not seem stalky or desperate. But once you figure out which managers might be a good fit for you, you can follow them on socials, Like their posts, watch their stories, see which artists they are interested in and following. Possibly collaborate with those artists (if you're in the same scene). Show up on their feeds—which this manager follows. Cover the songs of this manager's artists (tag the artist and use the appropriate hashtags). This is actually how Emily King's manager, Andrew Leib, discovered Victoria Canal and subsequently asked her to open Emily's show at the Apollo Theater in NYC (and eventually repped Victoria).

3) **A Lawyer** A more traditional way to get in with WCMs is from referrals from respected entertainment attorneys. More on how to find an attorney in a bit.

4) **Direct Contact** If you've done your homework, you can email a manager directly with links to your material. Begin the email to a WCM with compliments about him and express why you think you would be a good fit together; there's a chance the manager may dig in. Remember, you are bringing value to him. Respect his expertise and experience, but understand that you have something he doesn't—amazing music.

5) **Showcases** Many public radio stations, blogs, magazines and music conferences will hold showcases where they will invite managers out. Be careful, though; there are shady promoters and "talent buyers" who will try to get you to pay to play their "showcases," which are nothing more than regular club shows where you have to buy advance tickets to sell to your friends and fans. Do not take the bait. With legitimate showcases, you have to be invited to play. Many will have a submission process. Most won't pay, but they won't make you pay either. If you

have to pay, make absolutely certain you know the names of the people who will be there. "A&R" and "music managers" is not good enough.

6) **Public Radio** It's nearly impossible to get played on top 40 radio or other Clear Channel–owned stations without a big-time radio promoter. But NPR affiliate stations will regularly play local, indie and unsigned artists. Start with the stations in your town or the closest city to where you live that has a public radio station that plays music. Managers definitely tune in to discover new talent. One of the biggest music-based public radio stations is Los Angeles's KCRW, which gets over 550,000 listeners each week. They play pretty much every kind of music except mainstream pop. Study the music played by each DJ. DJs at KCRW (and most other public radio stations) have the autonomy to play whatever they want. So instead of submitting through the front door, go directly to the DJs who are playing music like yours. Be smart about this and do your research. Some DJs only play 1970s funk/soul, so don't submit your metal band's latest song to them.

7) **Business Schools** If you're near a business school, target your promotional efforts to these students. Promote your shows on campus and in the business school building. The business students who are interested in music management may come out to your show and offer to manage you.

AGENT

The day and age of not being able to contact industry
professionals is long gone.

JAIME KELSALL, BOOKING AGENT, APA

Agents book your shows. They typically do not promote these shows. They will book your tours, but you or your manager will have to work with them on the cities you want to visit. Agents will negotiate what you get paid at these shows. It is in their best interest to get the best possible deal because they only make money when you make money. Agents typically take a 10%–20% commission. Most club/festival agents take 10% and most college booking agencies typically take 15%–20%.

Despite what you may think, however, you don't need an agent to play shows or book tours. We'll get into this more in Chapter 7. Yes, agents are nice to have. As someone who has booked over 500 shows on my own, I can tell you, booking is not fun. It's a means to an end. I've booked many national tours on my own, for myself. It's definitely possible, but, believe me, you want to pass off the booking duties to an agent as soon as you can. Booking is incredibly time-consuming and emotionally taxing.

That being said, unlike managers, few agents are going to want to work with you just because they like your band. They're running a business and need to make money just like everyone else. Sure, they want to like the artists they book, but they're much more willing to take on a band they may not love, but has a proven track record of selling out clubs, over a band they love but hasn't ever played outside their hometown. You're going to have to put in most of the work on your own before any agent will take a look at you.

Once you've reached the level where it makes sense to find an agent, make sure you know who to sign with and why. Always ask the other bands on the agent's roster how their experience has been with the agent. Ask the bands the kinds of deals their agent has gotten for them.

Before you sign, ask the potential agent what their vision is for you. Where do they see you in one year, five years, ten years? Do they book national club tours or do they specialize in the regional pizza pub market? Will they be getting you guarantees or door cuts? What can you expect for income at each show? What kinds of festivals have they booked? What other acts on their roster can they pair you up with? Are they planning to book you on opening or headlining tours? Do they have relationships with reputable promoters or do they primarily work with talent buyers at clubs? Are you willing to play four-hour gigs for $100? Because some agents specialize in this. Do you want to live on the road or only play weekends?

You want to discuss all of these things before deciding to work with the agent.

There are scams out there where "agents" will try to get you to pay them up front to book you shows. If you can't find a legitimate, experienced agent, and really don't want to book your shows yourself, you're better off training and hiring a friend to book your shows and giving them the 10%. Do not pay anyone until you get paid. Playing live is a money-making venture. Of course, if you don't have a fanbase, then you're going to have to work that much harder to get people out to your shows, and it may be worth honing your craft at home and building an online presence before hitting the road. You don't want to lose money on tour. You can avoid this if you're smart about it.

You will typically receive the checks or cash from the club or promoter right after the show. Your agent will send you the agreement in advance of the show, so you can double-check that you receive all of the money you're owed. If there is a dispute, your tour manager should try to work it out on the spot. If he can't, your agent will step in.

Reasons to Sign

- He has connections you don't.
- You can spend time on things other than booking.
- She is a better negotiator than you are.
- He has a roster of artists you respect.
- The agent is not you.

Reasons Not to Sign

- You've never heard of any of the bands on their roster.
- She has a bad reputation from her other bands.
- Your visions don't align.
- You're the smallest band on the roster.
- You're the biggest band on the roster.
- Your gut says not to.

How to Find a Booking Agent

Make a list of 10 bands similar to you who you'd like to tour with. Research who their booking agents are (check their website, Facebook and research on LinkedIn). You can find contact info from *Music Connection* magazine's excellent list at www.musicconnection.com/industry-contacts. Simply shoot them an email with a link to a live video of yours or your EPK (Electronic Press Kit)—containing video of course—and your draw in your top five-to-ten cities. If they live in town, invite them to your next show. It's always best, however, to have a mutual friend (or band on their roster) make the initial introduction.

If you're going to be at major festivals like SXSW, Lollapalooza, Bonnaroo or Coachella, make contact months in advance to start the relationship and then a few weeks before the festival invite them to your slot. If you invite them to a club show, always put them on the list. Sure, they can afford a $10 cover, but it's a gesture that goes a long way.

RECORD LABEL

The major label music industry has completely
ruined every aspect of their business. At every step of
the way they've had the tools offered to them to create
an industry that works, and they've completely blown it.
That's why we never had any interest in signing a contract
with one of these companies because they're
clearly completely clueless.
—WIN BUTLER, ARCADE FIRE

Record contracts are just like slavery.
I would tell every artist not to sign.
—PRINCE

Our function is to make famous.

—AVERY LIPMAN, PRESIDENT, UNIVERSAL
REPUBLIC RECORDS

The bands who form to get a deal are the ones who usually miss.

—BRUCE FLOHR, RED LIGHT MANAGEMENT

You're not going to get a record deal by asking for a record deal.

—MARCUS GRANT, DEF JAM RECORDINGS

I don't think in the future record labels are going to own masters.

—TROY CARTER, FORMER MANAGER OF LADY GAGA, JOHN LEGEND,
MEGHAN TRAINOR

The goal of your music career should not be "to get signed." Remember the startling statistic from the introduction? Over 98% of all acts who sign to a major label fail. Success is not marked by getting signed. Sure, getting signed is a stamp of approval from people with money and connections. But, in no way does it mean you're going to be a star. Yes, the right label can help propel you to the next level of your career, but the wrong label can seal your demise.

Many artists these days are succeeding in the new music industry without a label. It's possible. It just takes a lot of hard work.

The biggest asset a label can offer is money and staff. They are your bank. And like a bank, if you don't pay them back, they will take everything you own. No, they aren't going to repossess your car to pay back the advance, but they will refuse to let you release any music you recorded on their dime and will hold on to your masters forever. Most contracts have rerecording clauses that prevent you from rerecording and releasing the songs you wrote while you were under contract with them. Did you spend three years working on your generation-defining masterpiece? Did you sacrifice your relationships, mental health and well-being to create a piece of art that you were certain would be worth it in the end? Your label may not see it this way, decide not to release it, refuse to let you out of your contract, "shelve" the album until you decide to break up. Tough luck. This, unfortunately, is not unique. But we never hear about these stories, because they aren't glamorous and they're from artists you, of course, have never heard of. But some of my favorite artists have gone through just this. It's depressing. And infuriating. Don't let this happen to you.

Major labels historically have disgustingly opaque accounting practices. If you try to audit them, they'll hand you a printed stack of 537,000 pages filled with single lines of sales and streaming royalties in 8-point-size font. Play by play. They do this intentionally so no one can even check if their reports are accurate.

It's well reported that the only way the Big 3 major labels—Sony, Universal and Warner—allowed Spotify to launch in the United States was by striking deals incredibly favorable to them, the labels, and completely unfavorable to the artists. The major labels owned equity in Spotify and cashed out millions when Spotify went public. A leaked Lady Gaga/Interscope contract from 2007 showcases how labels were able to screw artists out of streaming royalties altogether. It states, "No royalties or other monies shall be payable to you [Lady Gaga's songwriting company] or Artist in connection with any payments received by Interscope pursuant to any blanket license under which the Licensee is granted access to all or significant portion of Interscope's catalog . . ." Because the label licensed its entire catalog to Spotify, Deezer, Apple Music and other online services, Interscope doesn't have to pay Lady Gaga (or any other artist who signed this standard agreement) the money earned from streams of her music on those platforms.

Labels have always found ways to screw artists out of money. And as long as the labels make the artist famous, the artist doesn't seem to care all that much. And even if they do decide to investigate, they're handed a 40-pound stack of paper. There's absolutely no transparency when it comes to major-label accounting practices.

This is not because the data isn't there. It is. But it's in the labels' best interests to hide this data from their artists. So it's not surprising that so many huge artists and songwriters have jumped ship from their major publishers and labels to independent admin publishing companies and distributors who pride themselves on transparent accounting. The multinational admin publishing company Kobalt boast that they collect over 900,000 distinct royalty payments for artists and songwriters from around the world—without retaining any ownership. Clients of these types of companies, whether they are artists, managers, songwriters, indie publishers or indie labels, are able to log in and track revenue and streams from around the world.

When labels are courting you, they will make a myriad of attractive promises. They'll basically tell you anything they think you want to hear to get you to sign with them. Unless it's written on paper and signed, don't believe anything they say. Joshua Radin signed with Columbia Records because they promised him they could get him a tour with Bob Dylan. That never happened. Luckily he was able to buy himself out of his contract. Most artists aren't that fortunate. Radin said: "The major record companies are dinosaurs, it's impossible to get anything done with them. When I signed with [Columbia], originally it was to my understanding that I would have full creative control of what I released. And they were by no means dropping me; they just said, 'We want a single on here that's gonna make top 40 radio.' And I said, 'I don't do top 40 radio.' I don't listen to anything that's on top 40 radio. At the end of the day you have to be able to sleep and be able to look yourself in the mirror and say, 'I did what I believed in rather than what some guy in a suit in some office in New York believes in." Joshua Radin now has a very successful independent music career, regularly touring the world to sold-out theaters. He self-releases his music.

The major labels are multinational corporate conglomerates that must answer to shareholders. The company doesn't care about you or your music. The company cares about making money. Remember, even though you may love the people at the label today, they could be replaced tomorrow. You're not signing with people; you're signing with a company. A corporation. You're signing a 100-plus–page contract. You better know what every word in that thing means or have a damn good lawyer who can explain it all to you.

Now, there are some damn fine independent labels out there that could be a good fit for you. Indies are constantly changing their terms to be more favorable for artists. Many indies enter into partnerships with their artists and maintain a level of mutual respect.

In the 2010s, major labels got so desperate to stop their recorded music revenue from plummeting—due in part to the death of the CD, and the rise in piracy—that they rewrote their contracts to be even less favorable to artists than before. Didn't think that was possible? Well, think again. Instead of just taking around 82% of the artist's recording revenue (after recoupment—which rarely happened because of major-label accounting trickery), the majors came up with the concept of "360 deals." These deals mean that the label gets a piece of everything: recorded music, touring revenue, merchandise, sponsorships, the tip jar, your mom's allowance, your crypto earnings. Their reasoning was (is) that they helped propel you to stardom and deserve a cut of your entire career—not just revenue generated from your recordings. The problem with this is that the label starts dipping into so many areas that you will be left with nothing for yourself.

Now that global recorded music revenue has finally recovered from bottoming out in 2014 (thanks to streaming) and has finally surpassed the global recorded music revenue peak of 1999, the bleeding has stopped.

GLOBAL RECORDED MUSIC INDUSTRY REVENUES 1999–2021 (US$ BILLIONS)

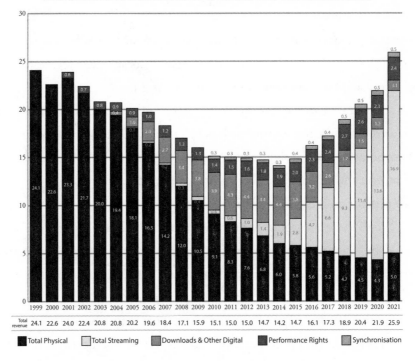

| Total revenue | 24.1 | 22.6 | 24.0 | 22.4 | 20.8 | 20.8 | 20.2 | 19.6 | 18.4 | 17.1 | 15.9 | 15.1 | 15.0 | 15.0 | 14.7 | 14.2 | 14.7 | 16.1 | 17.3 | 18.9 | 20.4 | 21.9 | 25.9 |

■ Total Physical   ☐ Total Streaming   ▨ Downloads & Other Digital   ▉ Performance Rights   ▤ Synchronisation

However, there is much more competition in the market now. The major labels have continued to lose market share to indie labels and self-released artists. In 2021, the majors only had about 65% of the global recorded music market—which is the lowest in fifty years, since the concept of "major label" was a thing.

Let me repeat this. Because it's a really big deal. The major labels have the lowest market share in over fifty years. Self-released, DIY artists and independent labels now make up over 35% of the global recorded music market. And in 2021, self-released artists collectively made $1.5 billion on recorded music revenue alone. Billion! With a *B*.

So, now the majors can't so easily get the artists they want to sign the abusive deals of yore. The major-label industry has changed more in the past three years than it has in the past fifty. Majors are now striking 50/50 licensing deals with artists. Meaning, you don't have to give up ownership anymore. These licensing deals usually last around twelve to fifteen years (but can be shorter or much longer). The label doesn't own your masters, and you are free to conduct your career however you please.

This all being said, not all majors have come around. (Yet. Give it a few years. They will.) And not all artists have educated themselves on this new reality. So, unfortunately, many young, naive artists are still signing the first deal thrown their way, which usually comes with a blindingly high advance (*cha ching!*) in exchange for giving up full ownership and control. Ever heard of a deal with the devil?

Artists, listen up! If one major label offers you a deal, most likely others will as well. Playing them off each other is common practice in every negotiation. You aren't at their mercy anymore. If you get a deal offer, you're most likely buzzing and can leverage that buzz into something wildly more favorable. If you're not buzzing, then you're not ready for a major label. And you don't want one. Because most likely you'll be forgotten, shelved, neglected and hung out to dry.

In the New Music Business, the artists hold the power. The indie labels and distributors hold the power. Sure, the majors still have a ton of money, connections and notoriety. Sure, if they want, they could turn you into a star tomorrow. But the majors know, now, that if they want to win a buzzing artist from the "label services" companies out there, the hands-on distributors, or even the hands-off distributors where most artists first find success, they have to offer more competitive, more favorable deals to artists than ever before.

In previous editions of this book, I spent a lot of ink on the reasons you should not sign with a major label because of their Draconian deals. And back then (er, five years ago) it was accurate.

Now things aren't as cut-and-dried. The majors are finally coming around.

Sony Music was the first of the "Big 3" (Sony, Warner, Universal—and their subsidiaries) to essentially admit their historical sins and wipe clean the debt of every act on their roster who signed prior to the year 2000. Meaning, no more needing to recoup costs before getting paid royalties. Because, the way the old record contracts were written, it was virtually impossible for artists to recoup (pay back the costs the label said it spent on the artist). (That private jet the CEO took to your concert? That's billed to your account. Good luck getting out of that debt.)

Fortunately, all of the majors have now followed suit and have done what's right. Hopefully, no more major-label deals will be written to screw artists anymore. Yeah, yeah, a boy can dream.

Understand that these deals *are* possible now (despite what the other *outdated* music business books written by attorneys say). Don't believe me? Think these deals are merely reserved for superstars? Think again. Listen to my interview with Ricky Montgomery on the *New Music Business* podcast. He got Warner Records to offer him a licensing deal with a fat advance. They wanted to keep this deal so under wraps that they actually demanded I strip out the parts of our conversation where he revealed his deal. I refused. And then I sent an email to the 50,000 music professionals on my list letting them know what Warner had done.

But you can't just march into Warner and demand a deal like this. They'll laugh you right out of DTLA. You have to earn it. How do you earn it these days? Unfortunately, talent has very little to do with it. Ricky had two songs go viral on TikTok and got a hundred million streams before he got courted by nearly every major label out there. You have to build up the buzz on your own first.

If you follow the steps in this book, you can maintain a successful, money-making independent music career. So when the labels do come a-knockin', you will be able to decide what's best for you at that time. Every situation is different. Every artist is different.

If you get offered a record contract (major or indie), the lists below will help you evaluate whether to sign or not:

Reasons to Sign

- You respect the other acts on the roster.
- The other acts on the roster are similar to you.
- Your visions align.
- The label has a strong track record.
- The term is short enough that you can get out if you're unhappy.
- You maintain ownership of your masters.
- The label isn't touching your publishing.
- The label is dedicating a lot of money to marketing and promotion.
- The label will get you on tour with other artists on the label.
- The label is offering lots of money up front in the form of an advance to record an album.

Reasons Not to Sign

- You are making a fine living without a label.
- You aren't similar to the other acts on the roster.
- You aren't a fan of the other acts on the roster.
- The label doesn't have a track record of success.
- Your visions don't align.
- The term is longer than three years (or 1 album).
- The label wants to own your publishing.
- The label wants to take a piece of nonrecording revenue (like merchandise, touring, crowdfunding, sponsorships).
- Your gut says not to.

HOW TO GET A RECORD DEAL

When Avery Lipman, president of one of the most successful record labels in the world, Universal Republic, was asked the question "How do you get a record deal," he replied, "Don't try to get signed. Try to become popular first."

Once you have become an unstoppable force, labels will come. If you have built up a substantial fanbase (tens of thousands of fans online and tens of millions of streams), you can hire a lawyer to shop you around at record labels. Or you can find a list of A&R reps on *Music Connection*'s industry contacts list (musicconnection .com/industry-contacts).

THE BRIDGE
How to Get a Record Advance Without a Record Deal

One of the biggest reasons that artists sign with major record labels is for the upfront cash.

Getting a six- or seven-figure check waved in front of their face is very attractive—even if it means they have to give up all of their ownership forever.

Remember, over 98% of artists who sign to major record labels fail. Meaning, of the 100 artists signed this year, 98 of them won't recoup the costs of their advance and will get dropped. Of course, they don't get their masters back. And all of the blood, sweat, pain and tears that went into that record is now (and forever) property of their former label. "Taylor's version," anyone?

There's also a chance that these artists will be shelved. Meaning, the artist delivers the required content (single, EP or album) and the label just decides not to put it out. Then the artist is left in some sort of purgatory, unable to do anything without the label's permission.

And far too often, artists sign with a label because they love the people at the label. Only for those people to get fired, replaced or move jobs. But, of course, you cannot move with them. You don't sign with people. You sign with companies. It's in black and white.

So, even if you sign with a person at a label whom you love, they may not be there next week.

And your cheerleader is gone. And no one left at the label cares about you. So you get lost in the mix.

Remember, to many labels, artists are just numbers. The executives need to balance the books. They're looking at spreadsheets, hoping for hits. The major record labels are no longer in the business of artist development. They are in the business of creating superstars. They aren't looking for talent. They are looking for hitmakers. Superstars. What's marketable.

Who are labels signing? Artists who have already built something substantial. Who are already starting to pop. The majors are good at giving proven artists a bump into the next level. Sometimes it works. Most of the time it doesn't. Or maybe it does for a short period of time, but then the buzz wears off, the advance runs out, and now the artist, two years down the line, is locked into a deal with a label that doesn't give a sh*t about them. And they are unable to move forward.

The major-label deal is the worst kind of loan in the history of loans.

What other industry does someone lend you money, collect all of their money back, then only pay you 18% of the money that comes in after that, and retain all of the ownership?

Can you imagine if home ownership loans were structured this way?

"Here's $500,000. Once you pay us back the money, you don't own the home. We still own the home. Forever. And all of the appreciation on the home, we will make 82% of that too. Sign here."

But sure, there is no question that major labels can (and do) create superstars. But not every superstar is on a major label.

Just look at Marshmello, Lauv, Chance the Rapper, Phoebe Bridgers. Not to mention the thousands of artists earning five-, six- or seven-figure incomes.

But it costs money to develop a music career. And most emerging artists, even if they've found a bit of success, don't have much up-front capital.

Companies like Sound Royalties, HiFi, Royalty Advance Funding, and Lyric Financial—along with a rising number of independent distributors—are offering advances on future streaming royalties (without ownership).

These companies look at your previous years' streaming revenue and approve a certain amount of up-front capital. Distributors will typically earn back their investment based on the commission they charge on all of your royalties, and other companies only earn a commission on the tracks you designate—capped at a timeline or earning threshold. However, some distributors will keep 100% of your royalties until they're paid back.

For clarity, these are not loans. No creditors will come after you. If you stop earning royalties, well then, you can just part ways.

Some of these deals work on a sliding scale. So, you could get, say, $15,000 up front by giving up 5% of your royalties. Or maybe you need more up front, so you ask for $50,000 and agree to give up 80% of your streaming revenue for the next two years (only of the songs you agree on).

If this really works, it could completely revolutionize the music business as we know it.

In the future, we're going to start seeing fewer artists sign to record deals because of systems like this.

And now blockchain-powered fan-investment models are popping up, so you don't even need to rely on companies to invest in you. You can turn directly to your fans. More on this in Chapter 12.

PUBLISHING COMPANY

As with record labels, there are major and independent publishing companies. They operate very differently. Major publishing companies (like major labels) will be able to give you the massive advances in the hundreds of thousands of dollars. But they will, in return, own all your songs. More on what publishing royalties are (and how to get them) in Chapter 13.

If you want to write songs for other artists, a publishing company may be a good fit for you. You can get a massive advance so you don't have to worry about money for a long while and just concentrate on writing music. Some of the biggest songwriters in the world today (you know, the zillions of names on Beyoncé, Travis Scott, Rihanna, Adele, Carrie Underwood, Toby Keith and Keith Urban songs), get paid a bulk amount up front (around $30,000 or so) by the artist's label to cut the song. Many times, these stars will get 50–100 songs submitted by publishers and the artist/label will choose their 10 favorites for the album. Meghan Trainor, Chris Stapleton, Bruno Mars, Julia Michaels, Carole King, Luke Bryan, Lady Gaga, Hunter Hayes, and Kacey Musgraves all started just as songwriters with publishing deals and wrote songs for other artists before they broke out as featured artists themselves.

I do not recommend signing a publishing deal if you're working on a career as an artist. We will get into how to collect all of your songwriter royalties in Chapter 13. You don't need a traditional publishing company to do this anymore. Yes, of course, many artists also have publishing deals, but like record labels, major publishing companies are very restrictive and require owning your songs.

Publishing companies also have licensing departments where they will work to get songs placed on TV, film, video games and commercials. There are many stand-alone licensing companies that you can work with who do only this and don't own your songs. This is a much better option in this day and age. More on this in Chapter 14.

Reasons to Sign

- You want to write songs for other artists.
- You love writing top 40 pop or country songs.
- You spend most days writing songs.
- They are offering a huge amount of money up front in the form of an advance.
- You like cowriting.
- You respect the other songwriters on the roster.
- The publishing company has a proven track record.

Reasons Not to Sign

- You want to own your songs.
- You have a career as an artist.
- You don't care for the songs on the roster.
- They aren't offering you an advance.
- Your gut says not to.

HOW TO GET A PUBLISHING DEAL

The big songwriting hubs are L.A., London and Nashville. If you want to be a full-time songwriter, you need to live in one of these cities. So step number one is relocate. Step number two is go out to songwriter nights around town and cowrite with as many people as you possibly can. You'll have to network your a$$ off. You can't just have voice memos on your iPhone of songs you've written. You have to get fully produced demos that sound like they could be on the radio. So if you don't have the production skills to put this together, you're going to need to find a producer or cowriter who does. Once you have a bunch of great-sounding demos, that's when it's time to shop around for a publishing company. You can hire a lawyer to get you in the door at publishing companies. However, the more people you meet and write with in L.A., London or Nashville, the better your chances are that one of them will have (or soon get) a publishing deal. Songwriters tend to find each other. There isn't a big division between songwriters with a publishing deal and those without. If you're focused on this singular goal, once you're in Nashville, London or L.A. (and your songs are undeniable hits), you will get a publishing deal. But your songs have to be hits. Publishing companies aren't looking for art songs. Artists write the art songs. If you want to be an employed songwriter, you have to write hits.

You can also find a very good list of publishers on *Music Connection*'s industry contact list (musicconnection.com/industry-contacts).

PUBLICIST

What sets you apart from every other artist out there?
The job of a publicist is creating that story.

—AMANDA BLIDE, TREND PR

I like to meet [artists] in person and have some sort of relationship because the more connection you have with somebody the more you want them to succeed.

—CAROLINE BOROLLA, CLARION CALL MEDIA

One thing that's important when you work with a PR firm is asking for a level of transparency and communication. Ask for weekly or biweekly reports. Working with a PR team that will be communicative and will send you updates is important.

—NINA LEE, THE ORIEL

A publicist remains a crucial element of an artist marketing campaign.

—REBECCA SHAPIRO, SHORE FIRE MEDIA

PR is a service industry, and like any other service industry, we should have to deliver in order to get compensation.

—MIKEL CORRENTE, PURPLE BITE

Want to know something startling? Most publicists charge $500–$5,000 a month. And you aren't guaranteed anything. They could get you on *The Tonight Show*, Joe Rogan's podcast and the cover of *Rolling Stone*, plus 50 blog articles, podcast, TV and livestream spots, or . . . nothing. Literally nothing. And they're paid the same either way.

Luckily there are some publicists who have changed this model a bit and cater to indie musicians. Some publicists charge per contact. Like $25 per email sent. This takes a lot of trust that she isn't just blindly sending out press releases but actually writing a personalized email to someone with whom she has a good relationship.

That's really what you're paying for with a publicist: the relationships.

Anyone can write a press release or send an email. But will your email get opened? That depends on who the sender is. If the publicist is known and respected, most likely she will get a reply. However, there are tons of publicists out there who charge an arm and a leg and literally just blast out press releases to every "music reviewer" on their master list. Let me tell you a little secret. There's this site called Cision, which is a master database containing contact information of anyone a publicist would ever need to contact. My contact info got included on the site (as a writer for *Digital Music News* and Ari's Take) and I get, on average, five press releases a day. Rarely are these emails personalized to me (other than a "Hi, Ari," which is a program they have set up within their email that inserts "First Name Here"). I feel bad for the bands these publicists are pitching me. 1) I don't review music, so I shouldn't be getting these press releases, and 2) I know that the publicists probably promised these bands that they had connections, relationships and contacts that they don't. Cision costs about $200 a month to subscribe to. Simply having a subscription to the site shouldn't give you the right to say that you actually have these connections. You want the music booker at *Ellen*? You can find it in thirty seconds in a Cision search.

A publicist can definitely help you come up with your story, image, strategy and schedule. But not every publicist will. That should be part of your initial conversation with your potential publicist. If they don't help you come up with a jaw-dropping story, then you shouldn't be paying them a jaw-dropping price.

Publicists operate on campaigns. Typically they'll require two to four months depending on the project (single, album, music video, tour, release show, benefit concert). And most publicists charge a monthly or campaign fee. The reason publicists need such a large window is because many reviewers need at least a month in advance of the release to cue up and assign stories. And then after the release date it may take another month or so for all stories to filter in. The publicist will want at least a month of lead time (before contacting press) to get all of the materials together, work on your story and PR campaign. So plan ahead. If your release is August 1, start looking for publicists in April.

Most important, if you choose to work with a publicist, they should be reputable and proven. Always, always, always check their references and talk to other artists they have worked with. Ask the company for references, but also go through their clients page on their website and hit up those artists and managers. There are a ton of PR scams out there that target independent musicians and managers. First off, if you get solicited by a PR company, that's a red flag. Most of the reputable ones don't need to seek out clients through spammy methods. I've encountered such scams personally. After receiving many complaints from artists and managers about a certain PR company, I decided to investigate and discovered that they were flat out taking artists' money, then disappearing. I wrote an article about them, and after they threatened to sue me multiple times (you can't sue if it's the truth!), they eventually conceded that they had messed up, and the company folded. Win for musicians everywhere!

This all being said, music PR has changed dramatically over the past ten years. A decade ago, if you charted on the blog aggregator site Hype Machine (which tracks hundreds of well-respected music blogs), you were almost guaranteed to get hit up by managers and labels.

Press used to move the needle. Now, not so much. It used to be that if you got a write-up on *Consequence of Sound*, *Pitchfork*, *Stereogum* or *Pigeons & Planes*, you would get hundreds of thousands of streams on SoundCloud. Now getting a great write-up on a reputable blog doesn't really do much other than give you bragging rights.

Did I feel good that *American Songwriter* did a full profile on me in advance of my new album, calling me "a DIY icon, a successful entrepreneur, a commanding performer and a world-class songwriter?" You better believe it. (Thanks, Joe Vitagliano!) I couldn't have paid for a better inclusion. Except, did anything really come of it? Not really. No streaming bump. No discovery. No doors flung open. Now, believe me, as a songwriter putting my heart out on the line in the form of an album, it's nice to get this validation from a well-respected publication. But validation doesn't pay the bills.

I paid a PR firm an arm and a leg to work my album campaign. They're one of the best in the biz. I had to see what the state of music PR was in 2021 (when I released my latest album)—and report back, of course. Well, they got me on a bunch of podcasts and blogs, some of which I'd never heard of, and a couple big spots. And that *American Songwriter* write-up. It felt good. But, again, it didn't move the needle.

If you're going to hire a traditional publicist, there has to be a bigger reason to do so other than that you're releasing an album, single or music video. If you have no real buzz or clout, a publicist won't be able to create buzz like they once could. Music publications aren't as influential as they once were.

If you're doing a collaboration with a well-known, respected artist, that's newsworthy. If you broke the Twitch single-stream attendance record, that's newsworthy. If you are the first-ever Grammy-nominated woman in the Best Engineered Album category (like Emily Lazar in 2016), that's newsworthy, and a publicist could help you land talk shows, radio, podcasts, and publications.

Just releasing music is no longer buzzy enough for a publicist to help virtually unknown artists. They'll take your money. They'll do their best. But nothing will happen other than getting a few people to write some nice things about you. Your ego will be stroked. How much is that worth to you?

Spotify says that getting press gives you a better shot at getting official playlist editorial inclusion. Maybe it will. It didn't for me.

PR and publicity are evolving. Publicists no longer just pursue press and appearances.

Many publicists are now expanding their operations to include brand management, social media management, digital marketing and creative direction. They have seen the industry shift. And they know that musicians don't care as much about a write-up in *Pitchfork* as they do about a placement in New Music Friday.

It used to be very frowned upon (slash illegal) to pay writers and publications to publish a story about you or your client. I once hosted a Clubhouse discussion on the state of music PR with seven reputable music publicists. We got on the topic of ethics. One of the publicists mentioned that it was unethical that the journalists weren't being paid a living wage to write about music. This publicist said he changed his business model, where he now pays journalists to write about his clients. The other publicists were in an uproar. This was against everything they stood for. Against their entire business model. Against all traditional journalistic ethics they had been taught in journalism school. They dug their heels in and patted themselves on the back for holding the line on traditional journalism, while this lone publicist stood his ground and began to build a new business— catering to the artists, labels, managers and publicists willing to pay for placement, and the publications willing to get paid for placement.

The thing is, nearly every publicist (including the ones on this panel) had used SubmitHub, paying journalists to *consider* inclusion. That's where they draw the line. It's acceptable to pay for consideration. Just not guaranteed placement. *Hmm.*

In the US, posting sponsored articles, tweets, Instagrams, TikToks, etc., without disclosure of the sponsorship can result in the publication or creator being fined by the FTC. But this is a common practice among marketing agencies, where they pay contributing writers to include links, mentions, or even full articles. And influencer agencies regularly get paid by labels, artists, and managers to get their songs used by their influencers on TikTok—almost always without disclosure.

And even *Rolling Stone* started a program in early 2021 called Culture Council where "a private, vetted community for influencers, tastemakers, and innovators" can pay $2,000 to have the ability to publish articles on

Rollingstone.com. These articles are labeled as Culture Council articles, but upon quick glance, they don't really look much different than any other article published on the website.

How much would you pay to get on *Rolling Stone*? That's the real question. Because when publicists charge $5,000–$20,000 for a campaign and only land you low-level blogs and podcasts, I'm pretty sure every artist on the planet would prefer to pay $2,000 for a guaranteed positive *Rolling Stone* review.

Which brings us back to our publicist who was attacked in the Clubhouse room for proclaiming that writers should be paid fairly. Most music journalists get paid a pittance for publishing blog posts in well-respected publications. Many get paid around $25–$50. Some get paid nothing— just the glory of having their byline in the publication (and the ability to make money off of SubmitHub submissions).

The state of music journalism is backward right now.

Which is why you must think long and hard about *why* you want a publicist. *Why* you want press or media inclusion. Would that $10,000 be better spent on creative development (music videos, photo shoots, style design, art direction) and paid marketing (social media ads)?

This is up to you to decide for yourself.

Reasons to Sign

- She has great ideas on how to craft your story, brand, aesthetic and image.
- He has a proven track record getting media placements for acts similar to yours (in size and genre).
- You can afford her.
- They believe in the success of your project.
- She likes your music.
- You are pushing out something newsworthy.

Reasons Not to Sign

- You don't have a headline-worthy event.
- You can't afford her.
- The publicist seems like he wants to work with you for the paycheck.
- She doesn't have a proven track record.
- He won't refer you to clients he's worked with.
- Her promises seem too good to be true.
- Their references don't check out.
- Your gut says not to.

HOW TO FIND A PUBLICIST

Make a list of some of the best blogs that review your style of music. If you don't follow any blogs currently, you can start with the ones cataloged on Hype Machine. You can also search mid-level artists' names and recent song or album titles to see what press comes up. Make a list of the artists that these blogs have reviewed. Then search for other blogs that have written about these artists. Hit up those who have gotten the most press (Instagram is totally fine) and ask them who did their press outreach. Most won't have a problem referring you to their publicist.

To organize this a bit, make a spreadsheet (I prefer Google Sheets so everyone on your team can work on this with you). Make seven columns: Artist, Campaign (single/album release, tour, etc.), Press Received, Date Range, Publicist Name, Publicist Website, Publicist Email.

If you're having trouble hunting down contact info or want a bigger list of publicists/PR companies you can check out *Music Connection*'s great industry lists at musicconnection.com/industry-contacts.

ATTORNEY

When you're ready, it's worth getting a lawyer who is excited about you to shop you around and open the doors you can't open on your own. But don't spend the money on these pursuits until you're ready. Meaning, if you're drawing only 50 people to your local shows and have very low social media engagement and low streaming numbers, you're not ready. If you're selling out 500-cap local clubs, are killing it in at least one avenue of social media, getting millions of streams, have a solid email list and are starting to tour, it's worth getting on people's radar. What people? Well, that's what you need to figure out. Refer back to your goals sheet. What kinds of people do you need to help you get there? Would a booking agent be most beneficial now? A record label? A hands-on distributor? A manager?

Once you find a good entertainment lawyer, you can contract her out for specific tasks. Or, if you're interested in getting shopped at a label, an invested attorney might take you on for a percentage of the advance. And remember, nothing is set in stone. Every attorney will operate differently. The young and hungry lawyers, especially, who are innovating in the new industry, may come up with a creative deal that works for you.

Eventually you'll have an attorney on retainer, but this won't come until you're using her services regularly (and, of course, can afford it). So for the time being you'll use lawyers for specific jobs like negotiating contracts, shopping you around and consultations.

HOW TO FIND AN ATTORNEY

Of course, finding an entertainment lawyer referred by someone you trust is best. First, ask around your scene. If you strike out there, check out *Music Connection*'s annual entertainment attorney guide—they have attorneys broken down by state. You can find a PDF of their annual guide online at musicconnection.com/industry-contacts. This is the best list out there. And the magazine is actually worth subscribing to. Full disclosure, they gave my 2014 album a very positive review and I've written a few articles for them (pro bono). But they ain't paying me for the recommendation.

Another option is to check out the Volunteer Lawyers for the Arts. Many states have active programs (google "California Lawyers for the Arts"), and you can contact them for free legal services.

Not All Lawyers Are Created Equal

After one of my shows at the Hotel Cafe in Hollywood, a guy in his fifties in a button-up shirt, unbuttoned just enough to admire his ample, greying chest hair, walked into the green room and handed me his card. He was an entertainment attorney. He told me he loved my set and was actually there to see the band after me. He told me that if I needed any help to give him a call. The following week I called him to ask a question about the flood of Music Reports Inc. (MRI) letters I was receiving. He explained to me that they were a rights-licensing and royalty-collections company and they were sending me NOIs (Notices of Intent) for their clients to use my songs on their services. I asked him what kinds of royalties do they collect and what rights do they license and for who. He said these are primarily mechanical royalties. I asked him, "Oh, like from Spotify and Rdio?" He said, "No, mechanical royalties aren't generated from streaming, only sales." Hold up. From speaking with multiple publishing administrators and the Harry Fox Agency (MRI's competitor), I had learned the contrary. (Rdio was actually a client of MRI at the time of this phone call.)

I pressed on, "Uh, I could have sworn streaming generated mechanical royalties."

"No, you're mistaken, they don't."

"OK, thanks for the help." I hung up.

He was flat out wrong. He didn't just give bad advice; he was literally incorrect about music facts. This music attorney didn't know basic music law. Granted, sure, when this conversation took place, streaming was still relatively new (this was early 2014), but still, shouldn't an entertainment attorney with a business card that says as much keep up with this stuff?

So, be careful. Just because they have a law degree doesn't mean they're always right.

Oh, and what the hell are mechanical royalties? We'll get into that in Chapter 13.

WHY EVERYTHING YOU THOUGHT ABOUT STREAMING IS WRONG

People have to see the future. Because free already exists. It's a flawed argument when you say "I don't want my music on any services that offers free" when free already exists. You're ignoring the future. Hurricane Katrina is coming and you're staying in the house right now.

—TROY CARTER, FORMER MANAGER OF LADY GAGA, JOHN LEGEND, MEGHAN TRAINOR

The narrative that streaming doesn't pay isn't completely true.

—VÉRITÉ, 350 MILLION SPOTIFY STREAMS

We all heard the stories like "My Song Was Played 168 Million Times and All I Got Was $4,000." Yeah, pretty jaw-dropping headline. Except, what you didn't hear about was that these were songwriter royalties, split among multiple writers. And this was from Pandora, a digital radio ("non-interactive") streaming service (which pays much less than "interactive" streaming services like Spotify or Apple Music). The artist actually made much, much more. We all were told over and over again that streaming was going to kill the music industry. Well actually, we were told first that tape recorders were going to kill the industry (because you could simply record the radio). Then it was burning CDs. Then it was downloads and Napster. Then it was Spotify. The thing is, innovations in technology are inevitable. You could fight progress by refusing to put your music on streaming platforms out of sheer principle (ignoring the fact that streaming now actually collectively brings in more money than CD or digital download sales) or you could work with technology, get creative and find new ways to make money with your music career.

Formats change. Price points change. People didn't like paying $18.99 for a full-length CD when they only wanted one song. So when downloads exploded and broke up the album, labels were furious because they couldn't get people to overpay for an album with one good song and ten filler tracks.

People will sacrifice quality for convenience. And pay for it. It's why cassette tapes were widely adapted when vinyl records sounded better. People could play them on the go in their Walkmans and car stereos. CDs were even more convenient (no more flipping sides or fast forwarding to your favorite track) and became popular despite the fact that audiophiles claimed that CDs (initially) sounded worse than cassettes or records. What stopped Napster? iTunes. Why? Because iTunes was more convenient. More reliable. iTunes downloads' sound quality was well below that of CDs (initially iTunes was 128kbps vs. CDs' 1411kbps). If the choice was between driving to the record store and buying a CD or downloading the song you wanted on Napster, people chose the latter. Not because it was free, but because it was easy. But many times the songs were mislabeled and things were not laid out very clearly. That's why iTunes caught on. It was a cheap and easy alternative to free and inconvenient. But what beat iTunes (and nearly killed piracy once and for all)? Spotify. Even more convenient.

We're never going back to downloads. Just like we're never going back to cassettes or vinyl (or flip phones). Yes, there's been a massive vinyl resurgence over the past few years, but it will never come close to its 1970s peak.

Withholding music from streaming because it doesn't earn as much as downloads is like a farmer refusing to sell eggs because they don't earn as much as the chicken. Sure, it may not make as much money *today*, but it will tomorrow. And the fact of the matter is, people want eggs, they don't want chickens.

Withholding your music from streaming platforms is the worst possible thing you could do to your career. Music fans have put their love of streaming platforms over their love of artists (unfortunately). If your music is not on Spotify and your fans are, they will move on to another artist. They will not go download your album for $10 when they can get nearly every other artist on the planet for $10 a month.

The alternative to streaming is not sales. The alternative to streaming is piracy. When Taylor Swift famously pulled all of her music from Spotify for her 2014 album, *1989,* you know what the #1 album on The Pirate Bay (the largest illegal downloading site at the time) was? You guessed it, *1989.*

And withholding your music from streaming services is extremely shortsighted. Remember, do not make decisions for your music career based on your bottom line (today). What do your fans want? If you alienate them by forcing them to consume music in a way that doesn't make sense to them, they won't stick with you.

Streaming eliminates piracy.

In 2009, 80% of Norway's population under 30 were illegally downloading music. In 2014 (after most of the under-30 population had adopted streaming), only 4% of Norway's under-30 population still used illegal file-sharing platforms to get ahold of music. In the United States, over 85% of the recorded music industry now comes from streaming. And after fifteen years of revenue decline from global recorded music, streaming fueled the comeback. Since 2015, the global recorded music industry has grown year over year and has finally surpassed its previous peak from 1999. So anyone who said that streaming would be the downfall of the music industry, once again, was incorrect.

Streaming is great for art. Streaming rewards artists for creating great music that fans want to play over and over. There's much more potential for the long tail. The more someone likes your album, the more she will play it. And you will get paid for every play. Over time, this will earn you *more* money than sales ever did.

Spotify has led the industry in streaming growth with their powerful playlists. It's now commonplace for independent artists to be able to quit their day jobs because one of their songs gets included in a few popular playlists. Many playlists have tens of thousands of monthly listeners. Some of these listeners turn into fans, but because every stream is monetized, the artist is getting paid regardless if they make new fans or not.

Before, your fans would buy your music to listen to it. You only got paid if you had fans. Now, people listen to your music first and become fans second. And you get paid for every play. Because so many people are using playlists to drive their listening habits, you could be making thousands of dollars a month in streaming revenue before having any fans willing to buy a ticket to your show.

We are nearing the end of owning data. It's pretty much already here for most under the age of 30. Who wants to clutter up their hard drives with files if they don't have to? That's why everything is moving to the cloud. Eventually, devices won't need to store any data natively because everything will be accessible at all times within the cloud and connectivity will be uninterrupted and ubiquitous.

There is a generational gap in ideology. Boomers cherish ownership and value things. Millennials embrace sharing and value experiences. Since boomers run the music industry and Millennials run the tech industry, there has been an ongoing battle for clarity.

One thing is for certain, you can't wait around for these two opposing forces to come to an understanding. You must move your career forward and exist in the realities of the day.

This all being said, it would be disingenuous not to mention the challenges independent artists who *have* fans face, when they haven't been anointed by the Spotify Gods by being placed on their coveted playlists. Yes, previously, if you had 10,000 fans who all bought your 10-song album at $10 and listened to it 10 times, you made $100,000. Now, if you have 10,000 fans who stream your 10-song album 10 times (1 million streams), you'd make about $3,500 (give or take). Yikes.

When streaming first hit, these were the arguments by the classic rockers and talking heads who didn't understand how streaming worked, and they manipulated the discussion to fit their narrative. However, we're comparing apples and oranges. It's not realistic anymore (if you do the work) to think that the only people streaming your music are fans. That's just not how streaming works. Songs get included on hot playlists all the time and end up with millions of streams (and very few fans). But those artists are getting paid for every one of those playlist streams—whether the listener knows who they are or not. This is not the record industry of your parents.

So, you do have to get creative. You have to find ways to monetize your fanbase—outside of simply getting them to stream (or buy) your music. Streaming is the loss-leader for future sales opportunities. The foot in the door.

When emerging independent artists, who are often located far outside the music industry hubs, get included on active Spotify playlists and rack up millions of streams long before they have any ticket-buying fans, is that bad? I would argue it's great. These talented artists are getting paid for their music.

In 2021, Spotify launched its Loud and Clear website, where it broke down some financial numbers based on the artists on the platform. This was in response to the criticism that Spotify isn't transparent enough with its payment structure. Spotify keeps this site updated, and I'd encourage you to see how many artists are earning money from Spotify.

Take a look at how many artists earned recording and publishing royalties from Spotify in 2021:

$1,000+: 203,300 artists

$5,000+: 81,500 artists

$10,000+: 52,600 artists

$50,000+: 16,500 artists

$100,000+: 9,500 artists

$500,000+: 2,170 artists

$1,000,000+: 1,040 artists

$2,000,000+: 450 artists

$5,000,000+: 130 artists

FANS AREN'T GOING TO PAY FOR MUSIC ANYMORE—AND THAT'S OK

It's almost a rite of passage every artist goes through in the modern music industry. The moment he accepts that he will not be able to rely on music sales to sustain his career. That people are not buying music like they used to. And never will again.

Just a few years ago it seemed like every artist was passing around articles chastising fans for illegally downloading music. How it hurts the bands. The producers. The session musicians. The labels. The songwriters. And the industry as a whole. We all remember the "illegally downloading music is the same as stealing a microwave from a store" argument. We all bought it. Well, musicians and the industry, that is. Fans? Not so much.

Since 2001, sales of recorded music have continued to drop like an anchor in a sea ruled by pirates. In 2021, 3.2% of the global recorded music revenue came from digital downloads. And under 20% came from physical sales (largely outside the US, where under 9% came from physical sales). We have to start embracing alternative monetization opportunities and accept that the traditional way that fans support artists is over.

It's time for a new mindset. It's a new era. People *are* valuing artists—but in the way that makes sense to them (not the current industry talking heads and classic rockers screaming the loudest). What's wrong with a 23-year-old who loves a band paying $250 for a Kickstarter exclusive, $5 per video released on Patreon, $25/month on Twitch through subscriptions and tips, $100 on their NFT, $35 a year on Bandcamp to be part of the fan club, an $18 ticket for their concert, a $25 T-shirt and a backstage "experience" for $50, but never download an album or buy a CD? What's wrong with that?

Fans aren't going to pay to own recorded music anymore. But that doesn't mean they won't pay you for making music.

The album gets the fan in the door. Gets her hooked. The album is only the introduction. No longer the end game. The album is the gateway. And the album is found online, for free, with a couple clicks.

And major label artists never made much from album sales anyways. They always had to rely on alternative sources of income (like touring and merch) to offset what their labels didn't pay them in royalties. Lyle Lovett admitted that after selling over 4.6 million records he has received $0 in record royalties from his label. But he's had a very successful career. Why are people silent when record companies (legally) steal from artists, but raise hell when fans do it?

I've never made a dime from a record sale in the history
of my record deal. I've been very happy with my sales,
and certainly my audience has been very supportive.
I make a living going out and playing shows.

—LYLE LOVETT

So, your options. You can either b*&ch about the "decline of the music industry," exclaim that fans aren't true fans if they don't pay for recorded music, *or* you can get creative, embrace the new technologies that build on the artist-fan relationship, and lead the pack in this beautiful new world full of alternative revenue sources. Your choice.

3.

RECORDING

A musician running software from Native Instruments can
recreate, with astonishing fidelity, the sound of a Steinway grand
piano played in a Vienna concert hall, or hundreds of different
guitar amplifier sounds, or the Mellotron protosynthesizer that
the Beatles used on "Strawberry Fields Forever." These sounds
could have cost millions to assemble 15 years ago; today, you can
have all of them for a few thousand dollars.

—STEVEN JOHNSON, *NEW YORK TIMES*

If you do something different, you excel a little faster.

—RIKI LINDHOME, GARFUNKEL AND OATES

The song can be no more or less human than you are.

—QUINCY JONES

'M GOING TO START OFF THE RECORDING CHAPTER WITH THE LEAST COOL
thing to talk about. You're going to have a knee-jerk reaction. Your
blood pressure is going to rise. You're going to want to fight me. Don't say
I didn't warn you. But hear me out. It's important.

Before you begin the writing process for the album, and definitely
before you start recording, you need to think of what's called in the marketing world Product Market Fit (PMF). Stay with me. Don't let your

eyes glaze over. I'm going to explain this as musicianly as possible. What Product Market Fit means is, do you have a product (music) that fits a market (fans). Simple, right? This seems like a no-brainer. And, of course, you probably just rolled your eyes and exclaimed loudly, *"Yes!"* Apologize to your neighbors in the coffee shop.

But, step back for a moment. Before you start the writing-recording process, you should know *exactly* who your fans are and what the purpose of this recording is. Most bands just make albums for themselves without thinking twice about it and wonder why they can't get anyone to listen and share it.

I know you think all you have to do is make "good music" and the fans will find you. But that couldn't be further from the truth. For one thing, "good" is obviously subjective. You probably think half the bands on the charts today are sh*t. But, clearly, others think they're incredible.

So, again, before starting the writing-recording process, make a document entitled "Our Fans." You should have a minimum of 20 points on this list. The more the merrier. It could look something like this:

Our fans('):

1) Are primarily male.
2) Are between the ages of 22 and 35.
3) Listen to KCRW, The Current and World Cafe Live.
4) Listen to podcasts like *WTF, Armchair Expert, Pod Save America* and *The Joe Rogan Experience.*
5) Favorite bands of the past decade include Alabama Shakes, the Black Keys, Cage the Elephant, Jack White, and Dawes.
6) Favorite bands from previous decades include Led Zeppelin, the Ramones, Nirvana and Pearl Jam.
7) Hang out in local coffee shops.
8) Read nonfiction philosophy books.

9) Wear leather coats, black jeans and boots.

10) Attend SXSW, Lollapalooza, Bonnaroo, and Governor's Ball music festivals.

11) Eat mostly local, organic foods.

12) Are early adopters of tech.

13) Are college-educated and probably studied philosophy or English.

14) Buy lots of vinyl.

15) Wear trucker hats.

16) Take public transportation whenever possible or own secondhand cars.

17) Shop in thrift stores.

18) Drink at bars like the Ye Rustic Inn, BLB, Herkimer and Liquor Lyles.

19) Eat at restaurants like Uptown Diner, Muddy Waters, Jitlada, Hunan Cafe.

20) Live in cities like Silver Lake, Los Feliz, Uptown Minneapolis, Portland, Williamsburg.

21) Favorite TV shows include *Silicon Valley, The Sopranos, Last Week Tonight, The Wire, Better Call Saul.*

22) Favorite movies include *Love and Mercy, Citizen Four,* Wes Anderson movies, Christopher Nolan movies, Quentin Tarantino movies, the *Godfather* movies, *Back to the Future, A Clockwork Orange, Fight Club* and *Casino.*

Now, of course, 100% of your fans will not meet each point. Your fan base is a Venn diagram of interests.

Understanding who the majority of your (prospective) fans are will help you craft your sound, image, merch and overall marketing and promotion.

I know it's hard to hear how calculated you have to be. The labels do this. They know who they're targeting. You're competing with them.

In 2015, in advance of the release of *25*, Nielsen (commissioned by Columbia Records) did a study of who fans of Adele are and they found (unsurprisingly) that more than half of them are women, most of whom are aged 25–44. But they also found, among other things, that most of them:

- Have children.
- Play soccer.
- Shop at Victoria's Secret.
- Drink Aquafina bottled water.
- Drink light beer.

Adele wouldn't release a song expounding the joys of a childless life. And she probably shouldn't bash soccer moms. Unless she wants to alienate 80% of her audience. Sure, this is inherent to who she is, and she probably didn't break out this study before the recording process, like I'm telling you to do, but she has a label to worry about these things. You don't.

To help you figure out what kind of music you want to record and release, what kind of fans you want to gain and what kind of career you want to have, you should think about these things before you lay down a click track.

If you want to get on top 40 radio, you have to understand what top 40 radio sounds like. You have to sound like that. If you want to get your songs placed in commercials, film and TV, you have to know the *sound* of songs that are getting placed the most.

Above all, you need to be thinking about your story. What is going to lead off your press release for this album? Are you getting over a tragedy? Is this album mostly about that? Did your band's van roll off the road on your last tour and you all ended up in the hospital but recovered and made an album about the experience? If you decided to make a full-length album (and not just singles or an EP), why? What is it about? The only reason to make a full-length album in this day and age is if you're making a statement. So what's the statement?

You can always update your story for each album. Or as often as necessary. As often as you evolve. But you always need that story that sets you apart.

The story is public. Your PMF research is private.

The best producers in the world analyze other successful producers' techniques. You need to analyze other successful artists' writing, recording and performing techniques, along with their image, personas and swagger. Every successful artist has a swagger. It's sexy. It's their own. And it's awesome.

All of this, when discussing recording, seems cold, calculated and unnatural. But it doesn't have to be. Of course, you're going to create music "true to yourself." But this could go in a million different directions. The song you heard in the bar last night influenced you whether you want to admit it or not.

So, do your research. Make a playlist of songs that you'll use as inspiration for your upcoming album. What is going to be the *sound* of the album? It will be a combination of all of your influences, of course, but get active with this process. Study what makes these songs great. Is it the guitar tones? The pocket? The hooks? The lyrics? The vocals? The groove? The syncopation? The raw passion? Once you've pinpointed what makes these songs great, then ask why? Why is the pocket so strong? Is it because ?uestlove and Pino Palladino are the rhythm section? Why are the lyrics great? Is it because they tell a story? What kind of story? And how do they tell the story? Is it literal? Metaphorical?

Remember, when reviewers talk about your music, they will talk about your story. They will not discuss these musical elements, because most music reviewers aren't musicians. They aren't going to say "the drummer lays back on the beat, the syncopated horn hits punctuate the Hammond

B-3 riffs." The musical elements that you and I get off to, music reviewers don't typically articulate. Of course, these techniques are important. You will perfect these in studio. But, never lose track of what the majority of the listening public will pay attention to: *the story behind the music.* Just getting great players on your album is not a story.

But, don't sacrifice quality because you don't think the majority will notice. Fellow musicians will notice and will or will not work with you based on the sound of your record. Do not make your music for the lowest common denominator. You must create great art first and foremost. Because if your product is not great, then your story doesn't matter.

I had the incredible honor of meeting legendary record producer Quincy Jones. It was at Capitol Records studio A where he was being honored with a lifetime achievement award by AKG. Jacob Collier performed a QJ tribute on the piano featuring songs by Michael Jackson, Frank Sinatra and George Benson. In one of the control rooms they had the original sessions of "Thriller" pulled up on Pro Tools where we could mute, solo or adjust the volume of every track. Pretty magical.

Because it was such an intimate event, I got a chance to chat with the legend himself. We got on the topic of fame, money and all of that. He leaned over and whispered in my ear, "If you do it for the money, God walks out of the room."

Welp. Life changed.

Music can be spiritual. You know that feeling you get when you're at a concert and everyone is connected? Levitating? That's what we're all striving for.

Even though this book is all about the business of music, you have to turn all of that off when you're creating if you want to affect people deep to their core.

If you want to make music for the sole purpose of making money, it can be done. But you'll be forgotten. No judgments. Just the truth.

Over the course of your music career, you are going to be making a lot of investments, like any business owner or entrepreneur. Early on, especially, most of these investments won't show an immediate return. Not all good investments return money. Some return art, music, passion, community, love.

You don't need to go into the recording process thinking, "Will I make this investment back financially?" Instead, it should always be, "Will I be proud of the work?" That's what will keep you going. And that's why you should continue to drop boatloads of money investing in your art when you know there's a chance it could be a financial loss.

It's always a love gain.

GETTING INTO THE MUSICAL HEADSPACE

The best art divides an audience. If you put out a record and
half the people who hear it absolutely love it and half the
people who hear it absolutely hate it you've done well.
Because it's pushing that boundary. If everyone thinks
"aw that's pretty good," why bother making it?
—RICK RUBIN

Maybe the truth doesn't rhyme.
—JONI MITCHELL

Once you know your PMF and are comfortable with the style of music you're going to make, you need to turn back into the artist. You can't write great songs with your business cap on. You need a clear head and an open heart to write songs that are meaningful to you and will connect with an audience.

Much of this book maintains the basic premise that your music is great. Music, of course, is subjective. A piece of music you absolutely love, others absolutely hate. That's what makes art great. But just because you believe your music is great doesn't make it so.

It takes a lot of failure to make great art. Andy Grammer wrote 100 songs before he wrote his top 10 smash hit "Honey, I'm Good." He said: "The first 50 that I wrote, I'm just being blatantly honest, I was trying to write a hit, and to me, when I listen back to all of them, they sound super sh*tty. They sound like a guy who is really scared and trying to write a hit. So then the next 50 were a process of me finding my way back to my genuine point of view."

And that's what you're trying to find: your genuine point of view. Whether you write pop, folk, soul, electronic, hip-hop, R&B, rock, metal or some hybrid of them all, people will only connect to your music if it's authentic. True to you. Whoever you are. It really doesn't matter what the music sounds like. It can be polished. It can be raw. It can be low-fi, high-fi. It can be recorded in a world-class studio or in your bedroom. It just needs to be honest. Authentic.

INSPIRATION QUESTS

You need to be inspired to create great art. Art cannot be forced. And inspiration doesn't just show up either. Inspiration is always inspired. Wait, what? Yes, you can create inspiration by embarking on Inspiration Quests.

Sitting at home all day every day pressuring yourself to create great art is the worst thing you can do. During your writing process, make sure you have an Inspiration Quest of some sort every day. Go out into the world. Go on a hike. Walk to a coffee shop and journal. Smoke a jay and actively listen to music. Go to the gym. Meditate. Do yoga. Go to a concert. Go to an art gallery. Go see a movie. Watch a TV show (this may seem like procrastination, but my biggest song to date came from watching a *Grey's Anatomy* episode—don't judge). Appreciating other kinds of art will inspire your own art.

Julia Cameron advises in *The Artist's Way* to journal a stream of consciousness every morning to get the creative juices flowing. She calls these "morning pages." This process can definitely help if you're feeling blocked.

Your Inspiration Quests can be anything *but* working on your art or your business. Because most of your life will be consumed by one of these two activities, your Inspiration Quests are a shift in your mind and your heart. Allow yourself to be open to things that have nothing to do with music.

And be careful with these. Home in on only positive IQs. Don't break up with the love of your life to get inspiration for your new album. That's a Destructive Inspiration Quest. It may work in the short term, but you will be miserable for the rest of your life. No matter how great the art you create, your overall happiness is more important. Don't ever lose track of that.

Right now, set the book down, and make a list of 20 Inspiration Quests and make a point to go on at least 3 a week. Keep this list open. It's a living document. Continue to update it with new ideas. And continue to explore. When you're in your writing mode, you may need more IQs, when you're on tour, you may get fewer. On your iCal or Google Cal or whatever synced digital calendar you use, make a new calendar, give it a color and schedule these in. Get an invite to a concert? Make that calendar event your IQ color. It counts. You don't need to go out of your way for every IQ. If you naturally explore outside of your daily routine, fantastic. Going to your day job, however, does not count. Because, let's be honest. How inspiring is that really?

ACTIVE WRITING SESSIONS

Creativity is the ability to take a risk. To put yourself on the line and actually risk ridicule. The creative process often takes place outside of your ego.

—STING

I wrote hundreds and hundreds of songs before writing (Justin Bieber's) "Sorry."

—JULIA MICHAELS

[Songwriting is like] a dirty tap. When you switch on the dirty tap, it's going to flow sh*t water for a substantial amount of time. Then, clean water is going to start flowing. Every now and again you're gonna get a bit of sh*t, but as long as you get it out of you, it's fine.

—ED SHEERAN

Practice doesn't make you perfect but it does help you stop thinking that you have to be.

—GUY RAZ, HOST *TED RADIO HOUR*, NPR

If you're not prepared to be wrong you'll never come at anything original.

—SIR KEN ROBINSON, AUTHOR, TED SPEAKER,
INTERNATIONAL ADVISOR ON EDUCATION IN THE ARTS

At some point, you need to channel that newfound inspiration into the actual writing. The creation. You can't continue searching until you're struck with the perfect song idea. Just sit down and start a song. If you've gone on Inspiration Quests, the ideas will flow once you're in your studio holding your guitar.

Unfortunately most artists can't spend all of their time creating art. Even major label artists with full teams around them still need to work at the business of their careers in addition to creating their art. Every artist needs to dedicate Active Writing Sessions. Most major label artists still maintain the traditional schedule of creating a full-length album, touring on it for two years and then spend the third year writing the next album. Indie artists don't operate this way. You should be constantly in and out of Active Writing Sessions. When you're not on tour or working on a new album, try to spend at least one day a week actively writing. Not every song you write will be gold, actually most will suck. If Andy Grammer, a chart-topping songwriter, had to write a hundred songs before he landed on the hit single, why do you think you can land on your hit at the first go? So keep writing. And don't worry about writing the best songs ever written, just write *your* best songs. To bring Rick Rubin back into it, he said: "If you're competing only with yourself it's a more realistic place to be. If you say I don't want to write songs unless I can write songs better than The Beatles, it's a hard road. But if you say I want to write a better song tomorrow than the song I wrote yesterday, that's something that can be done."

THE NEW STUDIO

It's no secret that great-sounding records these days are created in home studios. Did you see the Billie Eilish documentary? She made her breakout album with her brother Finneas in his bedroom. In their childhood home. That album won the Grammy for Album of the Year.

You don't need to invest hundreds of thousands of dollars in your recording like you did twenty years ago.

As we touched on in "The New Team" (Chapter 2), it's ideal if you can have your own recording setup in a "light switch" studio (a studio that is always set up and only needs to be turned on). This will enable you to record your rehearsals, demos, new song ideas and (potentially) official releases quick and easily.

The more you record, the better you will get at it. The more producers and engineers you work with, the more knowledge you will gain. Maybe someone in your band studied recording engineering and production in school. Maybe you're studying this right now. Fantastic! Build your own light switch studio and get to work. But also, take every opportunity you can to attend other studio sessions with producers and engineers who are more experienced than you. You will always learn something. Never get comfortable (or arrogant) with your recording techniques. There is always something to be learned. There is always room for improvement.

If you're like me and don't want to devote the time, money, energy and effort into building your own studio, then build up relationships with people in your scene who will work with you, regularly, on the cheap. Of course, pay them as much as you can afford, but when you're getting started, you won't be able to afford the best. Many up-and-coming producers and engineers are willing to work on the cheap (or for trades) to build their résumé. Start with your local scene.

However, if you're in a small community and there are literally no talented producers and engineers to work with, check out SoundBetter.com, AirGigs.com and Fiverr.com. These are online marketplaces of professionals offering their services remotely. You can record your album on your own and find an L.A.-based Grammy winner on SoundBetter to mix it. That's what the Tanzanian-based musician Geeva did. Need a violinist, drummer or singer for your project? These platforms have a plethora of them with full résumés and recordings. They will record their parts in their studios and email you the full WAV files.

If you decide to build your studio from scratch, you can learn everything you need to know about recording from YouTube.

HOW YOU CAN GET ANYONE IN THE WORLD TO WORK ON YOUR ALBUM

The most important thing you need to know going into the recording process is this: It doesn't matter *who* works on it, it matters *what* the finished product sounds like.

So many bands get approached by "big time" producers with their long lists of big-time credits who explain they will give you the privilege to work with them—for a fee, of course. An *enormous* fee, at that. Lucky you.

Don't take the bait.

You can get virtually anyone to work on your project and record in virtually any studio in the world if you can pay for it. And don't be fooled by these for-hire producers' credits. Fact-check them on AllMusic.com. If they're approaching you as a producer, but they were only a drum tech on one of their "big time" album credits, it's definitely not a good indication of their expertise. Where you record and with whom does not guarantee stardom. It doesn't even necessarily give you a leg up.

WHO DO I NEED TO GET TO DO THIS THING? HOW MUCH SHOULD I PAY THEM? WHAT ARE THE STEPS?

If this is your first recording or 500th, there are simple steps you can take to make sure you create the absolute best-sounding album for a very low cost.

Preproduction

This is an incredibly important aspect of your recording process. Maybe even the most important step. Working out as much as you possibly can before you step into the studio (on the clock) will save you a tremendous amount of money. You want to rehearse the studio version of your songs to the point where you could play them in your sleep. Get the arrangements locked in. There should be no debate about how to get out of the bridge when you're tracking. Have your guitar or keyboard player and singer record scratch tracks to the click (of the exact BPM you will use for the song). Write the tempo BPMs down for every song, so when the engineer opens the first song on day one, all you have to do is tell him "this song is called 'Maybe' and the BPM is 132." Don't waste time figuring out tempos in the studio. You should figure out what program the studio is using (Pro Tools, Logic) and if you can, record the scratch tracks in that program so all the engineer has to do is dump in those tracks. You'll most likely do much of the preproduction with your producer before hitting the studio.

PRODUCER

This is the most important person for your project. When you're seeking out producers, the first check you need to make is the gut check. Don't hire a producer before having an informal meeting, lunch, jam, whatever. This person will be with you every step of the way. You guys need to get along. You need trust. You need to know that she *gets* your project, your songs, your band. Figure out what her favorite albums are. Listen to some past records she's produced. Some producers will even offer to track one test song with you from start to finish for free. If you're on the fence about this producer, take her up on it—even if it's just in her home studio. It's worth it to get a feel for how she works and to see how well you vibe. You don't want to step into a $700-a-day studio and start fighting with this producer. Not only will it mess up the overall vibe, you'll waste a ton of money.

"Producer" is a broad term. Rick Rubin, one of the most successful (and versatile) producers of all time, was asked by Tim Ferriss on his podcast, "What do producers do?" Rubin responded "I honestly don't know. I can tell you what I do." That's the thing, every producer operates differently.

There are a thousand different producers out there, but most fall into one of four categories.

The Beat-Maker

The beat-making producer typically creates and mixes an entire electronic instrumental production on her computer and has the top line artist (the singer or rapper) come in when the track is completely finished. Some of these beat-makers sell these "beats" online. There are many marketplaces where you can purchase fully produced tracks from these beat-making producers. Most offer various price points based on the use. If you want the track exclusively (meaning, no one else can use it), it costs much more. Some will offer "tracked out" downloads, which contain every track in the mix so you can alter the mix if so desired. Want to mute the bass on verse two? You need the "tracked out" version to do this. Some beat-makers want to retain the rights, but will "lease" the beat to you to use commercially. And some will require credit to be given. Many producers embed self-managed audio stores like Airbit, Soundgine, Traktrain, Beat Stars and Soundee directly to their website to sell their beats. You can google "buy beats" and find a bunch of marketplaces selling instrumental productions ranging in price from about $15 to a few thousand dollars.

But, be careful. Make sure the beats you're buying are 100% original. Any samples used either need to be Loops from within a recording program (all professional recording programs like Logic allow you to use their royalty-free Loops and samples), from a certified marketplace with royalty-free samples and Loops like Splice, Loopcloud, Sounds.com or Landr, or recorded by the producer. Unless you get explicit permission (in writing) to use a recording (sample) from the owner (label or artist), you can't use it. Not 6 seconds of it. Not 2 seconds of it. Not 4 bars. These are all myths. Good rule of thumb: *If you didn't record it, you must get permission to use it.*

The Guru

The guru-producer is the guide. She has a network of diverse musicians and chooses the right ones for the project. She may not be a gearhead or know the shortcuts in Pro Tools, but works with her go-to engineers. She has relationships at the best studios in town at every price point. She is there every step of the way and manages every step of the process from preproduction through final mastering.

The Songwriter

The songwriter-producer cares less about creating a "sound" and more about getting the best possible song. This producer primarily works in the folk world. She has her go-to engineers who know all the technical aspects of the recording process. She doesn't typically take many production risks (you're not going to create the next *Kid A* with a songwriter-producer), but she does what's best for the song.

The All-In Producer

Today, the all-in producer is the most common producer out there. He typically has a home studio and will do the tracking, mixing and mastering himself. He knows how to create beats if need be and has a strong command over sound-mimicking software like Native Instruments and Alicia's Keys. And has Splice loaded and ready at his command. He is a multi-instrumentalist and can play every instrument for a basic production (or create the necessary sounds via his MIDI programs). He helps craft the sound and direction of the project and respects the power of the song (not just the beat). He is a part of the process from start to finish and works very quickly.

The thing that all producers have in common is they are idea people. They understand what it takes to craft a production to make it sound a certain way. Many producers, like Max Martin and Jack Antonoff, have distinct "sounds." Everything they touch is stamped with their trademark sound. Others, like Rick Rubin, aren't defined by genre or instrumentation.

Every producer's main goal, no matter which category he falls into, is to bring out the artist's best. Whether he is creating the entire production "in the box" (completely on the computer) or working with a 10-piece rock band, gospel choir and symphonic orchestra, the producer is there for the artist.

The producer is the architect. The artist is the homeowner.

How Much Do Producers Cost?

Of course, like everything, there is a range. Some will work on an hourly, daily or all-in basis. Their rate depends on their skill level and experience. Many "all-in" producers in L.A. charge about $50 an hour or $500 for a 10-hour day. If you're a more established artist and have a track record of heavy sales/streams or high-paying sync placements, you can negotiate a percentage of revenue. Like, $500 up front, all-in for a single, plus 20% of all revenue over $10,000. The $10,000 bench mark is so you don't have to pay out $2 checks every four months if the song doesn't make much money. But if it makes $10,000, you pay your producer from dollar one. So, if he's making 20%, he gets $2,000 for $10,000 gross song revenue. Often times, the song won't sell much but gets placed in a commercial for $200,000. (Yes, this happens to indie artists all the time. More on this in Chapter 14.)

There's a lot of confusion on the payment breakdowns and whether producers get a percentage of the master or publishing or both. So let's dig in.

How Do Producer and Songwriter Splits Work?

Historically, the producer stepped into the process after the songs were all written and ready to be recorded. The producer guided the process, working closely with the engineers who set up mics, turned the knobs, operated Pro Tools, etc. Oh, and historically, producers were paid a huge sum by the major record labels, in addition to "points" (we'll get to this in just a minute). Now that most producers are all-in producers, they are typically in the room from the get-go, working the song with the artist from the ground up.

Who's owed what and when? How is ownership broken down? What are split sheets? And what are producer points?

Before we get started, you have to understand a few things about how copyright and royalties are broken down. We're going to touch on both in this section for the sole purpose of understanding the working relationships between producers, songwriters and artists, but we'll go much deeper in Chapter 13.

Copyrights on a Recording

Every recording has two copyrights: one in the sound recording and one in the underlying composition (some call this the song).

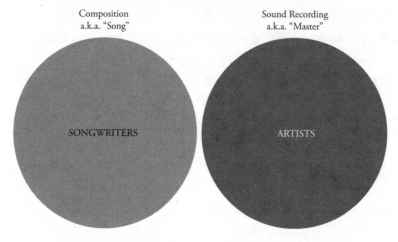

Composition
a.k.a. "Song"

Sound Recording
a.k.a. "Master"

SONGWRITERS

ARTISTS

Every recording has an underlying composition: the song that was recorded. An application to register a composition for copyright with the US Copyright Office would be on Form PA (called Work of the Performing Arts). The person or people who ordinarily would be entitled to register the composition would be the songwriter(s).

The "sound recording" is the actual recording. This is the term that is used when registering the recording with the US Copyright Office. It's Form SR (SR = Sound Recording). The producer has a hand in making the sound recording. As does the artist. In most contracts, "master" and "sound recording" are used interchangeably.

Songwriters write compositions.

Artists record sound recordings.

Sometimes the recording artist records a song that they didn't write, and many sound recordings are made by artists who didn't write the songs that they recorded.

If you record a cover song, you own the sound recording, and you can register that sound recording with the US Copyright Office, but you do not own the composition. If I cover your song, on the other hand, I own the sound recording, but you own the composition. Capiche?

If you bring a fully finished song to a producer to help record it, the producer may be entitled to co-ownership of the copyright in the recording, but typically the producer will not be entitled to any ownership of the composition copyright because they didn't write the song.

Ownership and Representation

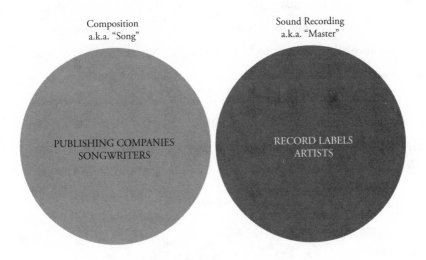

Composition
a.k.a. "Song"

Sound Recording
a.k.a. "Master"

PUBLISHING COMPANIES
SONGWRITERS

RECORD LABELS
ARTISTS

People like to toss around the word "publishing" a lot. "Who owns publishing?" "Am I getting the publishing on this?" "Where's my publishing money?"

"Publishing," "songwriting" and "composition" are all basically the same thing. You're talking about songwriting ownership and royalties.

Publishing companies represent songwriters and own and/or control compositions.

Record labels represent recording artists and own and/or control sound recordings.

If you don't have a publishing company or a record label, then you need to figure all this out on your own.

So, let's figure it out!

Various Music Producer Deals

Most of the time, a producer will get paid a flat fee for their work in addition to some royalties on the backend. An example would be a $1,500 fee to record the song plus 20% on the net (master) royalties.

For indie artist deals (self-released or small indie label) producers usually get 15–25% of net royalties on the master. "Net" is typically defined as after recording costs, producer's fees and other third-party costs like distribution and manufacturing, and is subject to recoupment. Sometimes marketing costs are included in that too. But that's negotiable.

Producer Points and Royalties

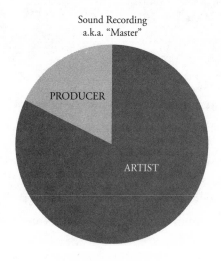

Sound Recording
a.k.a. "Master"

PRODUCER

ARTIST

For major-label deals, producers get "points." "Points" are simply defined as percentage points of the artist's royalty. So, if an artist gets 18 (percentage) points for a major record deal and the producer gets 3, those 3 get subtracted from the artist's points. If you divide 3 by 15, the producer is getting about 20% of what the artist gets. The label is still keeping 82%.

Producers typically receive anywhere from 3–7 points. The average for up-and-coming producers is usually 3 points; recognizable names typically get 4–5 points and anything over 5 points is typically for superstar producers. Producers get their up-front fee (an advance—after signing the contract), and then their points kick in after the recording costs are recouped. But, unlike how major-label deals are typically structured for artists, once the recording costs are recouped, the producer gets paid from "record one." Meaning, from the first sale/stream.

You can negotiate the backend percentage based on the up-front fee. More money up front, lower percentage on the backend. And vice versa.

So, maybe the producer wants $3,000 up front for a "buy out"— meaning no backend percentage and no ownership rights in the recording. But maybe the artist only has $1,500 up front to pay. In this instance, you might kick in 15% backend. Or maybe the artist only has $500 to pay up front, so then the backend could be 25%.

If the artist has no money up front to pay, then it's typically a 50/50 split of royalties—and usually co-ownership of the recording. But if you are the artist, and the producer is going to get ownership of the recording, then the producer should sign something saying that you can administer the track on your own: Since you, the artist, are going to be the one promoting the track and making all of the decisions, you don't want the producer to be able to hold anything up.

Where the percentage numbers come from for indie deals (15–25%) is based on the major-label point system. Since most producers get 3–7 points and most artists' deals are 12–20 percentage points of sales/streams, you divide the producer point by artist point. So, if you're working with a "3-point producer," you can divide 3 by 15 (typical artist points less the producer points) and get 20%. But these are obviously loose calculations because the artist royalty rate fluctuates based on the deal. I'm using these numbers for easy math.

Work for Hire

Here's the thing. Most producers never get ownership of any sound recordings. Most producers sign a "work for hire" deal, meaning they are paid for their job and may get royalties, but they don't have ownership of the sound recording. The artist (or label) can do what they please with these recordings and don't need the producer's sign-off every time. Whoever owns the masters has the control to do what they want.

In rare circumstances, artists and producers get into production deals, where the producer is essentially developing the artist and they may strike up some kind of co-ownership deal. Like they're in a band together. But this is rare for a per-project producer.

But under some circumstances, a producer still might get a cut of the publishing income generated by the underlying composition. Why? How? Keep reading.

Publishing and Songwriting

Composition
a.k.a. "Song"

SONGWRITER #1 SONGWRITER #2
SONGWRITER #3 SONGWRITER #4

Whoever wrote the song gets publishing.

If the producer didn't have a hand in writing the song, and just helped build a track to the song, the producer should not get any publishing.

However, if the artist and producer build a song from scratch and basically cowrite the song together, then, yes, the producer gets cowriting credit, co-ownership of all rights in that song and a share of all income that the song generates. Simply put, they get "publishing."

In Nashville they have the famous saying: "One word, one third." Which means, when there are three people in the room, no matter what you contribute (even if just a single word) you're entitled to equal song-writing/publishing credit. The idea is that you helped inspire the process and the energy shifted by you being in the room. The conversations you had and the ideas you tossed out guided the process.

But every genre operates differently.

In hip-hop, the producer who makes the beat will often demand 50%, and the other top-liners have to split up the remaining 50%.

In rock, sometimes the band will divvy up who did what. But this gets messy. Coldplay splits everything equally four ways no matter what. That's a safe bet to keep the band happy (and together).

If there's one thing to take away from this book, let it be this: All cowriters on a song should split publishing equally.

Let me repeat.

Songwriting = Publishing = Songwriting = Publishing = Songwriting = Publishing.

This is a concept that very few people grasp, and it gets confused way too frequently. The main reason for this confusion is that performance royalties in the US have traditionally been split between the "writer's share" and the "publisher's share" by two of the most well-known PROs, ASCAP and BMI. Those organizations pay 50% of the performance royalties from a song directly to the entity that is identified in the organization's records as the "publisher" and 50% directly to the person or people identified as the songwriter(s). Seeing this split, it's common for one person who cowrote a song to think, "If I'm the one taking care of everything over and above the songwriting, I should get 100% of 'the publishing,' and we can split up the songwriting 50/50." They think they should get 100% of the "publisher's" share of the royalties and also 50% of the "writer's" share of the royalties.

No! This is absolutely the wrong way to approach publishing-royalty income and registration, and thinking this way will royally mess up your registrations and royalty income across the board. Why? Well, for one, there are more publishing/songwriting royalties than just performance (what ASCAP, BMI collect). So, just because you got a song registered with a green check mark in that backend doesn't mean that it will be registered correctly in the other 80+ organizations around the world collecting publishing revenue. And you most likely won't get all your money because if it gets registered improperly one place, it's very hard to correct it.

Do not split up "songwriting" and "publishing" income anywhere.

If you cowrote a song with someone, you split *all* income 50/50. 50% of the money goes to you, 50% of the money goes to the other person. In ASCAP or BMI, and anywhere else that calls for it, list yourself as the songwriter and list your publishing company as your publisher (if you don't have a publishing company, you may need to create a "vanity publishing company"). We'll break this down further in Chapter 13. But for the love of your career, please don't try to split up "publishing" and "songwriting" again. OK? Thanks.

Words and Music

Most of the time when people write a song from scratch, the song is owned equally by everyone who wrote it. Music and lyrics. No one is counting words and notes to try and figure out the percentage. The only practical way that ownership of the copyright in the lyrics and the copyright in the music would get split up is if you put music to a poem or some other words written by someone else. And if you did that, then your song is a "derivative work" anyway, and you'd need permission from the poet or whoever wrote those words. Again, if the producer is in the room during the songwriting stage, they should get an equal cut. No one is really separating lyrics and music. Even in hip-hop, when the producer makes the beat and keeps 50% of the composition, the producer is usually listed on the copyright as owning the "words and music." Even though the producer didn't write any of the lyrics.

What Is a Remix and How Does That Work?

A remix is a new version of a recording that you get when you rearrange the different audio elements of that recording and maybe delete or add some elements. If the remix is sufficiently original (which has a specific meaning in copyright law), *and* the owner of the original recording authorized its creation, the remix may be a "new derivative work" of the original recording, which would be entitled to its own copyright registration. In that case, depending on the arrangement between the producer/remixer and the owner of the rights in the original recording, the producer may co-own the copyright in the remix and may be entitled to a cut of the income generated from the remix.

Usually, the remixer is paid a flat fee to remix the song and does that work on a "work for hire" basis, as more of a production service, without getting any copyright ownership. "Hey, can you remix this song for $500?" They do. Turn it over. And then you never have to pay them again or worry about filing a copyright registration with the remixer's name on it (although you may want to register the remix for your own purposes).

Sometimes, even if the remixer does not co-own the copyright in the remix, they will ask for a fee up front and a point or two on the backend for major-label releases. For indie releases, getting 10% or so is cool. But it's easiest if it's just a "work for hire."

More commonly these days, there's no money exchanged and whatever royalties the new master generates is split 50/50, artist/remixer.

Letter of Direction for Neighbouring Rights

If the producer gets backend points/percentages on the master, they are entitled to all the royalties that come in for the master (sound recording). One form of master royalties comes from sound-recording performance royalties. In the US, SoundExchange collects and pays these for digital radio royalties. PPL in the UK, Re:Sound in Canada (and most other countries' Neighbouring Rights orgs) handle digital radio, but also all "neighbouring rights," which are performance royalties for sound recordings.

Outside the US, these are not just for digital radio, but for terrestrial radio, TV, live venues, and any other public place music is playing.

Important thing to note: as the US was not party to the Rome Convention, the US doesn't recognize broad sound recording performance rights, and so not all "neighbouring rights" monies are due to US performers/producers.

For producers to get these royalties, the artist needs to send their local country's neighbouring rights organization (SoundExchange, PPL, Re:Sound, etc.) a "Letter of Direction" with the percentage the producer is entitled to.

If you're in the US, you can find SoundExchange's Letter of Direction form on their website. (Just google "SoundExchange Letter of Direction.") Fill it out and email it to accounts@soundexchange.com.

If you're outside the US, talk to your local neighbouring rights organization (in Russia it's VOIS and, again, in Canada, it's Re:Sound and in the UK, it's PPL). You can just google "[Your Country's Name] Neighbouring Rights Organization." And all neighbouring rights organizations have reciprocity. Meaning, you do not need to sign up with SoundExchange if you're signed up with PPL. And so on. It's easiest if you sign up with your own country's org.

So that there's no confusion here: Neighbouring rights covers rights in the master (recording). Not rights in the composition. Remember those copyright circles from a few pages back? Go refresh. There are two copyrights on every recording. Composition and sound recording. Neighbouring rights covers only the sound recording. And be aware that some people call the sound recording the "master." These terms can be used interchangeably.

Who Registers What

When it comes to publishing, each songwriter must register every song on which they are entitled to get royalties, and what their share of those royalties is, with their own publishing company (like Songtrust, Sentric, TuneCore, Kobalt, etc.) or directly with their own rights organizations (ASCAP, BMI, PRS, the MLC). But not both. Either register with a publisher or a rights organization. Their publishing company will then register the song with every organization around the world, including the songwriter's PRO.

If the producer doesn't have any writing credit and, therefore, doesn't get any songwriter income, but they get backend (master) royalties on use of the sound recording, it's up to the artist and/or the label to send the producer regular reports of the income received from use of the sound recording and to pay the producer their share of that income. Or, better yet, work with a distributor who can handle that accounting and those payments for you. Note, though, that if the producer is entitled to get a share of *net* royalties, you'll only want to start paying the producer after you recoup your recording costs.

Multiple Producers

It's common for multiple producers to work on a single track. Typically, each producer would split up the total "producer" percentage (if there is any other than the up-front fee). So, if the producer's backend is 20% for an indie release, and there are 3 producers, and they decide to split this equally, then each gets about 6.66%.

What Is Your Title?: Producer vs. Songwriter vs. Artist

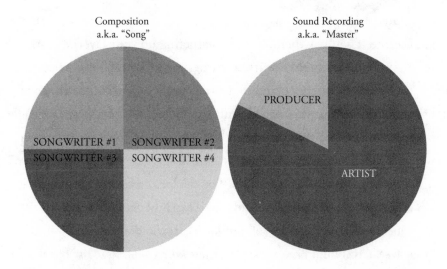

Composition a.k.a. "Song"

SONGWRITER #1   SONGWRITER #2
SONGWRITER #3   SONGWRITER #4

Sound Recording a.k.a. "Master"

PRODUCER

ARTIST

People in the music business may wear several different hats all at once or at different times. When you're registering a song or a sound recording somewhere, whether it's a PRO, your own publishing company, a mechanical rights agency, or the Copyright Office, it's important to know which hat you are wearing for purposes of that particular registration. For example:

When you register your song with a PRO, you are either a "songwriter" or a "publisher" or both.

If you produced a sound recording of someone else's song, you are not entitled to be listed in any PRO or mechanical rights agency database for that song at all unless you helped write the song.

If you produced or helped produce a sound recording, you may be a coauthor of that sound recording, but you cannot be the "author" (as it's called in the US Copyright Office) of the underlying "composition" unless you cowrote that song.

How to Find a Producer

As I stated a couple pages back, you can get virtually anyone to work on your record if you pay them. Start by gathering up your favorite all-time records (of the last twenty years, as earlier guys may be out of the game . . . or dead). Also gather up your favorite local records. Get a full credits list for all these records. You're mainly looking for the producer, since all other people will be worked out with you and your producer (you don't want to lock anyone else in before you lock in your producer). You can find most credits on Allmusic.com. For the local records you may actually need to message the artist and ask. They'll be flattered.

Once you have this list of producers, track down contact info (a Google search should be sufficient or the *Music Connection* list has many contacts [musicconnection.com/industry-contacts]) and send one a pitch email. Start with your first choices and work down the list. You should have one great-sounding demo of your best new song (don't send a crappy board feed from a live concert). Spend a couple hundred bucks to record a demo if you need to. Open the email with *specific* praise for her past projects. Ask her if she would be willing to work with you and what her rates are for a 10-song album (or whatever). Again, this will start the conversation. If she says "$10,000 is my rate for 10 songs, and I have hookups at studios and engineers to get us good deals on the rest," don't be afraid to write back and tell her your exact recording budget and ask if she can be flexible. No sweat off your back if you give her $15,000 to handle everything (studio, players, engineers) or give her $10,000 and you pay the rest directly.

Producers will pitch you their ideal rate for an indie record. Don't be scared off by the high price tag. If they pitch you $20,000 but you only have $15,000 budgeted for the entire record, feel free to write back and see if they will work with you for $10,000. Don't worry about insulting them. If they don't have any projects right now, they will consider your counteroffer. But remember, always have a meeting with them first before you agree to anything. Ask if they would consider tracking a test song.

THE BRIDGE
Music Split Sheet Example

This is not a legal document, and I do recommend getting a lawyer to draw up a formal agreement, but to get you started, it would be good to lay out these terms in the meantime before anyone releases anything.

An email with this information will suffice for the time being.

Artist: Brassroots District
Producer: Brett Nolan
Record Label/Distributor: DistroKid **Ownership?:** No
Automatic Payment Splitting?: Yes
Song Name: Take Allotta Sweat
Date: 3/3/2023
Up-Front Producer Fee (Advance): $1,500
Producer Royalty Rate: 20%
Recoupable: Royalties will be payable upon recoupment of producer fee (advance) and actual recording costs along with all personnel (producer, mixing engineer, master engineer, musicians, etc.)
Credit to Read: Produced by Brett Nolan
Songwriting %, PRO, Publisher and IPI#s:
Ari Seth Herstand = 25%, ASCAP, 123456789
Publisher: My Great Songs, ASCAP, 098765432
Admin: TuneCore Publishing
Brett Elliott Nolan = 25%, ASCAP, 234234234
Publisher: Brett Nolan Music, ASCAP, 987987987
Admin: Songtrust
Ursa Major = 25%, SOCAN, 345345345
Publisher: Downtown Music Publishing, SOCAN, 765476543
Admin: Downtown Music Publishing
Copper Jones = 25%, PRS, 456456456
Publisher: Sony Music Publishing, PRS, 345634567
Admin: Sony Music Publishing

THE RECORDING STUDIO

As with the producer, it doesn't matter how successful the previous projects that were recorded in this studio are; it matters that you like the sound of the albums. Sure, it's a fun tidbit to include in the album's press release, but at the end of the day all that matters is what your album sounds like. And these days, it's hipper to say you recorded the album in your older brother's bedroom (than a multimillion dollar studio). I recommend getting a studio with a great-sounding live room to record drums (if you're going to use live drums) at a minimum if you're creating a big rock or pop sound. You don't need a state-of-the-art studio to track vocals. You need a good vocal mic and an isolation booth (closet, sheet). That's it. But you do need a good-sounding live room to get good-sounding drums. The vibe of the studio is also very important, as are the house engineers, who will have the first hands on your project. While your drummer is tracking, you're going to be hanging out in the control room for hours on end. You want to make sure this room is comfortable. It should be bursting with energy to encourage inspiration, but also should be calming enough when you need some relaxation (or have a lounge that you can retreat to).

The ways studios get bands to block out multiple days, if not weeks, for their sessions are by offering top-notch gear, a vibey space and great amenities (coffee, fridge, Pac-Man, pool tables, couches, Nintendo). If you want to experiment with amps, drums, pianos, Rhodes, organs and guitars, then it may be worth it to find a studio with a plethora of these choices.

Get the mic and outboard gear list (most studios will have all of this info on their website) and do some research. Discuss with your producer what gear and mics are best for your project.

The studio's console is also a selling feature. Neve consoles populate some of the most well-known studios in the world, like Abbey Road, Electric Lady, Capitol, The Terrarium and Ocean Way. The Neve 8028 was the console that Dave Grohl went through such trouble purchasing and transporting to his home studio from the old Sound City studios where Nirvana recorded *Nevermind*. Because of Pro Tools and Logic, most sessions aren't actually mixed through the consoles anymore, but it's nice to run as many of the instruments through the console for warmth and vibe. It was fun to say most of the instruments on my album were run through the same console that John Lennon's "Imagine" was run through. But don't spend additional money to stay in that studio just for the console—99.99% of your listening audience will not be able to hear these nuances.

If your producer has a decent home studio with a few excellent mics and great outboard gear, and you're comfortable with all of the gear your band has, then all you need to do is spend a couple days in an expensive studio to track drums, then you can move to your producer's home studio to track everything else. Your vocals are going to sound nearly identical run through a U47 at your producer's home as they would in the big studio.

ENGINEER

This is the person who runs Pro Tools/Logic and other digital audio workstations (DAW) at the studio. They set up all the mics (after discussion with the producer). Some engineers will tune the drums. A good engineer will have the session open and ready (BPMs plugged in along with the scratch tracks) and have the room set up with all the mics you'll need for that day, before you arrive. They'll know the ins and outs of the studio (how to blow into the Mario cartridge to get it to work), the trick to get the pizza oven to not burn, to make the best cup of coffee and which amps need just the right tap on the left corner to get the sound you need. Some producers always work with the same engineers. On big sessions there will be the producer (who usually won't set up any mics or touch Pro Tools), her favorite engineer to run Pro Tools and set up mics, the studio's house engineer (to be the project engineer's assistant), studio interns to make coffee and wash dishes, and various drum/guitar techs. Small sessions will have just a producer (who covers everything above and more—except dishes: that will then be the drummer's job, clearly).

Mixing Engineer

Do not overlook the importance of your mixing engineer. Great mixing engineers can take a pile of sh*t and turn it into top 40 gold. You know the saying "You can't polish a turd"? Well, great mixing engineers actually can. Getting the right mixing engineer is almost more important than the producer, engineer and studio.

Mixing is an art form. I remember a conversation I had with my brother a couple years back when he showed me his friend's band. He said, "I know it doesn't sound very professional, but I can't put my finger on why. The singer is good. The playing is solid. But it just sounds very amateurish." I took a 30-second listen and confirmed my assumptions: bad mix.

You're going to want to work with your producer to find a great mixing engineer. Your producer most likely has her go-tos. But put your own list together as well. Even though some mixing engineers get hired frequently for one type of genre, a good mixing engineer is a good mixing engineer. Good ears are good ears. If they know how to mix Americana, they probably could mix R&B given the chance.

For my funk band's album, I contacted Mick Guzauski because I loved the sound of Daft Punk's *Random Access Memory*. The dude has mixed Backstreet Boys, Cher, JLo, Tyler, The Creator, LeAnn Rimes and a dozen other Grammy winning artists. I knew it was a long shot, but what the hell. If you don't ask, you don't get.

I sent him the rough bounces, and he got on a call with me. He spent the first 5 minutes letting me know how much he liked the songs, production, performances. Man, that felt good. And then we got into the money part of the discussion. He told me he gets $10,000 a song for major-label albums. *Whew!* I explained that this was a self-funded, indie project. He told me he normally gets $3,500/song for indie projects, to which I explained this was still out of range. He said he could go as low as $2,500/song because he dug the record so much. After a little bit more pleading, he said, "I really can't go any lower because then that becomes my rate." I thanked him for his time and kind words and told him I'd hit him back some day when I had that kind of budget. (Please don't go to Mick and say, "Ari said you would mix for $2,500 per song!"—his rates may have changed, and maybe he just dug the album. Everyone will cut people breaks if they really dig the project and believe in it. Mixing engineers [and producers] want to work on stuff they like. And have to work on stuff they don't for the paycheck sometimes. It is a business after all.)

In the end, we got Ryan Lipman to mix the album in our budget. He had never mixed funk prior to this album, but I really loved what he had done with the Jamestown Revival and Jesse MacLeod records, so I figured, good ears are good ears. I was right. And I've been using him for everything I've done ever since.

So, yeah, mixing engineers' rates vary quite a lot. You may find someone out there just getting started for $200/song. But most of the greats who do indie records are sitting at around $500–$1,000/song or more.

Mastering Engineer

I've had records mastered by Bernie Grundman, Scott Hull and Greg Calbi. These are big names. And they cost a lot. I didn't hire them to master my records because they've won Grammys (they have) or because they have countless platinum records on their walls (they do). I honestly couldn't care less about that. I hired them to master my records because they are the best at what they do.

In the world of mastering, there are only a handful of greats out there. And mastering is incredibly important, even though it's one of the most elusive parts of the recording process. But mastering can dictate the overall vibe and feel of a record. So it's important.

Mastering is the final step of the process. It gives it the sparkle that truly brings the track to life. Mastering brings out the highs and the lows and typically makes the entire track louder. Different genres demand different degrees of loudness. You won't master a jazz record the same way you'd master a pop record. Pop is typically mastered as loud as you can possibly get. In mastering, typically the louder you get, the more compressed the track. It's a trade-off. And only the truly exceptional mastering engineers with years of experience can keep a track open and big and bring up the volume without distortion or noticeable compression. If you get the chance to listen to unmastered final mixes and final masters (done by a professional) I highly recommend this. If nothing more, to train your ears.

Make sure you leave a budget for mastering. Heavyweights charge $2–4K per album (for indie projects) or $200–$400 a track. Some mastering engineers offer deals at slow times of the year. It may be worth calling them and asking if they do and when. Some will give you discounts depending on your situation. They'll send you a rate, but you can start the conversation from there. Some will budge, some won't. You don't need the best in the world, but get someone great. For my latest albums, we actually found an excellent mastering engineer out of Nashville for $60/song. If you hunt around, you can find some hidden gems of the industry. Some mastering engineers will agree to a test master of a song. That way you can A/B a few engineers you're considering. Some mixing engineers can also master. But, many swear by the rule that the person who mixes the track should not master it. Fresh set of ears. That sort of thing.

Similarly, listen to the records they have mastered and see if it's appropriate for your project. For instance, Greg Calbi's coworker (down the hall at Sterling Sound) Ted Jensen is also one of the greats; however, he masters in a complete opposite style from Calbi. Calbi's records feel like a lavender massage; Jensen's feel like a knockout punch to the face. It's all what you're going for.

What About Mastering Programs?

The most popular instant mastering platform on the market is currently Landr.com. You can basically upload your final mixes to their site, hit a button, and Landr's algorithm will master your track in minutes. You can master your entire album for about $40 (a fraction of what the pros charge). Does it get the job done? Will it replace high-priced mastering engineers? Well, it's an option. If you're on a tight budget, it's definitely worth exploring. Landr was initially built for DJs creating electronic music regularly. It wasn't built for bands creating full-length albums every couple years. That's why they started with a monthly price versus a per-track price. So, naturally, it will work better for electronic artists than for bands.

As producer, DJ, mastering engineer (and blogger) Brian Hazard put it: "The algorithm will get better over time, but it can never replace a professional mastering engineer, because it lacks musical understanding.

"It can't know whether occasional high frequency bursts are vocal sibilants that demand de-essing, or cymbal crashes. It can't tell if the excess energy at 200 Hz is the characteristic warmth of a rich fretless bass, or vocal mud that needs to be cut. It doesn't even know what genre your track is in. One size fits all.

"Most importantly, it can't tell you to go back and fix your mix!

"When I hear a problem best addressed in the mix, I ask the client for changes. That applies to everything from excessive sub bass to thin guitar tone to ultrasonic synth spikes to questionable vocal intonation. Maybe it's coincidence, but my clients' mixes tend to get better with every release."

Having a great album can bring you to the next level of your career. But once you have the album mastered, your work has only just begun.

THE HOME STUDIO

If you're interested in building up a home studio, great! Be the next Finneas. But it will take a lot of time and some money. You'll either need to invest in a recording school and work alongside knowledgeable instructors to help guide your process, or spend hundreds of hours on blogs, YouTube tutorials and in your home studio working out the kinks and learning how to make it work.

4.

THE RELEASE

Marketing is the final extension of your creativity.

—DEREK SIVERS, FROM *YOUR MUSIC AND PEOPLE*

Before it was all about week one. Today it's the opposite. It's all
about week 51. Week 151. Where you are after one week doesn't
really matter. Where are you a year later?

—CHAZ JENKINS, CHARTMETRIC CHIEF COMMERCIAL OFFICER

OH, HOW THE TIMES HAVE CHANGED. TRADITIONALLY, LABELS WOULD
release a full-length album once every three years for an artist.
The album was preceded by the lead single and an accompanying music
video. And once the album was out, every few months a new single would
be pushed at radio.

Most major labels still operate this way—despite the changing times.
You should not approach your release the same way major labels do. For
one, you don't have the bank account they do. NPR revealed that Def
Jam spent over $1 million to create, market and release just one Rihanna
song. You can't compete with that.

But what you have that the labels don't is an ability to try and fail.
Quickly. You can change course if something's not working without wor-
rying that you're going to hurt a record exec's ego. You can come up with

creative promotional strategies that have never been tried before without running it up the chain of command.

I, ARTIST

Before you even think about creating a release strategy that will give your album the recognition it deserves, you need to first figure out yourself. No, this book is not taking a hard right turn into a psychotherapy session. You're not on the couch. But the one major thing that separates the artists who have diehard fans from those who have merely passive listeners, or worse, pity supporters, is one thing: I, Artist.

We're all artists. We create art. But to become an Artist with a capital A requires a helluva lot more than just "great music."

So how do you go from an artist to an Artist? Of course, creating exceptional music is step one. But every great artist can do this. You need to showcase that you are so much more than just someone who can make great music.

Bob goes to work embodying the role of Company Man. He wears slacks, fancy shoes and a neatly pressed button-down shirt. He is cleanshaven, wears expensive cologne and his hair style is straight out of a Brooks Brothers catalog. When he walks into a conference room, he signals to everyone that Bob means business—of the office variety. He speaks with perfect diction. Looks people dead in the eye when he shakes their hand firmly. He performs in the conference room masterfully. As he presents his slide deck, he can answer everyone's questions with prowess and depth. He has worked out every angle and has thought through his concepts to their core. Not a hole to be poked. His coworkers leave the conference room inspired and impressed. Bob plays the role of Company Man flawlessly. He is cherished and rewarded. A promotion is in Bob's future.

Now, what does Bob the Company Man have to do with you the Artist? If you want to be an Artist with a capital A you need to embody the role of Artist to the core. Just like Bob had to learn how to dress, speak, present and interact with colleagues, you have to learn how to embrace your inner Artist.

Society encourages conformity. Falling in line. Keeping your head down. But Artists are leaders. Artists help people connect with their souls. Artists not only tap into a higher consciousness, but guide their followers to explore states of existence outside the daily mundane. Artists inspire those who are willing to open up and challenge their states of being.

The greatest Artists can inspire a generation into action. Or a couple into love.

Songwriters vs. Musicians vs. Artists

I know what you're thinking: "I just want to make music and I want people to dig my music. What are you even talking about?" Well, if you want to be a behind-the-scenes songwriter, you can move to a songwriting hub, write a million songs, get a publishing deal and be on your merry way. If you want to be a hired gun, you can follow your employers on stage and play your part in the background, conforming to these Artists' desires of how you should look, act and play.

But if you want to be *the* Artist, you can't just play the part. You need to be the part.

My friend texted me the *New York Times'* 6-minute *Watch How a Pop Hit Is Made* doc about Zedd, Maren Morris and Grey's "The Middle." If you've seen this video, then you may have asked yourself the same thing my friend asked: "Why didn't Sarah sing it?!" To briefly sum it up, a songwriting team consisting of Sarah Aarons and a couple producers made a great-sounding demo for a song they just wrote called "The Middle," in an attempt to get it cut by a famous Artist. The video details the process and struggle in trying to find the right singer for the song. Fifteen different famous singers sent in their own demos (auditions) to "win" the song. Every time the producers received another singer's demo, they felt more discouraged. Zedd recalled: "I'm looking for someone to sing it with the same intention as Sarah sang it. There were months we almost gave up because no one could sing it properly."

So my friend understandably wondered why not just have the best singer sing the damn song? She wrote it!

The simple answer is, she was not the best vessel to deliver this message. Sure, Sarah has a voice perfect for the song and is an undeniable hit songwriter, but she is not an Artist with a capital A. She is an artist, of course. But she may not be ready or prepared (or have the desire) to lead a generation.

What does this all mean? Why is this important? If someone digs "that one song" and they start exploring who the artist is, they start down a rabbit hole of information. If all of the socials are disjointed and confusing, the bio is bland and reveals nothing of interest or substance, and the photos and videos are forgettable, that potential fan will lose interest and move on. However, if this person unveils a beautiful, enticing, enriching and inviting world the Artist has created, that potential fan may turn into a hardcore, card-carrying member of the Artist's fan club for life.

Fans connect with Artists who help them reveal some truths about themselves.

Tons of people have great voices. Tons of people write great songs. Very few, however, are Artists who can bring their followers to spiritual heights. If it sounds cult-like, well, it kind of is. That's why people pay so much to attend huge concerts. It's not because they like "that one song," it's because they *love* the Artist and everything she stands for. And they want to join their fellow congregants in the church of that Artist for a night—levitating and connecting.

Creating the Artist World

So, you have to create your Artist world. Everything should be filtered through the lens of the Artist. You the Artist. Everything needs to be cohesive. If it's not, you will confuse your audience and they will move on. But how do you do this? There are a few concrete steps you can take to help you grow.

The Artist Vision

Just like politicians don't begin their campaigns without first working out their message and platform, you should not begin the release strategy without working out yours as well. What do you stand for? What do you stand against? What do you believe in?

I encourage you to create a My Vision document. List about twenty key words and phrases that you think the project is all about. Thoughtful, Playful, Fun, Aggressive, Heart-warming, Angsty, Sensitive, Hip, Brash, Sexual, Political, Activist, Coming of Age, Reflective, Colorful—you get the idea.

Once you have these key words, make another list of what the project is *not* about. And then start free-writing. Tell the story of the project. Have fun with it. You can always update this. And it will always evolve as you evolve as an Artist. This exercise is just for you. These lists and writing samples aren't meant to be public.

Your Vision should feel like your music.

The Artist Aesthetic

Defining your Artist aesthetic is crucial. It's the first glimpse into your world. The first touch. People remember visuals a lot more than they remember sounds. Your aesthetic is so much more than your image. Your image is a part of your aesthetic. The project aesthetic ties everything together.

The aesthetic should feel like your Vision. And should feel like your music. Are you seeing a pattern here?

The easiest way I've found to help solidify an Artist aesthetic is by utilizing Pinterest. First, create a "Vibe Board." The Vibe Board is the main hub other boards will stem from. Pin images to the Vibe Board that *feel* like your project. Everything and anything. Photographs, landscapes, colors, fashion spreads, logos, album covers, T-shirt designs. Go outside the world of music for this. It's more about capturing a vibe, feeling and energy than trying to find similar images in the world of music. You could save a photo of a ballroom dancer, an orchestra at Carnegie Hall and a painting from the Sistine Chapel. A photo of a model in a magazine and print of a candle. Don't rush this process. It should take you a few weeks at least, if not a few months.

Once you feel good about the Vibe Board, create more boards: Photo, Live, Fashion/Clothing, Music Video(s), Single Release, etc.

Your Photo Board may pull a few photos from the Vibe Board, but this board should only contain photos of people. Only pin the photographs you like the look and feel of. How they were shot. The energy you get from them. This is the board that you send to your photographer before a photo shoot. The biggest mistake bands make is that they lock in a great photographer and leave it up to her to guide the vision of the band. No one understands your project better than you. If you leave the visual direction up to someone else, they may come up with something completely off base. But it's not their fault. They have not been given proper direction. So send them your Photo Board.

Once you have your aesthetic on point, everything visual will fall into place. You'll never be at a loss for what to wear on stage or at a photo shoot. What to post to Instagram or your website. You will have no problems tossing away album cover or music video ideas if they don't fit within the aesthetic of the project.

The aesthetic is just a visual way of communicating your vision. It's an easy way for fans to enter your Artist world.

The Artist Story

Go back and read "Why No One Cares About Your Music" in Chapter 1. Keep this in the back of your mind when you think about what your story is. Yes, we are complex human beings with a million different stories, but, as we've established, people are not following you because they know or understand you as a complex human being; it's because they love you as an Artist. You need to come up with the most captivating story that feels like your music, your vision and your aesthetic. It should all make sense. Your story will evolve over the course of your career. Each huge release is a good time to rethink and rewrite your Artist Story. You need a main story of who you are as an Artist. The one thing people will remember about you. And you'll also need a story, per release, about the material—whether it's a song, album, music video or event. There is more on how to do this in Chapter 15.

The Live Show

And when you put on a live show, you'll have your aesthetic (and outfits) worked out from the Live Board. It should feel like your vision, aesthetic, story and recordings.

Staying Authentic

You may be feeling that this is all a bit too calculated and manufactured for your liking, but on the contrary, these are just tools to help you solidify your own vision. And your Artist World. Nothing will be fake or disingenuous. Everything will be honed and pointed. When someone dips their toes into your world because one of your songs came up on their Discover Weekly, they will be so enamored and connect instantaneously on such a deep level that they will dive in headfirst and forget to come up for air until they are gasping for the mundane once again.

Separating the Artist from the Person

We are all complex humans with varying states of being. Some days we fully embody the art—especially while writing, recording or performing. Some days we play the role of Bob the Company Man while at the day job. Some days we play the role of mother, daughter, sister, brother, father, son, aunt, uncle, niece, nephew, student, teacher, friend.

As the Artist, you should not showcase every aspect of your being. It would be pretty odd if your band website and socials were all about your best friend—her beautiful family and home, with stories and accompanying photos of how you're always there for each other, through thick and thin. Photos and videos of the trips you've been on—overseas and around the neighborhood. With a section devoted to her and her boyfriend that includes a full blog entry of their most recent vacation.

This, of course, sounds absurd, and I know you would never do this with your digital music profile, but you embody this when playing the role of Friend in your daily life. When you have your Friend hat on, you are all in. You are there for your friend. Her family and her significant other.

But as Artist, you don't need to showcase your world as Friend.

Now, this is not merely about what you can or cannot show on social media. It's about how best to showcase you as the Artist. So that when potential fans enter your world, it's understood and cohesive. Can you have photos of you and your friends, family, what have you? Maybe. If it's in line with your Artist Vision, Aesthetic and Story.

Singer/songwriters struggle more than most with what to share with the world via social media. Because their birth name is the name of the project, it can feel disingenuous *not* to show *all* of you. But no fan is following you the Artist because you are an amazing Friend (son, daughter, teacher, mother, uncle, etc.). That's why your friends stick around. Not your fans.

If you're a solo artist, it's a lot easier to create a different Artist name. What Melissa Jefferson did with Lizzo. Josh Tillman did with Father John Misty. Justin Vernon did with Bon Iver. Stefani Germanotta with Lady Gaga. Lizzy Grant with Lana Del Rey. Austin Post with Post Malone. Abel Tesfaye with The Weeknd. Donald Glover / Childish Gambino. Andrew Cohen / Mayer Hawthorne. Montero Hill / Lil Nas X. David Jones / David Bowie. Garrett Borns / BØRNS. Claire Boucher / Grimes. Kelsey Byrne / VÉRITÉ. Brandon Paak Anderson / Anderson .Paak. Sarah Borrello / Annabel Lee. The list is endless.

Creating an artist project with a new name enables you to separate you, the person, from you the Artist. But this doesn't mean you have to change your name. It's just easier.

Whether you change your name or not, whether you're a solo artist or a band, you need to filter everything through your Artist persona. Everything you put out from music, videos, photos, social posts, interviews, performances, email blasts, everything, is as the artist.

Matt Nathanson does a great job of this. His birth name is Matt(hew) Nathanson. He grew up as Matt Nathanson. Went to school and had jobs as Matt Nathanson. He's a singer/songwriter whose stage persona is equal parts comedy and music. He is fun, outgoing, hilarious, positive, uplifting, sensitive and down to earth. His Artist persona is just this. It's not some crazy alter ego. People love Matt Nathanson the Artist because he showcases this self to the world consistently. As a person, is he ever sad, angry, disgusted? Does he go to the gym? To the grocery store? Of course! He's human. But if he only showed his sad, angry, sweaty self to the world, his fans would drop off like flies. You understand Matt Nathanson the Artist. He's not being inauthentic by not sharing the parts of his (human) self that don't fit in his Artist persona.

Just like you, the Dutiful Employee, at your day job don't get sloshed and put on a strip tease in front of your boss (even though you may do so in other situations with other crowds), you, the Artist, need to play the part of Artist for your music career.

THE POWER OF VIDEO

I have good friends who don't even know a song is out until we
put out a video.
—JACK STRATTON, VULFPECK

It should come as no surprise that nowadays video is pretty darn important.

Unfortunately, most people are much more willing to watch a video than listen to a song. You can't just release a recording anymore. A video should accompany every song. Every time. And not just one video. Multiple videos in varying dimensions (aspect ratio), length and production value are needed for various platforms.

I know I just turned your world completely upside down.

YouTubers figured this out early on.

You don't need to make a $10,000 music video for every song (or even one music video that costs that much), but you must create multiple videos for each song.

Different platforms demand different types of videos. You need a short, vertical video for every song on Spotify. You need short-form videos for Instagram Reels, TikTok and the rest. Quick. To the point. Punchy.

Often these videos will get far more views than your high-priced, official music video.

Actually, the video that put Mothica on the map was simply a 15-second clip of her listening (crying) to her new song "Vices" in her car when she got the masters back. This video went viral on TikTok and got over 5 million views on the platform. She quickly put the song out (independently), and to date it has racked up over 30 million streams on Spotify alone. (The official music video for "Vices" only got 227,000 views on YouTube in the same time period.)

The video that helped propel Lawrence's single "Freckles" was 30 seconds of them performing the song live (with captions of the lyrics on the screen). It got 4 million views on TikTok and a million views on Instagram Reels. The official music video on YouTube got just 117,000 views in the same time period.

Remember your why. Why are you making a video? Are you making a high-production music video because you think you're supposed to, or because there's a story you want to help tell? Would a slew of short-form videos help you tell that story better? It would definitely give you more shots at the algorithm.

Artists (and labels) missed this boat early on. In the early days of YouTube, traditional artists only put up official music videos. But fans made lyric videos. Sometimes, these fan-made lyric videos became more popular than the artist's official music video—especially if the lyric video predated the artist-uploaded music video. Bruno Mars's "When I Was Your Man" fan-made lyric video got over 100,000,000 views. Talk about missed revenue. Had WMG (Bruno Mars's label) uploaded this video first and monetized it, they would have made much more money on the ad revenue than monetizing it after the fact on the fan's channel.

So, if you'd like to control your video presence (and make the greatest amount of money), be first. Be consistent. Be active.

HOW TO CREATE A GREAT-LOOKING MUSIC VIDEO ON A TINY BUDGET

Most of the time if you do a video, unless it's a Kanye West video or something, it doesn't have a real shoot. You scrape together a little bit of money and go out and do something.

—BEN FOLDS

It's hard to look good on camera. And it has nothing to do with your looks. The act of lip syncing (and acting on cue) is incredibly unnatural. But then again, so is performing onstage in front of a bunch of people. It takes practice to get good at. Whether you're creating a $200,000 music video with a cast and crew of 150 union members or a $100 music video shot by your roommate with a cast and crew of your girlfriend, brother and mom, there are some key components that every video needs in order to meet today's professional standards.

You don't need a ton of money these days to make a great-looking video. All you need is a great concept, people who know what they're doing, a little bit of gear and lots of time.

The Concept

An inexpensive creative concept will perform better than a high-priced paint-by-numbers video every time. So get creative. Obviously, if you're making a video for an intimate piano ballad, you aren't going to go skydiving for it. The concept, as creative as it may be, should match the song's vibe, energy and feel. The purpose of a music video is to enhance the song. Not detract from it. A supercreative video (that perfectly complements the song) is how you go viral. And it doesn't need to be expensive. OK Go were the first to prove this with their "Here

It Goes Again" video back in 2006. The video, which got over 50 million views, helped propel the single to the *Billboard* Hot 100 charts. The video cost very little. It was shot with a single, stationary camera and had no cuts. No edits. The band did a choreographed dance on six treadmills. It matched the tone of the song (and band) perfectly. Gotye exploded because of his creative, body-paint, stop-motion video for "Somebody That I Used To Know." Sia's near one-take video for "Chandelier" featured an uber-creepy, wildly talented and supercaptivating dancing 11-year-old girl. Kina Grannis spent over a year making her jelly-bean–themed stop-motion video for "In Your Arms." The Black Keys' "Lonely Boy" video is a single-take shot of a boisterous dancing businessman. Oren Lavie's "Her Morning Elegance" video is a single-angle shot of a bed while the sleeping protagonist gracefully explores pillow adventures through fantastical wonderlands all by the magic of stop-motion photography. Vulfpeck nearly broke the (musician) internet when they released their one-take, grain-heavy, live performance video for "Dean Town." Clairo was an instant viral hit with her "Pretty Girl" video which she created in 30 minutes (all by herself).

Drake ft. Trey Songz's "Replacement Girl" (2007) featured the artists and some friends just performing and dancing in front of different walls. It fit the vibe, aesthetic and energy of the song and artists at the time. Even two of the biggest stars in the world (with all the money in the world), Anderson .Paak and Bruno Mars, did a simple, (seemingly) one-take, performance video for their side project Silk Sonic's debut single "Leave the Door Open" (which ended up winning the 2022 Grammy for song and record of the year).

These videos were all created on a relatively low budget. But this takes convincing very talented people to work hours upon hours for free or very little. So, getting the right crew is crucial.

To help generate inspiration and focus your creative direction, make a list of music videos you love that don't look too expensive.

The Crew

Hollywood has special titles for every single person who works on a film set from Best Boy and Grip to 2nd AD and PA. Two minutes of network television could take 6 hours and 100 people to create. Your music video doesn't need fancy titles or craft services to be great. You need a dedicated crew of passionate people who all believe in the success of the video. For most of your early videos, you will wear most of the hats, but you'll need at least a few people to help out. You should learn as much as you can, though, so you can be as independent as possible.

Producer

Whether you're working on a multimillion-dollar film or a $100 music video, the producer is one of the most important people for the success of the project. The producer is the project manager. She finds and hires the entire crew, finds all locations and tracks down all necessary equipment. A producer who has tons of connections can get all sorts of deals. If she really believes in your project, she can call in all of her favors.

Director

The director is the brain. The leader. The idea person. He has the vision. The director will work with you on putting together the concept. He will, uh, direct everyone on set and has a solid understanding of everyone's role and the equipment necessary to achieve the goal of the video. He is a part of the project from concept to final editing. If he doesn't do the shooting, editing and coloring himself, he works alongside these individuals to attain his vision.

DP

DP means director of photography. This is the person who runs the camera. For low-budget shoots, it will most likely be the director or a fellow bandmate. For higher-budget shoots, a DP is hired specifically for her expertise and ability to realize the director's vision. Professional DPs know how to operate the most complicated (and expensive) cameras in the world and know what it takes to realize nearly any concept.

PA

PA means production assistant. These are your friends who have volunteered to help you throughout the shoot. They do everything and anything you need from positioning lights (when there are no lighting crew members), to running the playback, to making coffee, to running to Home Depot for an extension cable, to washing the windows you're shooting through.

Work with Students

Bring a film student on board to help with something. Call it an internship. Film students have access to state-of-the-art equipment for free. Regardless of their confidence level, most film students aren't experienced enough to create a video up to the professional standards you require on their own. But if you have one very experienced filmmaker to lead the operation, the film student can help with equipment and location needs (and more PAs), while getting great experience and building his résumé. Most film students would jump at the opportunity to work on a band's music video—no matter how low-budget it is.

The Performance

If you're going to sing in the video, you should practice re-creating the vocals from the recording to a T. Learn every breath and every inflection. If the visual vocals don't match up to the recorded vocals, it will be jarring to the audience. Sure, everyone knows this isn't a live performance, but make it look as close to one as possible. You should actually sing the part when you're shooting the video. People can tell if you're faking it. Actually sing. This goes for every instrument. The drummer should learn the part verbatim and play it like he's onstage in front of 10,000 screaming fans. The guitar player should plug into an amp, if possible, and similarly rock out like her tubes are reverberating through Madison Square Garden. Practice the performance before you get on set. Each band member should practice their performance on their own. If you're a live band and perform often, this will come much more naturally. It will feel unnatural to perform for the camera (and not a packed room of fans). Here's where the acting comes in. Each member should film and critique themselves before shoot day. Rehearse your performance, on your own, until it looks like how you think it should. If your performance looks dumb to you during your rehearsal, it will look dumb during the actual shoot (and to everyone when the video comes out). An expensive camera, lighting package and editor cannot save a sh*tty performance.

Camera

iPhones have come quite a long way. The latest ones are actually being used to create feature films. So it's possible. But I recommend either investing in a $1,000 DSLR camera and a couple great lenses or hiring a DP with a DSLR camera to shoot you. Freelance DPs typically range in price from $100 to

$500 for the day. Most will have their own camera, but some superprofessional DPs will only work on high-end cameras like a Red ($50,000) or Alexa ($100,000). In L.A., it's quite simple to rent these high-end cameras. If you have insurance, you can get a Red for about $500 a day or an Alexa for about $1,000 a day. But you don't want to just rent the camera if you don't know how to use it. These high-end cameras should only be handled by professional DPs.

Lighting

It doesn't matter whether you're shooting on an iPhone or an Alexa, if your lighting is sh*t, your video will look like sh*t. Plain and simple. At the very least, buy, rent or borrow a sufficient lighting package. If you're just shooting a simple solo performance video at home, a $150 softbox lighting kit from Amazon will do the job. Get the brightest lights available. And make sure the kit is for video (not just still photography). You can head down to a camera shop and ask them for recommendations. There are some great YouTube tutorials on simple video lighting techniques. If you're creating a multilocation, indoor, narrative music video, you'll most likely need to rent a lighting package. So be aware of this when coming up with your concept. Your DP will be able to instruct you on what she requires. But be careful, DPs aren't managing your budget. Make sure to rein them in. If they say they absolutely need a $1,500 lighting package, they may actually be able to (grudgingly) do it for a $500 lighting package. These are rental prices. You'll also need people who know how to set up and operate these expensive rented lights (so they don't explode on you—yes, this can happen if you don't handle them properly).

Shooting outdoors is the easiest way to avoid increasing lighting costs. The sun is the best lighting package on the planet. And it's free! All you'll need is a bounce (reflector disc) to help guide the light. These are $10 from Amazon.

Playback

This is one of the most forgotten-about elements of music video shoots. And it's the most important. Make sure you have an extremely loud sound system. And if you're shooting outside or in multiple locations, it needs to be portable. This is easier said than done. A little Bluetooth Jambox may not be loud enough—even if it is just you and your acoustic guitar. If your full band is performing, you may need a full sound system to get the playback loud enough. You'll want one PA on playback duty for the entire duration of the shoot. There will be lots of starts and stops.

Editing

You should learn basic video editing. This will save you tons of money down the line. It seems daunting to learn at first, but as someone who has taught himself Final Cut Pro (by watching YouTube tutorials), I can tell you firsthand, it can be done. And it's not as painful as you'd expect. It can actually be quite fun once you get good at it. You will be putting out lots of video content over the course of your career, and you don't want to have to rely on editors. Once you can afford to outsource the editing, then by all means, do it. But until then, it's much easier to just learn by doing. I never took a course or spent time practicing. I learned by editing a Christmas video of mine that had to get done.

For your official music videos, it will be worth hiring a professional editor if you can afford it. But for all other videos, you can edit yourself.

Coloring

What separates the amateurs from the professionals is color correction. There are people out there whose sole job is color correction. It's the final step of the workflow. Make sure every single one of your music videos gets color corrected. There are color correction plugins and presets you can purchase that when used effectively can give your video a Marvel comic look or *The Notebook* look. Sure, the camera is important, but color correction is what really gives it the "look." And if you don't color-correct, it will look like a home video shot by your mom. I've seen too many of these. Please, for your sake, color correct.

You Pick Two

No, this is not Panera's lunch special, this is the Iron Triangle of project management. And it applies to virtually every project from albums to videos to app creation. Everyone wants their project to be good, cheap and fast. But you can only pick two. Want something good and fast? It will cost a lot. Want something cheap and good? It ain't going to be fast. Want something fast and cheap? The quality will most likely be crap.

This Euler diagram will help illustrate this.

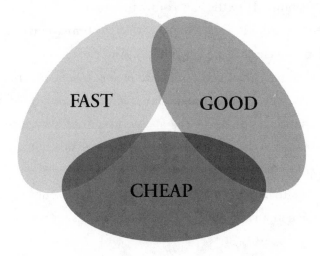

You Pick Two project triangle.

WHAT ALBUM CYCLE?

*Traditional music marketing strategies were really about release
dates and the first six months. The [TikTok] community is
starting to resonate with tracks that are 2, 5, 6, 7, 8, 10 years old.
It's breathing new life into it.*

—COREY SHERIDAN, SVP MUSIC, TIKTOK

Remember the first time you heard *The Dark Side of the Moon*? I do. And
believe it or not, I was completely sober. I was in tenth-grade English class
and, for some reason, our teacher cued up *The Wizard of Oz*, more specifically the second lion roar, with the DSOTM CD. And the class watched
in awe as the visuals from this 1939 film seemed to match up perfectly
with this 1973 musical masterpiece.

The Pink Floyd album is a true piece of art. Start to finish. It was
conceived as such. There are no breaks in the music and, it's said, the
five tracks on each side reflect various stages of human life. Pink Floyd
created an album. They did not throw their ten best songs together to
release a full-length LP. They worked within the limitations of the format
for which they were creating (a vinyl LP). And created a true piece of art.

Did you know that *The Dark Side of the Moon*'s run time is only
43:00? Know why? It's because a vinyl record can only hold about 22
minutes of music a side before the quality gets drastically reduced. Had
records been able to hold 35 minutes of music per side, *The Dark Side of
the Moon* could have been a completely different album.

It's funny that artists are still putting about ten songs together and
releasing them as an album. There are a few reasons for this:

1) Most of today's artists grew up admiring full-length albums.
   Albums (not singles) are why most of us fell in love with music and

chose to make it our profession. So artists want to create full-length albums—just like their influences.

2) Vinyl is back, baby! Like, in a big way. 2021 marked the first year that vinyl sales surpassed CD sales since 1986. Many artists are creating vinyl in lieu of CDs (excuse me, for you Gen Zers, a CD is a plastic disc that used to be how people listened to music before the internet).

3) Labels still want to release full-length albums because they can maximize their marketing efforts around one campaign (versus a bunch of smaller, single campaigns).

But there are no time constraints with the digital model. You could have a 1,000-minute album if you wanted. Hell, many people open an artist's profile on their favorite streaming service and just hit Shuffle anyway, in effect giving them an infinite playlist of their favorite artist. An infinite album.

Artists create for the medium of the times. Drake's 2021 album *Certified Lover Boy* has twenty-one songs and clocks in at one hour, twenty-six minutes. That does not fit on a vinyl record or a CD, but works perfectly on streaming services (with songs sprinkled throughout thousands of playlists). On Spotify, the duration of the top five streamed albums rose almost 10 minutes from 2012 to 2018, to an average of 60 minutes.

But creating longer albums isn't just for art's sake. Superstars make extralong albums to attempt to game the system. Both *Billboard* and the RIAA calculate an "album" at 1,500 on-demand streams. So, if you have diehard fans, and you release a ton of songs on one album, they'll spend more time listening all the way down. Chris Brown's 2017 album *Heartbreak on a Full Moon* had forty-five songs (clocking in at two hours and thirty-eight minutes!) and was certified Gold in ten days (without any hits).

But that doesn't mean more is always better. Olivia Rodrigo's break-out album *Sour* clocks in at only 34 minutes and was nominated for Album of the Year at the 2022 Grammys.

SHOULD YOU RELEASE A SINGLE, AN EP OR AN ALBUM?

If you're going to make an album, there better be
a reason for me to give a sh*t.
—BRUCE FLOHR, RED LIGHT MANAGEMENT

Despite what you see from the major labels still utilizing an antiquated release strategy, you should not be releasing an album every three years. You need to be consistently releasing music.

Unless you have a *Dark Side of the Moon* statement to make, you don't need to create an album. Spend your resources on creating a great song and great videos and get it out. Fans expect music so much more regularly now than they did ten years ago. If you don't continue the engagement and continue to feed them musically, they will move on.

Yes, artists still tour on albums. For one, it gives reviewers something fresh to talk about and the old guard still understands "album campaigns." But there's no need to create a full-length album unless you truly have a statement to make. So don't stress yourself out about building the funds for a full-length album.

How often should you be releasing music? That depends on a lot of factors. If you make electronic music in your bedroom, then you should be releasing a new song every month. If you're a full band and require a studio for every recording, you should still release a new song every month, but maybe a studio recording just every three months. You can release live versions, demos, covers and acoustic versions (on less formal platforms like SoundCloud, Bandcamp, and YouTube) in between the official studio releases.

Spotify has publicly come out and said they reward consistency. So, if you want to play the Spotify game and have the best shot at editorial playlist inclusion, you're going to want to follow their suggestions. Most artists these days are releasing songs every four to six weeks. It may sound daunting, but you can go in waves. If you want to track twelve songs at a time every year, great; then you can release one a month for a year. Or four singles in advance of an album, if you want to release an album.

ARE SALES DEAD?

Overall, album sales have been steadily declining since 2000. Digital download and CD sales are virtually dead, with streaming revenue now the dominant force in recorded music revenue. Vinyl has come back with a vengeance, with Gen Zers actually purchasing more than Millennials and Gen Xers.

The numbers would tell you that sales are essentially nonexistent. And on a macro level, they basically are. But the global music revenue report doesn't mean much to you when you're trying to figure out how to monetize your music, of course.

Above all, your fans want to support you. So make attractive ways for *all* of your fans to do this. Some will want to do it in the form of a vinyl record purchase. Some will back your crowdfunding. Some will subscribe to you on Bandcamp or Patreon. Some will tip you on Venmo or CashApp.

Some fans don't buy physical albums and exclusively listen to music on Spotify, YouTube or Apple Music, but still want to support you. So allow them to stream your music and give them opportunities to pay you in other ways. We'll get into more ways to do this all throughout the book.

DIGITAL DISTRIBUTION: HOW TO GET YOUR MUSIC ON SPOTIFY, APPLE MUSIC, AMAZON AND EVERYWHERE ELSE

CD Baby, TuneCore, DistroKid, Symphonic, ONErpm, AWAL, Route-Note, Stem, Amuse, Horus, Landr, or . . .

The major on-demand music consumption platforms of the world like Apple Music, Spotify, Tidal, Deezer, Amazon all require receiving their music from authorized distributors. And if you want to get paid for your music in China—the fastest growing music market in the world—you need a distributor to collect for you. Before CD Baby cracked this open in 2004, you had to be signed to a label that worked with a distributor to get your music into iTunes and the bunch. But over the past two decades, the field has been flooded with digital distribution companies accessible by millions of musicians looking to get their music out to the world. I keep an updated comparison on Ari's Take.

Things to look out for when researching which digital distribution company to use:

- **Cost**
  Do they charge you up-front fees? Yearly recurring fees? Fees per release?
- **Commission**
  What percentage of the royalties does the company take?
- **Speed**
  Some will get your music to outlets within days (or hours), others take weeks.
- **Number of Outlets**
  Most companies distribute to nearly all the most popular retailers; some just pick a few to work with.
- **Opt Out of Stores**

If you get a UK-only record deal, you want to be able to omit the UK region when you distribute to the rest of the world.

■ **Adding Stores**

Do they charge you to add new stores when they become available or do they add your music automatically?

■ **Custom Label Name**

If you have a record label you're working under, make sure you can use the name when you distribute.

■ **ISRC and UPC Codes**

ISRC codes are assigned per song. UPC is assigned per album. Some companies charge for these, some give them to you for free.

■ **Payment Frequency**

Weekly, monthly, quarterly, immediately?

■ **Payment Threshold**

$10? $100? How much do you need to make before they pay you?

■ **Payment Splitting**

Some companies will pay everyone who worked on the song their proper percentage. Have a featured artist and a producer who are entitled to a cut? Some companies will pay them directly what they're owed.

■ **Playlist Plugging**

Some of the more hands-on, top-tier companies will pitch you to playlist curators for inclusion in their popular playlists.

■ **Analytics and Data**

The distributors are increasingly more open about what data they will share. Some distributors interpret this data in an easily digestible way for you. Others make you download the data and work Excel magic.

■ **Offer an Advance?**

Similar to labels, some distributors will pay you an advance (bulk amount of money up front) if they believe you will make this money back fairly quickly.

■ **YouTube, TikTok, Instagram, Facebook Monetization**
Good to keep this under one roof.

■ **Flexible Admin Publishing Options**
Good to keep this under one roof if you wrote your songs. More about this in Chapter 13.

■ **Beatport and Pandora**
Both platforms curate their music. Some distributors will distribute your music for approval, others require you to submit your music for approval directly to the platform.

■ **Obtaining a License for Cover Songs**
If you distribute a cover song, you need to obtain and pay for a mechanical license. You don't need permission, but you still need the license. Some distributors will do this for you (for a fee); others require you to obtain it on your own.

■ **China**
Many distributors now distribute your music to the largest DSPs in China, and get you paid for those streams. But some still do not.

Self-Managed Download Stores

There are self-managed music stores like Bandcamp, Bandzoogle, Squarespace and TunePort where you can upload your music and sell it directly to your fans. These self-managed download stores take significantly smaller commissions than the big online stores and don't require a digital distribution company (some of whom also take commissions).

It's worth noting that even though global download sales from the biggest retailers (i.e., iTunes) have plummeted to nearly nothing, Bandcamp is still showing growth month after month, year after year. They have a running ticker on their website that tracks how much money fans have paid artists over the years (nearly $1 billion—not bad considering the platform doesn't allow major labels). And with Bandcamp Fridays, where the platform forgoes their 15% commission for the day, many artists take advantage of this to rally up their base to support them. Bandcamp's Name Your Price feature allows fans to pay as much as they'd like to their favorite artists. I once had a fan pay me $200 for my 12-song album—just because they wanted to support me.

Phoebe Bridgers and Maggie Rogers recorded a cover of "Iris" by the Goo Goo Dolls, releasing it exclusively on Bandcamp and donating all of the proceeds to charity. It was only available for 24 hours, but it raised an estimated $173,000 from 47,000 fans. And it debuted at #1 in the Digital Song Sales chart. This was in November of 2020. So, it can be done!

THE BRIDGE

26 Things to Do Before You Release Your Song or Album

1) **Market Research** How do you know if you suck or not? You're biased. So are your mom and your boyfriend. Your friends aren't going to tell you if they hate your music. They will come to your shows to support you. But to make sure your music is ready for primetime, you need some unbiased opinions. To hit the general public, you can use TuneCore's Fan Reviews. You don't actually have to distribute your music with TuneCore to get it reviewed. To get 100 reviews by these "music fans and consumers" (people who get paid to take surveys) it'll run you about $40. Otherwise, if you have a strong community around you, enlist some trusted ears to take a survey anonymously. You can use SurveyMonkey or Google Forms, and participants can rank songs in the order of their favorites, rate each on a 1–10 scale, and offer other kinds of feedback. If you're not super established, I recommend doing some kind of market research before releasing your music. It can also just help to know the order to release your singles.

2) **Make a Timeline** This should include all the elements below. A great song

needs a great strategy. The most important thing you can do is know exactly what you have to do each day and each week leading up to your release and what to do after. Be specific and thorough. At the top of each week, you should already know exactly what you need to accomplish. Which photos and videos are you posting? What emails are you sending? What stories are you telling? Once you have your timeline written out, make sure to use a system that will work for you so that you can execute it with precision. Maybe it's the calendar on your phone, maybe it's Post-it Notes on your wall, maybe it's a fancy project-management software. Whatever it is, stick to it. This is your roadmap to a successful release.

3) **Register Your Publishing** If you want to make sure you're collecting all of your publishing royalties, wherever they exist in the world, you're going to need an admin publishing company to help you (if you don't have a publishing deal). Songtrust, TuneCore Publishing, CD Baby Pro Publishing and Sentric are some admin publishing companies that any songwriter at any level can sign up for to get 100% of their publishing royalties collected.

4) **Sign Up for a PRO** In America, the most well-known Performing Rights Organizations (PROs) are ASCAP, BMI and SESAC. In Canada, the sole PRO is SOCAN. In the UK, it's PRS. You must be signed up with a PRO to get your performance royalties for songs you write. Most admin publishing companies will register your songs with every PRO in the world (including your hometown one), so you don't need to worry about registering each song with your local PRO as long as you register those songs with your admin publishing company. If you don't have an admin publishing company (uh, see #3), then you'll need to make sure you register every one of your songs with your PRO.

For every stream, there are two publishing royalties earned: performance and mechanical. If you only have a PRO, you're only getting about half of your publishing (songwriter) royalties. Admin publishing companies will collect ALL of your publishing revenue from around the world: mechanical and performance.

If you're scrappy and have a lot more time on your hands, you could register with a PRO and a Mechanical Rights Organization (MRO). In the States the only MRO is the Mechanical Licensing Collective (MLC). They will collect your mechanical royalties—for only US streams. They won't help you collect mechanicals from around the world. To do that, you need a publisher (or admin publisher). If you're located anywhere else in the world, your local CMO may be able to help you.

I like to save myself the headache and simply work with an admin publisher to do all of this for me. That way I know that I'm 100% set up with one-stop registration.

5) **Register with a Sound Recording Performing Rights Organization (Neighbouring Rights)** In the US, this is SoundExchange, in the UK, it's PPL, in Spain, it's AIE, Canada, it's Re:Sound. In most countries, its called a "Neighbouring Rights Oganization." These orgs will get you paid for all "public performances" of your master sound recordings. To clarify, this is for artists recording masters (not songwriters or compositions). We will break this down further in Chapter 13. Find the Neighbouring Rights Org in your country and register for it.

6) **Register Your Copyrights** You can currently register twenty of your unreleased songs for $85 with the US Copyright Office. You can do everything at Copyright.gov. Make sure you're protected so when the future Pharrell and Robin Thicke steal your song in thirty years, your kids will be able to sue for their retirement! If you don't register the copyright, you can't bring a suit.

7) **Pick Your Distribution Company** To get your songs on Spotify, Apple Music, Amazon, TikTok, Instagram and 100+ other DSPs worldwide, you need a distribution company. There are many distribution companies out there you can use. I keep an updated comparison article on many of these companies on aristake.com.

8) **Get a Sync Agent** If you're interested in getting your music in TV shows, commercials, movies, video games and trailers, you'll want to work with a sync agent. Some call these sync licensing companies. More on this in Chapter 14.

9) **Create the Folder of Assets** This will be the folder where everything lives. It will be quick and accessible to you and everyone on your team working on the release. More on what this is in a couple of pages.

10) **Get New Photos** You should build up a network of photographers in your city. You can never have enough high-quality photos. Every release is a new beginning. It's a time to update and enhance your image. To rebrand if necessary. Photos give your audience the first impression of the music. People will judge your project based on the artwork and photography before they choose to listen to the music. So, your photos should have the same vibe and energy of your release. Make sure your photographer listens to the new music. And make sure the photos you release alongside the new music make sense. You need to wear an outfit conducive to the new sound. Your new album needs a story. And those photos need to match the story. Put all the edited photos in your Folder of Assets. Create a separate folder for each single release with the accompanying photos for that release.

11) **Write a New Bio and Press Release** A new release demands a new story behind the music and an update on who you are. More on what these are and how to write them in Chapter 15.

12) **Clear All Licenses** If you are releasing a cover song or have samples in the track that you didn't create, you have to clear the licenses. For cover songs, most distributors will give you guidance on how to get the mechanical license (some distros do this for you—for a fee). If you used a piece of recorded music in your track that you didn't create from scratch, you have to make sure you're legally allowed to use it. Many recording programs (Digital Audio Workstations—or DAWs) allow you to use their sounds and loops, but if you took even a split second of a piece of someone else's recording, you need their permission. Don't think you'll get caught? Audio recognition software these days is incredibly powerful. Don't risk it.

13) **Cue Up Spotify for Artists** You want to make sure to distribute your song at least five weeks before the release date to have any hope at official editorial playlist consideration. You're also going to want to cue up the Canvas video for each song (which plays when someone streams your song on Spotify mobile). More on this in Chapter 11.

14) **Make a List of Playlists and Influencers to Contact** Make a list of user-generated playlists that your music would fit with and TikTok/Instagram influencers whose audience would respond well to your music. More on how to do this exactly in Chapter 5.

15) **Private Song Sharing and Storing** You need a private way to share new music with music supervisors, labels, agents, managers and blogs. Some of the most popular options to do this are Dropbox, DISCO, SoundCloud, Google Drive and Box. Put both wavs and mp3s in there, along with lyrics and any notes on the song. This will be the introduction to this project, so make sure whoever gets the link can understand the full picture. You only get one shot at a first impression! Get links for every song (make sure you click the Share button—don't copy the URL because it will make them login) and pop these links into your text doc in the Folder of Assets.

16) **Make a List of Press Outlets to Contact** More on this in Chapter 15.

17) **Create the Videos** TikTok, YouTube, Instagram, Spotify and so on. You're going to have tons of videos, long-form and short-form, that you're going to be releasing on all the various platforms. Instead of scrambling every day to try to make some, put together a content batching day once a week and bang these out.

18) **Put the Release on Bandcamp** Bandcamp is the #1 independent music store (even though it is now owned by Epic Games). The site now also has a popular music-review component, with music journalists and editors. Bandcamp is self-managed. You don't need to use a distributor to get on Bandcamp.

19) **Rebrand Your Socials and Website** Now that you have new photos, an album

cover and a bio, use these assets to rebrand all your social sites and your website. You are bringing an entirely new package to the world. Make it shiny, sparkly and tasty. And put a bow on it! It's a good idea to rebrand your website every couple years, regardless of if you have a new album or not. There are plenty of website builders that require no design or coding knowledge. They have beautiful templates to choose from and are very simple to use. I keep an updated comparison on aristake.com of some of the biggest website builders.

20) **Engage your Mailing List** If you don't have a mailing list yet, start one. This is the most important fan engagement tool you have. Of course, email is important, but text message marketing is becoming more widely used and is increasingly a must-have. Mailchimp is great for email. Community is an SMS marketing platform used by many musicians right now and enables you to build a text list and regularly engage your followers. Whereas email open rates sit at around 23%, text open rates are around 95%.

21) **Create New Merch** A new release demands new merch. You can create print-on-demand merch so you don't need to buy (or store) up-front inventory. The merch company will print and ship the item directly to your fan. I keep an updated comparison of print-on-demand companies on aristake.com. Also make sure to showcase your merch by linking to Spotify and your other profiles. You can do this via Shopify and other platforms.

22) **Cue Up the Ads** Digital marketing is now a must for every release. More on this in Chapter 5.

23) **Wikipedia Page** Even all these years later, Wikipedia is still one of the first places people go to get a quick glance at your bio. And it's almost always top of the list in Google search results. It validates you and helps the internet learn about you. If you don't have a Wikipedia page yet, there are plenty of people and companies out there you can hire to make you one. You just need a good amount of press under your belt. If you have a page already, time to get it updated. Wikipedia doesn't like when the subject edits their own page (and it can't read like a promotional bio), so ask your network to help with this.

24) **Trackable Links** ArtistHub, Feature.fm, Show.co, Linkfire and ToneDen all have ways for you to create custom links that you can use to track clicks on whatever you're promoting. They also enable you to create Spotify pre-save campaigns and a link-tree-style album landing page where the fan can choose their preferred DSP. Read a comparison of the services on aristake.com. Also, add a one-click landing page link, like linktr.ee, to your Instagram, Twitter, TikTok and other social platforms' bio section that directs followers to where they can learn more about you.

25) **Submit Credits and Lyrics** Most distributors now allow you to distribute your

lyrics and credits to DSPs (like Spotify and Apple Music). If you want this information to show up when people are listening to your music, you will have to make sure that this info (along with your music) gets distributed. Often it is an additional step in the backend of your distributor, but sometimes you will need to submit this info to your rep at your distributor (or label) or via Musixmatch. Make sure you do this. The trumpet player on track 7 appreciates it!

26) **Form a Corporate Entity (Like an LLC)** This gives you some legal protections and tax breaks. You should consult an attorney and accountant to make sure you form the right kind of entity for your particular needs and that you set it up properly.

THE FOLDER OF ASSETS

On your laptop, create a folder on your desktop and an identical folder in whatever cloud service you use (Google Drive, Dropbox, etc.). Title it the name of the new album. Inside the folder will be all of the assets you will need to access (and send out) frequently. The folder should include:

- Text doc of all lyrics.
- Wavs or AIFFs of every song (including instrumentals).
- 320kbps (metadata tagged) mp3s of every song (including instrumentals). More on metadata tags on page 516.
- High-res album cover (at least 3000 pixels x 3000 pixels).
- High-res album cover without text (to use for posters).
- Stems (for remixes). These are isolated vocals, drums, bass, guitar tracks.
- Print-ready promo photos (300dpi, no larger than 10mb in size).
- Web versions of promo photos (74dpi, around 1mb in size).
- Merch designs.
- All press releases.

- Text doc with album credits (break these down by song).
- Short and long bios.
- Promotional materials like advertising designs.
- Demos.
- Videos.
- Split sheets.
- Text doc containing login information to all your sites and links you will need to reference frequently (Dropbox, Box.com, DISCO, GSuite, Drive, Spotify, Bandcamp, etc.) or better yet, use a cloud-based password service like LastPass, Dashlane or 1Password.

HOW TO WRITE YOUR BAND BIO

Your bio is your story. It is the single most important piece of your release—next to the music, of course. It should reveal why people should care about you. What sets you apart? Why are you unique? And more specifically, what is the album's story? Go back and reference "Why No One Cares About Your Music" in Chapter 1. With this in mind, you can craft your bio. Many outlets will copy and paste your bio for their needs. Make sure you have three bios, a long one, a short one (1 or 2 paragraphs, definitely under 500 words) and an elevator pitch. Make sure every bio includes pronunciation of the name. Your bio should be written in the third person.

Your long bio can be structured like this:

Quote

Start the bio off with a quote from a well-known musician, celebrity or press outlet or a lyric from one of your songs. Something that will set the tone and is completely indicative of what your project is about.

Hook

The hook is your story. What makes you unique. Sets you apart from everyone else. Open with this. It doesn't need to be more than one or two paragraphs.

Accolades

Move right into discussing your accolades. Once your hook intrigues your readers, your accolades showcase that you are an artist on the rise, worth paying attention to. If you have well-known artists who have said something nice about you, include this here. Did a song of yours go viral on TikTok? Did *Rolling Stone* list you as an artist to pay attention to? List that here.

Newest Project

This is where you talk about your latest project. Most of the time it's the newest album. But you can also discuss music videos, tours or anything else that you're currently working on.

The Boring Stuff: Backstory, Influences, Song Meanings

This section is primarily for your die-hard fans who want as much possible information about you and for journalists doing their research. You don't need every band members' birthplace, but include interesting, pertinent information about how members met, how the band was formed and career highlights. You can also include some of your influences, back stories on songs on the record or any other interesting info.

———————

Your short bio should just have your hook, accolades and newest project. You don't need any of the backstory. DSPs (Spotify, etc.) need your short bio for your profile, so you'll want to have this at the ready.

THE ELEVATOR PITCH

Your elevator pitch doesn't need to be posted anywhere or sent out; it's just for you to verbally describe your band quickly and easily when people ask. You'd be surprised at how many musicians have a very difficult time talking about their own music. Pick two or three artists people say you sound like and use that. "David Bowie meets Bob Dylan." "If Janis Joplin got into a bar fight with Sly and the Family Stone." "If Bill Withers married Katy Perry." "It's Olivia Rodrigo for grown-ups." "Marvin Gaye meets Paul Simon in New Orleans." "Tame Impala flew into the 1975 while riding Train." We'll stop there. And obviously reference well-known artists. It's no use comparing yourself to an artist they haven't heard of. By doing this, it gives them a frame of reference. You may think your sound is unlike any which came before and that you shouldn't be pigeonholed by referencing one or two artists or genres, but believe me, you will drastically help your (potential) audience by giving them a frame of reference.

THE RULE OF 7

There's this old adage in the marketing world called "the Rule of 7." Basically, it states that a prospect needs to hear an advertiser's message 7 times before the prospect will take action to purchase. What this means for you, is that your fans need to be hit at least 7 times with whatever you're selling (album, song, music video, tickets, crowdfunding campaign) before they will even think of taking action. You may feel like it's overkill, most artists do, but it's science. And it's why marketing departments still employ these tactics. Just think about it, the first time you see a photo to an article on Facebook you typically ignore it if the topic doesn't immediately interest you. But if you see a bunch of your friends post the same article, you almost certainly click to read it.

Leading up to the release, there are tactics you can take to make sure your target audience gets hit at least 7 times and is certain to take notice.

THE ALBUM RELEASE TIMELINE

If you're planning to release a full-length album or EP, you can loosely follow this release timeline as a guide.

8 Months Before the Release

- **Launch the Preorder or Crowdfunding Campaign**
  The album cycle has totally changed. It no longer begins the day your first single is released, it now begins eight months prior. Before you step into the studio, set up a crowdfunding/ preorder campaign to, sure, raise the funds necessary to record and promote your new album, but also to invite your fans to be a part of the process. They will happily pay you for it. These are your hard-core fans who will be on the front lines helping you spread the word about your album when it's released. Some vinyl plants have built-in crowdfunding. So, if you don't want to run a full-fledged Kickstarter campaign, you can just run one for the vinyl using a service like Qrates. We'll discuss more fully how best to approach these campaigns in Chapter 12.

6 Months Before

■ **Order the Vinyl**

By this point, your album should be mastered. If you're ordering vinyl, start no later than 6 months out contacting the plant to make sure they will be able to turn your order around by your release date. Because vinyl has seen a massive resurgence over the past few years, vinyl pressing plants cannot keep up with the demand. So turnaround times are frustratingly long. And because of the nature of vinyl, a lot can go wrong, so leave time for all of this. Fortunately, because of the rise in vinyl popularity, more and more plants are popping up these days and rates are dropping. But it's not uncommon for plants to have an 8-month turnaround time from submission to delivery. So be prepared. Many might say 5–6 months, but make note, this is only *after* you approve test pressings—which can take 1–2 months to get to you in the first place.

Qrates is a great option, however, if you want to run a vinyl-only crowdfunding campaign. You can set the minimum number of records needed for the campaign at 100, and if you sell 100 records, everyone gets a record; if you don't reach the milestone, no one gets a record (but you also aren't out any money). Qrates also has non-crowdfunding options, like direct-to-consumer fulfillment and bulk pressing (if you need a bunch for tour). Qrates seems to be able to offer some of the quickest turnarounds in the industry. More on vinyl crowdfunding in Chapter 12.

5 Months Before

■ **Artwork**

Make sure your cover art is finished 5 months before the release. If you're hiring a graphic design artist for this, You Pick Two (good, cheap, fast) applies. The only exception, as I mentioned earlier, is if you find royalty-free images (but remember that those images don't come with the same legal protections as images that you license from, let's say, iStock) or images that are controlled by a Creative Commons license that specifically allows commercial use. Any fonts in image editing programs like Photoshop are fine to use. Other fonts that you download may have restrictions, so be sure to check the legalities of the font you're using.

All vinyl plants will send you art templates to design the artwork from. Make sure your graphic designer creates the art to their specs.

■ **Liner Notes**

Obviously, if you're creating vinyl, you need all of the packaging completed before sending it in. AllMusic.com will also require this info.

■ **Promo Photos**

You'll also want to get new promo photos done to potentially include on the album cover and within the booklet. If you're not including any promo photos within your vinyl packaging, then don't worry about this until 3 months out. But, it's nice to include at least one shot of the artist within the packaging. And yes, it should be a new photo, to capture what you look like now (not two years ago). People want to know what the artists looked like at the time of the creation and release of this album. The music is a snapshot of where you are in your life at the time of the recording, and the accompanying photographs should be the same.

■ **Route the Tour**
We'll get into how to do this in Chapter 8, but you'll definitely want to start about 5 months in advance to plan the tour supporting the new album.

■ **Record Release Show Holds**
If you do it right, this show will sell out. This will be a hometown celebration of all your hard work. You'll want to do this on a Friday or Saturday, and venues book these prime slots out well in advance. Make sure you get a least a few holds 5 months out.

■ **Pick the Lead Singles**
This is where Fan Reviews, Survey Monkey and Google Forms can come in. Do the market research to figure out which are your strongest songs. The answers may surprise you. You can also invite your crowdfunding backers into this process to help you decide. They are your biggest fans and are looking out for your best interests. Hold a listening party (in person or livestreamed) and ask your fans to rate each song from 1 to 5. If they aren't there in person, you can set up an online survey via SurveyMonkey for digital attendees. Ask your fans to associate words and feelings to each song. You can make a list for them and ask them to circle (or check box on SurveyMonkey) all the feelings they felt for each song: Calm, Mellow, Thoughtful, Relaxed, Loving, Sad, Happy, Joyful, Excited, Bored, Angry,

Inspired, Intense, Party and Horny. Oh, why not? Ask them to circle whether they are male or female and their age range (under 18, 19–22, 23–34, 35–44, 45–54, 55–64, 65+). Ask them what artists they think you sound like. This will help with your Elevator Pitch and your digital marketing campaigns.

■ **Pick Your Distribution Company**

Reference my up-to-date list on Ari's Take (https://aristake .com/digital-distribution-comparison) to figure out which digital distributor is best for you. Many companies can get your music to stores within hours or days, but some require weeks. And once in a while Apple randomly selects a release to quality-check, and it can delay your release by up to 16 days. Best to get on this quickly. It's worth noting that some companies, namely CD Baby, INgrooves and Symphonic Distribution, also offer physical distribution and fulfillment. If you have a significant national (or international) fanbase and think you could move some serious product, hit up your distribution company and see what the possibilities are.

■ **Cue Up the First Single**

Yes, you should be releasing a minimum of 3 singles in advance of a full-length album. But most artists these days are releasing 6+ singles before the album, utilizing the "waterfall" technique, where you continue to add songs to the forthcoming album with each release (more on how to do this in a moment). Every single release gives you an opportunity to pitch playlist editors, run new marketing campaigns, and engage your fanbase with new creative. Singles should be released every 4 to 6 weeks. Spotify editors like to receive playlist submissions 4 weeks in advance, and it takes a few days (sometimes longer) from when you hit Submit in your distribution portal to appear in your Spotify for Artists, giving you the ability to submit the song. And, as of now, you can't submit song #2 until song #1 is released. Which is why you need to spread out your releases. If you're going to also release your music on Bandcamp (you should), you can actually cue up all of the releases and album now and submit it to the blog editors.

▪ **Create the FanLink**
The FanLink is the album landing page with all of the DSPs. Services like ArtistHub, Feature.fm, Show.co, Linkfire and ToneDen have cornered this market. Ask your distributor which links they can provide to you in advance of the release. Most distributors will be able to give you at least Spotify and Apple Music. But others can give you more. And you can always grab your Spotify link in your Spotify for Artists. Include Bandcamp. Point everyone to the FanLink page.

▪ **Create the Videos**
Of course, you're going to be making many, many videos of varying production quality and dimensions, and for various platforms for months to come. Some of these will be spontaneous in the moment (remember the viral TikTok video of Mothica crying to her masters in her car), and some will be high-production music videos. Start to get the batch going. For the songs you want to turn into full-on music videos, you're going to want to start this process now. And of course, any single you release should be accompanied by a Canvas video and a music video or visualizer of some kind.

■ **Cue Up the Ads**

When your first single is released, you're going to want to run social media ads promoting it. This is a good time to start to learn how to do this if you don't already know. Instagram and TikTok ads have proven to be the most effective for bumping streaming numbers (at a low cost). However, it's worth looking into all other advertising platforms, like YouTube, Google and Facebook, if your target demographic spends more time there.

■ **Start an Influencer Marketing Campaign**

There are plenty of companies out there that will work within your budget to engage social media influencers in their network. You can also work this on your own without hiring an agency. More on this in Chapter 5.

4 Months Before

■ **First Single Gets Released**

■ **Start the Social Media Ads**

■ **Hit Up User-Generated Playlist Editors**

Now that the single is officially out on DSPs, it's time to promote it to user-generated playlists. More on how to do this in Chapter 5.

■ **Release the Music Video**

One to three weeks after the single gets released, release the music video for the song. Even if it's just a simple lyric video or visualizer, putting out a full-length video like this gives you another opportunity to promote the song.

■ **Cue Up the Next Single**

Using the waterfall effect, you're actually creating a 2-song album (rereleasing single #1 and single #2—using the same ISRC code). Use the album cover for this. Once the release appears in Spotify for Artists, submit the single to playlist editors.

■ **Create the Album FanLink**

The beauty of the waterfall effect with your releases is that once the 2-song album is up, the link to the album will never change. Eventually, it'll be a 3-song album. And then a 4-song album. On and on (as many releases as you'd like to do). And then when the full album is up, the link that you've been using for months is still the same. No need to keep switching out links and hunt down all the new pre-save or single links.

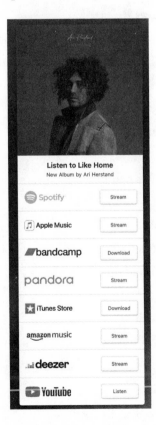

■ **Create More Video Content**

■ **Launch the New Website**
This is when you begin to let the world know about the upcoming album and release show. Sites like Bandzoogle and Squarespace make it easy to create a website and reskin it (change the design) at will, without having to beg your web developer to just update the header image one more time. I keep an updated comparison on ArisTake.com of some of the best website builders (https://aristake.com/website-builder-comparison). More on this in Chapter 11.

3 Months Before

■ **Second Single Gets Released**
If you used the waterfall effect, confirm that the 2-song album looks correct on DSPs (and stream counts and playlist inclusions have maintained). Now you can issue a takedown for single #1.

■ **Update and Tweak the Social Media Ads**

■ **Hit Up User-Generated Playlist Editors**

■ **Release the Music Video**
One to three weeks after this single gets released, release the next music video for the song.

■ **Cue Up the Next Single**
Using the waterfall effect, you're actually creating a 3-song album (rereleasing singles 1, 2 and now 3—using the same ISRC

codes). Use the album cover for this. Once the release appears in Spotify for Artists, submit the single to playlist editors.

■ **Create More Video Content**

■ **AllMusic**
It takes a while for AllMusic to process all of their info. To make sure they get your credit info up in time for your release, get your package to them sooner rather than later.

2 Months Before

■ **Start the Record Release Show Promo**
Now that you have triple confirmation from the vinyl plant that the shipment will arrive at least a month before the release show, lock in the date and start the promo campaign. We'll discuss exactly how to do this in Chapter 7. You will sell a lot of merch at this release show. Prepare yourself.

■ **Hit Up Local Press for Your Release Show**
Press outlets, especially those in print, plan far in advance. Start on this early. More on this in Chapter 15.

■ **Third Single Gets Released**
If you used the waterfall effect, confirm that the 3-song album looks correct on DSPs (and stream counts and playlist inclusions have maintained). Now you can issue a takedown for the 2-song album.

■ **Update and Tweak the Social Media Ads**

■ **Hit Up User-Generated Playlist Editors**

■ **Release the Music Video**
One to three weeks after the single gets released, release the music video for the song.

■ **Cue Up the Next Single**
Using the waterfall effect, you're actually creating a 4-song album (rereleasing singles 1, 2, 3 and now 4—using the same ISRC codes from before). Use the album cover for this.

■ **Create More Video Content**

The Month Before

■ **Fourth Single Gets Released**
If you used the waterfall effect, confirm that the 4-song album looks correct on DSPs (and stream counts and playlist inclusions have maintained). Now you can issue a takedown for the 3-song album.

■ **Update and Tweak the Social Media Ads**

■ **Hit Up User-Generated Playlist Editors**

■ **Release the Music Video**
One to three weeks after the single gets released, release the music video for the song.

■ **Cue Up the Album**

■ **Create More Video Content**

■ **Send Out All Crowdfunding/Preorder Packages**

■ **Listening Party**

Use a livestreaming platform of your choice to hold a virtual listening party for your new album. You'll get the first reactions from fans in real time. Or, even better, host a local listening party in your living room and livestream it out to people around the world.

■ **Run Contests**

To help promote the new music video, release show and tour, rally the troops and start running creative contests all the way up until release day. You should target your fans everywhere they are. Send an email out to your list to let your biggest fans know how they can get involved and help promote the album.

Here are some ideas on how you can use the social sites to run contests:

1. **TikTok**   Come up with a trend and encourage your fans to participate. Make sure they use your hashtag or Sound so you can track all of this.

2. **Instagram**   Have them post a photo or video of them listening to your new single. Start a hashtag like #newalbumtitle and encourage your fans to post photos of themselves doing something that relates to the album (or single) title. Then pick one for a special merch package to be sent to them in the mail (who doesn't love getting presents?) or given at the release show. Rachel Platten started a movement with her song "Fight Song," encouraging her fans to post photos of them-

selves holding up their arm making a muscle and then posting in the description what obstacles they have overcome with the tag #fightsong. A year after the song's release, the movement was still going strong. You can also use the same TikTok campaign as a Reel.

3. **Facebook**   Ask your fans to share your new music video (which you uploaded directly to Facebook) with the link to the album on their favorite DSP. Then have them write "Mission Accomplished" on your Musician Page. Pick one for a special merch package.

4. **Twitter**   Ask your fans to post their favorite lyrics or lyric meme (that you create) from the lead single with the hashtag #newalbumtitle.

5. **Spotify**   Ask your fans to add your new single to their playlists and pre-save the upcoming album.

6. **YouTube**   Ask all your fans to comment on your new music videos.

7. **Street Team**   Rally up the street team and start hitting your town with posters and flyers for the release show. Hit the coffee shops, record stores, college campuses and anywhere else your fans hang out. If the venue's into it, make coupons for drink discounts and include them on your physical postcard flyers (4 × 6). Give a small stack to each street team member. Put a number on each flyer and run an internal street team contest where whoever turns in the most drink coupon flyers at the bar gets a cash prize. This will really up the ante for your team. Of course, your street team gets free tickets to the show. You can do this in every city of your tour. Because so few people actually put up posters or hand out flyers anymore you will stand out. Make sure to get a QR code on there linking directly to the album landing page.

8. **Send Out Email and SMS Blasts** Lead off with the story of the album creation process. Be vulnerable. Be open. Be authentic. Don't just say, "This is the best album we've ever made." That's boring. Everyone says that. Why did you make an album? Use the hook from the press release (we'll get more into this in Chapter 15) and welcome your fans back to you. Or introduce them to the new you. Include a link to the preorder or album landing page site and focus on that. If you're running a preorder, include this link. Also include the contests you're running and invite fans to find you on the various social sites to participate. Gather more people for your street team. Link the music video in the blast. Invite them to your listening party.

You can utilize the platform Tunespeak, which enables you to run contests, promote merch, giveaways and preorders. It gamifies fan engagement by awarding points for every action taken (Spotify stream or pre-save, video view, creating a dream set list, viewing Instagram posts).

Two Weeks Before

■ **Send Out Email and SMS Blasts with a Timed Discount**
Yes, you sent a blast two weeks prior, but in this one, just include the preorder link (twice—beginning and end). It's good to give them a reason to preorder right now. Try a limited-time, free-shipping or discount offer, such as:

Subject: " 72 hours left for free shipping"

Body: Grab any *preorder package* (link it) in the next 72 hours and get free shipping. There are limited items left available for preorder and this will expire in 71 hours, 59 . . . 58 minutes.

Get it now (link)

Marketing experts will tell you that adding a "limited time offer" and "limited availability" pushes people to take action and gives them a reason to do so RIGHT NOW.

The Week Before

- **Create a YouTube Album Playlist**
  Upload all the videos that you have completed to YouTube, make the album playlist and schedule them to go public on release day. Remember, you need a video for every song, either a music video, lyric video or performance video. Yes, your distributor will automatically send your song to YouTube and YouTube will turn each song into a video with the single cover, but this may not notify the subscribers to your Channel, and if you have other videos you want your subscribers to see, get these up there and cued up.

- **Send Out Email and SMS Blasts**
  Yes, send another one. Push the preorder once again (twice—open and close), but this time, also include the behind-the-scenes video as a private link and explain that those on your list are getting a special sneak peek. Also, push the contest campaign once again. Yes, your distributor will automatically send your song to YouTube and YouTube will turn each song into a video with the single cover, but this may not notify the subscribers to your channel, and if you have other videos you want your subscribers to see, get these up there and cued up.

The Day Before

- **Create the Email and SMS Blasts**

  Now this is the big one. Launch day! Make sure it includes links to everything you're releasing. Prioritize Bandcamp and let your fans know they can "name their price" or subscribe to you (more on this in Chapter 12). Explain that 85% of the money from Bandcamp goes directly to you. Believe it or not, the fans who didn't back your crowdfunding or preorder your album may be happy to drop $50 on just a digital download of your album to support you.

- **Triple-Check All Your Links**

  Go through your Folder of Assets and make sure all the links are updated and correct.

- **Change the Preorder**

  Make sure your preorder switches over to purchase links.

- **Update Merch**

  Make sure your new merch, photos and bio are all up to date and will be synced everywhere to all platforms. Also make sure to link your merch to your Spotify profile (found in Spotify for Artists).

Release Day

It's here! All of your hard work and planning will pay off when you play to the sold-out club at your release show, start trending on TikTok, get added to popular Spotify playlists and take the whole project on the road. There are still a few things left to do to continue the momentum and have your album explode into the world.

- **Release the YouTube Official Album Playlist**
- **Release the Behind-the-Scenes and Other Videos**
- **Publish the Bandcamp Album**
- **Create an EPK on Your Website**
  EPK literally stands for "electronic press kit." This is the page that you send industry personnel as a snapshot of who you are. It may contain press quotes, videos, songs, a bio, social links and stats, tour dates/history and other exciting things you can highlight. Many people make this a hidden page on their website.
- **Send the Email and SMS Blasts**
- **Livestream the Release Show**

The Week Of

- **More Contests**
  Run some more creative contests to keep the buzz going strong.
- **Hit Up User-Generated Playlist Editors**
- **Update and Tweak the Social Media Ads**

Every Day After the Release

- **New Videos**
  You should be releasing new videos probably daily at this point. But these can be shorter, more candid videos on Instagram, TikTok, YouTube, Twitter, Facebook. Wherever your fans are, hit them with new videos reminding them of the release in creative ways. Acoustic performances. Remixes. Dances. Soundtrack to your grocery visit. Whatever. Regular videos, regularly.
- **Update and Tweak the Social Media Ads**
- **Hit Up User-Generated Playlist Editors**

■ **Go Live Frequently**

If your audience is on Twitch, TikTok, Triller or any other livestreaming platform, of course you should be livestreaming extra during this time period. Ari's Take Academy instructor and livestreamer extraordinaire Clare Means did a 12-hour livestream the day of her album release, and it helped propel it to #1 on the iTunes Singer/Songwriter charts.

This Campaign Is Carved in Play-Doh

Even though you just finished reading my very specific formula of how you can release your album, you should only use this as a guideline. Every project is different, and the beauty of managing an indie music career is, you have the freedom and flexibility to call your own shots and experiment. The indie albums that do the best are the ones that are not only undeniably great, but have creative release campaigns around them.

A FEW CREATIVE CAMPAIGNS TO GET YOUR JUICES FLOWING

■ **Enter the Haggis—Livestream Listening Parties**

Enter the Haggis released an album in March 2020—mere days before COVID-19 shut down the US. They had intimate, in-person album listening parties planned up and down the East Coast for their Kickstarter backers. Of course, those all had to be canceled. They decided to take these listening parties online. Each livestream, they would stream one of the ten albums in their discography. In order, chronologically. Initially hosted on Facebook (where the majority of their fanbase was active), they used Wirecast (a livestream production tool) to cut in behind the scenes videos, multi-square talking head lives (a la CNN), and music videos. They had GoPros and an ATEM Mini mixer to edit the live video feed on the spot. They linked to the tip page on their website. After Facebook shut down one of their streams for rights issues (I'm guessing Facebook didn't realize the owners of the recordings and songs were streaming their own music), they moved on over to YouTube and continued the monthly album listening party streams. Most of their streams were prerecorded, and they chatted with fans in the chat box. They embedded these livestreams on their Bandzoogle website, where they were able to seamlessly accept tips and sell merch—commission free. They averaged nearly $5,000 per listening party. Not bad for sitting at home.

■ RAC—Cassette Tape Digital Token

In May 2021, the Grammy-winning (independent) producer RAC released his album *BOY* and sold 100 cassette tapes as the token $TAPE on the Ethereum-based NFT marketplace Zora. Unlike most other NFTs or other digital tokens, this was tied to a physical item. Each token, which had a starting price of $28, represented one physical copy of the cassette, and the owner could redeem it for the physical item at any point—driving further scarcity for the token.

The price of a single $TAPE token peaked at $13,000—making it the most expensive cassette tape ever sold. Because this was traded on the Ethereum blockchain, every transaction was made publicly available. More on blockchain and NFTs in Chapter 12.

- **Kings of Leon NFT Album**

  For their 2021 album *When You See Yourself*, the band released it as an NFT (in addition to on streaming services). They minted a limited number of NFTs tied to the album. Each NFT contained the album and one-of-a-kind art designed by their longtime creative partner, Night After Night.

  What made this NFT drop unlike any other was that some of the tokens were tied to physical experiences. Whoever owns one of these tokens is guaranteed four front-row seats to any Kings of Leon concert during each tour for life. The token owner also gets a VIP experience that includes a personal driver, a concierge at the show to take care of their needs, a hangout with the band before the show, and exclusive lounge access. Upon leaving the show, the fan's car will have four bags filled with every item from the merch booth. And like other NFTs, these tokens could be bought and sold at will on the Ethereum blockchain—which prevents scalpers and hackers from interfering. Kings of Leon made $2 million on this NFT drop (and donated $500,000 to Live Nation's Crew Nation fund to support live music crews during the pandemic).

- **Esperanza Spalding—*Exposure,* a 77-Hour Album**

  In 2017, Esperanza Spalding camped out in a recording studio with other collaborators for exactly seventy-seven hours. She conceived, wrote, rehearsed and recorded ten songs in that time—while livestreaming the process out to the world (as a clock on the wall counted down). Fans could tune in at all hours of the day or night and watch as Spalding and team created the masterpiece (or slept). Think *The Truman Show* meets *Big Brother.* She had an extremely exclusive physical preorder available with 7,777 vinyl records and CDs (which contained pieces of the note paper she used during the session). She sold these packages for well above the standard rate ($60 and $50 respectively, and the autographed vinyl test pressing for $250) because they were exclusive, unique and limited. She sold out of all the inventory before the live stream finished. The album has never been available for digital download or streaming.

■ **Brassroots District—Phone Hotline**

Because the concept of Brassroots District is set squarely in 1973, we had to come up with ways to promote the debut single that was in line with the era. We put up posters all over Los Angeles. There were no websites listed on the posters. Websites didn't exist in 1973. We designed the poster after those of the era, included a few press quotes and put "Call to listen! (323) 596-1973." When called, after some theme music lead-in, you heard a sexy voice: "Welcome to the Brassroots District. Press one to preview the hit single 'Together.' Press two to visit New Orleans with 'Repetition.' Press three to get romantic with 'So Damn in Love.' Press four to leave reality with 'Takin' Back Daydreamin'.' Press five to learn more about Brassroots District." If you pressed five, you'd hear a cryptic bio with clues foreshadowing the first Brassroots District Experience. If you pressed one, on release day, you were sent a text message with a link to the FanLink to choose your streaming platform of choice to listen to the song. We retained everyone's phone numbers to let them know about upcoming events and releases. Were the quotes real or were they *fake news*? What is reality? What is truth? BRD's mantra is from the song "Takin' Back Daydreamin'": "We don't need reality, it's all for show."

■ **Transviolet—Anonymous Cassette Tape Packages**

In the summer of 2015, teenagers around the United States started receiving manilla bubble-wrapped packages with no return address. Each package contained a single cassette tape. On the cassette tape were the handwritten words "Just Press Play." When the tape was put into a cassette player, Transviolet's debut single "Girls Your Age" played. Also handwritten on the packaging of the cassette: "Don't have a cassette player??? Visual Shazam the other side." What was on the other side? Nothing. Just whiteness. But, sure enough, when you opened the Shazam camera and scanned the blank back of the cassette insert, the artist's Shazam profile appeared where you could play the song. Fans took to the band's Facebook Page proclaiming things like "Got the tape in the mail today.

I'm already in love. No freaking clue how you got my address, but A+ marketing. Hopefully all will be revealed soon so it will be less creepy . . ." The song got over a million plays on Spotify and 200K+ plays on SoundCloud within weeks of the tapes going out with virtually no other promotion other than a few blog articles. But word of mouth spread and even celebrities started getting in on the hype, with Katy Perry and Harry Styles tweeting about it.

■ **Beck—*Song Reader* Sheet Music Album**
In December of 2012, Beck released his new album. Except this time there was no audio, only sheet music. He released 108 pages of sheet music for 20 new songs (and 100 pages of art). His musical fans learned the songs and uploaded their versions to YouTube and SoundCloud. In 2014, Beck released an actual (audio) record of *Song Reader*.

■ **Nine Inch Nails—*Year Zero* Real Life Video Game**
In 2007, Nine Inch Nails ran a worldwide marketing campaign that included a cryptic YouTube video that you had to pause to decode, USB flash drives in bathrooms of venues the band played, and secret messages on T-shirts sold at the shows that when googled brought up even more confusion, with a webmaster email to contact that returned an autoresponse giving away a bit more of the puzzle. It was a real-life video game that Nine Inch Nails fans had to come together from around the globe via the Wikipedia page to complete. It all culminated with NIN's album *Year Zero*.

"The eighteen-to-thirty-five-year-old demo has grown up in a marketing-saturated environment and has developed a sophisticated set of tools for avoiding the vast majority of marketing messages," Jordan Weisman, the marketing director in charge of the project said. "As a rule of thumb, the bigger the neon sign, the faster they'll run the other way. So the premise here was, instead of shouting, go the opposite way and whisper."

■ **Sadie Jean—TikTok Open Verse Challenge for "WYD Now?"**
In October of 2021, Sadie Jean was in the process of writing and recording some new songs with a couple classmates from NYU. She posted a clip of them listening to a work in progress and captioned it "wrote this about realizing you still want to be with that person!" and included the lyrics on the screen. Her friend leaned over and said, "You have to send it to him." This video got over a million views on TikTok. So, a month later, she posted an Open Verse Challenge—a popular TikTok trend where the creator sings a bit of their song and then leaves space for others to add some of their own bars onto it via the Duet feature. Nearly 20,000 people took her up on the challenge and added their own verses—some sung, some rapped. Essentially, 20,000 collaborations on a song not yet out. Artists including Lil Yachty, Catie Turner, Zailk, Francis Karel, and Jewels participated in the challenge. Sadie re-Duetted some of them, which highlighted and propelled the trend even further. She quickly released the song (her debut) weeks later. And in less than a month, the official release had over 20 million streams on Spotify alone. Sometimes you don't make the release plan, the release plan makes you.

5.

BUILDING A FANBASE ONE FAN AT A TIME

You need to confidently exclude people and proudly say what you're not. By doing so, you'll win the hearts of the people you want.
—DEREK SIVERS, *ANYTHING YOU WANT*

An artist without a movement is soon forgotten.
—DAN WILSON, GRAMMY-WINNING SINGER/SONGWRITER/ PRODUCER

The music fan is more passionate about music than ever before. But they're not immersed in it. They're sampling. Everything is a charcuterie plate as opposed to "give me the steak and the potatoes and I'm diving in."
—BRUCE FLOHR, ARTIST MANAGER

In the past, the traditional approach was, you break an artist in the home market and then if the artist became super successful, you might be able to drum up some interest internationally. Because you had a blueprint. Today it's entirely the reverse. In the first instance you need to build a global audience.
—CHAZ JENKINS, CHIEF COMMERCIAL OFFICER, CHARTMETRIC

THE NEW FAN

The "rock star mystique" is all but dead. Before, the closest a fan could get to their favorite musician was by waiting at the stage door after the show hoping their idol would stop by for a few autographs and a photo. But many didn't. Many self-righteous rockers bolted from the venue to the tour bus in their shades without so much as a wave to their fans who waited for two hours in the rain to meet them. Now, a fan can literally get inside their favorite artist's pants (pocket, via a tweet to their phone) without having to wear a low-cut shirt. Oh, how far we've come.

Not only has social media broken down the barriers of access; it has created a new reality where it's virtually impossible for artists to hide their true colors—for better or worse. Fans have always been attracted to authenticity, but now one can more quickly and easily weed out the impostors from the true artists. You can't fake it and make it in the new era.

Similarly, the new music fan has a completely different set of expectations. If a fan DMs a band with just a few thousand followers and doesn't get a response or even just a heart, that fan feels snubbed. Obviously, artists with millions of followers won't be able to respond to every message (and it's not expected), but for up-and-coming bands, early engagement can be the difference between cultivating hard-core evangelists who talk about your band every chance they get and fair-weather fans who casually stream a playlist you're on from time to time.

Some artists these days, however, go a bit too far and overly engage with people who are not fans and who would rather not be spoken to by an artist they don't care about. There's a way to be respectful of your fans, to embrace the new reality while still maintaining your privacy.

A perfect example of how you can engage with a fan in an authentic, noncreepy way is offered by Brittany Howard, lead singer and guitarist of Alabama Shakes. It all started when a 24-year-old fan from Louisville Instagrammed a short video of herself playing half of the opening riff to "Future People," stating "Doing my best." She tagged Howard (@blackfootwhitefoot). Howard posted a response video on Instagram with a close-up on the neck of her guitar and finished the complicated lick for the fan, with "Here's the rest," and tagged the fan.

Every artist at any level can learn from this. You don't need to be a superstar to give back. Even if you have ten fans, make one of their days. Word will spread. But again, you don't need to be the creepy, overengaged Facebook responder. Sure, Like comments, respond occasionally, Regram, Duet, Stitch, Instaheart, but there's a difference between giving back and giving up your life.

Younger artists are much better at creating an authentic social media presence and knowing how to engage just the right amount to maintain a bit of mystique but also not insult their fan. Ashley Nicolette Frangipane (or as you know her, Halsey) is considered an overnight sensation by the music industry. She sold out her first tour ever (of 500–1,000-cap rooms) in 30 seconds with zero radio play, no album and no label. But she had been cultivating a loyal fan base for over six years. When she was 14 in 2008, she had 14,000 MySpace friends and at 18 she had 16,000 YouTube subscribers. She built her following online. Whereas most artists try to get the viral video, viral photo, viral song on TikTok, viral anything, Halsey worked on fostering a deep relationship with her followers. By staying open, vulnerable and intimate, her fans became loyalists. Halsey wasn't pushing or promoting anything. She was simply existing in a reality understood solely by those on the inside. So, when she had a piece of real content (her first song/music video "Ghost") to share, her fans were finally able to engage with something other than just a photo or a tweet. The track exploded online. Halsey told the *New*

York Times about her first meeting with Capitol Records. She said, "I remember walking into Capitol Records, sitting down with the executives and having them say, 'Look at what you did while none of us were paying attention.' That was one of the proudest moments of my entire life. I put all the groundwork in myself, and they let me do my thing, because it's working."

Engagement > Followers

Followers, plays and Likes can be bought. Everybody knows it. And you look foolish if your YouTube video has 200,000 views with only 7 comments and 12 likes or a million streams with only 1,000 monthly listeners. Those views and streams were clearly purchased from a bot. There's no point in spending money to puff up your numbers for vanity's sake. Advertising for real human followers is one thing, paying for bots to Like your page or watch your video is another.

Bots don't come to shows. Bots don't back your crowdfunding. Bots don't buy merch. Bots don't help you become a full-time musician.

Startup guru and angel investor Sean Ellis states that "focusing on customer acquisition over awareness takes discipline . . . At a certain scale, awareness/brand building makes sense. But for the first year or two it's a total waste of money."

Plays mean nothing if you have no way to connect with those listeners and follow up with them. That's why I completely tune out artists who tell me they got 100,000 plays on their most recent song. OK, but how many of those listeners signed up to your email list, bought a ticket to your show, followed you on Instagram and Spotify or supported you in any way financially?

THE PYRAMID OF INVESTMENT AND THE PYRAMID OF ENGAGEMENT

Every fan exists on a Pyramid of Investment. The fans who stream your music but never spend any money on you directly are at the bottom of the pyramid. Those who tip you during livestreams or shows are one level up. Those who come to your shows are a level higher. Those who buy your merch or music are a level above that. Those who back your crowdfunding campaigns are another level up. The fan club members (Patreon or paid subscriber) are yet another tier higher. And the fans who buy the high-priced, VIP experiences are at the top of the pyramid. You should give every fan, of every level, ways to support you financially.

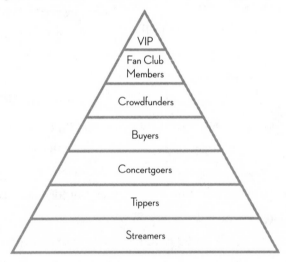

Pyramid of Investment.

But "investment" isn't just financial. Fans invest in artists with their time as well. The Pyramid of Engagement is nearly as important. Because the more engaged a fan is, the more she will be willing to purchase.

The fans who gave your Facebook Page a Like five years ago and haven't seen a post from you since are at the bottom of this pyramid.

Those who follow you on Instagram, TikTok, Twitter and everywhere else you may exist online are one level higher. The fans who actively Like, comment, watch, Stitch, Duet, retweet, vote and heart are a level higher. The fans who are on your email or SMS lists are a level above that. The fans who are not only on your list, but open and read everything you send, are a level higher. And at the very top are the fans on your street team engaging with every piece of content you put out and are constantly telling everyone they know about you. You know, like your mom.

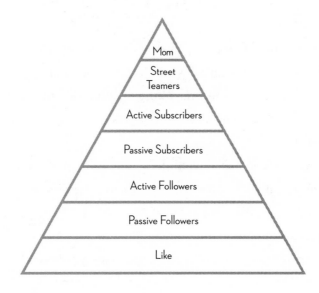

Pyramid of Engagement.

GET RICH IN YOUR NICHE

Own your niche. If you are an acoustic folk artist, get to know all the folk artists, listening rooms, labels and managers in your scene. Start there. Play the spots. Hang out at the spots when you're not playing. Cowrite with other folk artists. Find one to mentor you. Eventually, if you're good, word will spread. And then you expand to neighboring scenes.

But go deeper. Are you an acoustic folk artist who writes protest songs that appeal to college-age activists? Target that demo. But go deeper. Are you a blues artist? How about a blues artist from the south who only plays standards written before 1960? Target traditional folk lovers from the south. Embrace what makes your project unique. But go deeper. Are you a metal band? What kind of metal band? Metal-pop? Metal-core? Emo-metal? Are you a pop artist? Are you also Christian? Start with the Christian community. You don't need to label yourself a Christian artist, but target that community. Build your base of loyalists and let it spread from there.

You're not just a folk artist, blues artist, hip-hop artist, metal artist, pop artist, jazz artist, soul artist, singer/songwriter. Go as deep as you can with your niche to help you find your audience. The more that sets you apart and makes you unique, the easier it will be to target a demographic, a scene, a niche.

Once you've conquered your local scene, expand to neighboring scenes. The reason I say scenes and not towns is because not every town may have a scene in your niche. So do the research.

You can of course network online. The synthwave artist FM-84 was an active member of a 20,000-person Facebook Group of 1980s synthwave lovers. He regularly geeked out with the other members about everything synthwave. In advance of his album, he shared with the group new graphics he had created (at the time he was a graphic designer at Apple) to get their thoughts and prime the group for his forthcoming release. So, when he released his album, the only promo he did was within this Facebook Group. He shot to #1 in three categories on Bandcamp (including the Pop category) and got millions of streams on Spotify and Apple Music (it had been rumored that some playlist editors were also members of this Facebook Group).

Previously, social platforms were communities. In the late 2000s/early 2010s, there were YouTubers who cultivated community on the platform and launched their careers from their initial YouTube success. They also frequently collaborated with other similar artists on the platform.

Hip-hop artists, DJs, and producers found each other and collaborated on SoundCloud in the mid-2010s.

The late 2010s brought sub communities on Instagram like @pickupmusic, which helped propel the careers of Jacob Collier, Cory Henry, Madison Cunningham, Maddie Jay, Raquel Rodriguez, Elise Trouw and Emily C. Browning, catching the neo-soul wave of the late 2010s.

And recently, we've seen subcommunities continuing across Instagram, TikTok and Twitch, where musicians find and collaborate with one another on- and off-platform.

But, of course, these scenes didn't exist just a few years ago. Maybe there's another online community popping up that you feel connected to that you want to develop.

So, home in on your sound, your scene and your niche. And start there. And you want to surround yourself with like-minded individuals. They will influence you more than you know. If everyone around you is kicking a$$, working toward their dreams, you will be inspired to do the same. If everyone around is quitting music, starting families and settling into 9-to-5s, you will feel the pressure to do the same.

Your immediate community is so important. Which brings us to:

ARE YOU IN THE RIGHT CITY FOR YOUR MUSIC?

Of course, in the digital age, you can theoretically get your music out from anywhere in the world. But developing a music career where literally every other person in town is in a different field of work is unbelievably difficult.

Of course, you can start as "the guy" or "the gal" in town who plays music and initially gets hired for any event where they want some music. And it may work for a little while, but eventually you will most likely go stir crazy and yearn to get out. You don't have to go far either. Move to the nearest big(gish) city where there is a music scene. And more specifically, a scene of like-minded artists in your genre. And go from there.

Don't underestimate the importance of a physical community.

LOS ANGELES, NEW YORK, LONDON OR NASHVILLE?

Wonder why so many acts break out of L.A., New York, London and Nashville? It's because the industry exists in those places. And so many other like-minded musicians live there, constantly inspiring each other, collaborating and trading tips and tricks. If you live in one of these cities, you are constantly rubbing shoulders with the movers and shakers of the industry. They hang out at the same music venues, go to the same coffee shops, grocery stores and dog parks. You may get introduced to someone at a show and then see them the very next day at the gym and make a deeper connection. They may need a singer/guitarist/cowriter/producer/fill-in-the-blank and think of you first for the job because you're top of mind. Everyone knows someone in the industry, and even if a person is not in it, if they like your music, they may pass it along to their industry friend. Friends like helping friends out. And people trust their friends.

You don't need to be in these cities to "make it," of course, but it can definitely help to be there. That being said, each town has its own strengths and weaknesses, and you should not move to any of these cities before you're ready and understand why you're moving.

Before even considering moving to any city, make sure you visit and spend a good amount of time there exploring. And make sure you do your research about the city you're thinking of moving to.

The 2020 US Census revealed that there were 34,770 working musicians in the US. And the top cities where these musicians were concentrated along with their corresponding average hourly wages were:

City	Number of Musicians	Average Annual Income	Employment per 1,000 Jobs
New York City	4,520	$101,212	0.51
Los Angeles	2,880	$102,148	0.49
Chicago	1,590	$101,296	0.37
Nashville	1,230	$75,379	1.27
Seattle	1,040	$75,504	0.53

However, the cost of living in NYC and L.A. is far higher than Nashville or Seattle. So, you need to take that into account as well. This report also indicated that even though there are fewer total professional musicians in Nashville than Chicago, the concentration of musicians is much greater in Nashville. In Nashville, the "employment per thousand jobs" number was 1.27, whereas in Chicago it was only 0.37.

But even though we, as the human race, went through a massive structural refocusing since the pandemic, a few things still hold true: Los Angeles, London, Nashville and New York remain four of the biggest creative hubs in the world with still lots of talent (and industry) continuing to gravitate to these hubs.

LOS ANGELES

I moved to L.A. mainly to get away from the Minnesota winters. The fact that the industry is here was a bonus. The beauty of L.A. (unlike most other music communities around the world) is that it is incredibly diverse. There isn't a "music scene" per se; there is a singer/songwriter scene, a hip-hop scene, an indie-rock scene. There are hard-rock, pop, electro and jazz scenes. And every scene has artists fifty-deep. And many of the scenes have subscenes, like the under-30 singer/songwriter scene. The '80s-rockers scene. And so on.

It seems virtually everyone I know in L.A. is a creative of some sort. Musician, actor, screenwriter, director, filmmaker or industry personnel assisting and supporting these creatives. L.A. is a creative town. Even the agents, managers, attorneys, label people and those who work in the industry in other capacities are mostly creative. You have to be when you work in a creative industry. So, in L.A. you are constantly vibing off of the creative energies around.

But Los Angeles is not a town of hippie-dippy artists (well, Venice still is). It is a town of creatives who want to make a living with their art. The artists in L.A. are smart, driven, passionate and hardworking. No matter what field you're in, if you're in L.A. you have to *hustle your a$$ off.* You can't sit around, work a day job and hope to be discovered just because you're here. Everyone in L.A. who makes it does so because of their hard work. There is very little luck that goes into it.

The Three-Year Test

No matter what field of work you're in, if you can make it three years in L.A., you can make it in L.A. Making it in L.A. is defined the same as making it in the music business: survival. I've seen many people come, live in the city for a bit, realize it's not for them and take off. Within three years. Because it's a town of hustlers, nontraditional career paths and instability, you do what you have to do to get by and make a living. And pretty much everyone I know in L.A. does a million different little jobs to make up the whole pot of money they need to live in the City of Angels. Because, let me tell you, it's a wonderful place to live if you can make it. Yes, it's expensive (but not as expensive as New York). But what L.A. has that New York doesn't is the constant sunshine. Nearly every day of the year it is gorgeous out. Seventy-five degrees and sunny. Sure, there's some smog. But it ain't Beijing. And there's traffic. But now that the subway system is expanding, hopefully more people will take it and reduce the traffic and smog. L.A. gets a bad rap because of the plastic people and the traffic. But you don't have to surround yourself with the plastics. Yes, of course they exist. But they mostly exist in Beverly Hills. You know how often I go to Beverly Hills? Only when I stumble onto the other side of the city lines after leaving the Troubadour. And if you place yourself in a part of town where other, like-minded artists are, you won't have to drive much.

If you're thinking of moving, talk to a few musician friends and start there. Unlike New York, everything is extremely spread out. So if you live in Santa Monica and your bestie lives in Silver Lake, plan on seeing her twice a year and grabbing coffee over Facetime.

Here's how I describe the various neighborhoods.

West Hollywood

I'm starting with WeHo because it's where I lived for eight years when I first moved to L.A. It has a special place in my heart. If you walk down Laurel Avenue just south of Sunset, look down and you'll see my name carved into the sidewalk. WeHo is the gay capital of the country. It has been for decades. It's a great neighborhood—clean, comfortable and hopping. There are plenty of lower-key restaurants, cafes, bars, restaurants and, of course, music venues. The Troubadour is in WeHo. As are the Sunset Strip clubs. If you pick the right location, you can be in walking distance of Trader Joe's, cafes, bars, restaurants and a gym. (You soon realize once you settle in town, everyone goes to the gym—often. Everyone. It rubs off.)

West Hollywood is very centrally located—equidistant from the beach and the Eastside (25–45 minutes, depending on time of day). But it's far from the highways and the airport. There aren't a ton of musicians and artists in West Hollywood. Mostly actors. Beautiful people. To find most of the artists, you have to head east.

Hollywood

Don't confuse West Hollywood and Hollywood. Separate cities. Separate mayors. And completely different kinds of people and energies. Whereas West Hollywood is clean, comfortable and pleasant, Hollywood is rough, brash and flooded with tourists. There are lots of homeless people in Hollywood. The wealth disparity here is devastating. Hopefully by the time you're reading this, my city will have gotten it under control. All the bumping dance clubs with DJs are mostly in Hollywood. Bottle service galore, with promoters who literally scour the city all day to find hot people to stuff into their clubs and entertain the high rollers. But, that being said, there are a few really excellent music venues (and comedy clubs) in Hollywood, which is why I go there so often. Hollywood is significantly cheaper to live in than West Hollywood, so it may be a suitable option initially if you're looking to save money. Get some pepper spray though.

Downtown

Ten years ago Downtown was a ghost town at night. Nobody went down there. But today is different. Condos, apartment complexes, lofts, restaurants, bars, photography and recording studios, and music venues are popping up left and right. Many artists are renting lofts and setting up shop. Downtown definitely has much more of a New York feel than the rest of L.A. DTLA (as the locals refer to it) was also the location of Brass-roots District "Live in the Lot" 2021 summer Experience.

The downside is, Downtown is pretty far away from everywhere else. It's a solid 25 minutes from Silver Lake, without traffic. But there's always traffic. However, the subway will take you from Downtown to Hollywood in no time at all.

Silverlake, Los Feliz, Echo Park (the Eastside)

My new home. Man, when I moved to the Eastside from WeHo, I finally found my people. Artists are everywhere. Plenty of thirtysomethings and fortysomethings (with kids), but also some twentysomethings are settling in. It's gotten much more expensive since the first artist scene began in the early to mid-2000s. Many of those artists have stayed and started families, and you see them around the neighborhood. There's charm and there's culture. Energy and life. Unfortunately, the pandemic took a few of our beloved music venues, but fortunately, the area is still as lively as ever. Many more backyard concert series have popped up because of Covid and have continued on in some form or another.

Highland Park and Eagle Rock

Buying or renting a house near Miracle Mile, WeHo, the Eastside or on the Westside can be pretty cost-prohibitive. For the musicians who need more space or want a home studio that won't bother the neighbors, many have moved to Highland Park or Eagle Rock. These adjacent neighborhoods lie further east than the Eastside, but not as far removed as deep in the Valley, the beach or East Los Angeles. This area is actually quite up-and-coming, with cafes, restaurants, bars and some great music venues and private concert series.

Koreatown

Not much here except the 1,800-capacity Wiltern Theater and a ton of amazing Korean BBQ restaurants. It's definitely more affordable to live in Koreatown, but you're pretty far removed from the rest of the city— except Downtown, which is right next door.

South L.A.

This is just south of the 10 freeway, west of Downtown. Lots of families and more affordable homes. It is the home of the monthly Bananas Hip Hop Showcase and Blue Dream Studios backyard funk/soul/R&B concert series. Great jazz, soul, blues and hip-hop musicians have come out of South L.A. including Dr. Dre (and the N.W.A. crew), Kamasi Washington, Terrace Martin, Jhené Aiko, Dom Kennedy, Murs, Kurupt, Keb' Mo', Etta James, Montell Jordan, Patrice Rushen, and Schoolboy Q. It's a little removed from Hollywood and the beach, but you're about 20 minutes from the Eastside clubs or Downtown.

Santa Monica, Venice and Neighboring Beach Towns (the Westside)

Two words: beach air. Whenever I go to Santa Monica, I stop and take a deep breath and sigh. Fresh. Call me a hippie, but there's a heightened consciousness in Santa Monica. It's the hub of yoga and meditation in L.A. Many of the TED speakers who live in L.A. live in Santa Monica or Venice. Venice borders Santa Monica and there is still the Venice hippie/ surfer/artist culture on the beach and boardwalk. Not many music venues on the Westside though. However, Silicon Beach is here with Snapchat at its center. As is YouTube Space.

Pico-Robertson

If someone says they live in the Pico-Robertson neighborhood, they basically mean the one square mile surrounding the intersection of Pico and Robertson. It's where you'll find kosher markets, kosher delis and kosher Chinese restaurants (yes, they exist). The Mint is the closest music venue and Moshav Band hosts its annual Hanukkah party there. It's always sold out and oftentimes Matisyahu makes a guest appearance.

South Bay

This includes Manhattan Beach, Redondo Beach, Hermosa Beach and other nearby cities. It's very far removed from everything L.A. So much so that most don't really consider it L.A. It's a hike to get there and back. Most only go there to visit friends when their arms are twisted.

The Other Side of the Hill/the Valley

"L.A." is generally considered everything from the ocean (Santa Monica, Venice) to Downtown. The northern border is generally defined by the Hollywood Hills. Most people who move to L.A. populate L.A. proper. When you think of all the beautiful people of Los Angeles (and no, people aren't exaggerating), they mean south of the Hollywood Hills. But once they settle down and start a family, many move to the Valley (over "the hill") to raise kids. However, with rising rents south of the hills, many musicians are jumping over to Sherman Oaks, Studio City, North Hollywood and Burbank to get situated. It's much more affordable and really, not that far from Hollywood and the Eastside—without traffic, of course.

Culver City

Tech companies and movie studios heavily populate Culver City. It's also the home of Red Light Management's new offices. No one I know lives there, though.

Live Near Your Work, Play Where You Play

Above all, the determining factor of where you live should be proximity to work. If you get a day job before you move, live near it. The key to happiness in L.A. is avoiding traffic as much as you can. I'm very fortunate that my neighborhood is extremely walkable. I rarely drive. That being said, if you do end up living on the Westside, you will never want to make it to Eastside, Downtown or Hollywood venues. So be cautious of that. When you get to town, you need to be out most nights networking at venues around town. I recommend not getting a day job before you move and just find something near where you live once you settle in.

How to Make the Quick Bucks

If you're a touring artist and move to Los Angeles, you obviously aren't going to want to get an inflexible day job that will prevent you from hitting the road every few months. So you have to get scrappy on how to make rent money. Many musicians (actors, screenwriters, etc.) drive for Lyft, Uber or food delivery services like Postmates, Grubhub or DoorDash. If you love dogs, Wag is a great option and gets you a ton of exercise. Of course there's TaskRabbit if you don't mind doing mind-numbing tasks. You can sign on when you need to make some money and sign off when you have a gig, rehearsal or anything else.

Some musicians work catering/event staff jobs. There are a bunch of catering companies and they typically pay between $15 and $25 an hour.

Catering companies come and go. The best way to find reputable event staffing companies is to ask other musicians, actors, writers and other freelancers you meet once you get to L.A. It's hard to gauge from online searches which catering companies are worth it. You'll work a lot of celebrity events. Your first few gigs you may get a bit star-struck.

Many musicians teach lessons as well. But be careful not to take on so many students that you don't have any time for your own music. When you get to town, ask other music teachers about best practices for acquiring new students: hint, target the rich family neighborhoods. Price yourself high. You're a professional! You can get away with $100/hour easily in L.A.

If you're a player, you can freelance; however, it's incredibly competitive since there are so many available players. First step, though, is to get on the Jammcard app and start networking through there. It's the who's who of players in L.A. Singer/songwriters, music directors and band leaders typically only hire musicians their friends refer. And if a current player can't make a gig, the buyer will ask the player for a referral. So meet other players on your instrument. If you have a decent cover repertoire, you can get on The Bash and GigSalad to get hired for private events. More on these later.

Keep Your Problems to Yourself

When you first move to Los Angeles, if you don't already have serious passive income (like royalties), you're going to quickly realize how tough it is to get by financially. It is for everyone initially, so you'd think everyone would empathize. You'd be wrong. Needy people are unattractive. People like to surround themselves with winners, and complaining to your new friend that you have no money or how tough it is to make it in L.A. is a complete turnoff. It's tough for everyone. You're not special. Sure, pick people's brains on how the town works. People are happy to share their knowledge (if it works with their schedule), but no complaining. Stay positive. You can commiserate with other strug-gling artists if they bring it up first, but when you're meeting "impor-tant" people, this is not a topic of conversation to get into. I learned that the hard way. Many initial connections of mine became far less avail-able when I casually revealed in conversation how tough it was for me to make money in L.A. as a musician. I stopped making that mistake very quickly.

Building It Live in L.A.

You are not going to get a manager, agent or label to come see you just because you're playing a hot club in L.A. You need something happening online first. Or you need someone they trust and respect (like a manager, lawyer or musician) to get them there. Your email will go straight to the trash. Your box of cookies you send to their office will get eaten, but with-out any indication of who the box was from.

Believe me, I've tried it all.

Pitching yourself to important people in L.A. rarely works. You have to remember there are bands buzzing a hell of a lot more than you are, playing nearly every night of the week. Personally, I could go out every single night in L.A. to a show of someone I know who is per-forming. The city is unbelievably saturated with musicians. So, don't expect to get anyone out to your show if you have nothing happening online.

That being said, because of the saturation, most people (musicians and nonmusicians, in the industry and not) are constantly barraged with a slew of invites from their biannual Instagram friends who only send a message when they have a show (guilty!).

In other cities, you have many more friends who are not involved in the music industry and who actually enjoy going out to see live music.

The Clubs

It should come as no surprise that Covid really altered the music venue landscape in L.A. (just like everywhere). Fortunately, because of the Save Our Stages Act, many music venues that would have permanently closed were able to hold on (that's if they made it through the first year before the bill passed and checks were sent out).

This next section will be a combination of a brief history of the clubs of L.A. and where things are now.

Somewhat of a silver lining from so many venues shutting down is tons of backyard, parking lot, and house concert series. Unofficial "venues" are now all over the place, hosting regular music nights—of course, these are unlicensed, but the city has been looking the other way (for now).

■ The Sunset Strip

> To get in a van and drive out (to L.A.) to play the
> Viper Room so that I show up is a waste of time and
> money. I ain't going. So many people spend time on
> the sh*t that doesn't matter.
> —BRUCE FLOHR, RED LIGHT MANAGEMENT

Once you get to know Los Angeles, it's a lot less scary and daunting than it seems. Everyone knows of the Sunset Strip. Legendary clubs like the Whisky a Go Go, the Roxy, the Viper Room, the Rainbow Room, still exist. The House of Blues shut down at its long-standing location on the Strip and has been replaced by the social club The Britely (which hosts exclusive concerts and the occasional Dave Chappelle comedy jam). The Troubadour technically isn't on the Strip, but it's nearby and just as legendary.

Most of these clubs work with infamous, pay-to-play pro-moters (more on this practice in Chapter 7). These clubs pri-marily host hip-hop acts, rock and pop bands, the kind of music that made the Strip famous in the '70s, '80s and '90s. The only difference is, back in the day the Strip actually devel-oped talent and helped artists get known, paid and signed. Now, the Strip has all but become a museum. A relic of a time since passed. Young bands from around the country shell out hundreds of dollars for the opportunity to (pay to) play these interactive museums.

Let me make this crystal clear. Break out your highlighter. Type this out and post it in big letters on the side of your rehearsal space: YOU WILL NOT GET DISCOVERED PLAYING ON THE SUNSET STRIP.

Or any club in L.A. Live discovery rarely happens anymore. Promoters and venue bookers used to care about quality. They used to be respected gatekeepers. And if you got a coveted spot playing their club, people cared. Now, it seems that all venues and promoters care about is getting paid. Whether it's from the band's pocket or the fans'. There are definitely some exceptions, but not really on the Sunset Strip.

■ Eastside Clubs

This is where indie rock and electronic music live. Venues like the Echo (and big sister Echoplex) have some of the best live sound and highest-quality talent in town. Echoplex (700 cap) hosts a range of talent including electronic and hip-hop. Many young artists, especially indie-rock bands, start with the East-side clubs and develop in that scene, playing everywhere and anywhere to just get known in the scene, and then start spreading their shows out to actually build a fanbase. The Silverlake Lounge, Little Joy and other dingy (vibey) smaller clubs are scattered all over the Eastside. Unfortunately a few longtime clubs like the Satellite and the Bootleg didn't make it through Covid. A huge loss to the entire L.A. music community and especially the Eastside landscape.

■ **Singer/Songwriter Spots**

My area of expertise. The L.A. staples are Genghis Cohen and the Hotel Cafe. Genghis Cohen is literally a Chinese restaurant with a venue attached to it. The venue is fully seated with a capacity of 50. Nearly all the shows are ticketed. This is where I first saw a 19-year-old Phoebe Bridgers and 14-year-old Charlie Hickey share a bill (nearly seven years before they played the Greek Theatre together). Yes, L.A. natives get their start early around town. Sadly, the singer/songwriter incubator Room 5 closed down in early 2016, but the curators of the room now run the second (smaller) room at the Hotel Cafe. The Hotel Cafe has been a launching pad for acts like Katy Perry, JP Saxe, Theo Katzman, Sara Bareilles, Joshua Radin, Meiko, and Ingrid Michaelson. It's been my home ever since I got to town. To be clear, the Hotel Cafe is neither a hotel nor a cafe. But it is a spot where John Mayer, Ed Sheeran, The Roots, John Legend, Chris Martin and other superstar musicians will randomly show up and play an unannounced set. People love going to the Hotel Cafe. There's no pay-to-play here. The Second Stage at the Hotel Cafe still hosts the weekly songwriter showcase Monday Monday (originally started by Joel Eckels at Room 5 over a decade ago). Artists like JP Saxe, Theo Katzman, Annabel Lee, Rett Madison, Charlotte Lawrence, Jensen McRae, Charlie Hickey, Trousdale, and yours truly have frequented Monday Monday. Bar Lubitsch, Black Rabbit Rose and the Kibitz Room (attached to Canter's Deli) are also popular spots for singer/songwriters. Songwriter nights have started popping up around town as well, with many taking place in the Valley. Also, it's definitely worth getting involved with the Los Angeles Songwriters Collective (LASC). They have a supportive community of songwriters and hold events with guest speakers and performers. Attending these events is a great way to break into the L.A. singer/songwriter scene and make long-lasting relationships.

■ **Downtown**

Lots of hip venues are popping up (and shutting down) seemingly everyday Downtown. The Moroccan Lounge (with the best small-venue light show) and the Resident, both in the Arts District, are hip staples. The 600-cap Teragram Ballroom hosts mostly touring acts and larger locals. It was also the home of Brassroots District's first concert experience. The Edison has been a classy staple for a few years. It's definitely worth exploring some other spots—including the many secret loft shows and gallery parties.

■ **Hip-Hop Spots**

Aside from the Sunset Strip clubs which also book hip-hop, the Echoplex also hosts hip-hop regularly. And the Bananas Hip-Hop showcase in South L.A. has been going strong for over a decade. The World Stage in Leimert Park regularly hosts spoken word, hip-hop and jazz nights and open mics, along with educational workshops. Its mission is listed as "to secure, preserve and advance the position of African American music, literature and works in the oral tradition to a local, national and international audience."

■ **Jazz Clubs**

Unfortunately, Covid took L.A.'s renowned jazz club the Blue Whale. But we've still got the Baked Potato (recently celebrated fifty years running) and Vibrato, both in the Valley, Catalina in Hollywood, Sam First near LAX, and the World Stage in Leimert Park keeping the jazz alive in the City of Angels.

■ **Residencies**

In addition to the Mondays at the Hotel Cafe, the School Night series presented by DJ Chris Douridas of KCRW and promoter Matt Goldman, held at Hollywood's Bardot, features some of the best up-and-coming talent of L.A. (and touring artists). Billie Eilish, Dawes, the Naked and Famous, Two Door Cinema Club, London Grammar, Michael Kiwanuka, JP Saxe, Bruno Major and Kevin Garrett have all played it early on in their careers, and oftentimes surprise guests stop by like Ben Folds, Moby, Florence and the Machine, Stevie Nicks and Kimbra. All the events are free (with RSVP). Sign up on their email list to be notified about all upcoming events.

Also on Monday, Jason Joseph has been running his Super-Soul Monday jam for a decade featuring some of the best players in Los Angeles. Make sure to follow him on the socials and find out where his residency is housed now. Monday has become the hottest night in L.A.

If you're a player (freelancer, not a *playah*), you want to get involved with the Jammcard community (become a member in the app, follow them on the socials, read their blog).

They have been running exclusive (invite-only) jams (called JammJams), similarly featuring A-listers of the town—Beyoncé's players, Bieber's, Bruno's, Lady Gaga's, Migos's, Kendrick Lamar's, Ariana Grande's and nearly every other arena/stadium tours' musicians attend and play at the JammJams. They're held every couple months in different locations around town like the old Tower Records building and Capitol Records' Studio A. Curated and organized by Jammcard's founder, Elmo Lovano (drummer for Christina Perri, Myley Cyrus and Skrillex). The events always have an alcohol (and weed) sponsor. At the last event at Capitol we hotboxed Studio A alongside Ty Dolla $ign. Loooossss Angeleeess.

Don't Move to L.A. Before You Are Ready

This is important, so break out that highlighter again and pay attention. *Do not move to L.A. until you are ready.* How do you know if you're ready? Well, if you haven't played more than just a handful of shows, and want to be a live act, you're not ready. If you haven't established something in your hometown, you're not ready. Just because you have a good voice is no reason to move to L.A. People there hustle their a$$ off to make it as a musician. It's not a place to "see how it goes" or figure yourself out. Because, unlike your hometown, L.A. is very unforgiving. And unbelievably competitive. If you get someone, anyone, in L.A. to come to your show and make them pay $10 to watch you suck, they will never come again. Ever. You may think you're great because your mother tells you how amazing you are. But unless you look, sound and perform like the next big thing, no one is going to care. I can't tell you how many local artists' shows in L.A. I've been to that are awful. L.A. has some of the best talent in the world, but it also has some of the worst.

The only exception is if you're young. Like under 20. People are much more forgiving of youth. Not only will you be relegated to the few 18+/ all ages spots in town, you will play many more makeshift, DIY, pop-up venues early on. The Eastside and Highland Park scene has a lot more youth and a lot more "local" clubs. So start there if you're young and need the experience.

So, if you're thinking of moving to L.A., wait until you're great and are ready to make that leap.

NEW YORK CITY

While there is an incredibly vibrant music scene in New York and the (talent) level is still *very, very* high, the business seems to have fallen away. The record business, publishing business, and recording studio business, all of which were major engines of the musical economy for years, have all fizzled from what they once were. One does not really get the sense that this is the place to *take creative risks.* Nobody can afford to.

—LEO SIDRAN, OSCAR- AND GRAMMY-WINNING PRODUCER, SINGER/ SONGWRITER, MULTI-INSTRUMENTALIST AND HOST OF *THE THIRD STORY* PODCAST

Music here is amazing because of all of the players, and the music scene is thriving. However, expect to hustle hard and potentially work a daytime job, because the cost of living keeps going up, while musicians' pay has stagnated.

—LAUREN SCALES, ARTIST, VOCALIST, SONGWRITER

There's so many amazing artists here that have zero online presence. They have local impact and are happy with that.

—AUSTIN ZHANG, JAZZ SAXOPHONIST

NYC's got its own special brand of music and people that make it. We're a bit more rugged, but very authentic. Many musical genres started here for a reason. The new renaissance is starting now—I can't wait to see what we create.

—MILITIA VOX, SINGER, SONGWRITER, MUSICIAN

New York City is my favorite city in the world. Don't get me wrong, I love L.A. and the sunshine, but nothing beats the energy of New York. Life moves fast in the Big Apple. The people are always on the go and move a million miles a minute. It's a true melting pot of cultures, backgrounds, races, religions and ethnicities. You can walk four blocks and hear six different languages. If you walk four blocks in L.A., it's because you couldn't find parking any closer. I love the walking culture of NYC. My iPhone told me that on my last weeklong trip to New York I walked an average of five miles a day. I'm lucky if I walk five miles a week in L.A. Actually, unlucky. Again, that means my parking luck was off.

I create better art in New York. I'm more inspired there. I can walk outside and the inspiration starts flowing. I don't have to seek it out—it finds me. When I walk outside in L.A., I just smile because it's so darn gorgeous out. It's more difficult to create great art when you're happy all the time.

Because there are so many band leaders in New York (and theater groups), you can make a decent living as a freelancer. There's always someone looking for a hired gun. But, as in L.A., it takes a serious hustle.

The time to have moved to NYC was February 2021—nearly a year into the pandemic. There was a massive exodus from the city in 2020, and rent plummeted to nearly one-third less than what it had been a year prior. But just like Spike Lee (and his interviewees) said in his *Epicenter* documentary, "New York always comes back."

Well, rent prices sure have. As of August 2021, rent prices were back to what they were before the pandemic. Which is too damn high!

And now, once again, in the United States, the borough of Manhattan is the most expensive place to live. The average rent for a one-bedroom apartment is a cool $3,500 a month. And now Brooklyn, as a whole, is pretty darn expensive as well, with average one-bedrooms costing around $3,000 a month. So, if you're just moving to New York, Queens may be your best bet to start out and until you figure out how to make a living. Queens averages about $2,300 a month for a one-bedroom. Of course the further away you get from Manhattan, the cheaper it gets (and the more space you can afford).

Just getting started in New York, you'll most definitely need a few roommates and a big savings account.

Like L.A., you want to find your scene. New York is such a massive city, with so many artists and musicians, that it's best to start with your genre of music and the clubs where it's hosted.

It's worth noting that, from the first edition of this book to the second, ten music venues that I previously profiled had shut down (mostly in Manhattan). And this was pre-pandemic! The new ones seem to be popping up in Brooklyn. This is a pretty clear indication that the local music scene of Manhattan is slipping. But it's not surprising. As rent continues to skyrocket, it pushes out the artists (and smaller clubs).

Fortunately, most venues were able to screech by through Covid, in part due to livestream shows and the Save Our Stages Act, which was the initiative spearheaded by the National Independent Venue Association (NIVA) and was passed in December 2020 as part of the COVID-19 relief bill. It helped secure grants for music venues equal to 45% of their 2019 revenues.

For this edition, I took to the Ari's Take community to crowdsource much of this info. After interviewing about fifty NYC-based musicians, I concluded that NYC is still alive and well for musicians of all persuasions.

Most musicians are living in Brooklyn and around Bushwick, Bed-Stuy and Clinton Hill these days. Much of the new scenes in indie rock, hip-hop and experimental are in Brooklyn. Williamsburg has gotten too expensive for the artists and many have left. That being said, there are many artists way uptown in Harlem and Washington Heights, over in Queens and even on the outskirts in New Jersey—all cheaper places to live. But if you're looking to jump into the thick of it and want to be among the most artists, Brooklyn is where it's at.

If you're a producer in NYC, it's worth checking out the Anti-Social Producers Club network. Founded by producer, songwriter, artist (and all-around great dude) Danny Ross, this network of Grammy-winning and Platinum-selling producers holds writers' camps and helps connect and support NYC producers and writers. Danny and I also host the annual SongCon in NYC, bringing together emerging songwriters from around the world mentored by Anti-Social Producers.

The Clubs

- **Jazz**
  Few cities in the world have the reputation that New York has for jazz. And for good reason. Of course there are strong traditions in many American cities, like Chicago, Kansas City and New Orleans, but New York's jazz scene remains one of the best. New York jazz musicians may tour, they may move, but they always seem to return home. Clubs like the Blue Note, Birdland, Smoke, Minton's Playhouse, Iridium, the Village Vanguard, The Flatiron Room, Smalls and Zinc are New York institutions, while fabulous dives like Mezzrow, Barbès and 55 Bar are hopping most nights of the week as well.

- **Singer/Songwriter**
  The New York counterpart to the Hotel Cafe is Rockwood Music Hall. Most singer/songwriters in New York make this

their home, and for good reason. Initially, just a tiny, 70-cap (that's generous) room, Rockwood has now expanded into three music venues (in the same building): Rockwood 1, 2 and 3. Most shows are free and on Saturdays (in Rockwood 1) music starts at 3 P.M. This is a great spot to go and hang out if you're a singer/songwriter. You'll meet fellow singer/songwriters and build up your community. Rockwood 1 and 3 are much more intimate spots (caps at 70 and 64 respectively), whereas Rockwood 2 typically has bands and has a sizable cap of 300. Other spots in town frequented by singer/songwriters are the legendary Bitter End, Rough Trade, City Winery, the Mercury Lounge and Pianos. The Sidewalk Cafe, Pete's Candy Store and the Owl Music Parlor are great spots to start out with—and pop in for the open mics. The New York Songwriters Circle has been hosting songwriter rounds (more on what these are in the Nashville section) since 1991 and have showcased artists like Norah Jones, Lana Del Rey, Vanessa Carlton, and Gavin DeGraw over the years.

■ **Indie-Rock and Other Bands**

The indie-rock tradition is still going strong in NYC. Clubs like the Mercury Lounge, Bowery Ballroom, Gramercy Theatre, Music Hall of Williamsburg, Arlene's Grocery, Pianos, Le Poisson Rouge, Rough Trade, Muchmore's, the Bowery Electric, Knitting Factory, Brooklyn Bazaar and elsewhere are all solid spots to find some of the best up-and-coming indie talent out there. While Baby's All Right, Secret Project Robot, Saint Vitus, Living Gallery, and the Owl are hot DIY spots for more punk and experimental projects.

Brooklyn Made is one of the hottest new spots to hit in Brooklyn, with Jeff Tweedy, M. Ward, Matisyahu and Vundabar all making early appearances at the club. And Elsewhere in Bushwick is a multi-room venue that has a DIY ethos (primarily because the founders, PopGun Presents, have a long history in Brooklyn of running DIY venues). Brooklyn Music Kitchen is also a hot new spot which opened in the summer of 2021 and hosts mostly local talent. Skinny Dennis, a self-proclaimed "honky-tonk bar," is your home for country and roots music in Brooklyn. And believe it or not, there is a reggae scene (and ska is coming back!). If this is where you're focusing your efforts, check out the occasional shows at Wild Birds and Natty Garden.

■ **Hip-Hop/R&B/Soul**

Aside from the bigger rooms that host a range of genres, such as Bowery Ballroom, Music Hall of Williamsburgh, Knitting Factory, Joe's Pub, Brooklyn Bowl, Baby's All Right and SOB's, more intimate spots like Shrine, the Bell House, Pianos, Nuyorican Poets Cafe, Village Underground and DROM have hip-hop, R&B and soul nights, but most feature all kinds of music. It's also worth checking out the rich poetry scene New York has to offer and get started there as well. And there's an entire Brooklyn drill scene now, made famous by Sheff G, Pop Smoke, Fivio Foreign, Sleepy Hallow, and 22Gz.

■ **Residencies**

As in L.A., many artists get weekly residencies at hotels or lounges that pay a guarantee. Oftentimes this is a two-to-three-hour gig. DJs and producers as well as singer/songwriters are seeing most of these residency opportunities. Pay is typically $100–$500 a night. Don't do them for "exposure."

NASHVILLE

So many people get record deals in Nashville
and they don't ever get an album.

—LUKE BRYAN

There isn't anywhere else in the world where on a Monday night,
if I'm out of money and need to pick up work, I can just call a
couple of friends or post on a Facebook message board, saying,
"I'm available to play _____ instrument tonight from 6–close"
and have someone reach out and say, "Hey, can you play at
Tootsies tonight from 10–close?" And then 20 minutes later have
another friend say, "Hey, I need a keyboard player from 6–10 at
the Stage." And suddenly, because you're a multi-instrumentalist
who people know, you're working a "double" and are going home
with a minimum of $200 before tips on a Monday night.

—TYSON LESLIE, NASHVILLE-BASED KEYBOARD PLAYER

If you're a country singer/songwriter, Nashville is where you need to be.
Plain and simple. Music City, as it's known, is a songwriter's town. And
not just country songwriting. But country music is the city's heritage—
almost as much as Hot Chicken.

Nashville, despite what you may think, is a relatively small town.
And it definitely has that feel to it. The people are polite and have that
famous southern hospitality. It's not spread out like L.A. or built up (literally) like New York. The people are much more laid back. And unlike
in L.A. and New York, pretty much everyone you meet works in the
music industry.

Like Austin's 6th Street during SXSW, the bars on Broadway have
live music (mostly country) from 11 A.M. until 2 A.M., 7 days a week.

During the daytime, you can find songwriter rounds with a mix of up-and-comers and, believe it or not, hit songwriters, at many of the hot spots, like Tootsie's, but come nightfall, nearly every club turns the party on with mostly country cover bands rocking the strip. Honky-tonk, bluegrass, country-pop, bro-country-rock, all of it is showcased at different clubs up and down Broadway. The street is packed with mostly tourists, but country-loving locals are often scoping out the talent as well. If you're a player looking to break in, this is where you want to be hanging. Every country-rock band knows 75–100 country staples. If you're a guitarist, bassist, fiddle player, keyboard player or drummer, learn these tunes and you will find work. If you're the best on your instrument, word will spread and your work will improve. If you're the best on your instrument and you're a great hang, you will work often and be well compensated. But, of course, it takes time. But it takes less time the harder you hustle and the more you network.

Believe it or not, most bands and songwriters aren't getting paid much (if anything) to play the clubs on Broadway, but they can make a decent amount in tips. Some get cuts of the bar for the time they're performing. None of the clubs have a cover and most are packed every night. Learning to work the room (and get the most amount of tips) is an art in itself that is mastered by working Broadway musicians.

Songwriter Rounds

The songwriter round is an honored tradition in Nashville. Despite what the name suggests, most songwriter rounds don't actually take place "in the round" (except at the Bluebird Cafe). Two to five songwriters typically sit in a line on stage and each trade off playing a song. This goes round and round (hence the name) for hours. Occasionally you can find a songwriter round in L.A. or New York, but those in Nashville happen multiple times a day, every day, at various venues around town. Songwriter rounds are not open mics. The rounds are booked with top-notch talent, of, you guessed it, songwriters playing mostly their original songs. Many songwriters who participate in the rounds aren't aspiring to be artists. Most of them are seeking a publishing deal (or already have one and are testing out their new material). It seems like many more writers in Nashville get publishing deals than do those in L.A. or New York (just by the sheer number of great writers in town), but most initial deals may just be for a single song, or 18. A typical initial writer's pub deal in Nashville is what's known as the 18-18-18: 18 songs, for 18 months, for $18,000 (or less). Which isn't much of a commitment on the part of a big publishing company. Publishing deals these days (in Nashville, L.A. and NYC) with a major publishing company can pay hundreds of thousands of dollars up front. This, like a record deal, is not a paycheck; it's a loan that is paid back in royalties. The platinum-selling, country act Cam turned down her first publishing deal offer. She told *Billboard* magazine, "The next time I show someone my music, they're not going to underestimate or undervalue me." She was right.

Many songwriter clubs have 6:00 and 9:00 shows. If you're new to town, start hanging out at the 6:00 shows. This is where your community is. The 9:00 crowd is made up of established Nashvillians. Most people's initial community is made up of other newbies. Nashville is all about the community, from the get-go.

Open Mics

Open mics, unlike rounds, are open to anyone who wants to sign up. Like most places around the country, you arrive early (or call in) and put your name on the list. There are many popular open mics that happen multiple times a week around Nashville at venues like the Tennessee Brew Works, the Commodore Grille at the Holiday Inn Nashville-Vanderbilt, the Bluebird Cafe and the Listening Room.

PROs and NSAI

The PROs (ASCAP, BMI and SESAC; more on these in Chapter 13), along with the Nashville Songwriters Association International, are extremely helpful resources for getting your songs critiqued and passed along. Get in touch with your PRO when you move to town (once you have a batch of killer songs) and join the NSAI.

Breaking In

Before you move to Nashville, make sure you visit at least once to get a feel for the town. One of the best times to go is during the Tin Pan South Songwriters Festival in the spring. I also highly recommend getting Liam Sullivan's book *Making the Scene: Nashville: How to Live, Network, and Succeed in Music City.* He gives great tips on venues to check out, neighborhoods to live in, restaurants and bars to frequent and even where to buy a mattress. He also interviews some big players in town about their tips on how to break into Nashville.

Above all, Nashville is a networking town. Even more so than L.A. or New York. The most important thing to do in Nashville is get out and meet other songwriters. You also want to play everywhere and anywhere all the time. This gives you a chance to showcase your songs in front of other writers, make tips and, more important, make connections.

And unlike in L.A., publishers do actually frequent open mics and songwriter rounds to scout out talent. You most likely won't get signed off of a single performance at an open mic, but you may get a meeting.

Nashville is all about the community. You can't bust into town and carry yourself like you're the greatest thing since Garth Brooks. That may work in L.A., but in Nashville, people top to bottom, left to right, appreciate humility. Yes, your songs have to be top-notch, but above all, people want to work with those they like. If you're a d**k, you won't get anywhere. Be humble, be gracious, be kind and be awesome.

The Demo

Many songwriters seeking publishing deals (or even artists seeking major record deals) first cut demos. What's the difference between demos and albums? Demos aren't released, but merely pressed on CDs and put up as private links online. They are meant to pitch publishers to get your songs bought and recut by a current star. Every songwriter signed to a publishing deal, in any city, records demos, but typically these are funded by the publishing company. Because there are so many unsigned songwriters in Nashville, many demos are made on spec and the demo recording business is strong. You can find an engineer, producer and studio to track your demo for about $500, start to finish. But you'll also have to hire your players. The demos, many times, sound good enough to be on the radio, but they're meant to shop, not publicly sell. That being said, many songwriters do sell (or just give away) their demos at their gigs. And a business card is always included. You don't build a local following in Nashville like you do in other cities in the country. It's a totally different scene.

However, many noncountry musicians and songwriters live in Nashville. Many L.A. and NYC singer/songwriters have migrated to Nashville. East Nashville, like East L.A, is the hipster part of town and is becoming rapidly populated with musicians of all sorts. There are rock clubs where local bands do build followings (like they would in other towns), and there are growing rock, funk/soul and hip-hop scenes outside of the city's country music epicenter.

LONDON

It is possible to live just out of London and commute in for gigs
and meetings. Though I'm still of the opinion that living in
London is best so that you're available at the drop of a hat.
—SHAODOW, LONDON-BASED HIP-HOP ARTIST

London has a very vibrant music scene, with live music in lots
of venues and work available for musicians. The network of
musicians here is very large and quite interconnected. There is
a strong sense of community between the musicians, which is
one of the things I love. I discovered this when I first moved to
London [from New York City].
—ACANTHA LANG, SOUL SINGER, SONGWRITER

London is a city of extreme variety, and moving even less than a
mile between neighborhoods within one of its 33 boroughs can
result in a significant change in atmosphere and makeup—be it
historical, demographic, architectural, cultural or religious.
—JACK RENNIE, LONDON-BASED INDIE ROCK ARTIST

Outside of the US, London is the other music hub. There's quite of bit
of industry in town. If you're a pop songwriter, you either want to live in
L.A. or London. The population is double L.A.'s and the city is even more
spread out. However, the thing London has that L.A. does not is a robust
public transit system—namely the Underground (the tube).

Like NYC, London has increasingly become a wildly expensive city,
displacing artists and music venues over the years.

BBC Music Introducing

Of course what's unique to London is BBC Music Introducing, which is how independent artists can get played on BBC radio stations, at BBC events and festivals, and appear on BBC playlists. If you're London- or UK-based, you should definitely register an account and upload all of your new tracks to their platform. Technically, anyone in the world can sign up, but they give preferential treatment to local musicians (especially with the local stations). And they ask for your PRS ID (to get paid). With thirty-three boroughs, London can be a quite intimidating place to begin to make your way if you don't have any local connections.

Camden, Islington and Hackney

The highest concentration of small- and midsize music venues is in Camden. Venues like KOKO, the Roundhouse, the Electric Ballroom, the Underworld, O2 Forum Kentish Town, the Jazz Café, the Camden Assembly (formerly Barfly), Green Note and the Dublin Castle are all in Camden. This part of town is very vibrant and now a popular tourist destination. Because of this, it's gotten quite expensive. So, many of the artists have moved to Hackney. Namely the Shoreditch and Hoxton areas. But right in between Camden and Hackney is Islington, which has great venues like Scala, the Library, the Islington Assembly Hall (a shout-out to Youngblood Brass Band, who I saw here during my first trip to London), the Islington, the Garage, the Lexington, Union Chapel, Old Street Records (for acoustic acts) and O2 Academy.

London Jazz

If you're in the jazz or blues world, Soho is your part of town. Clubs like Ain't Nothin But the Blues, Jazz After Dark, Ray's Jazz Cafe, PizzaExpress Live and the legendary Ronnie Scott's are all in Soho. But they have great venues for other styles of music as well, like the 350-cap 100 Club and the superintimate Spice of Life (where celebrities oftentimes make appearances). But there's a cool jazz wave scene happening in South East London as well.

South London

Many musicians and artists now live in South London because it's cheaper. Grime music is quite prevalent here. Grime isn't necessarily known much in the States (as hard as Drake is trying), but it's huge in London. You're going to find more urban styles of music in South London, including Reggaeton (spearheaded by musician and promoter Harold Guerrero), Latin, Soul and of course Grime and hip-hop. Hootannany, O2 Brixton Academy, Brixton Jamm, the Blues Kitchen and ElectricBrixton are all in Brixton. The newer 350-cap Omeara is fantastic and located in Southwark. Peckham is becoming an artist hub as well. Lots of cool little scenes are popping up in South London.

Getting Plugged In

If you're new to town, there are some networks that would be good for you to get to know. As stated before, getting involved with BBC Music Introducing is step one. If you're a songwriter, London Songwriters, run by Murray Webster, hosts regular events and has a network of about 4,000 songwriters. Check out Open Mic Finder and London Unplugged to find great open mics all over the city. If you're into hip-hop/Grime, GRM Daily and Link Up TV are great networks to tap into.

Cool jams happen at Mau Mau Bar, Troy Bar, Ruby Sings (upstairs at Ronnie Scott's) and Ciro's Pomodoro. Sofar Sounds is also very active in London and very supportive of the music scene. If your show works acoustically, it's a great idea to get involved with the Sofar community. The Sofar network is well respected and active in the States as well, so if you connect in London, they may be able to set up some stops when you cross the Atlantic. Definitely check out the London Musicians Network Public Group and join the Musician's Union.

Club Booking

When you're just starting to book shows at the smaller clubs, you'll work with promoters putting bills together and venue talent buyers about equally. There are some shady pay-to-play deals, but most of the deals you'll find will be the "Sneaky" deals (reference "Performance Deals" in Chapter 7), where you'll only get paid after a certain number of people come to see you. They'll have a tick sheet at the door. However, there are some "Standard" deals, where you get a solid percentage of the door (often 100%) after expenses.

Busking

Busking is legal in most public areas around London. Most of the touristy locations require a busking permit if you use amplification. You actually have to audition to be approved for most of these permits. One of these approved buskers, Harry Pane, makes around £60 an hour busking primarily in the Underground. Harry says the best spots are the touristy areas like Tottenham Court Road, Leicester Square and Piccadilly Circus. Charlotte Campbell is also a staple in the London busking scene. She prefers South Bank next to the River Thames, but also frequents Covent Garden and Trafalgar Square in addition to the spots Harry plays. Most busking locations are regulated and buskers are limited to one to two hours of performing. If you want to busk in the Underground, you have to sign up, in advance, online for your slot and location (they call it a "pitch").

The Pubs

The cover/tribute band scene is quite huge in pubs around London and you can make some decent money doing it. If you have that repertoire, it may be worth tapping into. Or at least stopping in to meet other musicians to collaborate with.

Above all, even though London is so spread out, everyone goes everywhere because the tube goes (nearly) everywhere. If you're thinking of moving to the city, find some open mics or jams, get on BBC Music Introducing and get out to see live music often. There's only so much you can accomplish behind a screen. Get out and experience everything the town has to offer.

HOW TO FIND WHO YOUR FANS ARE

Remember when you made an "Our Fans" list back in Chapter 3? Now it's time to actually figure out where they exist. Geographically, demographically and internetgraphically (yeah, I know, that's not a word).

First, make a list of artists who you sound like. Or at least, artists whose fans will get into your music. This list is now going to help you to set up direct marketing campaigns to target your potential fans. You're going to want to master the Meta (fka Facebook) Business Manager platform (which controls the ads for Instagram and many other placements around the internet). TikTok Ads Manager has come leaps and bounds in the past couple years and proving to be very effective as well.

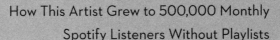

THE BRIDGE
How This Artist Grew to 500,000 Monthly Spotify Listeners Without Playlists

In early 2016, the northern Virginia conscious hip-hop artist Lucidious was struggling to get listeners to his music. He had about 150 monthly listeners on Spotify (no, I didn't forget a zero) with merely 45 followers, and about 1,500 followers on Instagram and Facebook. He was making less than $100 a month from his music.

Fast forward to 2019—three years later, he was at 500,000 monthly listeners on Spotify (no, my finger didn't get stuck on the zero key), over 50,000 followers on Spotify, 250,000 Likes on Facebook, 150,000 followers on Instagram, 5 million streams a month, over 100 million total streams across all platforms, making around $20,000 a month just from his recorded music.

Oh, and he got all this with no label, no manager, no publicist, no agent and zero official Spotify playlists.

I'll pause as you pick your jaw up from the floor.

These are real fans. Not bots. Human beings. He showed me his Instagram inbox, which is flooded with fans telling him how his music, which focuses on mental health awareness, saved their lives.

So how did he do this? He utilized direct marketing strategies on Facebook and Instagram to find his audience and get them into his world. Specifically, he mastered the Facebook Business and Ads Manager and ran all different kinds of video ads targeting fans of similar artists.

They came pouring into his world, and eventually he was getting fans to click his ads at around $.02 per click—putting every marketing expert to shame. Spending about $10 a day, he was pulling in around 500 new fans per day. And because his music is great and his Instagram is engaging (i.e., he is very active on there—responding to comments and messages), these people who started off as passive observers turned into diehard fans.

Yes, I know that you've probably run Facebook ads in the past and were less than thrilled with the results. Me too. I've wasted thousands on Facebook ads. If you don't know how to utilize them effectively, they won't work for you.

Yes, mastering the Ad Manager takes a bit of time. But anyone can do it. You just have to hunker down and make it work. You can learn to master this either by enrolling in an online training or by putting in the time researching blogs and YouTube tutorials.

So, instead of posting incessantly on Instagram begging people to share your stuff, go directly to the people who would dig what you're doing.

IS RADIO STILL IMPORTANT?

To get a song on the radio is expensive. If you just
have radio leading the charge and you swing and miss,
you just bet $200,000.

—BRUCE FLOHR, RED LIGHT MANAGEMENT

Before, you saw direct impact from radio to artists to sales,
whereas now it's completely TikTok.

—LISA KASHA, HEAD OF DIGITAL, EPIC RECORDS

Radio is still how superstars are born. But commercial radio no longer breaks acts like they used to. Radio gets to the party last—only after the act is proven and getting serious traction across other mediums like Spotify, TikTok and YouTube. Commercial radio rarely takes chances anymore. It's a complete waste of time for you to hire an expensive radio promoter. Even if you get a $200,000 investment, this is not a good use of your money. I've seen very talented acts blow this kind of money attempting to break pop radio. Lay the groundwork. Build the fans. Grow loyal followers. Get some traction online first. If you're not getting serious Spotify or TikTok numbers, radio will completely ignore you. That being said, the only reason radio plays indie acts is because they have serious traction already.

Ingrid Michaelson had her hit single "The Way I Am" not only in a popular Old Navy commercial, but it was featured in *Grey's Anatomy* (in 2007 this was a big deal) and she got on the front page of the *Wall Street Journal* for it. Not to mention the millions of plays on MySpace (remember that?) she was receiving. Using that ammunition, the radio promoters at Sony RED Distribution (who Ingrid used for physical distribution) were able to go to AC and AAA radio stations and pitch it confidently. Same with Macklemore & Ryan Lewis's "Thrift Shop." They already had a massive YouTube following when "Thrift Shop" was released and the video went viral. Like Ingrid, they used a major distribution partner (ADA under Warner Music Group). Although it was released in August of 2012, it didn't actually crack the top 10 on the *Billboard* Hot 100 until January 2013. But it became the second-best-selling song of 2013. And it sold over 10 million downloads in the United States alone. And because they released it independently, the duo got to make the record in the way they wanted and kept the majority of the revenue without having to recoup (pay back) a major record-label advance.

Lauv's first single released in 2015 hit #1 on Hype Machine and cracked the Spotify Global Top 100. But it wasn't until he released his 2017 single "I Like Me Better" that he cracked top 40 radio. That didn't just happen, though. The song had massive traction on Spotify and had been out for nearly six months before it hit top 40 radio. Unlike Ingrid Michaelson and Macklemore, Lauv utilized an indie distributor, Kobalt (now AWAL), for distribution and in2une Music for radio promotion. Lauv has remained independent and is well into the billions of streams.

Chance the Rapper's first charting album was the *Coloring Book* mixtape he released via TuneCore (where he kept 100% of the money). This album was preceded by a mixtape he released for free on DatPiff, where it was downloaded over a million times. *Coloring Book* had collabs and features from the who's who of hip-hop and R&B of that moment. The album instantly received critical acclaim, earning a 9.1 rating from *Pitchfork* and topping endless "best-of" lists. Chance got his fans to request "No Problem" at their local radio stations on Twitter via a site he launched, RapperRadio.com. This campaign was so successful that "No Problem" cracked the *Billboard* Hot 100 and *Coloring Book* became the first streaming-only album to hit the *Billboard* 200 album chart. He didn't need a third-party radio promoter or record label to win over the radio stations. If you have enough listeners requesting a song, the station will eventually give it a spin. And because of his collabs with the likes of Kanye West, Lil Wayne, T-Pain, Future, Ty Dolla $ign, and Anderson .Paak, it was an easy sell to mainstream radio even though there was no label attached. If you get enough heavy hitters to sign off and guest, no one's asking for label credentials.

Lorde's song "Royals" also didn't break into America until Sean Parker (of Facebook and Napster fame) included it on his wildly popular Spotify playlist, Hipster International, two weeks after the song was released. Six days after Parker included the song on his playlist (of 800,000+ followers at the time), "Royals" debuted on the Spotify Viral Chart. Less than a month later, "Royals" was #1 on the Spotify Viral Chart. And then a month after that, "Royals" hit alt-radio. And a month after that, it cracked the *Billboard* Hot 100. By year's end, it was the third-most-shared track in the country.

As stated earlier, Halsey self-released her song and music video "Ghost." Because of her massive Instagram, Twitter and YouTube following, it quickly went viral. Labels approached only after she was wildly successful. And her song "New Americana" was an easy sell to radio because she was already a proven artist.

Gotye's "Somebody That I Used to Know" was recorded in Gotye's parents' basement and initially released by an Australian label, Eleven Music, in July 2011. Powered by a stop-motion body paint video, it gathered 200,000 views in the first couple weeks. Hip music blogs quickly took notice and shared the video. By December the video had gone viral, with millions upon millions of views. Universal Republic swooped up Gotye and pushed the song at US radio (even though many stations had already begun playing the song). By January 2012, the song cracked the *Billboard* Hot 100, and a few months later you couldn't get away from it. *Glee* was covering it. *American Idol* finalists were singing it. It hit #1 on the *Billboard* Hot 100 and in 2013 the song won two Grammys. All from a very creative music video (and an incredibly personal, yet ever-so-relatable, song).

Lil Nas X first released "Old Town Road" in December 2018 on SoundCloud. He made the song from a beat he bought for $30 from a teenage producer from the Netherlands (we'll get into the legal complications in Chapter 13). Lil Nas X made about 100 memes promoting the song. He had years of experience making memes and going viral on Twitter long before he released this song. One finally caught on TikTok with the Yeehaw Challenge in March 2019. He tagged the song as #country and it rose on the SoundCloud charts. After the song became a viral TikTok sensation with millions of people making their own videos to the song, radio finally started playing it. When it first hit radio, "Old Town Road" hadn't even been officially released to major DSPs—radio programmers had to rip it (illegally from YouTube) to play it. After a controversy surrounding classification on the country charts, Billy Ray Cyrus added his vocals to a new remix. "Old Town Road" became the longest-running #1 single in history.

Similarly, Olivia Rodrigo's first hit "drivers license" spread on TikTok initially as a trend started by a 20-year-old fan. Fans filmed themselves lip-syncing the pre-chorus dressed down and then when the chorus hit, fell backward, and with some 2021 video-editing magic, they were fully dressed up, lying on a bed with the sparkle filter on. Over a million people created videos with this song, and the hashtag #driverslicense amassed over 888 million views in one week. One week! It was quickly added to radio and rose to #1 on the *Billboard* Hot 100 chart, where it sat for 8 weeks.

But again, radio didn't lead the charge here either. They rarely do. They want something proven. Unfortunately, quality and taste have very little to do with it anymore.

PLAYLISTS ARE THE NEW RADIO

What I love about Spotify is that it's a very honest platform. We play a game called best song wins. It doesn't matter if you're the biggest artist in the world or an act that was on SoundCloud and finally went to TuneCore and uploaded on Spotify, the listeners don't lie. This isn't "call-out radio research" or anything like that—this is actual people leaning into records, and you're finding out whether things are fake or real really quick. And I think creators and artists having access to that sort of platform is powerful, and I think we're already seeing that the entire business is going to be reshaped.

—TROY CARTER, FORMER GLOBAL HEAD OF CREATOR SERVICES, SPOTIFY

In today's streaming world, consumer consumption doesn't necessarily mean fandom. It's not hard to stream a song. And it's not hard for a lot of people to stream a song from a popular playlist. That doesn't mean that you have millions of fans—it

means you have millions of people who happen to hear your song.
Who knows if they even dug it.

—NICK BOBETSKY, STATE OF THE ART MANAGEMENT

Music discovery has evolved from night clubs, to print reviews, to radio, to blogs, to Hype Machine to Spotify playlists to TikTok. Sure, people "discover" music by all of these means still, but the past few years, the music industry has become obsessed with Spotify playlists because the discovery (and stream boosts) are so powerful. John Mayer brought on The Night Game as his tour opener after discovering one of their songs on Spotify (via his Discover Weekly customized playlist). Discovery is real on Spotify—at every level from fan to superstar.

Entire industries have popped up utilizing the Spotify ecosystem focused squarely on playlists (much to Spotify's chagrin). As the industry realized how powerful Spotify playlists were, the playlist editors became the new radio programmers. Some labels found ways to woo the editors to the point that even Spotify felt a bit squeamish with how it was all working. They officially came out against the practice of paying to influence playlist inclusion, but that didn't stop individual playlist editors from taking bribes under the table and keeping it hidden from Spotify. And, payola is only illegal when it comes to traditional radio, not Spotify.

I know I know, you're wondering how to get included in Spotify playlists when you can't afford to bribe. Well, first you have to understand what kinds of playlists exist.

There are 4 kinds of playlists on Spotify:

1) **Official Editorial Playlists**

   The first category is something everyone is familiar with. These are the playlists "Created by Spotify."

   Basically, playlist editors employed by Spotify curate both genre and mood playlists (head of hip-hop, head of chill, focus, workout, sleep, etc.). These people have the same kind of power that the biggest DJs in the world did back in the day.

However, Spotify has also been relying heavily on their analytics to see which songs people are responding to. And Nick Holmsten, Spotify's head of shows and editorial, told *Wired* that artists/labels "can't beg, borrow or bribe" their way into the Today's Top Hits playlist: "There's absolutely no way to push our team. It's no one person's feeling that matters."

You can kind of think of official editorial playlists as a pyramid. At the bottom are all the various playlists with thousands (or hundreds of thousands) of followers, like Funk Outta Here, idk, Bedroom Pop, Relaxing Spanish Guitar, Soul Revived. And as you make your way up, fewer playlists have millions of followers, like Hot Country, Are and Be, Hit Rewind, Baila Reggaeton, Chill Hits, Peaceful Piano. At the very top are RapCaviar with over 14 million followers and Today's Top Hits with over 30 million followers.

Unlike the Clear Channel–owned radio stations or the biggest stations of yore, no one person decides Today's Top Hits. The songs that get included in that playlist have been relentlessly tested in less popular playlists. If they do well (users add them to their personal playlists, save the song, listen to the song longer, don't skip the song), they move up the pyramid. And eventually they could make it to Today's Top Hits.

For a while, it was very difficult to break into the official Spotify-curated playlists without a label, manager or distributor who regularly talk to these editors. However, now that Spotify officially opened up the pitching process to anyone with a Spotify for Artists account (and are guarding their editors like the Queen of England), the editorial process is becoming more based on the artist's streaming history and industry buzz. For as much as Spotify likes to highlight the indie success stories, the majors seem to still have guaranteed placement slots in many top-rated playlists. That being said, indie artists do get included daily. If you follow Spotify's release schedule suggestion, you dramatically increase your chances at editorial inclusion.

2) User-Generated Playlists

The second category is playlists created by users of Spotify (yes, anyone can create a playlist) or a company, blog, label, org, what have you. Spotify has stated that there are over 4 billion playlists (mostly created by users). The major labels also have created their own numerous playlists (Topsify by WMG, Digster by UMG and Filtr by Sony). It's the cool new thing to have a hot Spotify playlist. It's like you're the owner of a radio station. And if you run multiple hot playlists, it's like you're the owner of a radio network.

3) Algorithmically Generated Playlists

The third category isn't human generated. These are the Discover Weekly, Release Radar, Daily Mix (which are actually customized per user) and Fresh Finds. Around 2017, if you got included in Fresh Finds you were almost guaranteed a couple hundred thousand plays. Now Fresh Finds is much more fragmented, broken up by genres.

4) Hybrid Playlists

This category of playlist is a mix between editorial and algorithmic. All of the songs on these playlists are handpicked by Spotify editors, however, the order of songs is determined by the user who's listening. The algorithm creates the order that it thinks the user will like most, based on their listening history. Playlists like Beast Mode, Songs to Sing in the Shower, and Happy Hits fall into this category.

HOW TO GET INCLUDED

Now that you understand what kinds of playlists exist and the landscape, here are some ideas on how to get included.

Get Featured in Blogs

Most Spotify playlist editors read blogs and follow the Hype Machine charts. If you get written about by a top blog like Complex, Consequence of Sound, Stereogum, Pitchfork, etc., it can help your chances of getting included in playlists. The Spotify for Artists playlist pitching form asks for this info.

More on how to do this in Chapter 15.

Pay for Play

In the heyday of radio, paying DJs to play the labels' songs could almost certainly guarantee direct sales. Which in turn brought direct revenue.

Now, getting songs included in big playlists almost certainly guarantees direct streams. Which in turn brings direct revenue.

But this isn't just happening with big labels paying (er, treating to VIP events) official Spotify editors. User-generated playlist editors are very openly taking money to insert your song into their popular playlists. This is against Spotify's terms and conditions. If they catch a UGP (user-generated playlist) editor charging for inclusion, Spotify will shut down the playlist without blinking. I've seen people spend tens of thousands of dollars on ads building up playlist networks, to then get these playlists removed overnight because Spotify caught them charging for inclusion. Even though these listeners were actual humans (not bots), Spotify does not support paying for inclusion.

There are flat out scams that exist where a questionable entity charges artists to get a set number of streams. These streams are not from real listeners but rather click farms and bots. Spotify has gotten very good at spotting bot listeners. They monitor the play-to-save ratio and the time listened. When Spotify catches what they think are inflated, bot plays, they rip down the songs and halt royalty payments. If most of your plays are 31 seconds (Spotify counts 1 stream at 30 seconds) with no saves, most likely bots are listening to your songs.

Playlist Pluggers

There are playlist plugging companies (kind of like publicists, but for playlists) whose sole job is to pitch you for inclusion in playlists. But be very cautious with this. Campaigns range from $100 to pitch just a few smaller playlists all the way into the thousands to pitch to a bunch of very popular playlists. Mind you, these are all user-generated playlists (not official "Created by Spotify" playlists). And nothing is guaranteed. A manager told me that he once spent $5,000 on a campaign with one of these companies and got 0 playlist inclusions.

There are also platforms like SubmitHub, Songrocket, Groover, Playlister Club and PlaylistPush where you can pay (via their platform) to pitch the playlist editors directly. Technically, this isn't against Spotify's terms because you're not paying for inclusion, only consideration. But be very careful paying to pitch "popular" playlists. Follower numbers don't mean anything anymore. It matters how many (real, human) listeners you will generate from getting included in the playlist. Once playlist editors started getting compensated for submissions to their playlists, they inflated their numbers by purchasing bot followers. Or using "gates" to incentivize people to follow their playlists—even though they'd never actually listen to the playlist. You can always check out how many listeners (and streams) you gained from a playlist inclusion in your Spotify for Artists account. Playlist plugging is big business. There are UGP editors out there who are paid five to six figures a year just for listening to submissions.

Contact Playlist Editors Directly

Contacting official Spotify playlist editors directly was the common practice for a few years, but has become increasingly less effective. Yes, Spotify playlist editors have relationships with every major label (and many big indie labels). Yes, they (typically) answer their calls, open their doors and their emails. But I recently heard that some editors are receiving around a thousand emails an hour! So cold emails to the biggest editors is probably not your best bet anymore. Especially because their contact info has leaked in a massive way and people are now selling lists with Spotify playlist editors' contact info.

That being said, you can get creative with the ways you contact editors. I spoke to a DIY artist who found the contact info of the biggest playlist editors at Deezer. She sent them personalized postcards in the mail (from locations she had stopped at on tour) with her artist name and three songs she thought would be a good fit for that editor's playlists. And it worked! She got responses back and inclusions on some huge playlists. *Boom!*

This same artist told me that she actually went up to an official Spotify playlist editor at a music conference after the panel. She handed the editor a napkin, similarly with her artist name and three song titles that she thought that editor would like for her playlists. Three days later this artist had those songs included on gigantic playlists. She now has 10 million collective streams because of this short interaction at a music conference.

This, my friends, is how you get creative and make sh*t happen. (Of course, it goes without saying your music has to be great and similar to the other songs on the playlists you are going after.)

Get in Touch with the User-Generated Playlist Editors

It isn't very difficult to find the editors of many of these user-generated playlists—since most users link their Facebook to Spotify (so you can see their actual name). Don't just hit them up asking for inclusion. That's the wrong way to go about it. You can contact the person and compliment them on their playlist. Once you've developed a respectful relationship then you can pitch your music. This editor will definitely check out your socials and what not, so your stuff better be up to snuff.

And of course, you have a much better chance of making contact with editors of playlists with fewer followers (because fewer people are hitting them up). So don't just go after the biggest ones.

You can check chartmetric.io to validate and verify the playlists and get more detailed info on most playlists on Spotify.

Keep your research organized: Create a Google Sheet with nine columns: Playlist name, Editor Name, Follower #, Genre/Vibe, Last Updated Date, Editor Contact, Notes, Added By (team up with your artist friends to work on this), Playlist Link (oftentimes playlists will have the same name).

However, most UGP editors these days aren't just doing it for the love of music. They know the kind of money that can be made, and most require you to submit via a paid-submission service or will ask you flat-out for payment for inclusion. But again, never pay to be included in a playlist. If Spotify finds out, they will promptly remove the playlist and then you're SOL.

Love for Love

If you point people to Spotify, Spotify may point people to you. Spotify has also said that they like when artists fill out their Spotify profiles (bio, links, features) and create playlists themselves and promote them to their followers. If you show Spotify you are an active user they may show you some love.

Playlist Owners?

More recently, users who created popular playlists have been offered lots of money from labels and playlist-plugging companies to sell the control of their playlists. This is very much against Spotify's terms, but that's not stopping this underground marketplace. Dollah dollah billz ya'll!

Streams ≠ Fans

This all being said, just because you get a million streams from being included in a few hot playlists, doesn't mean you will get a million fans. You may not even get a thousand true fans. And even though streams now pay (a little), it's fleeting. I've heard of people quitting their day jobs because they were making thousands a month from Spotify because their song got included in a huge playlist only to have to ask for their job back when their song got removed from that playlist. Live by the playlist, die by the playlist. Getting included in playlists can be great, but it's not the be-all end-all.

Playlist inclusion comes and goes. Never lose track of your ultimate goal: to build a loyal fan base that will support you over the course of your entire career.

THE BRIDGE
How I Gained 50,000 Followers to My Spotify Playlist

Here's a fun little story. In advance of launching Brassroots District, I decided to create a funk/soul playlist. I curated it months before the release of BRD's first single. I called it "Low Volume Funk" (based on a Vulfpeck fan club phrase) and promoted it in the "Vulfpack" Facebook Group. For months people would ask for music suggestions other than Vulfpeck. I kept a running list of all the suggestions and added the ones I liked the best to the playlist and spent a long time on the order (I put as much loving care into this playlist as I did the mixtape I made for my girlfriend in high school). I then promoted the playlist pretty much solely in the Vulfpack Facebook Group. Since I had been an active member of the group for months, many people knew my presence and thanked me profusely for taking the time to put the playlist together. So when Brassroots District's first song came out, you better believe I inserted it into the playlist. We got thousands of listeners right off the bat directly from followers of the playlist. *Score!*

Since then, I've run Instagram ads (from the Facebook Business Ads Manager), which have brought in over 50,000 followers to this playlist. The playlist is still active and growing. Most UGP editors run ads to grow their playlist following.

It's a good idea to create your own playlists and promote them in a unique way that makes sense for your project.

TIKTOK DISCOVERY

> TikTok is the only thing that really moves the needle when it comes to streaming.
>
> —LISA KASHA, HEAD OF DIGITAL, EPIC RECORDS

In late 2021, TikTok revealed in a study with MRC Data that 75% of their users discover new music on the platform, and most of them then seek out those songs on music-streaming services. This study was conducted when TikTok had nearly a billion users. Far more than Spotify.

It seemed that the 2020/2021 music industry could be equally defined by TikTok's influence as by the pandemic. Artists of every level, from Lil Nas X, Megan Thee Stallion, Olivia Rodrigo, and Doja Cat to Lizzy McAlpine, Mothica, Ritt Momney, Ricky Montgomery, Zai1k, and Trousdale had their careers launched because of TikTok. There has never been an app in the history of social media that spread songs quicker than this platform. Nearly every artist signed by a major label in 2020 found their success from TikTok.

And as previously discussed, Sadie Jean had her debut single, "WYD Now?," go viral on the app through the Open Verse Challenge when nearly 20,000 people created collaborations to her song—many of these before it was even officially released. Selene Records quickly scooped her up and helped her release the song, which translated into 20 million streams in under a month.

Arizona Zervas initially released his song "Roxanne" via DistroKid and it went viral on TikTok, with over 2 million videos created using the song (this was propelled by the influencer marketing agency Flighthouse Media—more on influencer marketing in a minute). That traction translated to Spotify, where the song hit over 1 billion streams. Zervas ended up signing with Columbia Records with a multimillion-dollar deal.

Ricky Montgomery similarly had two of his songs go viral on TikTok in 2020. This quickly translated to Spotify streams, where he racked up over 100 million for each. Mind you, these songs went viral on TikTok before he even had a TikTok account. Nearly every major record label offered him a deal and he got into a bidding war to the point where he was able to negotiate a previously unheard-of licensing deal with Warner Records; not only did he get a fat advance, but he retained ownership of his masters with a 50/50 royalty split. The majors have gotten so desperate to compete with the indie labels and DIY distributors (as they continue to lose global market share) that they have had to change their business model dramatically. Ricky revealed to me on the *New Music Business* podcast that when he showed another major label the deal Warner offered him and asked them to top it, they said, "We would only offer that deal to Beyoncé." The times, they are a-changin'.

And with the launch of TikTok's DIY artist-direct tool, SoundOn, artists can help propel their music on the platform in a much more streamlined way.

INFLUENCER MARKETING

And of course, as TikTok creators gained massive followings, influencer marketing on TikTok was born. Influencer marketing essentially involves hiring people ("influencers") with moderately popular social media accounts to promote your song (or product).

We've come a long way from the Fyre Festival days of paying the biggest models in the world to promote a doomed festival in the Bahamas. When "influencers" only existed on Instagram, you had to pay a lot of money to those with big followings. Because the way Instagram worked at the time was that users would only see content from accounts they followed. This practice was virtually out of reach for most indie artists and labels.

TikTok, however, changed all that. It has never been easier to go viral on a platform. Because of the For You Page (FYP), which is the default homepage for all users, videos go viral all the time from accounts with very few followers. The TikTok algorithm rewards videos that get early engagement versus those from accounts with a ton of followers.

Because of this, the way that influencer marketing works now is that the client (artist, label, manager, agent, promoter) pays a bunch of influencers with varying follower counts to promote a song. Sometimes a concept will be worked out (like a dance or a meme), but most of the time, the client just asks the influencer to get creative and use the song in their own way. Clients engage as many micro-influencers as they possibly can (and sometimes big influencers as well) for the campaign. It's more shots on goal.

In the era of TikTok, it's better to pay $50 to 100 micro-influencers than $5,000 to one big influencer. Reason being, the big influencer's video may flop. Even though they may have millions of followers, the algorithm may crush the video's reach and no one may see it. Whereas of the 100 micro-influencers, there's a much better chance that one will go viral—which will then inspire many more people to use that same "Sound" (song) for their own videos.

And as of today, it's probably safe to pay influencers to make videos with your song. The FTC continues to crack down on brands, and even on individual influencers, for not disclosing sponsorship or other influencer compensation, and it is possible that, in the future, there will be greater financial penalties. But it's currently the Wild West, and many people are not revealing that they're being paid to promote a song.

Unlike paying playlist editors on Spotify to include your song in their playlist, TikTok actually encourages the practice of brands and businesses paying creators to make videos via the TikTok Creator Marketplace. Any registered business can browse the creators listed on this marketplace, negotiate a price to promote your song or product, and get it going.

The amount fluctuates quite a lot per TikToker, but some influencer marketing agencies have revealed ballpark numbers. Austin Georgas, a senior account manager at Flighthouse, said that influencers with 50,000–150,000 followers can earn anywhere from $20–$150 per post. Devain Doolaramani at the Fuel Injector noted that influencers with

200,000–300,000 followers who get around 20,000–30,000 Likes on a video earn around $200 for a song promotion. Jesse Callahan at Montford Agency had a fairly straightforward calculation: $200–$300 per post for every million followers. And Griffin Haddrill, the CEO of VRTCL, said that the top 30 creators on the app earn anywhere from $8,000–$50,000 per post.

These are some of the bigger influencer agencies out there. Hiring them will cost you a high five figures per campaign. So, it might be more economical to start with the TikTok Creator Marketplace.

And just like playlist-plugging companies, there are quite a few companies that will connect you with micro-influencers to run campaigns. This will help you save costs, but will be far more hands-off and less transparent. These companies are coming and going pretty frequently.

THE MAILING LIST

I remember in 2008 when every band on the planet's entire online promotional plan revolved around MySpace. And why wouldn't it? It was the most popular social network in the world. And the band profiles were easily customizable. MySpace profiles became most artists' primary website. Artists grew massive fanbases on MySpace, and fans loved the access it gave them to their new favorite artists. MySpace seemed to be breaking artists left and right, and play counts and "friend" numbers were the new musical currency. Facebook was, of course, rapidly growing, but at the time it was still primarily just used by students. And never for music.

But then, in 2009, something happened. People started leaving MySpace in droves. By 2010 it was all but a ghost town. It became the slums of the internet. You didn't dare visit.

What's the big deal, right? Well, all the artists who built up their fanbases on MySpace couldn't reach them anymore. Some haphaz-ardly attempted to transition them over to YouTube and Facebook, but most didn't. I went on a national tour supporting a MySpace star after the death of MySpace. Even though this artist had millions upon millions of plays on MySpace, the fans didn't transition to Facebook, YouTube or the artist's mailing list. We grossly undersold our tour projections because the artist didn't have a way to reach the fans and let them know about the tour. The fans were still listening, but now they were listening on YouTube. To fan-made lyric videos. So this artist couldn't even add annotations to the videos letting everyone know about the tour.

And we all remember Vine. There were huge Vine stars who simi-larly built up massive followings on the platform but never transitioned those followings anywhere else. So when Vine died, those creators lost their entire fan base. Similarly, there was this livestreaming platform for a hot minute called Busker. It was positioning itself to be *the* livestream-ing app for musicians. A few musicians built up huge followings only to lose them when the app died, leaving those musicians without a way to get in touch with their hard-earned fans.

What's the lesson here? Build up your email list! Jamie Foxx told Tim Ferriss on his podcast, "I was social media before there was social media." Jamie built an audience while he was working the stand-up circuit of L.A. in the early '90s. He used to hand out 3 × 5 cards at his shows and asked people to write down their pager numbers so he could text them when he had upcoming shows.

The mailing list remains the best way to communicate with fans. All the contacts on your email or SMS list, you own. All the Likes on Face-book, Followers on Twitter, Instagram, TikTok, Twitch and Spotify, Sub-scribers on YouTube and Friends on Snapchat, you rent. Any third party can change their terms, and overnight you could lose access to all your hard-earned fans (like Facebook does all the time). Even though average music email open rates sit at just 23%, social media engagement rates are abysmal.

Average Social Media Engagement Rates:
Instagram = 0.83%
Twitter = 0.05%
Facebook = 0.13%
TikTok = 5.96%
(Socialinsider 2022)

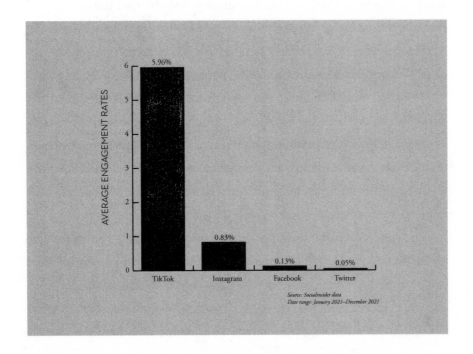

Whereas when a fan opens your email, they've engaged with it (clicked open). Oh, and the SMS engagement rate is around 95%. When was the last time you didn't open a text?

Make sure your email sign-up on your website is prominent and that there is an incentive to sign up, and make sure that you have a prominent notice that says that each person who signs up is giving you consent to send them marketing emails. This may seem unnecessary and just common sense, but given the very strict privacy laws that continue to be passed, especially the EU's recent GDPR (General Data Protection Regulation), it's recommended that you include that language. Signing up on the website from home is very different from signing up at a concert. There isn't the buzzing energy (or a band member's personal encouragement to do so), so incentives like exclusives, raffles and full-quality songs help.

And how do you get people to your website these days? Well, pop that link into your bio and put an incentive for people to click it. Many artists also have a "Text me at this number" on their socials as well. I'd encourage slipping an incentive in there, like "Text ARI to 55-444 for a chance to win free tix to my next show"; you can run contests or give away livestream tickets to your text-message subscribers.

It's much more difficult to get people on your SMS (texting) lists than to follow you on social media, but once you do, you'll get them to convert a lot easier. New single coming out? Send a text and watch the pre-saves pour in. Tour dates announced? Send a text with a pre-buy link. Running a vinyl crowdfunding campaign? Text your fans about it. Tracking isn't quite up to the level of email yet, but it's getting better every day.

For your shows, put up signs around the venue with "Text us for free merch and updates: 55-444" or pop in QR codes for your email list. You can even have a moment during the show when you announce, "Everyone pull out your phones. Text OURNAME to this number, 55-444, and you'll get an instant text with a link to this song before we finish it. It's unreleased, so you'll be one of the only ones to have it." Come up with an incentive that makes sense and get those sign-ups at every show. I've seen bigger artists put on the jumbo screens before the show to text a number to win merch packages or backstage passes for after the concert. Talk about instant gratification! Other artists have texting campaigns for charities they've partnered with.

With many texting services, you can set up an autogenerated welcome message that asks the user to input more data, like location, name, favorite song—the kind of stuff that helps you with sorting. Or, at your Minneapolis show, have people text MINNEAPOLIS to your number, and they'll get auto sorted by location; that way, when you return, you can let them know. And you can follow up the next day with a live recording from their show.

The texting platform Community has been leading the front in the music space for SMS marketing, but there are many other great options to check out (that are far cheaper). Search around a bit and you'll find a suitable option for you. It is time to get an SMS list going, that's for sure.

But email is still incredibly valuable. Yes, open and engagement rates are lower than SMS, but tracking is far superior and it's *much* cheaper to run an email list than a texting list. And the etiquette is very different. Sending an email with five paragraphs and eight links is pretty common. A text message with five paragraphs and eight links? Yikes.

So! At your shows, collect those emails. No need to pass the iPad around anymore or decipher drunk handwriting. Just get a QR code up at the merch table (and maybe on stage if it fits your vibe) and incentivize people to sign up from their phones. Make sure everyone signs up. Especially at house concerts. People are very willing to sign up on your list during house concert experiences. And you absolutely want everyone's email at these shows so you can hit them up for your club appearance when you return to town.

Make sure building your email and SMS lists are the first priority. Email isn't going away anytime soon and remains the only constant in an ever-changing digital world. Building a grass-roots music career is about gaining fans, one at a time, and keeping them engaged and respected.

As far as who is the best mailing list provider? Mailchimp has become the industry standard, but there are many great options out there. I've used a few different services and most have pros and cons.

Things to look out for when you're researching who to use:

■ **No Double Opt-In**

Meaning, if they sign up on your clipboard at the show, you should be able to import the name to your list online without them having to confirm it. And if you're changing mailing list providers, you want to be able to import your current list without the users having to opt in (again) to the new provider's list.

■ **Automations**

Most mailing list providers have this. This means, when someone signs up, they immediately get a welcome email in their inbox (that you customize) containing links to the incentives. Others enable multiple autoresponders. The provider can send an initial autoresponse to new sign-ups immediately, then another automated response one day later and then another autoresponse a week after that. A stream of welcome emails.

Once you have a digital specialist/marketing manager on the team (remember that from Chapter 2?), they can master the automations and set them up for every variable. Somebody visited your store's checkout page but didn't complete the purchase? Automation sequence commence! Want to only send a message to people who opened your last email? Or clicked the tour dates link? You can with some email list providers. Some get very nuanced. For example, you can send someone four emails over the span of the next nine days. If they end up buying the record, you can choose not to send them any more emails in this automation. You see where this is going. And you now see why you need that digital specialist on the team ASAP.

■ **Analytics**

You should be able to see how many opened the email, who clicked on each included link and from which geographic location.

■ **Location Sorting**

Some mailing list providers will grab the subscriber's location automatically when they open your email. Having the ability to sort by location is especially important when you're touring so you can send out targeted emails to the cities you are visiting with specific details (and reminders) about their show.

■ **Reuse Past Campaigns**

Considering the template for most email blasts will be very similar, you should have to design it only once and then be able to reuse it (changing out the body info).

■ **Not Using Your Physical Mailing Address**

In America, the law requires that any email that promotes goods or services (and concerts are services) include the physical address of the "sender," which is the person on whose behalf the email is being sent. For that reason, some providers will require you to put your own, personal address. Others will put their company's address. It's nice if you don't have to give all of your subscribers your home (stalker-friendly) address, even though that doesn't comply with the US law.

■ **Groups**

You should be able to filter your subscribers by location, open history, click history, and then add them to groups to email directly. You should even be able to create a street team group and other filtered groups to mail separately for things that may not concern the entire list.

■ **Customer Service**

This is key. The best services will provide you with a phone number or online chat. It's also good to test customer service email turnaround time. Things come up. Glitches occur. Being able to contact a human is a must.

THE TRIPLE CHECK

This is a tactic you should employ with everything in your music career. The last thing you want to have happen is send out a blast to 5,000 people with a link to your new album, only to realize that your link doesn't work. No brainer, right? Well, I can't tell you how many emails I've received from artists with broken or incorrect links. Always, send yourself a test email and text (every provider allows this) and open the email on your desktop *and* your phone. It should look great on both. Click each link to make sure it's good. And it's good to click the link in an "incognito" window. Incognito windows are available in Chrome and enable you to create an entirely new session with none of your settings saved (and fresh cache). This is crucial to test your links, because many times links may work for you when you're signed in, but no one else. Perfect examples are Dropbox, Google Drive and PayPal links.

If you edit a blast, send another test. Edit it again, another test. Train yourself to use the triple-check method in everything you do.

6.

PLAYING LIVE

Bands should not be trying to play in front of 1,500 people
because they've got one song in heavy rotation and they literally
weren't a band a year and a half ago. They might get away with it
for a little while, but I can tell you a bunch of bands that I
heard on the radio two years ago, you ain't hearing about
them now. Because they couldn't bring it live.
—BRUCE FLOHR, RED LIGHT MANAGEMENT

You really don't know how something's going to
play until you test it.
—B. J. NOVAK, WRITER/ACTOR/COMEDIAN

People are nervous for no reason, because no one's going to come
out and slap you or beat you up.
—JAMIE FOXX

WHAT HAPPENED TO LIVE MUSIC?

Boy, did it take a global pandemic shuttering the live music industry for
us to realize how important live music actually is. It shouldn't have, but
by god, if you didn't feel it before, you felt it then. There were spurts of
concerts that happened (sometimes when they shouldn't have) through-

out the pandemic. Some safe. Some not. But all needed. Desperately needed, no doubt.

Live music is spiritual. Live music is cathartic. Live music is important. And can never be replaced.

I was fortunate enough to put on a sixteen-show (outdoor) concert-theatrical experience with my immersive 1970s funk/soul project, Brass-roots District, in the summer of 2021, in Downtown Los Angeles. What I witnessed from the stage was a joy and euphoria only achieved by sweating with other humans having a collective experience. Together. With the band. As one united spirit. One energy, transcending the lethargic confines of the depressive physical realities of the moment. And embracing the spiritual possibilities of the future.

(Photo by Nick Cimiluca)

That's what live music is. Well, should be. If done right.

Remember what you have the power and ability to create with your gifts. Yes, there is more competition—now more than ever—for people's attention. Not only do we have to convince people that they should choose our concert over all the others in town that night, but even more so that we can offer a more memorable and life-altering experience that is unattainable sitting at home on their couch. Even with how good television has gotten.

I have no doubt that we, as a music community, can achieve this. Don't let the pessimists convince you that TV can hold even a glimmering candle to what we have the ability to do. In the end, we remember the experiences we had. The music we saw. Not the TV shows we watched.

I have faith in you.

Speaking of which, why not set this book down for a minute and plan out the next show you're going to see this week? The community stays alive only if we keep it alive.

THE PURPOSE OF PERFORMING LIVE

I love playing live. I love connecting with an audience. I love elevating a crowd to new heights. I love creating a beautiful, shared experience that people walk away from inspired, uplifted, invigorated and fulfilled. But I realize not all artists like or want to perform. Many very successful producers, session musicians and artists I know have no interest in performing or touring. They make enough money for them to live on and that's totally fine. And, of course, professional songwriters rarely, if ever, tour. They cowrite day in and day out and hope their song gets cut by a big star and becomes a hit. All they need is one hit a year and they're set.

However, most artists want (and need) to play live. So ask yourself what kind of artist you want to be. Does playing live interest you? If so, you need to have a killer live show. And the only way to get better at performing is by performing. So, start by playing as much as you can. Anywhere and everywhere. You need experience more than anything early on. Get onstage whenever you can. You won't be getting paid for these early shows, but you don't deserve to be just yet. You deserve to get paid when your act merits it and when you can consistently get crowds out to your shows.

WHEN TO CHARGE FOR SHOWS

There will come a point when there is a shift in your audience's reaction. It will go from a polite, respectful (pity) applause to a rousing, enthusiastic, fervent one. Your friends will compliment you with a hint of disbelief in their voice and people you don't know will start coming up to you gushing about your show. People (if you do it right) will start coming back to your shows and bringing friends. At some point you will look out at the crowd and there will be more faces you don't recognize than those you do. That will be the moment you know you're onto something.

Once people start requesting to book you, you need to know what (and if) to charge. Obviously, you can do benefit concerts for free if you believe in the cause. But always ask if they can give you a "stipend" to at least cover your expenses. Or charge them a very reduced rate. And make sure the gig will represent you well and will cover all of your necessary technical requirements. You don't want to take a benefit concert only to find out that you're going to be playing in the corner of the cafeteria, without a stage, through a sound system that only half works, with one mic on a shaky stand in a fluorescent-lit room. Or worse, a completely unlit "stage." I've done it all. So, if you take a free gig, send your tech rider and compromise on less.

We'll get into negotiating techniques, price points and tech riders in the next chapter, but don't undervalue yourself. If people are asking you to play, and you've proven yourself over and over and over again, then you can ask to be paid. If you're still green and need the performance experience, ask if there is compensation, but if there's not, you probably should still just play it.

THE PERFECT 30

Put every show you play to the Perfect 30 test:

Payment = 10
Career building = 10
Enjoyment = 10

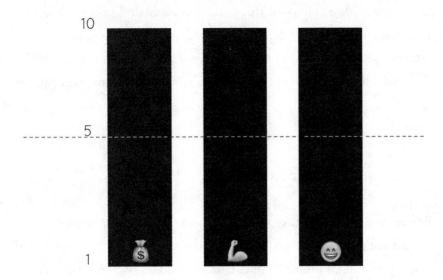

The Perfect 30.

You don't want to play any shows for less than a total of 15 on the scale. If the payment is incredible (10), but there will be very little career-building potential (3) or enjoyment (2), that equals 15. If there is decent payment (5), but will bring great enjoyment (9), but little career-building potential (1), that also equals a 15. Take these shows. The shows you shouldn't take are the ones for little to no money (1), very little career-building potential (3) and very little enjoyment (3) = 7. Pass!

But, career-building potential doesn't just happen. You have to *make* it happen. If you play a show outside at a beer garden for 2,000 people, it could be a 10 for career-building potential if you have volunteers walking around with flyers/business cards and a mailing list sign-up sheet/iPad. It could also be a 10 on the payment scale if your volunteers walk around selling merch, holding a tip jar, and you have a manned merch table set up.

A funk/reggae band I used to manage got a chance to open for Damian Marley at Summerfest in Milwaukee in front of nearly 3,000 reggae lovers. We employed this exact approach, and not only did their roaming volunteers sell $2,400 in merch during their ninety-minute set; they sold tickets (and passed out flyers) to an upcoming Milwaukee show which ended up selling out. This Summerfest show was the Perfect 30.

THE POWER OF THE TAG

Before you play your next show, make sure every piece of your gear is labeled with your name on it. Every pedal, every cable, mic, mic stand, amp, everything. I use white duct tape and make a two-inch tag on every cable and then write my name on the tape with a Sharpie. You can even get craftier and print out your name on a sheet of paper and then cover it with clear packing tape. Whatever you do, make sure all pieces of your equipment (especially cables) are tagged. This will save you a tremendous amount of money (and stress) in having to purchase all the cables accidentally stolen by other bands or the club. The last thing you want to have happen is to show up at a club the next night and realize your one-of-a-kind power cable that powers your mixer was grabbed by the previous night's sound guy, mistaking it for his own, and you have to play tonight's show acoustic. (This may or may not have happened to me . . .)

BEHIND THE BANTER

Practice what you're going to say in between songs. Rehearse stories and jokes and write notes on your set list for what you are going to say. Come up with "safety stories" just in case the crowd doesn't give you much energy to play off of in between songs and you need to pull these stories out.

The Grammy-nominated folk duo the Milk Carton Kids have some of the best live banter of any working act today. Fun fact: Their first tour was supporting me for a string of shows in the Midwest. They reciprocated and gave me my first California tour supporting them. I've seen their banter evolve over the years. Lead story teller, Joey Ryan, has an extremely dry sense of humor. And he plays it up. Who you are onstage should be a heightened version of yourself. Or, if you've created a character, it's the best version of that character. I saw the Milk Carton Kids captivate the 1,600 in attendance at the Theatre at Ace Hotel in L.A. The show was equal parts music and comedy. Joey with his dry wit and subdued stage persona had the entire theater rolling. Joey and Kenneth played off of each other effortlessly. It felt fresh and spontaneous, when in reality much of it had been worked out over hundreds of shows. None of it felt rehearsed—that's when the banter is the best. There were definite moments when the banter was actually spontaneous, like commenting on the theater, the audience or responding to a heckler.

Eventually you will become so comfortable with any crowd that you will effortlessly be able to switch between old jokes, rehearsed stories and spontaneous jokes and comments. Once you have the audience in the palm of your hand, you can virtually say anything and they will go along with you for the ride.

THE BRIDGE
When Greeting Fans, Never Say "Nice to Meet You"

When you're at a show, you are onstage from the moment the doors open to the moment they close. Even if you're not physically standing on the stage. You are the artist and there is a spotlight on you, even if you're hiding in the corner trying to get ready. If you're being loud and obnoxious at the bar during the opener's set, people will notice. If you make out with your girlfriend by the stairwell, yeah, you're gonna lose a few fans. PDA not OK! People are watching you and judging your every move. If they talk to you, your little twenty-second interaction will remain with them for a very long time.

I still have fans who come up to me after shows and remind me of the conversation we had three years prior. Of course I can't remember it (or them), but they retell it like it was yesterday. To me, that was hundreds of shows and thousands of postshow conversations ago. To them, it was the only conversation they've had with one of their favorite artists.

You're going to meet fans after shows, on the street, in coffee shops and at other bands' concerts. Greet everyone like you've met before. Replace "nice to meet you" with "nice to see you." Because, if you've met once (or four times) before and you say "nice to meet you," they will, at best, feel bad that they aren't memorable enough to remember or, at worst, be so offended that they will turn on you, bad mouth you around town and never return to one of your shows ever again (it can happen, trust me).

There's no way you're going to remember every fan, every conversation or even every show. So fake it. Pretend like you remember them. It will make their night.

THE BRIDGE
10 Things You Should Never Say Onstage

1) **We're Having Technical Difficulties** Even if your guitar just caught fire. Well actually, that would be hilarious if you said it then. But when bands sheepishly admit it into the mic, it's uncomfortable and kills the vibe. Technical difficulties are your fault. Even when they're not. Your amp will crap out, your guitar cable will short, your batteries will die, your tuner will get dust in it and short out, the DI will die, the mic stand will fall apart and all of this

you're going to need to know how to deal with on the spot, in front of your audience.

It's your stage. It's your show.

I once had a venue's DI die on me during my first song in front of a sold-out show in San Francisco. I had just built up a 12-track loop with beat boxing, trumpets, bass, keys, guitar, the works. So when it crapped out, it felt like Satan had just burst through the floor, grabbed my sound and blazed out the back door leaving only awkward silence.

However, because I knew my setup so well, I quickly went through the checklist of everything it could be and realized within four seconds it was the DI. Without missing a beat, I got the crowd 1 2, 1 clapping while I told the sound guy I needed a new DI. He ran up, switched out the DI, the sound came back and joined the crowd's 1 2, 1 claps almost right on beat where I left off.

I could have smiled awkwardly at the crowd, pissed myself, then curled up in a ball on the center of the stage crying "There's no place like home" while clicking my heels, but that wouldn't have accomplished anything. That's basically the same as saying "Uh, we're having technical difficulties" while looking awkwardly at your band members hoping someone will fix it for you.

2) **I Forgot the Lyrics** If you can't memorize your lyrics, then bring a lyrics sheet on stage as reference. Or get good at making them up on the spot.

The only thing worse than bad lyrics is forgotten lyrics.

Don't ever step on stage unprepared. Not at an open mic; not at a talent show, not at a songwriters showcase and especially not at a show where your name is on the bill. The stage is not a time for you to "see how it goes" or to practice. Rehearse on your own time.

3) **I Want to Thank My Significant Other** It's like having a one-on-one conversation with someone in the audience off the mic. Uncomfortable for everyone else in the house.

Leave your lover out of it. If he or she did something truly awesome, then you can say something like "We'd like to thank our friend Sarah for getting this song into the hands of the music supervisor for Euphoria."

If your significant other needs to be publicly thanked as your significant other, then you have bigger issues you have to work out.

4) **I'm Sorry** Don't ever apologize onstage. It makes you look weak. I don't care if you just dropped a baby. Don't apologize.

Making excuses for your lack of preparation makes everyone in the house uncomfortable and feel bad for you. I hear it all the time: "I forgot the rest of the song. Sorry." "I'm sorry if this song sucks, we just wrote it." "I'm sorry there aren't more people here." "We haven't rehearsed this much, it might suck."

Own the stage. Own the room. Own your set. Or don't show up.

5) **Your City Sucks** Should be a no-brainer, but I can't tell you how many touring bands I've seen make fun of the city they are in—*onstage*. It may be fun to joke about in the van, but your audience takes pride in their city. No matter if you think their city is cool or not.

Never say anything negative about the town you are in while onstage unless you want a beer bottle thrown at you.

6) **This Song Is About My Grandma Who Died of Cancer. Love You, Nana.** Don't depress your audience. You can play a song about your dead grandma, but you don't need to tell the audience that's what it's about. Can you play sad songs? Of course! Many artists make careers of this. But make sure your shows are inspiring and enriching.

People don't pay money to come to shows to be sad. They come to be happy. To have fun. To be enlightened. To be inspired.

If you can't communicate the power of your song by just playing it, then maybe the song isn't really that good. That being said, telling stories about songs—especially at folk shows—is extremely important and impactful. Work out your stories so you don't ramble.

7) **I'm Broke** Don't make your audience feel bad for you. It removes the mystique and coolness factor. You can say "Pick up a T-shirt and help us get to the next city." That offers an emotional appeal in a positive light.

Guilting your fans into buying your merch never works.

8) **You Guys Suck** Even if 95 out of the 100 people are screaming above your acoustic set while smashing glasses and vomiting in the corner, 5 people are engulfed in your set. Never insult your audience. They always have one ear to you—even if you are just background music.

9) **Any Requests?** You're never going to get the songs that you actually have prepared, and there will always be that one a**hole who yells "Free Bird" as if he just came up with the joke.

10) **How Does It Sound?** This is a slap in the face to the sound engineer. Never ask the crowd that. It should sound amazing. If it doesn't, then it's either your fault or the sound engineer's fault. Either way, you just pissed off the one person not in your band who can actually make you sound worse.

DON'T PLAY TO THE A**HOLES

We've all experienced the drunk a**holes. My first instinct is always to engage. Sometimes you have to. If they're making themselves a part of the show (like yelling at you or talking loudly, disturbing the show for others), you have to engage. It's awkward not to. *But* you don't have to do what they say. Actually, you should *never* do what they say. It only encourages them.

There's a huge difference between taking requests from fans and appeasing drunk a**holes. Drunk a**holes are just there to party and make themselves look cool around their friends. Unless you're a cover/party band, these people are not your crowd. You don't want them at your shows. They are an unwelcome detraction for the people who *are* your fans and are actually there to see you.

Remember, there are always people in the room who want to hear *your set*. They are holding on to every word you sing and every note you play. Don't play to the a**holes, because the show is not meant for them. It's meant for the fans (or potential fans) who are actually into your music and will stick with you for the rest of your career. You don't win fans by appeasing drunk a**holes. You win fans by shutting them up (humorously) and kicking butt with the set you prepared. If the a**holes leave, so be it. Better for everyone.

Take a three-step approach to dealing with loud a**holes:

Step 1: Humorously Engage

If there's a loud conversation going on at the back of the room and everyone else is silently listening, you can whisper through the mic and (politely) discuss the wardrobe of the offending party until they notice and take the hint. If there is someone who is constantly yelling out requests of cover songs you can say, "So I only know 2 cover songs and I already played them. However if you have any (fill in your band name) originals you'd like us to play, let us know!" That should put them to rest. Many times they'll realize that you're not into making the show about them and they leave. Good riddance.

Step 2: Show a Bit of (Reserved) Annoyance

If the humor doesn't work (it almost always does), try engaging in a bit more assertive, albeit still polite, manner. Look them directly in the eye with a "why are you f'ing up my show?" look that they will recognize and others will appreciate. Or if they're close to the stage, you can hop off the mic and ask them to stop. With a smile.

Step 3: Kick Them in the Head

Now, I only know of the Brian Jonestown Massacre actually doing this literally. And I definitely don't recommend it. But take the figurative approach. Stop the show. Make it known that you don't like what they're doing. Get them kicked out (or ask them to leave). Florence and the Machine stopped the show because of a fight. The way Florence approached it was brilliant.

You don't want a**holes at your show. It makes you look bad. People come to concerts for the scene as much as the music. If your shows turn into douchefests, then the crowd you really want will be driven away. Catch this early on. Make every one of your shows *your* show. Take control. Command *your* stage. Play to the supportive faces in the room. Play to those who want to be there. For those who ended up at your show and are working their damnedest to destroy it? Kick them in the f%*&ing head. Figuratively, of course.

Your Audience Is a Direct Reflection of You

Venues know it. Promoters know it. Agents know it. And fans know it. An audience is a direct reflection of the artist. An artist is essentially the CEO of their company. Their attitude seeps into everything their organization does. Artists' fans emulate the artist. If an artist is aggressive and careless, the entire organization (including their fans) will be aggressive and careless. If an artist is sensitive and considerate, their fans typically follow suit.

In November of 2021, the world watched in horror as ten people died at the Astroworld Festival in Houston, Texas, organized and headlined by Travis Scott. Besides the safety measures that may have been overlooked or neglected, the fact of the matter is, when Travis took the stage, his audience pushed and crushed people to their deaths.

As the *New York Times* wrote, "Travis Scott's concerts are known for their chaotic energy." And at Astroworld, moments before people were crushed, Travis yelled into the mic, "I want to see some rages. Who want to rage?"

You are responsible for the kind of show and audience you want to have. How you carry yourself on and off stage determines this. Your fans will look to you for cues as to how to behave at your shows. What kind of environment do you want to create?

It is your responsibility to keep your audience safe.

DOES THIS MUSTACHE MAKE MY A$$ LOOK FAT?

It's not cool to your dude friends to fret over your image, but your image is almost as important as your sound. If you look like an idiot onstage, half of your audience will think that you sound like one (and the other half may not care, but you just lost half of your audience before your first note).

They say that 80% of what the audience remembers is visual. So even if you sounded like Led Zeppelin, if you looked like Weird Al, that's what they're going to remember.

Image is extremely important in music. You won't hear most musicians talk about this because it's not cool to talk about how much time went into their outfit or hair. Fans love thinking that your outfit is just what you normally wear and is an artistic expression of who you are.

Your image should represent your sound appropriately. When was the last time you saw a folk artist get up on stage looking like Kiss? If you want to be taken seriously, then look, act and sound serious.

I can't tell you what your image should be, but I can say it is extremely important.

You should have a look that separates you from everyone else. If you look like everyone else, then you're admitting that your sound has no originality and you should get written off as just another pop/jam/acoustic/blues/college/rock/hip-hop/whatever act.

You know how when you're at a concert the band stands out from everyone else? They didn't always have "the look." They grew into their look. Clothes are an expression of who you are and so is your art. This should be taken into consideration. However, sometimes a group of artists who all have a similar external way of expressing themselves get together and form a band and they never discuss or need to think about their image because it all just clicks. This is ideal. Eventually when you mature into yourself, your onstage and offstage look will be the artistic expression of who you are and it will feel comfortable.

Or if you create a persona, like a Lady Gaga or Lana Del Rey, you embody a character when you step on stage or into the studio. You're like an actor, in costume, playing the part.

Or you can just have everyone in the band literally wear costumes. Like Phoebe Bridgers. Her entire band wears skeleton costumes for every show. The skeleton costume has become her thing. She's featured it in music videos, photo shoots, and now on stage. People now associate the skeleton costume with her everywhere. Talk about branding!

It's quite rare for young artists to wear outfits that are different. It's uncomfortable to stand out, and even very talented artists succumb to peer pressures and conform. Be an outcast! Some of the best artists of all time were outcasts and weren't really comfortable with themselves or anyone around them and they expressed this through their art.

Also, many music reviewers will (believe it or not) start by reviewing your image and the culture surrounding your music before (if ever) they review your sound.

HOW TO HIRE FREELANCE MUSICIANS

As a singer/songwriter or musical director, there are a few very important things you need to understand about hired guns:

■ **Freelance Musicians Aren't Playing Your Music for Fun**
Sure, all musicians love the art. Love the craft. Have a passion that bleeds out of their eyeballs. It's the only reason they chose such an unstable career.

But musicians, like all other humans, need to eat. Just because they're holding a guitar instead of a hammer, you shouldn't value their craft any less. Just like a carpenter isn't going to build your fence for the love of the craft, don't expect a professional freelance musician to play your gig for free either.

Young musicians will tend to take gigs for free, however. For experience. Some friends might even agree to play your gig as a favor. Or because they believe in you. They may even say "for fun." But be very cautious about getting a volunteer band together. If they get offered a last-minute paid gig the same night as your show, you may be left without a drummer hours before you hit the stage.

By paying your musicians (regardless of the amount), you can demand (politely) a level of professionalism. If they're playing "for fun" or as a favor, prepare yourself for flakiness.

However, "sitting in" is an honored tradition, and many artists sit in with friends all the time—for, of course, no pay.

■ **Discuss All Details Up Front**

You can't just ask someone to play the gig for $100 and then spring three rehearsals on them the week of the show and assume they'll be OK with this. Make sure you discuss all details up front: rate, rehearsals, show date(s), per diems and sleeping arrangements (if it's a tour), how many songs you want them to learn, if you require them to be memorized or if they can have charts on stage, rehearsal length (three hours is typical), show length, gear they need to bring, if you want them to make charts or if you're providing them and anything else you'd like from your musicians.

■ **Get the Scene's Going Rate**

In L.A., the typical going rate is $100 for the gig and about $50 per rehearsal. This varies depending on the musician's reputation and experience. Some ask for more and some will accept less. If you've never hired musicians before, ask other singer/songwriters or music directors (MD) in your scene what they pay their players.

I don't recommend asking them what their rate is because most likely it will be way more than you were prepared to pay and then you'll feel like an a**hole for undercutting them and they'll feel like a noob for agreeing to a rate so much lower than their "normal rate." Pitch them all details including the rate from the get-go.

And remember, just like every contract agreement, you can always negotiate. But be respectful. If you ask someone to play the gig and two rehearsals for $50 and he replies saying he needs $150 for that, try to make it work, or pass. Don't tell him his mother only goes for half that.

All details should be worked out up front. Once both parties have committed, there should be no more haggling. This is an easy way to get blacklisted in the scene. Both sides should respect the offer and accommodate. They shouldn't spring a "cart fee" on you to bring their gear and you shouldn't spring extra rehearsals on them.

■ **Send Streaming and Downloadable Links**

I hate downloading music. When I freelance, I want practice tracks sent as streamable links. I want to listen to them when I'm driving. I want to dedicate a few minutes here and there to run them in my home studio. I don't want to spend fifteen minutes downloading, importing, labeling and syncing to my iPhone. DISCO, Dropbox, Box and Drive allow you to stream the song online *or* download it if you want. They're the most flexible for your players. SoundCloud also has this option, but you have to enable it. Some will prefer to download so they can pop it into their DAW to rehearse with, others only want to stream.

Give your players options.

■ **Be a Leader**

You need to lead your rehearsals. Your players have agreed to play *your* gig with *your* name on the bill. They may be the lead songwriter and front person of their main project, but for this gig, they defer to you.

Make sure you show up to rehearsals prepared. Know what songs you want to rehearse in the order you want to rehearse them. Don't spend ten minutes in between each song deliberating over the setlist. This is your responsibility. You can ask their opinions if you want, but you know your audience, act and songs best.

You should be familiar with every player's part. Be able to answer every player's question decisively. Confidently. Don't say, "I don't know. Do whatever you think." Yes, you can trust their talent, expertise and craft, but it's your gig and your songs. Know your songs and know your show.

■ **Set Expectations**

In addition to discussing all details up front, make sure you let your players know what you expect from them. Will you have charts available, or do you want them to learn the parts on their own?

Let the players know what to wear to the show.

It's your responsibility to lock in a rehearsal space, but feel free to ask if they have suggestions.

Are you adamantly against alcohol? Make it known that the tour will be dry. Don't wait for show number three on a fifty-date tour to bring that up.

■ **Have the Money at the Gig**

This is the most important rule. Don't make them hunt you down for the check. If you become known as someone who never pays (or delays payment), you're going to have a very difficult time finding players. Hand them the check before they hit the stage. Or Venmo them at sound check.

If you can't afford to hire a band, you can't afford to have a band.

I never recommend singer/songwriters split the door with their free-lance players, because it's a slippery slope. If you somehow get your musi-cians to agree to split the crappy door cuts with you, they're going to expect the same when you get the huge check.

It's your name. Your image. Your reputation. You are making all of the management decisions and you are setting up the shows. If you get a $2,000 check, then you should pay your players a fair wage and then invest the rest in the career. If you get a $100 check, then you take a loss and pay your play-ers the same fair wage.

You're the entrepreneur. It's your project. And your career.

Early on, your gigs will not pay for your band and you'll have to take losses. But those early investments in your career will pay off when you're selling out venues with the same players who have felt respected and cher-ished from day one.

THE BRIDGE

9 Things Every Musician Needs to Know About the Sound Guy

As much time as you spend in your rehearsal space perfecting your sound, it won't mean anything if it's botched coming out of the P.A. All the money you spent on new pedals, amps, guitars and strings doesn't matter if the mix is off in the club.

The sound guy (or gal) is the most important component of your show that most bands don't really think about. He can break your set (few sound guys can actually *make* your set if you suck). First off, they like being referred to as front of house (FOH) engineers. So, this is a good place to start.

You have to know how to approach sound guys right and get them on your team for the short amount of time that you have with them.

1) **Get His Name** The first thing you should do is introduce yourself to the sound guy when you arrive. Shake his hand, look him in the eye and exchange names. Remember his name—you're most likely going to need to use it many times that night and possibly a couple times through the mic during your set. If you

begin treating him with respect from the get-go, he will most likely return this sentiment.

2) **Respect Her Ears** All sound guys and gals take pride in their mixing. Regard-less of the style of music they like listening to in their car, they believe they can mix any genre on the spot. However, most front of house engineers will appreciate hearing what you, the musician, like for a general house mix of your band's sound. Don't be afraid to tell her a vibe or general notes ("we like the vocals and acoustic very high in the mix" or "we like keeping all vocal mics at about the same level for blended harmonies" or "add lots of reverb on the lead vocals, but keep the fiddle dry"). She'll appreciate knowing what you like and will cater to that. She is most likely a musician herself, so treat her as one—with respect. She knows musical terms—don't be afraid to use them.

3) **Don't Start Playing Until He's Ready** Set up all of your gear, but don't start wailing on the guitar or the drums until all the mics are in place and the sound person is back by the board. Pounding away on the kit while he's trying to set his mics will surely piss him off and ruin his ears. Get there early enough for sound check so you have plenty of time to feel the room out (and tune your drums).

4) **Have an Input List** Print out an accurate, up-to-date list of all inputs (channels). A stage plot can also be very helpful, especially for bigger shows. Email both the stage plot and the input list in advance. The good sound engineers will have everything set up before you arrive (this typically happens only at BIG venues). If you're at a line-check-only club, then just print out the input list/stage plot and hand it to the engineer right before your set.

There are some great stage plot software options, like Stage Plot Designer, that allows you to simply create a graphic stage plot without needing image-editing software. At the very least, though, print out an input list like this:

Channel 1—Kick Drum mic
Channel 2—Snare Drum mic
Channel 3—Hi Hat mic
Channel 4—Tom 1 mic
Channel 5—Tom 2 mic
Channel 6—Drums Overhead mic
Channel 7—Bass Amp DI (upstage right)
Channel 8—Guitar Amp mic (upstage left)
Channel 9—Fiddle DI (stage right)
Channel 10—Acoustic DI (center)
Channel 11—Keyboard DI (stereo-L) DI (stage left)
Channel 12—Keyboard DI (stereo-R) DI (stage left)
Channel 13—(lead) Vocal mic (center)

Channel 14—Vocal mic (stage left)
Channel 15—Vocal mic (stage right)
Channel 16—Tracks DI

5) **How to Insult Your Sound Guy** Address him as "yo, sound man" if you want to piss him off. You got his name—use it. Or ask him politely again if you forgot. Don't tell him that the house mix is "off" or "bad." Everything is subjective. It may not be what you like, but it's obviously what he likes. He most likely has much more experience mixing than you do. So get specific about what you like and don't like for your band's house mix from the beginning or keep quiet.

6) **Know Your Gear** Know how you like your vocals EQed generally so you can say that. You can say, "Can we drop some of the highs on the vocals in the house?" You shouldn't say, "The vocals sound piercing—they hurt my ears." You should know how your gear works inside and out, so if anything goes wrong, you point to the sound gal last. Pointing to her first is a sure way to piss her off.

7) **He's Part of the Club** The sound guy, door guy, bartender, booker, managers and servers are coworkers. They hang out, have work parties, hit the bars together and they talk. If you're a d**k to the bartender, he'll tell the sound guy and the sound guy may then decide to ruin your set out of spite. Or just not put any effort into mixing you.

8) **Everyone Wants a Great Show** Believe it or not, your sound gal wants to perform at her best just like you do. Make her job easy by showing up prepared and not sucking. She most likely has her sh*t together so make sure you have your sh*t together as well. Remember, the stage is not the time for you to "see how it goes" and try stuff out. That's what rehearsal is for. Show up prepared.

9) **The Chip** There are sound guys out there (we've all worked with them) who seem like they have a massive chip on their shoulder from the moment they step into the club. These guys are typically older, failed musicians who have been at this club for decades. They are hardened from years of working with holier-than-thou musicians who not only suck, but believe they are rock stars and that the sound guy is a peon—and treat him as such. You may not be able to change his outlook on life, but treat him with respect and dignity from the get-go and he may lighten up just enough to put some effort into mixing your set.

Even though it should go without saying, apply the golden rule. If you treat your sound guy as you'd like to be treated and work with (not against) him on putting together a great show, you most likely will have one.

THE ONLY WAY TO PREVENT BAD SOUND

The only way to make certain you won't have a bad-sounding show is to bring your own sound engineer. Find an FOH whose mixes you love, get her rate, and treat her like a member of the band. If she's your only call, then book shows around her schedule. Pay her like you pay a freelance musician. Most going rates for one-off sound guys is $100 a night. It's worth the investment. Unfortunately, too many clubs around the country employ very terrible sound guys. So remove the variable, hire your own.

And, no matter how nice the sound guy is, the only thing that really matters is what his mixes sound like. So just because you love working with your church sound tech, he may not be that good. And he may not know how to mix any system other than the church board. You want someone versatile who can work with any system, digital or analog, in any venue. Someone who knows how to tune a room and can rewire the entire system if necessary. Because you will run into issues—especially while on tour.

So get out to shows around town and find someone whose mixes you love. Compliment her at the show on the mix, ask her if she freelances and get her number. A great sound technician is very hard to come by.

If you absolutely cannot find someone just by going to the local clubs, check on SoundBetter.com or AirGigs.com. Many live sound engineers have profiles on the service, and you can filter by location to find one in your town.

HOW TO PUT TOGETHER A LOCAL HEADLINING SHOW

When you're just getting started in your local market, most gigs won't be technically "headlining" or "opening" (no matter what number you are on the bill) because most local bands typically start off on a level playing field.

It may feel like once you are officially anointed as a "headliner" for a show (or tour) that you have made it. The worst thing you can do is act like a headliner and treat the openers as unworthy peasants.

If you're headlining in your local town (and actually headlining—not just playing last) it's your job (if the talent buyer, stage manager or FOH don't do this) to tell the opener(s) their set time/length and ask them to stick to it. You have earned rights to the best merch location, but definitely leave room for all other bands to set up their stuff as well. If you're running the night, you'll want to make sure that the openers know their load in/sound check times and know what the drink/food deal is. Don't expect them to know this info. Give them an allotted sound check time—to make sure everyone gets enough time to check. Be courteous of their time and don't run your sound check overtime either. If you're paying them a flat amount, come to the venue with your checkbook just in case the venue pays you in a check. Or ask them if they're cool being paid via Venmo or PayPal, and if the answer is yes, do it from your phone, right there. There's nothing worse than having to track down a check, especially from fellow musicians. If you're giving them a cut of the door, then make sure you get a rep from each band to settle up with the venue at the end of the night so there's no confusion on what was brought in and what was paid out.

You'll most likely be in charge of promo if it's "your" show, but it's totally acceptable to ask the openers to pull their weight in promo as well (especially if they are getting a cut of the door). However, if you're paying them a flat amount, you can't expect them to go all out with promo (because they have no financial interest in this show's success). So, it may be to your benefit to give them a cut of the door.

HOW TO HEADLINE ON TOUR

Now, if you're headlining on tour with local openers, it's a little different game. The promoter or venue that booked the local opener will most likely negotiate the deal with them. Confirm with the talent buyer (promoter or booker at venue) the opener's set times/length and make sure your pay is not affected by theirs. I always like to get the local opener's contact info and touch base with them a couple weeks in advance and get them excited for the show and help promote it. Remember, you'll most likely need some of the local opener's audience to fill the venue.

When you're at the club, make sure to introduce yourself to the local openers (sometimes they'll be huge fans and too nervous to come say hi). The short amount of time you have with them will leave a huge, lasting impression of what kind of person you are. They will either turn into life-long fans or vocal haters. Hang out with them in the green room. Get their story. Take a photo together, post it on Instagram and tag them. Do it in the green room and I guarantee they'll get all their friends to check out this photo on *your* Instagram account. Show some fun back-stage shenanigans.

And, above all, watch their set. It's totally reasonable to hang out on the side of the stage and not in the house, as most people in the house will want to talk with you (which takes them away from the opener's set—and you should preserve your voice if you're the singer), but watch at least a couple songs and compliment the local opener on their music. It means a lot more than you may think.

It's also a good idea to have your tour manager (or you if you don't have one) to go over the set times again (just to make sure everyone's on the same page and make sure they won't go over their time). I've had headliners in the past (when I've been the local opener) ask me before the show to not hang out by the merch table when the headliner is performing. If it's a small club, this will be very noticeable (and quite annoying) to the headliner if the opening band is taking photos and chatting with fans during your set (especially if it's a quiet singer/songwriter show). It's fine during set breaks, but once the show starts, the opener should go hide at least for a few songs. Be polite about this and feel it out. If it's a big club, this is probably not necessary to mention and the openers could take this the wrong way.

Every band believes that once they become a headliner they will always remain one. This isn't the case, no matter who you are. So, make sure you treat your openers with respect—they may be your headliner someday very soon.

HOW TO BE A GREAT OPENING ACT

Being the opener for a more established act can be one of the best ways to make new fans. I can pinpoint specific opening gigs where I gained a large number of fans who are still incredibly supportive to this day. I love opening slots for more established acts because I get to win over new audiences. I sometimes prefer playing in front of a room of people who've never seen me before rather than a room full of fans. Sometimes.

When you get an opening slot for a touring or established act, make sure you approach it right. *The number-one rule about opening is to play one minute less than your allocated time slot.* Meaning, if you get a 45-minute set, play 44 minutes, pack up your gear quickly and get off the stage. I don't care how good you think you are or how much the audience is loving you, never play long. And especially if it's a local show with four bands on the bill, it's just disrespectful to play longer than your time slot. This signals to the other bands that you think you're better than them and the audience prefers to hear you more than them.

You have to understand the purpose of being selected to open an established act's show. The main reason you are on the bill is to bring people out. Even established acts that can get a few hundred out still would like an additional fifty that you could bring as the opener. You're expected to pull your weight somewhat when asked to open. It also looks good to the headliner's fans if your fans are in the crowd singing along and enjoying themselves.

Sure, the promoter or venue chose you to open the show because you have a similar sound or vibe, but the reason touring acts ask for a local opener and don't bring one themselves is because they need the audience buffer with the local's draw. Local promoters have their ear to the ground; they are living in your city and they know the pulse of the scene. If you go all out and promote the show that they asked you to open, they'll see this and appreciate it tremendously (because it's unexpected) and they'll ask you to open more shows and give you more opportunities. They'll also be much more willing to help you if you need a venue in the future or a festival spot or something.

When I was just getting started in Minneapolis, I was asked to open a show for a UK star right when she blew up in the UK (but was virtually unknown in the States). The promoter told me point-blank that I needed to bring people because tickets weren't really selling. This promoter was the biggest promoter in Minneapolis and this was the first opportunity he gave me. I went all out. I printed up 200 posters (on my dime) and plastered downtown Minneapolis and the University of Minnesota campus (and near where the promoter's office was, of course). I made it sound like the biggest show of my career. I talked it up to everyone. I got about 60 people in there (that was really good for me at the time). The promoter was very happy, and you know what show I was asked to open next? The sold-out 800-person Joshua Radin show.

PLAYING LIVE FROM HOME

The pandemic really pushed livestreaming mainstream. When it was the only kind of performing artists could do, well, they did it. And many artists made very, very good money doing it. Often more than they made performing IRL concerts. It seems new livestreaming platforms are popping up every day. Some are free and open to all, like Twitch or YouTube Live, and some are ticketed, like Veeps or StageIt. And of course, there's Zoom for everything and anything. I'm going to get deep into how livestreaming works now and how you can be successful livestreaming from home in Chapter 11.

THE BRIDGE
8 Things You Don't Want to Forget to Do on Show Day

You should make sure to schedule your load-in as early as the venue is comfortable with. If you're a solo act, two hours before the doors open is sufficient. If you're a band, you'll want at least three hours.

Most musicians don't understand everything that needs to get done before the doors open. The obvious necessities of loading your gear in and setting it up is understood. Many bands don't fret over sound checks, with an "it'll be fine" attitude.

1) **Leave Enough Time for Sound Check** Fret over sound check! It's incredibly important. Sure, there will be shows with venues that are so put together that everything runs smoothly and sound check takes ten minutes or the engineer mixes you on the fly with no major issues, but you can't plan on that. Always plan for something to go wrong. Even if the equipment all works flawlessly, every room is different and responds differently to your sound. The room wasn't built for your band so you have to allow time to let the engineer feel out your sound in the room. You don't want the first three songs of your set to sound like butt, cluttered with feedback, because the engineer is attempt-

ing to mix you on the fly (giving the audience an unsettling opening feeling about you).

You want time to feel it out on stage and get comfortable with the space. I've played too many shows where a sound check wasn't possible or was cut too short and I hated performing because it felt awful on stage and I couldn't settle in to my performance and therefore put on a bad show. This can be overcome by setting aside enough time for the sound check.

And yes, of course, there are venues that just do line checks—especially in L.A. and NYC where they book bands every night on the hour. Nothing you can do about that! Bummer.

2) **Set Up the Merch** Once the sound check is finished, your night has just begun. Setting up your merch is the next step and almost equally important as getting a good sound check. If you aren't touring with a tour or merch manager, you should designate one band member who will be in charge of the merch for the entire tour. She should be responsible and decent at math. She'll need to count in and out the money and inventory every night, and she should also be friendly enough to train your merch seller (fan) for the night. And make sure your display is big, organized and in a prominent section of the venue near the door (or the place the venue has designated). You should bring lights for the merch display because many times venues will not have well-lit merch tables.

3) **Get a Merch Seller** You see touring bands post about this all the time: "Need someone to sell our merch tonight in Lincoln. Get into the show for free. DM us!" Until you're packing theaters, you most likely won't be able to afford to bring a merch manager on the road with you, but you *must* have a seller at the table before, during and after the show. Not having someone by the table while you're playing will cost you. If someone wants your T-shirt or record but has to leave early and glances at the merch table on his way out and there's no one there, he'll leave without buying anything. No one's going to go out of their way to try to pay you. And they definitely won't go online and buy it once they leave the venue.

4) **Park** Many venues will allow you to load in near the stage door but won't have a spot for you to park and will need you to move your car from the load-in door. This can be a huge hassle if there isn't a free, dedicated parking spot. I've had to spend up to thirty minutes finding parking and walking back to the venue. Be mindful of this and plan accordingly. And to make sure you avoid this hassle, always go over parking when you advance the show with the venue a week or two beforehand.

5) **Set Up the Room** This is typically overlooked by most artists. It's your night at the club and you want your fans to have a good show, so look out for them.

Many venues (and especially colleges) will be able to set up their room multiple ways. Sometimes the way a room is set up needs to be changed for your show. For instance, if you want people to dance, but the room is full of chairs, all it takes is asking your point person at the club if you can get rid of the chairs or shift them around to clear a dance floor.

Nearly every college I've played (over 100) I've had to rearrange the room to make sure people would be comfortable. No one knows your show experience better than you. Take initiative and work with your point people to rearrange the room to fit what's best for your show and your sound.

6) **Hand Off the Guest List** You then need to make sure the door guy has your guest list. Some venues require this list to be emailed well before the doors open. Make sure to go over this information when you advance the show.

7) **Settle Up** You should also find out who you are settling up with at the end of the night. Hopefully that person is the same person you advanced the show with. Before the show, go over the other agreed-upon details that are in your email confirmation and that you advanced: drink deal, food deal, lodging, door cut or guarantee, set length, curfew, etc. And *always* count the cash in front of the manager. It's not insulting, it's expected.

8) **Dinner** It may seem like musicians NEVER forget to eat, and most of the time you'd be right, but I can't tell you how many shows I did when I didn't actually schedule time to eat, got caught up in all the other show prep, and felt lightheaded by the end of my set because of my growling stomach.

7.

BOOKING AND PROMOTION

Some people believe that musicians live in this romantic,
fairy-tale world where only artistic integrity matters and trying to
make a buck where and when you can is "selling out." In reality,
these bands have to make a f%*&ing living and apply
some real business strategies to survive.

—ANDREW LEIB, ARTIST MANAGER

HOW TO BE A STAR IN YOUR HOMETOWN

As important as establishing yourself online is, everyone has a local community they come from. You don't compete in a NASCAR race before you've earned a driver's license; similarly you don't book a sixty-date tour before playing your hometown. I'm a strong believer in establishing yourself at home before you hit the road.

Supporting your local music community is the single most important thing you can do for your career. When you're not playing a show, you should be out seeing a show. If you're in a fairly big city, there should be various local shows happening around town nearly every night of the week. Get out to these shows and meet the community. You'll soon figure out which venues cater to your style of music and which don't. Start to frequent the clubs where you want to play. Get to know the staff and the patrons. The more you show your face, the more the regulars will warm up to you. Meet the other musicians and hang out at the after-parties. When you're establishing yourself in a scene, you need to be out in the world, often.

We hear all the time about artists who start to break online who have played only a few shows locally. These artists completely ignore their hometown and believe they are above it. They may see some initial success in other communities (or overseas) where local tastemakers have taken a liking to their music. Don't be like them. If you don't lay the groundwork, eventually people may lose interest and then you'll have no one to go back home to. You'll have no support group. No hometown following. No home.

Start local.

Your Scene

I want to make clear that the tactics I'm laying out to approach your local scene do not really apply to L.A. or Nashville. Or New York, to some extent. These towns operate completely differently (as described in Chapter 5) and the ways to approach them are different than most other cities. That being said, even if you do live in L.A., Nashville or New York, keep reading, as you will gain some perspective.

How to Crack the Local Gatekeepers

No digital message or phone call can replace the electrifying experience of a physical encounter.

Every scene has them. The bloggers, the playlisters, the radio DJs, the music editors, the local Instagram or TikTok stars, the club and festival bookers. Gatekeepers are an elusive group of somebodies who once were nobodies.

What they all have in common is that they love the culture of music. They're typically not musicians and have very little actual music (theory) knowledge. They know what they like and know what they hate. But becoming a local star requires that you crack this inner circle. At least somewhat.

■ **Hang Out with the Cool Kids**

This isn't a lesson middle school guidance counselors would ever reveal, but cool begets cool. Most gatekeepers respect other gatekeepers. The radio DJ will meet up with the music editor and grab drinks with the club booker. They are a tightly knit group who see each other at the buzz shows.

So, find out what those buzz shows are and go there. Find a mutual friend of a friend to introduce you to someone in that crowd.

The way you're going to work your way in is not by handing them a record or sending a cold email, it's by being welcomed in by a fellow insider.

■ **Follow Them on Twitter and Instagram**

You want a newspaper review? A blog review? A show at their venue? A song on their playlist? A song played on their local show? Step 1 is to get on their radar. You're not going to break this crowd in a day. Or a month. It takes time. You have to start somewhere. Follow all of the local music journalists, club and festival bookers and radio DJs, and learn. What shows are they frequenting? Who are they tweeting? Most likely it will be other gatekeepers. What is their personality?

Anyone is flattered when they are followed on Twitter and Instagram. After some time, start to interact with them. Favorite a tweet here and there. Like their photos. Comment occasionally. Reply to their Stories. Retweet them once in a while. Reply to tweets with something witty or brilliant.

Above all, don't creep. Following on Instagram and Twitter is totally acceptable. Friending on Facebook is not. You can search for mutual friends on Facebook or LinkedIn, though, and ask for an intro the next time you're all at a show together.

■ Show Some Love

You want something from them? Give something *to* them first. Read the reviews and comment (occasionally) on the articles. Most of the time they won't get any comments, but if they see your name giving insightful (or just praiseful) comments to their articles, they will remember you when you meet in person. But don't overdo it. Keep some level of mystique. Be flattering, not gushing. Share their playlist in your Story and tag them with a link. Duet or Stitch their TikToks. Use their Sounds in your videos.

■ Go to the Spots

After you've been following them online for a bit, you'll know where they hang out. Where they like to see live music. So go to those spots. And if you're trying to get a show booked at a venue, frequent it. Go hang out and be a pleasant presence in their club. Tip the bartenders. Buy the band's merch. Pay the cover price. Meet the door people and bartenders. If you get known as a positive energy in their club, they will be much more receptive when you eventually ask them for something (like a show or a review). Which brings me to my next point.

■ **Meet Them in Person**

Again, no digital message or phone call can replace the experience of a physical encounter. Even just a thirty-second interaction with a few jokes (or shots) will get you further than twenty beautifully crafted emails. So get out often. The way you're going to be a member of the scene is to get out into the scene. Physically.

■ **Don't Bad-Mouth Anyone**

The worst thing you can do is trash-talk. They may do it, but don't stoop to that level. If you get caught up in the negativity, you will eventually talk sh*t about the wrong person or band, which could turn *you* into the punch line of their next meetup. Rise above and be a positive presence in the scene.

■ **Ignore Them**

Or, you can disregard everything above and make killer music, draw big crowds and make them come to you. There's nothing they love more than befriending the hottest band of the moment.

Don't be sleazy about any of this. That's a quick way to ruin your reputation. If you can be a supportive, positive presence in the scene, then word will get around. They'll eventually want to meet you.

The Venues

Believe it or not, venue owners, talent buyers and bookers want you to succeed. The reason they are in the line of work they are is the same reason you are: love of music. If they didn't love live music, they wouldn't have it. It's too damn tough to run a music venue. Talent buyers (bookers), who many times are the owners of small venues, want to host great talent. But, more than that, they want a packed club of drinkers. A venue owner's best night is a packed club, record-setting bar sales, a lineup of acts she loves, a respectful audience and no major catastrophes.

Always look at booking a show as a partnership between you and the venue. It's never you versus them. If you have a great night, everyone wins. Put yourself in the venue owner's shoes. If she books too many shows where no one shows up, she will go out of business. You must remember this every time you're corresponding with venues. They are always on the defensive because they've been burned too many times. They assess the risk for every show they host.

If you convince a booker to give you a night at their club and no one shows up, they will never have you back. Everyone loses. So don't book a show until you have a promotional plan set out.

THE BOOK SHEETS: PICKING YOUR SPOTS

Open a Google Sheet, invite all your band members, your manager and anyone else on your team, and title it "Our Venues." This will be a living doc that can be updated by all members on your team. The best resource to find venues in your town is IndieOnTheMove.com's (IOTM) Music Venue Directory, which has some of the most complete lists of venues around the United States. You will see all venues within your selected location listed by capacity, genre and ages. When you select a venue, the week's upcoming shows will be listed (along with how to book the club with name, email and phone numbers of the booker). You should also use Songkick and Bandsintown apps to see the hot upcoming concerts in town.

On this spreadsheet, add all of the local venues that you want to play. Make 3 headings: This Year, Next Year, 3 Years. Like your 26-Year Marathon goals sheet, you are customizing a local venue goals doc. Make 9 columns: Venue/Festival, Website, Capacity, Ages, Booker Name, Email, Phone #, Bands, Notes. The first 7 columns can be filled out from the information provided by IOTM. If IOTM isn't in your country yet, you will have to do this the old-fashioned way. Look on the Venue's website and social platforms or call the place and ask for contact info. Under the Bands column list other local bands who have played the venue. Under Notes, list any thoughts you have about the club from when you've visited or played it, or what the word on the street is about it (like "Brad and Angela both book. Brad is friends with Alex from Roster McCabe. Angela is friends with George from This World Fair. The bouncer's name is Joe and his wife is Alicia from All Eyes). This information is important, for when you visit the club, you can ask Joe at the door how Alicia is, and if you go with your buddy George, ask him to introduce you to Angela. This is how you get to be known as a positive presence in the scene, make connections and get it done.

THE BOOK SHEETS: FINDING LOCAL BANDS

Make another shared spreadsheet and title it "Local Bands." Make 6 columns: Band, Members (include email and phone numbers), Website, Social Sites, Draw, Venues/Festivals, Notes. All the local acts you meet, see, play with and hear about, add to this list. Check out the Song-kick and Bandsintown upcoming show list for your city, note all of the bands and include every local band on this sheet. Of course the draw is an estimation and fluctuates, but if they headline a 400-cap club and sell it out, you can safely say their draw is 400, even if they had a couple openers. List all the venues and festivals they've played within the past year (or have upcoming on their calendar). Under the Notes section, keep it positive. Even if the drummer of the Future Antiques slept with your girlfriend, you don't need to list it or call him names (good luck to you if this doc ever gets out). Reiterate to your band members to keep the notes positive. You can invite other artists in town to help collaborate on your lists and really start to build up a community of dedicated artists like you.

EPKs and One Sheets

EPK stands for electronic press kit and it has evolved through many iterations over the years. It used to be a 3-to-5-minute promo video showcasing the artist and new album and was typically put on a VHS tape and mailed out. I still have John Mayer's *Room for Squares* EPK somewhere lying around. Obviously, this is not how it's done anymore. For a while, most in the industry were utilizing "one sheets," which were (clickable) PDF docs that had only pertinent information that the industry would need. Since everyone hates attachments, the PDF One Sheets were typically hosted on Dropbox or Drive and the link was included in the email.

But now that anyone can create a beautiful-looking website with no coding or graphic design experience on website building platforms like Bandzoogle and Squarespace, the EPK has moved to the website. It's typically a hidden page on the site not visible to the public, and the link is only sent out to industry people (talent buyers/promoters, press, labels, agents, etc.). If you're superfamous and don't want just anyone finding it, you can make it password-protected; just remember to include the password in the email!

THE BRIDGE
11 Things Your EPK Needs to Have

Make sure your EPK is in line with your branding. It should match your artist aesthetic and vibe.

1) **Bio** This is the promotional, short bio that you wrote in Chapter 4 with just your hook, accolades and newest project.

2) **Photo(s)** You want to display prominently your most recent promo photo, which will set the tone and vibe of the project. You can have other photos in a slideshow. They all need to be downloadable for print and web. JPEGs are best.

3) **Music** Embed a music player. Make sure it does not autostart. Don't include every song, just three to five of your best. If they want to hear more, they can click on your Discography or find you on Spotify.

4) **Tour History and Upcoming Shows** If you have an upcoming tour, list every date. If you don't have an upcoming tour, but have had a previous one with impressive venues, list it. If you've never toured, just list past venues you've played (if they're of note) and note the sold-out shows.

5) **Videos** Make sure you embed videos. You should have both live and music videos. But live is most important, so talent buyers can see what your live show will be.

6) **Social Links** You can just link all your socials at the bottom with icons.

7) **Discography** You can embed all album covers that link to Spotify or Bandcamp. Or you can embed square Bandcamp players (that look like album covers).

8) **Any and All Accolades** These can be impressive social or streaming stats, radio play, sync placements, chart rankings, award wins/nominations, TV appearances, tour or local show history with big shows that have sold out.

9) **Press Clippings** You can pull the best quotes from your recent press and link to the articles, or if you have a ton of great press, you can just put the images of the outlets (that link to the article).

10) **Assets** This includes high-res photos, logos, poster designs, your stage plot/input list, recent press release.

11) **Contact** Put all contact info for everyone on your team: manager, agent, label, publicist, licensing agent, lawyer, tour manager, everyone.

How to Book Local Shows

The best way to get in at a club is through another band, manager or agent. From your Book Sheets, pick out a few bands to put a show together with at a club they've played before. It's best to hit up the bands you have an established relationship with. That's why it's so important to meet them in the scene. *Never email a band and ask to open for them.* This signifies that you have no idea how it works. There are no real openers or headliners in your local community. Sure, there are the outliers who are very established and are headlining the biggest clubs in town, but you're not concerned with them. You want to approach the artists who regularly play the clubs you want to play. Once you have rehearsed your a$$ off, have a 45-minute set that is solid and undeniable, have played a myriad of free shows in town, and have a solid online presence (more on this in a minute), you are ready to start setting up real shows at clubs in town. So, start with your friends' bands. Talk to them about putting a show together. What this means is that you put a complete bill together (three or four acts) and take it to the booker at a venue. Know what the typical club deal is (your friends who have played it will let you know). Since you're organizing the show, you can hit up the club (unless another band on the bill has a strong connection). But this will give you a good opportunity to make the connection with the club. It's best if you've met the booker at their venue. And, if you've done your job right, you will have.

Email Pitch

Email the booker and put in the subject line: Dates—bands ("August 5, 6, 9, 15—The Alarmists, White Light Riot, This World Fair, Ari Herstand"). Lead with the band who is most established at the club. Since it's a local show and you're not routing a tour, you can give a date range or a few dates. First check to make sure the dates work with your lineup (and that they are open at the club). Keep your email short and to the point. Your email should not be more than eight sentences. You don't need to include your bio or all of your accolades. Just hit the booker with the important points: How many people you expect, a few promo tactics you're going to utilize and your previous show turnouts in the area.

Your initial email can read like this:

Subject: aug 5 , 6, 9, 15—the alarmists, white light riot, this world fair, ari herstand

Body: hey eric, great meeting you last week at the debut's show. i'm putting together a show with the alarmists, white light riot and this world fair (link them) and we're calling it The Unknown Order where we will draw names out of hat right before each set to see who will play. I brought 70 to my show june 12th at the whole, the alarmists just played the Rock the Park (last week to 500), wlr brought 200 to their fine line show in may, and this world fair just had 150 at their last varsity show with you. we expect to get 500 out for this show. we will be promoting with posters, handbills, a street team, facebook ads, heavy instagramming. andrea at 89.3 has agreed to help us push it and we're sending out press releases. bauhaus beer is down to help with promo through their networks if we can work out a beer special that night. looking at august 5, 6, 9 or 15th.

> let me know if we can lock in a date
> Alarmists EPK: http://alarmists.com/epk
> WLR EPK: http://whitelightriot.com/press-page
> TWF EPK: http://thisworldfair.com/epk
> Ari Herstand EPK: http://ariherstand.com/epk
>
> ~ari
>
> P.S.: who mixed the Luci show last week? it sounded incredible in there!

Boom. Eight sentences. Add in a flattering P.S. And remember to link to everyone's EPK (or at least yours if the others don't have one). And yes, you should use all lowercase letters. It's less formal and how most in the club booking world communicate. Use proper spelling and proper grammar, but all lowercase. All lowercase is more approachable, friendlier and signifies you're too busy to use caps.

If you haven't heard anything from the local booker after a week, your follow-up email can read:

> **Subject:** Re: aug 5, 6, 9, 15—the alarmists, white light riot, this world fair, ari herstand
>
> **Body:** hey eric, checking in to see if i can grab one of these dates for this Unknown Order show. we'll get 500 out for this. thanks!
>
> ~ari

Always reply from your initial email so the booker can just scroll down to see the details. For local shows you can definitely follow up every week. If you haven't gotten a response after the third email (or sooner depending on the timeline) pick up the phone and give a call. This seems so obvious, but so many musicians are deathly afraid of the phone and have gotten so accustomed to just interacting over email, text, Instagram and Facebook that they sometimes forget that phones actually function as spoken communication devices. And, believe it or not, some bookers still only book over the phone.

I've actually called a venue after four emails with no response and the phone call went like this:

"Warehouse."

"Hi, is Steve in?"

"Speaking."

"Hi, Steve, this is Ari Herstand, I'm looking to get into the Warehouse on June 10."

"Oh yeah, I think I got a couple emails from you about this. So what's the show? What's your history in the area?"

"I just played the college down the street for 300 students and want to follow this show up. I have a student street team ready to promote this show."

"OK, let me see, June 10. Yeah, it's open. OK, sounds good. Let's do it. $8 tickets? 7:00 doors, 18+. We do 70/30 split. Cool?"

"Yup, that works."

"OK, it's confirmed. Send me a promo photo and bio that we can get up on the website along with links."

Boom! Show booked at a venue I'd nearly given up on because of no email response.

THE BRIDGE
The Reason You Never Get an Email Response

We've all been there. You're attempting to manage your business, but one extremely necessary party isn't responding to your emails.

I know this can be awfully frustrating when you're contacting clubs for potential shows, music supervisors for placement, other musicians for favors, press for reviews, editors for playlist inclusion, or festivals for booking and no one is getting back to you. So what do you do?

Follow up. *The key to this industry is polite persistence.*

I've gotten nearly everyone to reply to my email through this method (even rock stars and big-time managers). If after three beautifully crafted emails they still haven't gotten back to you, don't get discouraged. They'll scan your email each time—if not just the subject line or sender field—and each time they'll make a mental note (always Reply from the original email so they can see the thread and the subject line says "Re:___"). If they see a seventh email from you with each one more polite than the last, they'll eventually write you back.

If people don't respond to your email, it isn't because they hate you. It isn't because your music sucks. It isn't because they found out you slept with their ex (well . . . maybe).

It's because they just don't have the time. Right. Now.

I know it's tough to say the same thing over and over again, but find a way to be just as kind each time with different wording. And above all, *Keep the emails short*. One of the reasons people don't respond is because they open your email and see it's a mininovel. No one has the time for that. And remember, keep your initial email under eight sentences. "But Ari, I just spent three weeks crafting the most poetic, perfectly worded essay explaining why there has never been a band more ideal than us to play this club." Don't care. Delete. Rewrite. Eight sentences! No more!

It's also about timing and luck. Some days they're putting out fires, and other times they're staring aimlessly at their computer screen when your email comes in and reply right away.

Also, to help curb your neuroses, install a mail-tracking plugin to see who has, in fact, opened your email (syncs with Gmail, Outlook and Apple Mail). You'll at least know if the other party was interested enough to even give it an open. If not, maybe you should update your subject line (but still reply from the original email with the "Re:__." But even if they do open it (as noted above), they may just not have the time to respond or deal with it. So, again, follow up.

Once you do get an email response, *you* should reply *right away*. Do *not* make them wait (like they made you wait). This is not a dating game via text. If they've finally taken the time to devote the mental and emotional effort it takes to fully concentrate on your issue in this moment, every passing minute from when they hit Send to when you reply, they will increasingly lose interest. And if you wait too long to reply to their response, you may have to play the follow-up game all over again.

On one occasion, I had been trying to get into a club (that will go unnamed) for months (years). One day I finally got a response. I *immediately* replied back, and then the booker immediately responded back to me. And we basically had about 20 back and forths within the span of 10 minutes. I was top of mind, so it was supereasy to just continue the conversation. Show booked, negotiated, locked down (with some jokes thrown in for good measure), in 10 minutes (+ 3 years).

WHAT DO YOU MEAN WE DON'T GET PAID?!

The Confirmation Email

Once you have a show confirmed, you should send one final email that includes all of the necessary details. This acts like a contract. Most venues with capacities under 600 don't typically work with contracts, especially when booking directly with the artist. Even if they do work with contracts, it takes way too long to send one over, have them sign it, send it back and confirm everything. Most venue bookers won't take the time to do this. Just send them an email that looks something like this (see below). Fill in all the information that you are certain of (what had been discussed in previous correspondences) and highlight the areas they need to fill in.

Note that your band's promo bio is included at the end.

Date:

City:

Venue:

Bill title:

Lineup:

Ages:

Cost:

Capacity:

Venue website:

Artist websites:

Advance tickets link:

On-sale date:

Guest list #:

Door time:

Set times/length:

Curfew:

Compensation:

Drink/food deal:

Number traveling in band/crew:

Load-in time:

Sound-check time:

Advance with: (name)

Phone: Email:

Venue day-of contact phone #:

Production contact #/email:

Artist day-of contact phone #:

Venue address:

Load-in directions:

Parking:

Other instructions:

Promo photos: (link)

Stage plot & tech rider: (link)

Promo bio:

PERFORMANCE DEALS: FROM THE WORST TO THE BEST

When you start booking shows locally and around the country (or world), you'll come to experience all of the various deals venues and promoters work out. From booking over 500 shows around the country myself over the past ten years, I've experienced virtually everything a small-to-mid-level artist deals with. Here are the worst to best deals currently being offered at clubs around the world.

The Worst

Pay to play.

What Is It?: Typically this happens with "promoters" who scour Instagram and Bandcamp, find naïve bands and promise them slots at well-known venues or festivals. All you, the band, have to do is sell 35 tickets (which you must purchase in advance). But hey, you get to keep $3 for every ticket you sell. What a deal! Except you have to buy the tickets for $12 and sell them for $15. If you do the math, you are making 20% of the cover from the people *just* there to see you—which is the sh*ttiest deal in the history of sh*tty deals. Or, I've also seen scenarios where you must buy 50 tickets up front for $10 a pop ($500) and then you get to keep 100% after you sell all 50 tickets at $10. So, if you sell 60 tickets, you walk with $100 (and the "promoter" walks with your $500 plus all of the other bands' $500 for the night—ouch). These "promoters" usually present about 5–15 bands on a night, who each play about a 20-minute set. And the bands almost never fit together musically. And many times they won't give you a set time and tell you that set times will be figured out the night of the show based on who sold the most tickets. So, of course, your fans must get there at 6 P.M. and may have to stay until 1:30 A.M., when your set time actually comes around. And these "promoters" don't actually do anything to promote except post the event flyer on their Instagram.

And more recently, especially in the hip-hop and hard core/metal scenes, there is a practice of flat-out charging bands to open for established acts. Like, "Venmo me $1,000 and you can open for Wiz Khalifa for 15 minutes." Besides this being slimy AF, it's been well reported that often these are complete scams, and when you show up, the venue staff will have no idea this went down and you will not be on the bill (and the "promoter" has completely disappeared). Mötley Crue once charged a band $1 million to open their tour and, according to a lawsuit filed by the band, not only was the band forced to play *before* doors opened; they were terrorized and abused by the crew the entire tour. Pass! (Btw I don't know how the lawsuit turned out, but you are forewarned that if you pay to play, prepare for the worst.) **Is This Fair?:** No! How these "promoters" get away with this is by preying on young bands who don't know any better (now you do!) and will do anything to just play the venue or festival, including paying lots and lots of money for this. As tempted as I am to name the names of these promoters who do this (and boy would I like to), I will not and hope that enough of you band together and collectively tell these promoters to politely go f*&k themselves when they contact you (as I have many, many, many times).

Fun story: My final year in Minneapolis, one of these promoters kept hounding me to play a club I had actually headlined many times. I told them that I typically get 500-plus people to my headlining shows and I'm not interested in their offensive deal (as I had a very good relationship with the club already). They responded explaining how much money I could make with their horrendous deal if I brought 500 people (duh). I responded by telling them no thanks and to please not contact me again. I was then hit up by the same "person" with the same form email multiple times. Each time my responses got more and more annoyed, until finally I contacted the owner of the club and told him what was happening and how it was giving the club a bad name and that they should stop working with this promoter. The owner canceled the promoter's upcoming show and hasn't worked with them since. *Boom!* More bands need to do this in more cities.

LESSON LEARNED: Don't pay to play cool venues or festivals or to open for big artists. You will be paid (a fair amount) to play these cool venues when you are ready and can draw a substantial crowd.

Bad

Venues charge a "rental fee."

What Is It?: Music venues that also host private events like weddings got smart to the fact that they were making a boatload more money when they got wedding parties to rent out the venue than if they book a night of music. So, these venues figured, "why not ask bands to pay nearly the same amount to book a night in our beautiful venue?" They'll make you rent the place for, say, $1,500. You can charge whatever cover you like and will make 100% of it (if you're lucky). You are essentially acting as the promoter. Oh, you play music too? Eh.

Is It Fair?: Well, it's not ideal. The venue is basically completely covering their a$$ and will make out on this deal regardless of whether you bring anyone. The venue is basically admitting they have zero faith in your draw and they are doing *you* a huge favor in letting you play their club (for an exorbitant fee).

LESSON LEARNED: I would say pass on this deal typically. Play a different club that gives you a fair and standard deal. Or, crunch the numbers, and if you think you will bring enough people to make this deal worthwhile, then go nuts. It helps to fill a promoter's shoes once in a while.

Sneaky

Venues only pay you after a certain number of people come to see you.

What Is It?: I've only really seen this kind of deal in Los Angeles and New York (some other cities are catching on though). Basically, the door guy has a tally sheet with each band's name on it. The venue works out a separate (standard) deal with each band. Typically, you get paid *only* if a certain number of people (I've seen 15–75) pay to see you (and not the others on the bill). You then get a cut of the door after the minimum number of people come. Meaning if the minimum is 35 people at $10 a head and you bring 33, you walk with $0 (and the venue takes your $330—and all the drinks your fans buy). However, if you bring 35 (and your deal is 70%) you walk with $245. However, I've also seen requiring a minimum number of people and only getting paid a cut after that minimum show up. So if your minimum is 35 and 36 people show up at $10 a head, you walk with $7 (if your deal is 70%). If you bring 35 you get $0.

Is It Fair?: Kind of, but not really. On the surface it looks like they are just covering expenses, but if they have 5 bands on the bill and each one is required to bring 35 people at $10, the venue is getting way more than just the amount to cover expenses. If every band brings 30 people, the venue makes $1,500 (30 people × $10 × 5 bands) and each band makes $0. Yikes!

LESSON LEARNED: I don't like these deals because it encourages competition among the acts and not a "we're all in it together" approach, which I stand by. You have zero incentive to work with the other bands on the bill to make it a great night—encouraging fans to stay from beginning to end. Because of this, bands in L.A. and New York don't get to know each other that well and typically show up right before their set and leave shortly after. "Hit it and quit it." Which rubs off on the fans too. It's very unique to see fans in either city come for a full night of music (because of this practice). Venues don't realize that if they stopped working their deals this way and started encouraging complete bills and promoting the entire evening of music, they would get more people in their club for a longer period of time (i.e., more drink sales). But hey, I don't run the clubs.

Standard

Venue takes expenses off the top.

What Is It?: A venue will take an amount off the top to cover expenses before they split the door with the organizer of the show (the headliner—you). The standard is about $50–$350 depending on the size of the club. A club that takes more than $350 for an under-300 capacity room is screwing you. And this isn't $50–$350 off the top per band. It's $50–$350 off the top of the total, and the rest is split with the organizer of the show, who then pays out everyone else on the bill.

Standard door splits after expenses:

70%–100% cut (in your favor) for 21+

70%–85% cut (in your favor) for 18+

50%–70% cut (in your favor) for all ages

Is It Fair?: Sure. They wouldn't need to hire a sound guy or a door gal if you weren't playing that night. This money (typically) does directly go to those people and then the venue splits the remaining money with you fairly. But, just remember, they are making bar sales, from which you don't get a cut. So if they take more off the top, you should negotiate for a higher cut after expenses or a good guarantee. The reason the split is lower for all ages vs. 18+ nights is because venues typically need to hire more security for all-ages shows and enforce an earlier curfew (less drinking time for the drinkers).

Good

Door split from dollar one.

What Is It?: Many venues are happy to have you and will split the door with you from the first person who pays a cover. This is ideal.

If 10 people come at $10 a head and you have a 70/30 split with the venue, you walk with $70.

Is It Fair?: Absolutely. I see this deal occasionally, but most will at least take $50 off the top for the sound guy.

Great

Guarantee vs. % of door (whichever is greater)

What Is It?: Talent buyers will do this to get you to play their club (and not the many other options in their city). Because of your proven history, they feel confident that with the amount of promo that they will do, they will be able to get enough people out to your show to make it financially worthwhile for them.

Example: $1,000 or 80% of the cover—whichever is greater. So if 500 people come at $10 a head, you walk with $4,000 ($10 × 500 × 80%). If 50 people come at $10 a head, you still walk with $1,000 (the guarantee). *But, if this actually does happen, give some money back to the club/promoter.* You don't want your low turnout to get them to default on rent that month. They'll never forget you did this and will absolutely have you back.

Most of the time only promoters offer these kinds of deals. They then work extremely hard to promote your show. They have serious skin in the game now.

Is It Fair?: Absolutely. You earned this!

There's a fine line between what is acceptable, ethical, smart business, and career advancing.

Look at it from the venue's standpoint: They are taking a risk every time they open their doors for a show. If no one shows up, then they do lose money (door guy, sound guy, bartender, electricity, heat, AC, on and on). If they are strictly a music venue and don't open unless they have a show, then they really are losing money the moment they open the doors, until people (ideally drinkers) enter their club.

The biggest misconception bands have about venues is that the venue is supposed to promote their show and bring people to the club. Venues think bands should promote the show and bring people to the club. In the end, neither end up promoting the show and no one shows up.

The reason all the clubs in L.A. and New York can create such horrible deals for the bands (and fantastic for the club) is because there are so many bands willing to take these unfavorable deals. If one band refuses, there are ten more waiting in line that will take the deal. Venues in smaller cities tend to create better deals to lure in the good bands who will bring a crowd. They realize that if they offer insulting deals and enough bands pass on the deals, there will be no bands left to play their club and they'll go out of business.

The most important thing to remember is: *Don't play a big venue if you can't fill it.* Take shows at smaller clubs and fill them. Open for bigger bands at bigger venues to build your crowd. Keep selling out the small clubs and eventually you'll be able to move up to the big clubs with enough clout to get a fair deal.

WHAT ARE PROMOTERS?—AND HOW TO GET OPENING SLOTS FOR TOURING ACTS

Most cities have local promoters. Promoters are booking agents' go-to people in town. These promoters are not to be confused with the pay-to-play, shady ones who prey on local bands—like the "Worst" deal from a few pages ago. The legitimate, local promoters know all of the venues and have great relationships with all of the talent buyers at each venue. When agents book tours for their artists, they rarely go directly to the venue; they typically work with a local promoter in town to set up the show. The promoter will typically rent out the venue or work with the venue to put together a favorable deal. Much of the risk and responsibility falls on the promoter. But, if the show is a success, the promoter has a lot to gain. Venues like working with promoters because they are proven and trusted. There is very little risk to a venue when they work with a promoter.

As I said earlier about my experience working with a local promoter to open for the UK star, promoters also know the local talent. Many times national booking agents will ask the promoter to find local support (opener). There is one and only one reason for this: crowd buffer. If all they wanted was a great opener, they would bring one with them on tour. Promoters will build up relationships with local artists and know how hard each artist works on show promo, what kind of crowd they draw and what kind of music they play. A promoter will not put a local metal band on to open for a touring singer/songwriter. The lineup still has to make sense.

The promoter is typically in charge of ticket sales and will know if tickets aren't selling as they should. The promoter will find local acts who can help promote the show and increase ticket sales. Typically, promoters will pay the local opener a set guarantee (like $100). *Don't value these shows based on the amount you receive in a guarantee, but rather the fans you will gain and the merch you will sell.* This show can be a 30 on the Perfect 30 Scale (even with a low guarantee) if you do it right and sell lots of merch.

And when you get an opening slot for a touring act, this is your moment to shine. Make sure you bring your A game. This is a chance for you to win over a ton of new fans. Push your mailing list and merch. Have volunteers at the door handing out flyers for your band as people leave.

And maybe, just maybe, if the headliner happens to check out your set and likes what they see, they may invite you to open future tours.

THE BRIDGE

The Troubadour Said This Was the Best Booking Email Ever

After being in the music scene in a city long enough, you get to know everyone. L.A. is no different. I had become friendly with the talent buyer at the Troubadour. She would put me on the list for shows I wanted to see and usually hooked up a few drinks. (Thanks, Amy!) But even being friends with the booker, it didn't change how I went about helping a friend book a show.

Only later did she tell me that a pitch email I sent to her was the best booking email she had ever received. So, in all its (underwhelming) glory, here is the email I wrote to the Troubadour talent buyer pitching a friend for an opening slot. Disclaimer: The artist did not have an electronic press kit (EPK) or one sheet, hence why I included links directly in the email. And for club booking, they don't need the fluff. Just the facts, ma'am!

Subject: annabel lee x marian hill may 15

hey amy! did you catch annabel lee at school night monday? didn't see you there. she really brought it hard. and it was completely packed—couldn't move in there. ask sharyn about it :)

does marian hill have an opener may 15th? i think annabel would be great and she's a big fan of theirs.

annabel's L.A. history:
School Night: 250 RSVPs to her personal list
200 at satellite
150 tix hotel cafe

School Night full band performance: https://youtu.be/4o66OI-I7Rg
Solo: https://youtu.be/8IspVBOU24A
Spotify: https://open.spotify.com/artist/05uHL3asnUSGm2jQJIggJl?si=XDGj4IPiRne_zH_1A037Hw
Instagram: https://www.instagram.com/yourannabellee/

thanks!

THE BRIDGE
11 Things to Do Once You Book the Show

1) **Create Smart Links** Once you have the ticket link and Facebook event links, create trackable links so you can see how your promo efforts are going. There are many trackable link services out there, like Bitly, Short.io, Ow.ly, TinyURL, and Rebrandly.

2) **Add the Show to Your Tour Calendar** You can embed a Bandsintown or Songkick calendar to your website. Even if you don't, you need to add your shows to these sites. Bandsintown and Songkick have each built up communities of active users, over 75 million users collectively, who use the apps to track artists and get notified when they come to town (via push notifications and customized emails). If you're routing a tour, you can schedule the shows to go public at a certain time. Triple-check the ticket link and don't publish the show until you have the ticket link included (because if fans get a notification about your show and click through but find no link to the tickets, they won't be able to buy and may forget about the show). Songkick and Bandsintown have partnered with many digital platforms like Spotify and Shazam. If you're wondering why your concerts aren't being listed on various platforms online, it's most likely because they aren't on Songkick or Bandsintown.

3) **Create a Facebook Event** Bandsintown can actually autocreate Facebook Events for every date, but you'll want to double check that all of the info is correct, with the proper banners, links and info. Having a Facebook Event for every show is crucial for building buzz, gaining interest and making contact with the local market. Facebook now also allows you to sell tickets directly within Events. Make sure you work this out with the venue, though, so as to not confuse your audience.

4) **Create a Show/Tour Poster** Hire a graphic design artist to create something truly eye-catching and interesting that represents your image and vibe.

5) **Create Videos** You're going to want to make multiple videos for all platforms that you can regularly roll out to promote the show/tour.

6) **Print Up Physical Posters** I know, I know. Who prints physical posters anymore?! Exactly. If you get some posters around town (with QR codes), you will stand out because ain't no one doing this anymore. I've found that Vistaprint has the cheapest and highest-quality options.

7) **Send Posters to the Venue** Bandposters will print, label and ship five very-high-quality, full-color (no-bleed) posters to each venue for $15 a pop. Totally worth saving the time, Sharpies and hand cramps.

8) **Send an Email and Text Blast** Include the ticket link and show promo video.

9) **Write a Press Release** See Chapter 15.

10) **Restock Your Merch**

11) **Split Up Promotional Duties** Work with the other bands on the bill to figure out a cohesive promo plan and delegate jobs to your other bandmates and street team members.

HOW TO DOUBLE YOUR INCOME

When you're on tour, merch can be your number-one income generator. Believe it. Bands stress over their guarantees, door splits and turnouts. If you want to survive financially with your music, you must understand the importance of merch sales. I've played shows where 10 people showed up, but they had such an amazing time and I so stressed the merch to them that all 10 people bought something averaging about $15. That's good for any night.

The tour merch tracking platform atVenu has calculated that for 500–1,000-cap venues, the average dollar per head (DPH) is $3.65. Meaning, if 200 people show up, you can estimate to make $730 in merch. However, this doesn't just happen because you offer merch. The dollar-per-head number will fluctuate based on how well you sell your merch, how attractive your merch items are to your audience, how attractive the merch display is and how good your sellers are. Ingrid Michaelson's manager, Lynn Grossman, stated that they have "become much smarter" about what merch items Ingrid's fans like. She stated that by adding vinyl they increased their dollar per head quite a bit. Her fans also buy songbooks for piano and ukulele—which obviously may not do as well for a hard rock project. Ingrid's dollar per head fluctuates just as much as that of the next act, and Lynn stated that their range has been as low as $2/head all the way up to $8/head. Even though Ingrid is playing to an average of 2,000–5,000 people a night now, she still goes and checks her merch display every night to make sure it is set up just right.

Vulfpeck's online merch operation is incredibly strong with their vinyl preorders, holiday drops, custom fonts, audio plugins, bobble-heads, and signature bass models. But live, it's gotten even better. When they headlined the Greek Theatre in L.A. in 2019, they hit an astounding $7.37 dollar per head in sales.

AVERAGE DOLLAR PER HEAD PER GENRE

GENRE	AVERAGE	MAX
SINGER/SONGWRITER	3.52	7.35
INDUSTRIAL	6.23	8
JAZZ	3.15	6.66
GOSPEL & RELIGIOUS	4.18	10.87
HEAVY METAL	3.08	6.67
METAL	4.75	7.28
REGGAE	3.95	6.49
SPOKEN WORD	4.46	5.85
CHRISTIAN & GOSPEL	3.51	13.1
COUNTRY	3.18	16.25
HIP-HOP/RAP	3.59	10.76
BLUES	3.17	7.01
INDIE ROCK	2.13	4.34
HARD ROCK	7.16	9.53
PUNK	4.38	5.63
ROCK	3.77	19.32
ALTERNATIVE	4.08	44.81
WORLD	5.33	10.08
FOLK	4.58	7.57
POP	4.47	17.34
R&B	4.28	7.74
ELECTRONIC/DANCE	2.25	7.79

(atVenu 2015)

The Display

You should have an impressive merch display. It needs to be big, attractive, professional and well lit. For all intents and purposes you are traveling salespeople. So make your displays as appealing as possible. If your display consists of CDs tossed in a dimly lit corner of the room, you aren't going to sell anything. Bands complain that their fans don't buy merch. Bull. Every fan buys merch. If you sell it right, they'll buy.

The Pitch

Musicians are traditionally horrible businesspeople and that's why managers exist. Most musicians hate having to "sell" to their fans. The most charismatic front person who can captivate every single person in the room while singing can be the most introverted, bland, unimpressive and embarrassing salesperson when having to talk about the merch.

You have to get over this. Getting your merch pitch down is almost as important as getting your live performance down.

Depending on how attentive your audience is, you may need to stress the merch a few times during a show. But don't overdo it. There are classy ways to do it and annoying ways to do it. This takes practice and feeling out the audience.

Combos

Make combo options. For example, "Records are $25, T-shirts are $30, but if you get both, it's $50," and then not only announce this but emphasize it. I spend about forty-five seconds every show to explain what I have for sale. You may say this is a vibe killer and stops the flow, but on the contrary you can make it a part of your show. My stage banter is a big part of my show, so I incorporate it into my banter and turn it into a joke. For one tour (back when CDs were a hot seller), I titled the 3-CDs-for-$25 combo my "Midwest Combo" because, I say, "I'm born and raised in the Midwest and we love bargains there, so I like to pass along the Midwest bargain wherever I go." People came up to me after the show and, with a smile on their face, handed me their credit card and said "give me the Midwest bargain."

Take Credit and Digital Payment

Just having merch isn't enough. If you're cash only, your sales will suffer. For one, who carries cash anymore?! Take every possible payment method available: credit, Venmo, CashApp, PayPal, whatever. It's not hard to set these up and most platforms are free. Credit card readers are free with low transaction fees these days. Print out big signs with the digital payment QR codes and credit card logos on them so people can scan it from far back in line. Maybe even have a separate line just for digital payments.

The Merch Seller

Bringing a merch person on the road with you is best, but expensive, and you probably won't be able to afford that for a while. Not having someone sell your merch, though, is not an option unless you play very short sets and are certain people will stay for the entire show and you can run over and man the table yourself after you finish playing. But most likely, not everyone will stay the entire time, especially if there are multiple bands on the bill or you're playing a late-night, four-hour bar gig.

Bands think that if they didn't sell any merch it was because people didn't want to buy it. But what if they *really* wanted to buy something but they had to leave at 11:00 because they have to wake up at 6:00 and you didn't take the stage until 10:30 (when you advertised 9:00) and you are playing a 90-minute set. They glance at the table on the way out, but no one is there to sell them something so they leave.

You will double your sales by having someone at your merch table during your set. Find a couple fans in each city to help you with this for free admission.

If you push your merch from the stage, take digital payment, and have a merch seller at your table, you will absolutely increase your yearly income. Doubling your sales by taking digital payment and doubling them again by having a seller at the table during your set can take your yearly income from $10,000 to $40,000. And now you're a full-time musician.

Your pitch for them to buy your stuff starts with a killer performance and ends with you standing by their side after the show with a Sharpie out ready to sign your record.

Keep It Organized

I once toured with a band who put a lot of money into creating a lot of merch. They played after me, so after I finished my set, I hung out by the merch table during their set. People came over to me wanting to buy the other band's T-shirt. However, all of their shirts were tossed with no rhyme nor reason into several bins. I put in solid effort sifting through hundreds of shirts attempting to find the correct design in the right size, but eventually, with a line piling up, I had to give up and apologize that they either didn't have the size or I just couldn't find it. I told them to come back when the band finished and they could spend more time searching. Sometimes they'd ask if I had their size in one of my designs. Eight seconds later I pulled out their size, swiped their card and just made $20 for being organized.

A good way to keep your shirts organized is to roll them up, put a strip of painter's tape around the rolled shirt and write on the tape the size.

Place the shirts in a long, clear bin from Target with the sizes ranging from XS to 3XL left to right. If you carry women's shirts (I recommend it), put the women's shirts in one bin and unisex shirts in another. Label the women's shirts "WS" for women's small and the unisex shirts just label "S."

Sell Quality

Merch is an incredible money-maker and should be looked to as such, but it's also a promotional tool. You want to sell fans shirts that they'll actually wear with your band name displayed on them to promote you to their friends. It's a conversation starter. I've gotten tweets from people saying they met new friends from wearing an Ari Herstand T—and someone actually got a first date out of it once! True story.

Order brands that are comfortable and hip. You're not just selling a design; you're selling a feel and the vibe. If people get your shirt and after one wash it gets deformed and becomes uncomfortable to wear, they'll associate your band with that discomfort.

Offer Creative Options

Use your creative talents to offer items that are unique to you. Are you a painter or photographer? Sell your artwork. Are you a calligrapher? Sell lyric sheets handwritten by you. Can you screen-print? The more unique the merch item, the more it will sell (and be talked about). Nikki Lane is a visual artist (in addition to being a musician). She visits thrift shops and rummage sales while on tour and creates art pieces and customized merch items from her travels. Visiting her merch table is an experience in and of itself. I've seen artists sell paintings, framed photographs, coasters, jewelry and everything else you can imagine.

Make a shared doc with your band and keep a living list of creative merch items you can offer.

Have the Right Sizes

Make sure you never run out of a T-shirt size. Keep good inventory and reorder when you're running low. If someone wants to buy a shirt, but you don't have their size, they will leave without buying anything. They aren't going online when they get home to order it from your online store. The energy is at the show, while you're at the table so you can sign the shirt.

Stand by the Table After the Show

Until you're headlining gigantic theaters, you should be back by the merch table after the show meeting your fans, getting mailing list sign-ups and signing merch. Fans will remember their twenty-second interaction with you by the merch table for the rest of their lives. If people see you are there signing merch, they'll want to buy something you can sign. And if they meet you, they'll become lifelong fans.

GOING RATES FOR TOURING BANDS PLAYING UNDER-500-CAP ROOMS

T-shirt (Bella+Canvas or equivalent) = $30

CD/Coaster = $20

Vinyl Record = $30

Large Screen Print Poster = $15–$25 (depending on size, quantity, limited edition, etc.)

Standard Tour Poster (11" × 17") = $10

Sticker = free with mailing list sign-up

Hoodie = $40

USB sticks (with album(s), artwork, videos, extra goodies) = $15

If you're selling these, make sure you have a large, clear display of all that is included:

INCLUDED

- Both of our albums (22 songs)
- Full liner notes and artwork
- 2 music videos
- Exclusive studio documentary (not on YouTube!)
- Super, special, hidden, secret goodies

Combos:

T-shirt + Vinyl = $50

CD + T-shirt = $40

THE BRIDGE
10 Steps to Sell Out Your Show

1) **Spread Out Your Shows** Even if your favorite band played in your city every week, you wouldn't go to every show. What makes you think your friends and passive fans will want to come see you every other weekend at various bars around town? They'll just think, "Eh, I'll catch the next one. They play all the damn time!" So don't play all the damn time. I recommend setting up a big show every 6-12 weeks locally and 4-6 months nationally.

2) **Get a Street Team** The greater number of people who work on the show, the greater number that will be invested in its overall success. I used to get a street team of 10-20 people for all my big local shows to hit the town at night, in smaller teams, with staple guns, tape, black winter caps and secret code words. I called my team "The Street Stand" (play off of Herstand) and I sometimes provided pizza or took them out to hot chocolate after a cold Minnesota postering evening, but they always got into the show for free and were, of course, invited

to the after party. In addition to the postering evenings, I gave them flyers to hand out at their work, on campus, at the bars, and some nights we had Facebooking parties where we all promoted the show video and Event on all our friends' walls.

3) **Show Videos** Create multiple creative videos that you can regularly roll out for all the social platforms. The more fun and creative the better. Work with the other acts on the bill and make as many of these videos together as you can. It's always fun to see more than one artist in a video. And don't forget to include the link to buy tickets.

4) **Shows Sell—Events Sell Out** Make each show unique. Why people will come out to this show versus a random four-band-bill Wednesday night show is because this is an *event*. Giving the show a title automatically turns it into a talked-about event. "Are you going to the Unknown Order show?" Versus "Ari is playing Room 5 on Thursday. Want to go?"

5) **Create a Show Poster** Get a graphic design artist to create a special poster for this one show (with the show title, of course). You can find a designer on 99designs, Guru or Fiverr if you don't have any in your local community who are great. Depending on your budget, you can screen-print a limited number and get all the bands to sign a few. Then either sell them or get ticket holders to win them. This show poster should be used everywhere: Bonus points if you do a photo shoot with all the bands on the bill for this event and roll these photos out along with your videos for weeks leading up to the show. The more people who see the poster image, the more they will talk about it and the more likely they will actually attend the event.

6) **Sell Tickets in Advance** Always try to sell tickets in advance whenever possible. Getting people to purchase tickets in advance ensures they will actually come. It also gets them to encourage their friends to buy tickets so they can all go together. Having advance tickets also legitimizes the show and makes people feel more comfortable coming out.

7) **Run Contests** As you ran contests for your release, run various contests for promo efforts and advance ticket purchases. For one show, I gave advance ticket holders goodie bags containing a poster, stickers and other random fun knickknacks from each band. It might be good to give out the bags after the show, though, as people are leaving—biggest complaint was that they had to hold on to the bag the entire night. Also, run contests on your socials to encourage people to share the show video, poster and ticket link. Maybe run a contest on TikTok where you encourage your audience to Stitch you, explaining the first time they discovered your music. "Everyone who does this will be thrown into a drawing to win a T-shirt and poster at the show. Must be present to win." Then onstage at the show, announce the winner.

8) **Include Other Buzzing Bands** Maybe you got 50 people out to your last show, the Alarmists got 80 to their last show, White Light Riot got 70 and This World Fair got 40. If there's no overlap, that's 240 that will most likely get out to this show (because it's an event). Those in the local music scene will also love to see four buzzing bands on one bill together. Get together bands who are good and buzzing. If they aren't buzzing yet, well, get bands who are hardworking and who will work just as hard as you on promo. Don't bring on a band unless they are willing to follow the promo necessities.

9) **Contact Local Media** Because this show is now an event, you have the ammunition to get the local media's attention. If none of the bands could get more than just a mention in your local newspaper, bringing them together for this talked-about event will get the paper to write about it. More on this in Chapter 15.

10) **Get a Sponsor** Find a local company (like beer, wine or gear), brand, newspaper or radio station that will get behind the event. This is a partnership for the evening. What the sponsor gets is being associated with a hot event and getting included in all promo, and in return, what you get can be anything from airtime, ad space in the newspaper, a write-up on their (high-traffic) website with many social posts, alcohol, cash, printing and so on. The best show-specific partnerships deal in trades, not cash. We got a wine company to sponsor the Unknown Order show and they printed all of the full-color posters (some 400 to be put up around the city), donated a case of wine per band (which was nearly finished during the show—glad I didn't perform last!), an ad in the weekly variety newspaper, some air time and other promo. This show sold out 10 minutes after the doors opened, with 200 people turned away. We'll dig into how to approach sponsorships in Chapter 10.

THE BRIDGE
9 Things to Consider When Choosing a Venue

1) **Capacity** Every booker wants to know what your draw is. Locally, once you're experienced and have a name around town, when you book your big shows every 6–12 weeks, you'll have a pretty good idea of the number of people you can bring consistently.

   When you can, always book a venue slightly smaller than your draw. Meaning, if you can draw 500, book a 450-cap room. If you can draw 50, look for 45-cap rooms. It's better to sell out a 200-cap room than play a 500-cap venue and have it two-thirds empty. Sure, it's cool to put well-known venues on your tour calendar, but it's better for your overall career to pack people in and give the best possible show to a full house, regardless of the size. Those who get in will be buzzing with excitement that they can experience an exclusive (to ticket holders) event and those who get turned away will know that, your next time through, they'll need to get tickets quickly.

2) **Ages** If your target demographic is 12–19, you don't want to play 21+ rooms. If you're a bar band and need a bottle of Jack on stage with you at every show, you don't want to book the all-ages (dry) teen center. I try to book all ages or 18+ shows whenever possible. I remember what it was like before I was 21 and couldn't get into clubs to see my favorite bands.

3) **Reputation** You should use Indie on the Move in the US, the Unsigned Guide in the UK, TripAdvisor and Yelp when doing venue research. Indie on the Move has band reviews for most venues (and full contact, capacity info). The Unsigned Guide has festival, venue and promoter contact info. Yelp and TripAdvisor have mostly customer reviews. You can get a great sense of the venue by reading reviews. If the customers don't like the place, then you're going to have that much harder a time getting people out. If the bands have a horrible time there, then you're most likely not going to have a good show. Choose a venue that's generally liked by both the patrons and the bands.

4) **Vibe** Metal bands shouldn't play coffee shops and singer/songwriters probably don't want to play S&M clubs. Every venue has a vibe, and you have to figure out which kinds of clubs will help provide the most enjoyable experience for your fans.

5) **Payment** There are venues out there (typically run by musicians) that make sure their deals are fair and favorable to their guests (musicians). Some venues (typically run by d**ks) try to screw the musician out of any possible money and all but turn each band member upside down at the end of the night and furiously shake them down for loose change. Remember, nearly every deal (outside of L.A. and NYC) is negotiable.

6) **Promo** Most venues will not do anything to promote your show except display a few posters (that you provide) inside their establishment and list you on the website concert calendar. However, some venues take out ads in the entertainment weekly newspaper. Some venues have street teams distributing flyers for upcoming shows. Some venues exclusively work with promoters that handle this (and you'll then have to book your show with the promoter). It's good to know going into the show what promo the venue does and what promo you're expected to do as the band. Some venues have marketing departments that will poster the town, run Facebook ads and get press, but most don't and will expect you to do virtually all the promo. However, some may give you a little budget to run ads or work other promo efforts. It can't hurt to ask!

7) **Advance Tickets** Most venues have a way to set up advance tickets, if it's not done by default. But some venues are stuck in the dark ages and, oddly, do not. Check the calendar on the website to make sure that they actually sell advance tix and get them set up for your show. It's best if you can control the ticketing directly so you can get everyone's email who purchased a ticket (and can track how well your ads actually convert). Most venues are locked into ticketing deals and don't allow this, but if you can sell tickets on your website, that can be tremendously helpful for data. But, do not pay to play. You should not be on the hook for unsold tickets.

8) **Sound** The sound engineer is the most important person for your show. Try to book venues that have a good reputation for sound—or bring your own FOH.

9) **Perks** One of the perks of working with a promoter (instead of the club) is that they will typically fulfill riders (veggie tray, tub of beer, bottle of Jameson, don't ask to remove the brown M&Ms though). They'll also provide parking for your bus, van, car and sometimes lodging. But you have to ask.

Venues rarely provide any of this when booking directly with bands. But some will. Most venues will have a green room, but not all. If you need a space to clear your head, dip away from the crowd, warm up, rub ice on your nipples or whatever weird preshow routine you do hidden from the audience, you're going to want to make sure the club has a green room. So ask.

The venue is a direct reflection on your band. Your fans will associate your band with the venue they saw you in—for better or worse. So don't pick the wrong one.

WEDDINGS, CORPORATE PARTIES, PROPOSALS, BAR/BAT MITZVAHS AND THE WEIRD, WILD, PROFITABLE WORLD OF PRIVATE SHOWS

How to Get the Best Deal for the Gig

Around the holidays, musicians are especially in high demand. Playing holiday parties is an entire business in itself. Learn a handful of holiday songs and you will become much more valuable come December.

Whether you're doing a holiday show, a wedding, a bar mitzvah or bat mitzvah, a lunch-in or any kind of private party, if you don't have an agent, you need to learn to agent (yes, it's a verb—in L.A. at least) a bit.

Never Accept the Asking Price

When a buyer pitches you a rate for a gig, always negotiate this. Never settle for the asking price. This goes for when promoters and other bands offer you a guarantee for a club show as well. You don't need to go all Ari Gold on them, but if they pitch you $100, ask for $300. You'll most likely settle at $200.

Have a "Normal" Rate

More times than not, a buyer will ask you what your rate is. It's good to always have a rate (and set length) you fall back on. You can set your "normal" rate at, say, $1,000 per show up to 2 hours (for private events), with a "normal" set length of 70 minutes. I've done 70-minute gigs for way more than my "normal" rate and for way less, but, by default, I ask for my "normal" rate plus expenses. Remember everything that has to be factored into this price: (local) travel, rehearsal, equipment, years of practice honing the craft, writing the songs, recording the album, creating the website, building your reputation, and so on. And above all, you're better than anyone else they will ask who is cheaper! Sure, the buyer could get his brother to play, but he only showers once a week, gets drunk before his shows and is kind of racist.

Also, the further out you lock in a gig, the higher your price should be. If you reserve a date, that means you have to turn down other (potentially higher-paying) gigs.

Price Points

Set different price points depending on time:

    0–2 hours = $1,000
    2–3 hours = $1,500
    3–4 hours = $2,000

The reason I say 0–2 hours and not set a specific set length is because once you are set up it's not much of a difference if you play 15 minutes or 120 minutes (if you have the material). You're there, so why not play? The work is getting to the gig. And they will think you're charging based on performance time. They'll try to get extra services out of you. "So since you're only playing for 75 minutes but you're charging for 2 hours, can you give my son a guitar lesson for 45 minutes?" This is how I learned to charge for 0–2 hours—after I gave her son a guitar lesson.

Feel Out the Gig

If a company hits you up to play their holiday party, you can bet they have a large budget. Pitch them your "normal" high rate. They can always come back at you and say that's more than they have budgeted and you can negotiate from there. If you ever pitch a rate and they immediately say "sounds good," you undersold yourself. Up your rate.

Get All Details Up Front

Do they provide sound? Lights? Stage? Seating? What kind of event is this? Can you sell your own merch? How many sets? How many breaks? Do they provide dinner and drinks? Lodging? All of this factors into the price. Have a normal rate plus sound, lights, food, lodging and travel. If they don't provide any of that, then factor that into the price and explain that to them. Your rate could be $2,500, but once you work out plane tickets, sound and light rental, hotel, dinner and rental car, it may cost around $4,000.

Have set points of expenses that are factored in:

- hotel buyout = $150 (either they provide one or add $150 to your check—if you have more band members, factor in the extra rooms)
- food buyout = $20 per member
- plane and rental car you'll have to look up and factor in per show basis

The Massage

If you pitch a rate way above their estimated budget, they may not respond to your email. You may need to follow up and ask if your rate is in their budget and if they are "ready to move forward and discuss details." Massage them—metaphorically, of course . . . or in actuality . . . whatever works. If they reply stating that your rate is way out of their budget, come up with an excuse as to why you can be flexible with them (you like the organization, it's last-minute and you're free, you have a close mutual friend, whatever), and ask what they can afford. Then negotiate from that point.

The Perfect 30

Put this gig to the Perfect 30 test and decide if it's worth it. Most private events are going to be around 2–3 for enjoyment and a 2–3 for career potential, so your compensation better be a 10.

Send a Contract

For these private gigs, always send over a contract that lays out all the details, including the performance fee. It makes them feel like you are professional. It's best to have a lawyer write something up for you, but if you can't do that, at least have something that simply states the facts of the event and makes sure everyone is on the same page.

ARI HERSTAND

Road Contact: Andrew Blieb Email: a.bleib@ariherstand.com and Phone: 323-555-5555

PERFORMANCE AGREEMENT

This Performance Agreement is made this 30th day of January, 2023 between Ari Herstand hereinafter referred to as "Artist," and Joe Schmo hereinafter referred to as "Buyer"

Buyer Joe Schmo   **Name of Venue** The Pause

Mailing Address Joe Schmo, Podunksville, PA 19610

Address of Venue 103 St. Olaf Drive, Podunksville, PA 19610

Contact Joe Schmo Email jschmo_85@email.com

Title of Event (All promotions shall be written exactly as stated)
        Ari Herstand concert

Indoor/Outdoor Indoor   **Rain Site** N/A

Load in instructions Drive into alley behind main building. Call upon arrival.

Day of Contact Name Shayna Rox Cell Phone# 608-555-5555

Artist Road Contact Andrew Blieb Email: a.bleib@ariherstand.com and Phone: 323-555-5555

Day of Show Wednesday, March 21st, 2023

Solo or Band? Solo   **Load in Time:** 5:00 PM

Sound Check Time 5:30 PM

Name and Phone # of sound engineer Gremlin: 414-555-5555

Door Time 8:00 PM **On Stage Time** 9:00 PM **Set length** 70 minutes

Other acts on bill ReadyGoes   **On Stage Time** 8:15 PM

Open / Closed to Public? Closed   **Ticket Price** N/A

Sound and Lighting Provided by Rapid Productions
Contact Name and Phone number Joe Le | 763-555-5555

Contract Price $1,500
Hospitality Dinner provided by Buyer
Travel Cost $475   **Lodging** $150 buyout

Total Cost To Buyer $2,075

Cancellation. If the Buyer cancels the engagement less than five weeks before the performance, Buyer will pay Artist 50% of the total price (**$1,037.50**) If Buyer cancels the engagement less than two weeks before the performance, Buyer will pay Artist 100% of total price (**$2,075**). The parties agree that such payments are reasonable in light of anticipated or actual harm caused by the cancellation—and the difficulties of proving the actual damages—to Artist. If any of the aforementioned stipulations—or stipulations listed in the Rider—are not met by the Buyer, Artist has the right to cancel the engagement without advance notice. If Artist is forced to cancel the engagement because of Buyer's refusal to meet an agreed upon stipulation, Buyer owes Artist the full cancellation fee (**$1,037/2,075**). Artist may cancel the engagement for any reason not explicitly expressed to Buyer no less than 30 days prior to the engagement. Artist may cancel the engagement less than 30 days prior to the engagement if unforeseen circumstances occur that prevent Artist from attending.

Payment. 50% of the guaranteed payment shall be given to Artist at least 30 days prior to the Event. The remaining 50% shall be given to Artist directly following the Event. All payments shall be given in check form or PayPal.

Make checks out to ARI HERSTAND.

Send check to:

Proud Honeybee Productions
1234 My Street
Los Angeles, CA 90028

Or PayPal to: ari@ariherstand.com

Force Majeure. If because of: Act of nature, inevitable accident; fire; lockout, strike or other labor dispute; riot or civil commotion; act of public enemy; enactment, rule, order or act of any government or governmental instrumentality (whether federal, state, local or foreign); failure of technical facilities; failure or delay of transportation facilities; illness or incapacity of any performer; or other cause of a similar or different nature not reasonably within either party's control, either party may cancel the engagement with no penalty.

General. Nothing contained in this Agreement shall be deemed to constitute either Buyer or Artist a partner or employee of the other party. This Agreement exhibits express the complete understanding of the parties and may not be amended except in a writing signed by both parties. If a court finds any provision of this Agreement or the accompanying rider invalid or unenforceable, the remainder of this Agreement shall be interpreted so as best to affect the intent of the parties. This Agreement shall be governed by and interpreted in accordance with the laws of the state of California. In the event of any dispute arising from or related to this Agreement, the prevailing party shall be entitled to attorney's fees.

Ari Herstand	Date	Joe Schmo	Date

Cancellation

And make sure you always have a cancellation stipulation in the contract. I always require 50% of the money up front as a deposit (that is not returned no matter what), and if they cancel the performance less than 30 days prior to the event, the remaining 50% is required.

How to Get Private Shows

If you build up a hefty cover repertoire, sign up for The Bash, The Knot, Thumbtack and GigSalad. These platforms allow buyers to shop for talent for their event. The most popular gigs on these platforms are weddings (ceremony and reception), corporate events, parties (graduation, retirement, quinceañera, bar/bat mitzvah, holiday) and, believe it or not, marriage proposals. A few singer/songwriter friends of mine have played quite a few proposals (surprise her in the park; as the couple walks by, a busker just so happens to be playing her favorite song as the dude [the buyer] drops to a knee). There are literally hundreds of various kinds of events that hire musicians through these services. The Bash boasts nearly 4 million events secured through its site. The more gigs you play and the more reviews you get, the higher your ranking will be on the site. The higher your reviews, the more you can charge. It costs about $100–$300 a year to become a member (depending on your membership level). But you will typically make back the fee after one booking.

Event Planners

Another way to get in with your local private events market is through event and wedding planners. Just google event and wedding planners for your local city or neighboring communities. You can email them and offer to take them out to lunch to get acquainted. You want to get on their radar so they will think of you first when they're booking the next Coca-Cola event and have a $20,000 budget for an incredible dance band. Or the wedding planner needs her next cocktail-hour singer/songwriter.

Sample email to event planner:

Hello,

My name is _____ and my band/I play [briefly describe band/music]. I'm looking to get a better idea of what working with musicians is like from a planner's point of view so I can better anticipate your needs as well as your clients'. I'm hoping you might be open to providing some insight. I was very impressed with the clarity/organization/look/etc. of your website and would love to chat with you about what you're looking for when you work with musicians. Would you happen to be free for a phone call or to maybe get together for lunch or a cup of coffee sometime this week (my treat!)?

Looking forward to hearing from you. Thanks so much for your help.

Best,

HOW TO MAKE OVER $100 AN HOUR STREET PERFORMING

The downside of being a street performer is the perception
that you're either homeless or you suck.

—KATIE FERRARA, AWARD WINNING,
WORLD-TRAVELING STREET PERFORMER

If you're a singer/songwriter and don't want a 9-to-5 day job, it's definitely worth exploring street-performing options in your city. Street performing takes a lot of work to master. Approaching a street performance is very different from approaching a club show. For one thing, on the street you have to grab people's attention as they walk by. In a club, people have paid to be there.

In Los Angeles, the most popular street performance location is in Santa Monica on the 3rd Street Promenade and Pier. It's where Andy Grammer started his career (long before his chart-topping hits and guest appearances with Taylor Swift). One summer I got an acoustic trio together and we busked 4 or 5 times a week for an average of 4 hours a day for about 4 months on the Promenade. It was definitely a learning experience. And, actually, a pretty decent way to make money. The Santa Monica Promenade is incredibly regulated. You need to get a permit (which only costs $37 for the entire year), and you must follow all of their guidelines to a T. Because if you don't, you will get ticketed by the "Promenade Ambassadors" who walk around with decibel readers (I kid you not) and rulers to measure your volume. On the Promenade, there are designated performance spots (you can't set up closer than 40 feet to the next performer), and nearly every performer uses amplification (less than 85db measured at a foot away). The Promenade, though, is unbelievably saturated with street performers (mostly break dancers who have so many in their crew that they crank up their volume (way past 85db) and one person's job is to just be the lookout for Ambassadors. This is one of the reasons many singer/songwriters have fled the Promenade for other locations around L.A.

Wherever you decide to perform, check the rules and regulations. The easiest way to do this is just ask other street performers who are there already or the manager of the event where you're thinking of street performing.

In New York, to perform on the subway platforms, you must follow the MTA's Rules of Conduct. Also, the Music Under New York (MUNY) program auditions and books performers at the most popular subway platforms, like Grand Central Terminal, Penn Station and Atlantic Terminal. You have to become a member of MUNY to apply to get booked. But you don't have to be a member of MUNY to perform on other subway platforms. And you don't need a permit, even with amplification (as long as it is below 85db measured at 5 feet away). To perform in New York City parks with an amp, you need a permit that costs *$45 a day*—yikes! So the subway is your best bet.

Regardless of where you perform, here are a few tactics that will help your earnings.

■ **Nothing Draws a Crowd Like a Crowd**
  If you've ever walked down the Santa Monica Promenade, Hollywood Boulevard or explored the New York City subway system, you've no doubt been drawn to . . . wait for it . . . a crowd. Sure, they're surrounding a street performer (or group of ten break dancers), but the reason they have such a big crowd is because they started with a little crowd. When people see a crowd nearby, they want to see what all the fuss is. If nothing very interesting is happening, but there's a big crowd, they'll hang out longer than they normally would because they think the others there must know something they don't.

The best street performers spend the first few minutes of each set getting a crowd—however possible.

■ **Short Sets**

The purpose of street performing is to make money. Plain and simple. People aren't hanging out at your set to go on a musical or spiritual journey. They have stopped to tune in for a couple minutes because something you said or sang caught their ear. They will not stick around very long, however, so the best way to sell more CDs and make more tips is to engage with them after your set. And the more set breaks you take the more opportunities you will have to cash in. Try playing sets of just five songs. Once you're done, leave your guitar case open by your performance area and go around the crowd with your CDs and a tip jar.

■ **The Performance Space**

The thing that sets the pros apart from the amateurs is the performance space. Setting your space up to feel cozy and unique to you should not be underestimated. Bring a rug to designate "your space." Set up a card table for your CDs, mailing list and a tip jar. Hang a large poster with your name, a professional live shot (of you looking amazing under the lights in a club), and your social links and QR code to your virtual tip jar (and social links).

■ **The Sound System**

You don't want to street-perform unplugged. No one will be able to hear you. Get an amp or portable PA that is loud enough for your space. The louder the better—but, of course, stay within the regulations. Check out the Roland CUBE Street Ex and the Fishman Loudbox Mini.

- **The Tip Jar**

  It's best to have a clear plastic tip jar. Plastic because with all the traveling you're doing a glass one will most likely shatter—ours did. And fill it with lots of $5s, $10s, $20s and a few $1s. Believe it or not, you will make more tips if the jar is full (because those who want to tip will be encouraged by how many others have tipped you as well—they'll think they have good taste). Having an empty tip jar is just sad. People will not tip you out of pity. They'll just keep walking. It's exciting to see a load of cash. They'll happily be a part of the action. And remember have a big QR code by your tip jar for people to tip you virtually. Bonus points if you have your phone out and call out the tips that come in.

- **The Mailing List**

  Make sure every person who buys your CD also signs your email list. And at each set break, encourage those who have stuck around to also sign your email list. You can also set up an inexpensive texting service which enables someone to text a word to a number. The user will automatically get subscribed to your list and the texting service can send them an instant reply with a link. So you could have a sign that says "Text KATIE to 55-4444 to get free, unreleased music." Even though they only heard a couple songs, they may become lifelong fans if you lock them into your list. And then they may buy tickets to your club show.

- **What My Friend the Banker Taught Me**

  One of the members of my acoustic trio worked at a bank during the day. Don't worry, he got out and is now doing music full-time. But what he explained to us was that the $20 bill is the most popular bill in rotation. It's the bill you get from ATMs. It's the bill everyone has on them (if they carry any cash). So create $20 merch options. Sell a 3-CD pack or a USB stick loaded with music, videos, lyrics, and other special goodies for $20. Just create a $20 option. Oftentimes, though, many regulated street-performance locations will not allow you to sell merch other than CDs, so always check.

■ **Have a Seller**

Having someone walking around with your CDs, mailing list and tip jar will drastically improve your earnings (and email sign-ups). Make sure this person is very charismatic and outgoing. You can cut your helper in on the sales too. Give her 20% of everything you make that day.

■ **Have a Cajon Player**

The thing I learned from Andy Grammer when I picked his brain about street performing was that having a cajon player makes it an event. It becomes a true performance. Two performers is much cooler than one. A million people play acoustic guitar and sing, but very few have a rocking cajon player with them. The cooler your cajon player looks and the more animated he is, the better. Give him or her 20% of your earnings or $50 for the day, whichever is greater.

■ **Covers**

And, of course, having a healthy cover repertoire will help increase your tips (and traffic). Learn the current hits, but also mix in your favorite oldies. And also learn some more obscure songs that you love, because the few who actually know the song you're playing (and similarly love it) will absolutely stop and enjoy and most likely give you a big tip, buy a CD and become a lifelong fan. That being said, Clare Means street-performed on the Promenade and Pier for a decade and played very few covers and has made a solid living doing just this. She started livestreaming her street performances in September 2015 and in just under a year built up tens of thousands of (paying) followers who became fans of her original music. More on how she did this in Chapter 11.

▪ Competition

Katie mentioned that she left the Promenade because there were just too many street performers and loud break-dancing crews. She found that it's best to seek out more obscure locations like farmers markets and malls. Talk to the market manager of the farmers market about setting up and performing. Some even have a budget to give performers a stipend of $100 or so. So definitely inquire.

▪ Keep It Fresh

The biggest thing you need to look out for if you're planning to street-perform regularly is to make sure you don't burn out. You should challenge yourself to learn a new cover every week and retire the songs that you're bored with.

▪ The Ego

The most difficult part of being a street performer is dropping your ego. Sure, most people who walk by you will think you're a struggling artist, but what they don't know is that you're pulling in $50–100+ an hour.

And if you're ever feeling down on yourself that no one is stopping by or giving you tips, just remember that Joshua Bell, one of the most famous violinists in the world, played a $3 million violin in a D.C. subway station for 43 minutes (incognito), and only made $32 from 27 people (as 1,070 others hurried by, ignoring one of the greatest living violinists playing some of the most challenging pieces ever written on one of the most expensive instruments in the world).

FESTIVALS ARE NO LONGER JUST FOR HIPPIES, MAN: HOW TO BREAK INTO THE FESTIVAL CIRCUIT

Festivals are a discovery mechanism—a live version of streaming.
—BRUCE FLOHR, RED LIGHT MANAGEMENT

You've heard of Coachella, Bonnaroo and Lollapalooza. But so has everyone else. Getting into a huge festival on your own is nearly impossible. If you don't have at least a manager or agent on your team (and serious online buzz), you're going to have a very difficult time breaking into one of these huge festivals. But you don't want to play such a festival until you're ready.

Festivals can break artists to the next level. There are always one or two bands that nobody expects that breaks from Bonnaroo or Coachella.

If you have an opportunity to play one of the huge festivals, you have to approach it right. Aside from putting on a great show, your online presence needs to be fresh. "You've got to make sure the looks you want line up to when you're peaking," artist manager Bruce Flohr advises, "otherwise, you're playing a festival that's really important and you're not quite where you want to be." When a big festival finishes and 80,000 music lovers disseminate and get home, they'll be asked what their favorite shows were. They'll say, "I saw My Morning Jacket and Radiohead, and there's this new guy." Make that new guy you.

But if everyone starts checking you out online all at the same time and you have an album that's three years old, no upcoming shows and a stale social media presence, that was a wasted opportunity.

So, despite what you think, you don't want to play an influential festival until you're ready—until you have a big fall tour set up, a new album to promote and a team of passionate people ready to push you hard.

That being said, there are a zillion little festivals around the country that you can play. Getting in at smaller festivals is far less difficult than getting in at a big one where everyone is competing for the spot.

Friends Like Helping Friends

Most cities have festivals of some sort over the summer where either music is the main attraction or a featured component. Whether it's the 400-person Folk the Park or the 100,000-person Brat Fest, start with your local festivals. Put the word out that you're looking for anyone involved in your local festivals, and track down how to play. Oftentimes there will be an open submission, but other times you just need to know the bookers.

When They Book

Many of the big festivals begin booking the following year's lineup the day after the festival finishes, and the big ones get 80% booked up less than a month later. The rest of the year is spent finding all of the hot up-and-comers and securing the big headliners. It's a good rule of thumb to start your outreach for summer festivals right after the festival finishes.

It's definitely worth looking into winter cruise-ship festivals like Jam

Cruise, Rock the Boat, Cayamo, The Outlaw Country Cruise and 70000 Tons of Metal. Sixthman runs many of the biggest cruises on the seas, so it might be worth making contact with them. Festivals skew younger and cruises skew older. It's good to keep that in mind when planning how you want to build your audience.

If you think playing the festival circuit is the best way to go for your project, create a shared Google spreadsheet and make nine columns: Festival, Location, Dates, Attendance, Other Bands, Submission Process, Contact Name, Email, Notes. Some festivals take applications directly on the website. But big ones are only booked via connections. So you'll have to get scrappy. Submit through the front door, but also hunt down personal email addresses of the organizers. And try to find mutual friends to make intros.

Music Festival Wizard has the most complete listing that you can filter by genre, location (worldwide), type and date. Indie on the Move has a good amount of US listings with links to submit. And the Unsigned Guide has a great listing for UK festivals.

Festivals are most interested in what you look and sound like live, so having a very high-quality live video is crucial. They also want to book buzzing bands. So gather up all of your accolades. Getting featured on hip blogs or hot Spotify playlists definitely increases your chances of being selected. We'll dig into this more in Chapter 15.

The Street or the Ground

There are two main kinds of festivals out there: the Street and the Ground. These are my terms, by the way.

The Street festivals work with local venues, like bars, cafes and, of course, music venues to host music from open to close where music typically wouldn't necessarily be hosted. The most popular Street festival is South by Southwest (SXSW) in Austin. The official SXSW-sanctioned clubs require badges or wristbands to gain entrance, but because of the influx of fans, musicians and industry to the area during SXSW, more and more venues unofficially host live music in the same area and only require an ID to get in. Walking 6th Street in Austin during SXSW, it's hard to tell which clubs are official and which are unofficial. Most artists play multiple "showcases" throughout the festival. Street festivals are becoming more popular around the world and many, like the Mile of Music festival in Appleton, Wisconsin, are popping up all over the place.

The Ground festivals require you to purchase entrance to the grounds. Once you're inside, you can see any act you want. Many times there will be multiple stages hosting music simultaneously. Often there is a camping section and the majority of attendees camp. The most famous Ground festivals hosting all genres of music are Bonnaroo and Coachella. Cruise ships also fall into the Ground category and they take place—you guessed it—out at sea.

Summerfest in Milwaukee, which boasts it's "The World's Largest Music Festival," and Lollapalooza in Chicago don't allow camping (and kick people out every night), but have multiple stages set up throughout the grounds where you can see any act you choose once inside. Brat Fest in Madison, Wisconsin, hosts over 100 bands on 4 stages and is actually free for all attendees.

There are genre-specific festivals like EDC and HARD for electronic music, WE Fest and CMA for country and Jam Cruise and Summer Camp for jam bands. And hundreds more.

Once you get booked at a festival, there are ways to maximize your appearance. For Ground festivals, if you're playing early in the day or on a small stage, you'll want to promote your slot to attendees so you're not playing to an empty lawn. Make sure you print up a bunch of flyers and walk around the campgrounds meeting people and passing out flyers. Be friendly and make sure you're chill about this process. Don't be sleazy.

Festivals are all about the vibe and the hang. So make sure you're keeping a cool vibe when you do this. Enlist the help of your friends, fans and street team members who are at the fest to help you promote your slot. You can also work the Facebook, Instagram, TikTok, Google and YouTube advertising angle—targeting festivalgoers for your appearance a month leading up to the fest. If you're the first act of the day on the small tent stage but you pack the tent to the brim, the festival organizers will take notice and most definitely have you back the following year for a much better slot.

It's much more difficult to promote your set for Street festivals. At SXSW everyone and their mom (literally) is promoting their showcases. You can't walk five feet without seeing a poster on a pole or being handed a flyer. To promote your sets at Street fests, you'll want to do all the heavy lifting well in advance of the festival. Most people will have all of the acts they want to see planned out before the festival starts.

Pay-to-Play Festivals

Every legitimate festival will pay you to be there. Many think that SXSW doesn't pay. They do, but it's not much. No matter who you are. SXSW offers artists (of every level) two options for payment. They can either get paid $250 (for a band) and $100 for a solo act, or get artist wristbands which lets band members attend all festival activities. There are also sponsored showcases at SX, where the sponsor woos larger artists to perform with fat paychecks. SXSW actually encourages this practice. But SXSW never requires artists to pay to play. There are some unofficial "festivals" that occur during the same time as SXSW that require bands to pay to play. You should never, never, never, never, never pay to play a festival. No exceptions. I have to mention it and emphasize it with five nevers because these kinds of festivals exist around the country and unfortunately are gaining in popularity. Let's band together to crush them. OK?

The way many pay-to-play festivals work is, organizers of the fest first secure fairly well-known headliners (who, of course, get paid). Once they've secured the headliners, the organizers hit up young bands and offer a "great slot near the headliners" if they sell a set number of tickets. To get your tickets, you have to purchase them up front. They require you to Venmo or money-order the money up front. And before you're allowed inside the grounds, you have to turn in all of the tickets you didn't sell. The closer your set is to the headliner's is based solely on the number of tickets you sell. Note, that "near" is a very loose term. I've heard of bands getting slots on a side stage (not the headliners' stage) with a set time *after* the headliner's set and getting their time cut from the typical 25-minute set to 5 minutes because the festival was running behind. There's an amazing video on YouTube of a pissed-off band who got their time cut short being physically ushered offstage by security because the festival was shutting down. Yes, these festivals cram as many bands in who will pay and therefore keep set times and changeovers as short as possible. There are unfortunately countless examples of bands (and hip-hop artists—this is sadly very prevalent in the hip-hop and metal communities) paying hundreds (or thousands) to play a festival with impressive headliners. However, when they arrive, either the festival has shut down, doesn't have enough stages to accommodate the pay-to-play artists, or is so completely mismanaged that the artist never actually gets a slot to play (and never gets their money back). If you want to read some horror stories, look up my article on *Digital Music News*: "Festival Owner Charges Bands to Play, Cancels Fest, Skips Town with the Money."

I was clued in to one of these shady pay-to-play festivals by a musician friend who had been hit up by one of the bookers. This guy was booking the festival via text. So, acting as a young, dumb band, I texted the self-proclaimed "booking agent" (the title is wrong on so many levels) of the festival and said "I want to play the festival." I never gave my name and gave him a fake band name (had he spent 10 seconds to google the name, he could have called my bluff). This festival, mind you, was taking place in two weeks. Two. Weeks.

We went back and forth over text for a solid hour during which I got the full rundown. By the end, he offered me a slot at the festival— *without ever hearing my music.*

The deal he offered for a "good" slot "near the headliners" was to buy 40 tickets. I got two options: I could buy the 40 tickets up front ("send money via PayPal or money order") at $18 a piece ($720) and then sell them for $20. I would also get 40 more tickets to sell on my own (and keep the dough). Or, if I couldn't shell out $720 up front, I could buy only 10 tickets up front ($180), get 50 total tickets and then turn in the rest of the $720 three days before the festival (via PayPal or money order). Total potential for option number two if I sold all 50 tickets (mind you, two weeks before the show)? $280. That's 28% of what I sold. And that's ONLY if I sold all 50 tickets. If I sold only 35 tickets, I'd be out $90.

Here's a good rule of thumb: If anyone asks for a deposit or asks you to purchase tickets up front (for a festival or club show), run the other way as fast as you can. It's the festival's job to book a mix of talent that will draw the crowds, along with new talent (who they love) to showcase amid the lineup. And it's the festival's job to promote. Sure, every artist should do their fair share in helping promote through their social media networks, email list and possibly some press appearances, but in no case, ever, should the band be on the hook for unsold tickets.

Legitimate festivals make their money on sponsorships and ticket sales. Not off the backs of young bands who don't know any better. If the festivals are incapable of securing enough sponsorship money to cover their costs, it is their fault. Not the artists'.

GIG RESOURCES YOU NEED
TO KNOW ABOUT

In addition to The Bash, Thumbtack and GigSalad, if you have a home studio setup, you should register a profile on SoundBetter (now owned by Spotify), AirGigs and Fiverr. These marketplaces connect musicians with other music pros to help finish a song. You can hire a singer from Australia, a guitar player from London, a percussionist from Brazil and a mixing engineer from L.A. all within the platform. Mixing and mastering engineers and freelance players and singers are the most popular services offered, but recording studios, live sound engineers, top-line writers, beat makers and full-demo production services also exist.

Fiverr's community is by far the largest, as it appeals to mostly non-musicians and advertises services ranging from social media marketing, cartoon making, voiceovers and crowdfunding managers.

And if you're looking for more freelance work, you need to be on Jammcard. It only allows A-list talent, but it has become the go-to app for music directors looking to hire their bands (for every level of tours from clubs to stadiums).

8.

TOURING

We never did anything that we lost money at. Driving her mom's minivan with her friend all over the country and staying at people's houses along the way doesn't cost very much.
—LYNN GROSSMAN, INGRID MICHAELSON'S MANAGER

WHY HIT THE ROAD

Too many bands go on tour just to say they're going on tour. Yes, it seems cool to your friends, but do you know what's not so cool? Playing empty shows in every city, sleeping on beer-stained couches, getting your gear stolen from an unguarded green room and having your van break down 200 miles away from the nearest gas station.

The road is an unforgiving beast.

Like moving in with a lover, hitting the road with other musicians will bring out the worst in them. But putting up with five other smelly musicians, clashing personalities, cramped living quarters, a fast-food diet and endless miles of nothing but cornfields instantly becomes worth it when you step onstage in front of a crowd of screaming fans (and, of course, see your bank account swell).

But what if you step out onstage and instead of a crowd of screaming fans there's a crowd of 7 playing pool in the back. Less awesome.

The road isn't for everyone. But if you want to be a live artist (IRL, we'll get into livestreaming in Chapter 11), taking your show on the road will be a must if you want to grow past your local scene.

Tour revenue has become a lot more democratized over the years, and more indie bands are seeing serious success on the road. In 2000, the top 100 tours captured 90% of all revenue, while in 2019 the top 100 captured only 42%.

The most important thing to remember: *If you don't promote your show, no one will show up.*

Just being listed on a hot venue's website and being a touring band will not get people to show up to the show. Very few venues in the world have built-in audiences. So, step one is to build up a fanbase and tour where those fans are. If you start to gain traction online, make sure you grab email addresses (with zip codes) so you can promote directly to these fans when you visit their town.

If you have very little traction online and are itching to hit the road, it's possible to book a successful tour, but it takes a lot of creative promo tactics. More on this in a bit.

WHERE TO TOUR

Once you have built up a good following online, you need to find out where these fans exist. YouTube, Pandora, Spotify, Bandcamp, Instagram, TikTok, along with the analytics platform Chartmetric, provide excellent metrics of where your fans are located (and how engaged they are). You should also check the geographic breakdown of your fans on Bandsintown and Songkick. Make sure to register yourself as an artist (via Bandsintown.com or Tourbox.songkick.com).

But above all, you want to get your fans on your email list. Most email list providers can track where your fans are located. Nino Bless (and his manager Circa) set up a Google Form to ask his fans where they were located, grab their emails, and if any of them were bookers. They sorted the spreadsheet by location. By using this data, Nino set out on an international tour where he sold out nearly every date.

HOW TO BOOK A NATIONAL TOUR

Timeline

You need plenty of time from beginning the booking process until the first show. For a tour containing mostly cities you've never been to before, I recommend starting this process at least six months out if you're touring your home country and 9–12 months out if you're touring internationally. You should have nearly all of the shows booked two months in advance of the first show so you have plenty of time to promote the tour.

Most likely you're going to spend the first month routing the cities, researching venues and gaining contact info.

Routing

Your routing will never be perfect. Meaning, you have to expect you'll do a little bit of backtracking and have a few off days because it's impossible to get every venue's schedule to line up with yours. You want to keep the backtracking and off days to a minimum though, obviously.

First, on a map (Google Maps works) plot out the cities you want to visit. Try to keep drives shorter than 6 hours on a show day and shorter than 10 hours on a non-show day. You're going to spend most of your time on the road, but spreading out the long drives will save you from burnout (and murdering your band members). You also want to plan for about an hour of stops for every 4 hours of driving. And of course if you're traveling in an electric vehicle, you're going to need to take charge times into account.

The more members you have on tour, the less each member's driving burden, but the greater your tour expenses.

Open a shared calendar in Google Calendar or iCal and share it with everyone on the tour. Put in "held dates" with city names. When you get a "hold" at a venue, change the color of the "held date" and title it the city along with the venue name. When you get a "confirmation" change that color again and title it the city with the venue, and in the notes of that event, list all details: talent buyer name, email, number, day-of contact, venue address, time of show, set length, load in time, door time, set times (for all acts), compensation, hospitality. This will all get confirmed in your confirmation email. (Remember that? See Chapter 7.)

These held cities will undoubtedly shift, so make sure you keep an updated calendar—especially if you have multiple members booking.

Finding the Venues

Once you have the cities you want to visit, you have to find the venues that are appropriate for your sound and your draw. If you've never been to this city before, it's going to be much more difficult for you to convince the talent buyer (booker) at the venue to give you a night, but it's possible.

First, you have to decide what kind of rooms you want to play. Are you a mellow singer/songwriter? Seek out art galleries, listening rooms, museums, cultural centers, black box theaters and living rooms (more on these in a minute). Are you a rock band? Seek out rock clubs, basement venues, festivals and block parties.

Indie on the Move (IOTM) in the US, the Unsigned Guide in the UK, TripAdvisor and Yelp are some of the best resources to use for venue research. Yelp and TripAdvisor are great for audience reviews of the venue and to get the vibe of the club. Spend time reading these reviews and get a feel for how your project could (or could not) fit in the venue.

Indie on the Move is specifically for bands booking their own tours. They have a great list of venues, contact info and band reviews of the venues. To save time, you can hire IOTM to customize and send out initial emails to venues meeting a specific criterion that you set in each city (like, clubs under 300 cap that are 18+ and host rock music in a 10 mile radius of Atlanta). Currently, IOTM has reps you can hire to help you customize and automate this process. As someone who has booked 60-date national tours on my own, any way to expedite this process is worth the financial investment. Believe me.

The Pitch

Most talent buyers prefer to work over email. Do not DM them on Instagram. Some older, hardened buyers (usually the owners of small clubs and bars) may respond well to a phone call. So, if you're not getting a response over email, pick up the phone and give it a try.

Similarly to how you pitch local clubs, your initial email pitch should be short and to the point. Well, all your emails should be short, but especially the initial one.

Make sure you check the venue's calendar first and make sure that date is open.

Keep the email under eight sentences. Write it in all-lowercase letters (if you can stomach it—I know you grammar nerds out there will fight me on this; that's cool—do what feels right for you). Talk about your history in the area (if any) and explain briefly how you're going to promote the show. Link your EPK which will contain your bio, press clips, music player, videos, links to socials, tour history, and other accolades. Most important, say how many people you expect to get out for it. This is what 98% of talent buyers care about.

Sample Email:

Subject: oct 23—pink shoes and thom johnson

Body: hi tony, minneapolis-based pink shoes is passing through on oct 23 with thom johnson. last time through we played the rhythm room and drew 75. we have an active street team on the ground in phoenix (with 175 phoenix subscribers on our email list), we'll be contacting all local media and will be running facebook, instagram and youtube ads for this show. we expect 150 tickets sold. can we grab a hold?

Pink Shoes (Minneapolis based) - **epk**
8 million Spotify plays (Phoenix 11th most popular city)

Praise from Consequence of Sound, Stereogum and Paste (link each
word to the article)
"Seven Letters" music video has 3 million views (link "Seven Letters" to it)
Debut album Blue Socks releasing October 1st.

thank you,
~ari

Manager/Guitarist—Pink Shoes

Pink Shoes Ent, LLC

http://pinkshoes.com/epk

PINK SHOES LOGO

Local Openers

Most venues will want you to put the bill together, but sometimes they
will happily place a proven local act similar to your style on the bill. It's
best, though, if you can take a complete bill to the venue.

When MySpace was around (RIP), it was very easy to find bands similar to your style in any city and quickly listen to them and see what kind
of buzz they had. Now Bandcamp can be used to find for this purpose.
But it's not a completely exhaustive list.

Always cross-check these bands on Facebook, Instagram, Spotify and YouTube to check out their numbers and engagement. Once
you've narrowed down the list by location and genre, check out their
tour calendar. See what kinds of venues they play. Take a look at their
past shows by viewing their Bandsintown or Songkick data. See if they
tour or exclusively play local. Are they playing local every week or every
couple months? If they're playing local all the time, they won't be able
to bring many people out to your show. Find bands that have a decent
social presence and seem to pull well locally. Shoot them an email and
ask them to open your show. Explain all the details up front: time slot,

payment and draw request (we need the opener to help get the word out and draw at least 30). Remember to start off with a compliment about their music and how you found them. Give them $50 or 10% of your cut, whichever is greater, so it will encourage them to promote.

If it's getting closer to your tour start and you don't have a show booked, it may be worth searching for concerts in the city and hitting up the bands or the venue listed on the date you need, to see if you can hop on the bill. Pay won't be great, but you will hopefully make up for it in merch sales.

Show Trades

Once you've established yourself in your hometown and can draw decent numbers, you have something to offer. You can team up with other bands from other cities and offer them an opening slot at one of your big headlining shows in exchange for an opening slot at one of their big headlining shows. Ideally, you find similar bands with similar hometown draws.

You have to be careful, though, that you don't promise this to too many bands, as it may take you an awfully long time to fulfill the hometown promise if you play a big local show only every six to twelve weeks.

Payment

Reference the worst-through-the-best deals from the last chapter before getting into negotiations over payment. Most original music clubs will not offer guarantees if you aren't proven in their club (or with the promoter). But some will and you can definitely ask. You don't have much negotiating power if it's your first time through and aren't proven, so you're going to basically take what you can get. But these are good guidelines to stick to so that you know when you should be moving on to another venue in that town. Expect to set (or pitch) your ticket price around the same as most shows on their calendar. Meaning, if you contact a club and every show's cover is $15–$25, don't expect to charge $6 for your show. Most clubs will allow you to set your cover (within reason). I always recommend up and coming touring acts to set their covers around $10–$14. Fans understand that you're on the road and they will pay a little more for touring acts.

COVER SHOWS

If you have a large cover repertoire, it's a completely different ballgame. Most cover bars are located in the suburbs of big cities. If you can play three-to-four-hour cover sets, by all means work these into your tour.

You'll have to do a bit more research to find the bars that hire cover bands, but a good place to start is searching Indie on the Move. These shows typically pay a guarantee, and sometimes they will throw in a percentage of the bar.

The beauty of the cover bar circuit is if the bar is located in a city far away from any major metropolis, the bars are much more willing to throw in a hotel, food and drinks in addition to the guarantee because they want to keep high-quality talent coming to their small town.

Lodging

Once the tour is completely routed and confirmed, you'll want to start figuring out sleeping arrangements. For your first few tours this will mean finding friends in each city with couches or floor space (invest in air mattresses and sleeping bags). Try to figure this out before the day of the show, but as a last resort you can announce onstage that you're looking for a place to crash that night. More times than not this works. Not very rock-star—but neither is sleeping in your van.

TOUR RESPONSIBILITIES

The more successful your tours are, the more people you will be able to afford to bring on the road with you to handle necessary tour duties. Until then, you need to manage everything on your own and delegate when you can.

TOUR MANAGER (TM)

When you're on the road, the tour manager is the liaison between the band and everyone else: venue, promoter, fans, street team. The tour manager should have all of the contracts (or confirmation emails) organized and readily accessible. The TM should either have a physical tour binder with day sheets, maps, directions, addresses, contracts and notes printed out, have all of this organized on the tour iPad or use a platform like Master Tour or Artist Growth. The TM makes sure the night (and day) goes smoothly. She makes sure the doors of the venue don't open until sound check is finished and the band is in the green room. She makes sure the room is set up the way the band likes it (this should be discussed during the advance call). The TM schedules the oil changes or clocks out charging times and locations and finds laundromats. And of course, the TM collects the money at the end of the night, counts the money in front of the venue manager and makes sure it is exactly what was discussed in the contract/confirmation email and advance call. If there is a per diem, the TM distributes these as well.

DAY SHEETS

The day sheet lists all the info everyone on tour needs to know about the day. It should include:

- Band name | Day of tour #
- TM name, number, email
- Today's date
- Travel

    Starting and ending points with distance and time
- Ending location address

    Typically venue or crashing pad
- Bus (or van) call time
- Venue info

    Name, address, capacity, phone, website, parking info, load-in info, load-in time, sound-check time, door time, onstage time
- Venue day-of contact name/number/email
- Production (house sound guy) contact name/phone/email
- Dinner info and time

    Is the venue providing food? Are they giving you a "buyout"? Or are you stopping somewhere before or after sound check.
- Meet-and-greet time and location
- Merch seller's name/phone/email
- Sleeping arrangements

    Hotel info (name, address, phone, website, Wifi password, gym, hot tub, etc.) or crashing pad names/numbers and relationship to band (drummer's friend, found through Instagram).
- Departure time

    Either that night (if you're driving through the night on a tour bus) or the next morning from the crashing pad.

Young Canyon - Almost Famous Tour

Saturday, May 20, 2023
Hi-Dive - Denver, CO - Mountain Time
Venue Address: 7 S Broadway, Denver, CO 80223

Schedule:

Bus Call: 9:00AM

Drive: Lincoln -> Denver = 7:00hrs

Time Change: Central -> Mountain (Gain 1 hour)

Load In: 5:00PM

Sound Check: 5:30PM

Doors: 8:00PM

Local Opener TBA @ 8:30PM

Milk Carton Kids @ 9:15PM

Young Canyon @ 10:15

Curfew: Midnight

Hospitality:
Meal tickets for neighboring Mexican restaurant (1 entree)
Draft beer, wells all night
Gram of marijuana (sativa by request)

Lodging:
Stay with Hutchinsons
1234 Chambers Rd
Aurora, CO
31 minutes from venue
Phone: 720-555-3212
OzarkHutchinson@email.com

Promoter Contact:
Dave@coloradoshows.com
303-555-9752 (cell)

Venue Day of Contact:
Matt@hi-dive-venue.com
303-555-6123

Tomorrow:
Bus Call: 4PM
Denver -> Boulder = 42 min

Sample day sheet.

It's best to print these out and tape a copy inside the bus/van and in the green room. The TM should also create a digital day sheet on the shared calendar or a shared Google Doc so band members can view them at will on their phones. Bring a small mobile printer on the road with you to print these (and set lists). You won't be able to make day sheets too far in advance of the show because variables will change (like load-in time, merch sellers, crashing pad, etc.).

ADVANCING SHOWS

One of the most important jobs a TM has is to advance the show with the venue. What this means is calling and/or emailing the contact person at the venue (usually the production manager, bar manager, or house sound guy) at least a week before the show to confirm all details like load-in and sound-check times, how the room is set up (standing or seated show), payment details, who the day-of contact person is, guest list protocol, dinner details and parking info. This information is how the day sheet will be created and finalized. Details change from when the show was confirmed months prior so whether you have a dedicated TM on the road with you or not, every show must get advanced.

Guest List

The TM will handle the guest list and follow the venue's protocol on how to get it to them. You should create a dedicated shared calendar just for guest list each day of the tour, so any band member can add names at will. The guest list number will be on the contract (or confirmation email) and the TM should write the number on each day's calendar event so members know not to go over—first come first serve!

THE BRIDGE

It's Not a Meet and Greet—It's an Experience

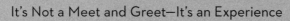

Every band, big and small, should organize some form of preshow, VIP meet-and-greet package.

Abney Park offered "afterparty" livestream tickets for $100—held directly following their ticketed livestream concerts (during quarantine—and beyond). The afterparty show was essentially the same as their livestream concert, except the band members did shots in between each song and interacted with the chat box a lot more. Emily King offered fans a meet and greet/photo op, group Q&A, commemorative laminate, signed poster, crowd-free merch shopping, along with early entrance to the venue for $50. My Morning Jacket offered a ticket in the first eight rows, signed poster, some merch items, and an "on-site host" for $200 (ticket included). The Disco Fries challenged fans to a backstage NBA Jam game preshow for $30. Ron Pope challenged fans to Pop-A-Shot preshow for $150. Ryan Beatty offered fans a pizza and a movie date for $500. Jana Kramer challenged fans to Ping-Pong and Cornhole preshow for $60. Experiences are a great way to make extra money on tour and get to know your biggest fans on a more intimate level. Wild Child claimed they doubled their net touring revenue (drawing 100–500 a night) by offering experiences at every stop.

The TM will get in touch with each day's VIP guests and arrange all the details. It's fun to make special lanyards with laminated passes that say ARTIST NAME | NAME OF TOUR | VIP. They will cherish this souvenir forever, and it will be a constant reminder of the great time spent before the show. For bigger tours, the promoter may have a VIP package option. Otherwise, independent companies like CID can run your VIP experiences.

Believe it or not, many fans will pay good money for VIP experiences. A 2013 Nielsen study revealed that fans would spend up to $2.6 billion more a year on music if "they had the opportunity to snag behind-the-scenes access to the artists along with exclusive content." This study also revealed that 40% of US consumers are responsible for 75% of music spending.

You can offer a portion of all VIP package proceeds to go to the charity of your choice.

LODGING

A TM is also responsible for arranging the lodging. If it's a crashing pad tour, have every artist search Facebook for "my friends who live in City" and go from there. Great ways to save on hotels is by using Priceline's Express Deals, Booking.com or Hotel Tonight. Hotels that have empty rooms will list them for supercheap (like 60% off normal price) a day or two before to try and fill them. I've booked 4-star hotels for $45 using this option. Airbnb is also a great option to find cheaper lodging in cities. Try not to drive very far after the show (if you don't have a dedicated driver) to the crashing pad or hotel. It will drastically reduce your post-show hang time, bar hopping and overall tour enjoyment. Exploring each city's nightlife is one of the best parts of being on the road.

MERCH SELLERS

You need someone selling your merch every night. Even if you have a merch manager on the road with you, you should still have a few sellers to help out. These can be fans (sought out via social media or your email list) or sometimes the venue will provide some merch sellers (for a fee). Offer the fans free entrance to the show. The TM will be the point person for the merch sellers and train them on how everything works. The merch sellers should be positioned at the table when doors open until doors close. Hook them up with free drinks and free merch.

PER DIEM (PD)

For bigger tours, each hired gun and crew member typically gets a per diem, which is a daily amount to be spent on food. "Per diem" literally means "per day." It can range anywhere from $5 to $50. Typical per diems sit around $20. But for most early tours, there are no per diems.

As you can see, the TM has a ton of responsibilities and it's crucial that you have a very organized and responsible one. Oftentimes, a sound engineer or merch manager will double as a TM. Or many times, for singer/songwriter tours, hired freelancers will double as the TM. If you're just a 4-piece band on tour with no extra help, have the most responsible member be the TM.

MERCH MANAGER

Many tours will be profitable based solely on the success of merch sales. The merch manager counts in and out all inventory and cash every night, makes sure the "bank" (change pouch) is full of small denominations for change ($5s are best—don't have any of your merch packages cost amounts requiring singles). The merch manager keeps track of inventory and knows when to reorder to make sure you never run out of anything. She should be very organized and very charismatic to be able to upsell each customer.

FOH

FOH stands for "front of house" and just means the sound guy. The first person you hire to bring on the road with you after the musicians should be the FOH. The venue's house FOH does not know your sound and may have completely different taste. Many FOH's will be able to double as TMs.

50 IS THE MAGIC NUMBER

Remember, the number-one thing venues care about is turnout. So when booking your tour, you're going to have to figure out how you're going to get people to every single show. Unless you're booking venues with built-in crowds (like restaurants, house concerts, or casinos), you will need to work to promote the tour.

You can book a financially successful tour around the country a lot easier than you think. In pretty much every major city in the country, there will be a small venue with a capacity under 300 that will be conducive to your sound. Nearly every under-300-cap venue in the world will be satisfied with a 50-person turnout on a week night and even some on the weekend if they haven't filled that date with a sure thing. If you tell the club that you can get 50 out, you can probably book the club.

So that's step one. Now that you have the shows booked, how do you actually get the 50 to come? You have to find your niche. Break out that Our Fans sheet again. You should look at groups and organizations as a main target when promoting the show. Sure it's nice to grab one kid's attention from a TikTok ad, but it's much more effective if you get an entire group excited about you.

Does your music appeal to college kids? Line up promo shows at dorms, frats, and sororities in that town a day before or the day of the show and offer them a table at the venue to take donations for their philanthropy project. Are you a chess master? Contact the local chess clubs and offer them discount tickets and run a tournament preshow where the winner will get free merch. Are you Jewish? Hit the local Hillel houses, synagogues, Moishe Houses, summer camps. Are you gay or trans? Hit up the local LGBT organizations. Are you a theater nut? Contact local playhouses and offer them music to play before the show and at intermission and have discount tickets available in the lobby.

Just find a niche or an organization that you can contact locally that you can get excited about your band. Personalize your pitch to them and your reason for wanting to work together. It's a minipartnership for that day (or months leading up to the show), so you should point out how it will benefit them. You should contact a few organizations for each city and not bank on just one—in case the one falls through or doesn't work.

Once you find a way to get 50 people in any city to come to your show, you're now a headliner. Start with your local market and figure out what works there and then take that strategy on the road.

I once booked a 10-city high school tour. I spent a week in each city (most of which I had never been to) and went into the local high schools during the weekdays and then had an all-ages club show booked on that Saturday. I performed a couple songs and talked to the music students about how a music education helped me get to where I was. I offered to visit the high schools for free in exchange for allowing me to sell my merch and promote my Saturday show. I was the talk of the school that week and every club show that weekend was filled with these high school kids who bought lots of merch. I promised every club at least 50 (even though I'd never been to that town before and had no online buzz) and I had 50–250 at every show.

HOW TO MAKE $500+ PER HOUSE CONCERT

A lot of us musicians have big egos and we've all been brought up with this mantra that it's about more tickets and more people in the room and more albums sold. Quantity. I got to a point where I was having these magical experiences that were super out of the ordinary. I connected with a lesser quantity of people, but it was more of a connection.

—GRAHAM COLTON

If your footprint can't be wide, let it be deep.

—DAN MANGAN, JUNO-WINNING SINGER/SONGWRITER AND COFOUNDER OF SIDE DOOR

House concerts are not a new thing. There is a long tradition in the folk world that dates back to the '60s. However, they seem to have had a massive resurgence over the past decade of singer/songwriters trading in club touring for house shows. Personally, I've played about 30 house concerts and these shows have been some of my favorite (and most profitable) shows of my career. Nothing beats the connection of a room full of supporters sitting merely feet from you, soaking up every note, every word, and every beat. A living room concert is one of the most memorable concert experiences a fan (and artist) will ever have.

And house concerts aren't just for tiny singer/songwriters. Artists like Vance Joy, David Bazan (of Pedro the Lion), Jeremy Messersmith, Julia Nunes, Califone, Mirah, Laura Gibson, Tim Kasher of Cursive, S. Carey, Richard Buckner, Alec Ounsworth of Clap Your Hands Say Yeah, and John Vanderslice have set up house concert tours over the past few years.

With house shows you don't have to deal with bad sound guys, drunk a**holes, empty clubs, or the headache of promotion. Shannon Curtis has a great book on how to book a house concert tour called *No Booker, No Bouncer, No Bartender: How I Made $25K on a 2-Month House Concert Tour (And How You Can Too)*, which I highly recommend if you're thinking of getting into the house concert game. You can also check out ConcertsInYourHome, which is a community of house concert hosts around the world. If you are accepted as an artist into the network, you can set up full tours to cities you've never visited in great homes of acoustic fans.

And when Covid shut down the entire live music industry, many DIYers got creative, putting on drive-in, driveway and backyard concerts. We at Ari's Take put on a drive-in concert in the summer of 2020. This was one of the first concerts to take place since lockdown in Los Angeles County. The artist Annabel Lee headlined the event and celebrated the release of her song "Los Angeles." We promoted it on Instagram and required fans to text her (SMS service) for more info (which auto-returned a link to buy tickets). We sold tickets (price per car—people packed their household into their cars) through Splash and hosted the concert at a friend of a friend of a friend's big open lot (because the owner of the parking lot we had booked got Covid five days before the show!). Fortunately, we didn't release the location, via text, until the day before the show. We handed out an instruction sheet to every car (via a grabber stick), which had instructions on how to tune in (via the car radio), how to buy merch, social, stream and download links (via QR code, of course). We had a dedicated merch person managing the Venmo account, running around to cars with their merch items.

I wrote more about it and how you can put on your own drive-in concert on aristake.com.

The show went off without a hitch. Live music had been officially shut down for four months at this point, and this concert was desperately needed by Annabel, her band, her fans and everyone else involved.

After having his summer 2020 tour canceled, Toronto-based singer/

songwriter John Muirhead reached out to his local community offering driveway concerts and booked 10 driveway concerts in the Toronto area. And then in early 2021, once he had started to build up his TikTok presence, he compiled some footage from the previous summer into a little advertisement-style video. It spread on TikTok extremely quickly (racking up nearly 30,000 views) and returned more requests for driveway concerts in Ontario than he could handle (hashtags worked wonders). John filled up his entire calendar with these throughout 2021. He charged hosts a guaranteed minimum around $200–300 CAD, and averaged around $7 CAD per head in merch sales. Win!

The Nova Scotia–based company Side Door, co-founded by singer/songwriter Dan Mangan and music industry professional Laura Simpson, connects artists with hosts and helps them facilitate private concerts—both in person and online. All payments are taken digitally, and the money is kept in escrow until the show happens. The host and artist negotiate a payment split on the platform. They have name-your-price ticketing, global transactions, and geotargeting. Artists can even facilitate tours by automatically selecting the locations they are looking to tour to, and the registered hosts in those areas get notifications and can decide whether to host the artist.

Side Door currently has 2,000 venues and hosts registered in North America, and more popping up in Europe and around the world. They've facilitated shows with Vance Joy, Broken Social Scene, Feist, Barenaked Ladies, Tom Odell, Said the Whale and thousands of others.

The quirk-rock band More Fatter set out on a 43-date backyard concert tour in the summer of 2021. Half the shows were ticketed ($30 through Eventbrite), and the other half were $30 suggested donation. Some shows had 50+ people packed into the backyard. And other shows where they didn't have much of a base and the host didn't promote it super well had 5–10. They sold T-shirts for $40 and burned CDs of new demos for $20. They completely sold out of all their merch after multiple reorders. They toured in a 2005 Toyota Sienna and crashed on couches to keep expenses down. In two months, they made $25,000. That's the thing with house concerts. It's such a magical experience that you can get away with selling your merch much higher than you would at a club. It's much more personal. People aren't simply buying your merch for the item, they're buying it as a souvenir from the night. And to have a special connection with you when they make the transaction.

The Booking

The beauty of house concerts is that you only need one superpassionate fan per city to set up a house concert. Put out feelers to your email list and on social sites. Set a guarantee plus a percentage of tickets, or you can play for tips.

You'll have to designate Fridays and Saturdays (or Sunday afternoons) for house concerts, since most hosts have 9-to-5 jobs and won't want to organize it for a weekday. But some may. Plan your house concerts about two to three months in advance. Give your hosts plenty of time to invite guests and get excited.

You'll want to tour with an amp or PA (and all mics/stands/cords) to plug in your guitar, keyboard and vocal mic. The host will most likely know nothing about sound and have zero sound equipment. You should be able to set up anywhere and play. Don't forget your extension cords and power strips.

The email I send out to potential hosts usually looks something like this (feel free to copy whatever you want):

Ari Herstand Living Room Concert!

What the . . .?
I'd like to set up shows in people's living rooms/backyards/dorm
lounges/etc. and have a very intimate experience—something that isn't

necessarily possible in many clubs I play. I'm going to play many new, unreleased songs for these performances—many songs that translate very well to the living room, but maybe not so well to the club.

Interested?

If you'd like to host a living room concert, all you need to do is reply and fill in the information below and I'll get back to you with possible dates for your area. I need you to bring at least 20 people to the concert—hey you have home turf advantage!

What I charge.

The concert costs $350 + 80% of admission after $350 is met. This means, if you charge $15 a head (what I recommend) and 30 people show up, that equals a total of $450. I end up with $430 (you end up with $20) at the end of the night. If 20 people show up, that equals a total of $300. I end up with $350 at the end of the night (you have to cover the remaining $50). If you're confident you can bring 24 people at $15 a head, everyone who lives in the house basically gets a free concert because I don't charge the hosts and hostesses. Just so you know, this is much lower than my normal "private concert" rate, but because I want people who really dig my music—dare I call them fans—to be able to afford this and not have to pay an exorbitant amount out of pocket, I've reduced my rate for these house concerts. I used to take 100% after $350, but I've added the 20% to the host idea to give you an incentive to provide simple snacks/drinks for your guests and so you don't lose money.

What to provide.

All you need to provide is a big enough space to hold everyone. Also, make sure my performance space (corner) is well lit with upright bright lamps or something and then the rest of the room can be dim with candles or other lamps. People are most comfortable sitting on chairs, couches, benches, husbands, boyfriends, girlfriends, etc., so it would be great if you had enough seating for everyone. Maybe encourage people to bring a pillow, blanket, or lawn chair to sit on if you don't have enough chairs. Make sure you have a key person who will collect money from everyone at some point.

How long is the concert?
The concert will last about 2 hours. The first 45 minutes I'll play an acoustic, mostly unplugged (chill) set. Then take a 15-minute intermission and the next hour will be a full looping show—plugged in. Make sure your neighbors are OK with this. Won't get too loud, though. I'm looking to start at 7:30 for most places.

Notes for this experience:
Please let your guests know that this is an intimate, private concert by a touring musician. This is not a party. Promote my music to all guests and get them excited about the music if they don't already know my stuff. This is not a drinking party with your best bud providing the entertainment. While alcohol is absolutely OK (and encouraged if somehow a Guinness ends up in my hand), this is not a time to get wasted.
Also, please inform your guests, maybe at the start (because I don't want to look like the bad guy), that talking is very uncool during the performance.

Anything else?
I'll most likely need a place to crash that night, so if you have a couch, that would be fantastic. If you provide dinner for me as well, I'll love you forever.

Please fill in this info and I'll get back to you with open dates:
City, State:
Are you in high school or college (please list where):
If in high school list parent's name:
      and email:
How many live with you (are they ok with this):
Do you live in a house, dorm, apartment, etc. (elaborate):
Expected number of attendees:
Where will this be held (living room, backyard, dorm lounge, etc. please elaborate):
Exact Address:
Contact Phone Number:

Hopefully I'll see you soon!
~Ari

And once you confirm a date, make sure you send them a confirmation email. Here's what I use:

Details:
Saturday, March 17
Contact: Mickey Mouse
Phone Number: 612-555-5555
Exact Address:
1234 Beautiful Lane
St. Paul, MN 55104
7:30–9:30 (you can change this if need be)
$15 a person (hosts excluded)
$350 guarantee + 80% of cover after $350
Make public (upon request) or keep private?
Load in: 6:00
Sound check: 6:30
Provided equipment: lamps to light my performance area (corner), mood lighting for the rest of the room
Sleeping accommodations? yes

**CANCELLATION POLICY
Because I am routing a tour around this show, once this is confirmed, we cannot cancel it. Please do not confirm this unless you are certain you can afford the concert and/or can get enough people to attend. If you have to cancel the show less than 3 weeks before the date, I will still need to receive 70% of payment.

Please confirm these details and we're set! Thanks!
~Ari

People have organized pot lucks, birthday, graduation and anniversary parties around these. You will have a lot of fun with house concerts, and even if you're a full band, as long as you tour with a full PA system, you can set up backyard and basement concerts. Customize this for you.

You will build lifelong fans this way. Attendees get a very personal experience, get to hang out with you before and after the show, and typically buy tons of merch.

Make sure you pass around the mailing list clipboard or iPad and get every single person's email who comes. If 30 people show up, the next time through you can book a club and you can estimate that each of them will bring at least 1 more person and now you have a solid 60 for your club show.

Shannon Curtis typically works solely on tips and merch sales for her living room concerts, and it has worked out very well for her. If you're just starting out, you can go this route as well. But make sure the host discusses the importance of the tip jar (she advises not to include a suggested donation because if you say the show is worth $10, no one will drop a twenty in). The tip jar (and merch) should be placed right near the front door so it absolutely cannot be missed.

Companies like Sofar Sounds, Side Door and ConcertsInYourHome organize (or help artists and fans organize) house concerts. Sofar Sounds has set up intimate, living shows with oftentimes famous artists like Hozier and Karen O of Yeah Yeah Yeahs.

House concerts are a beautiful, unforgettable experience for everyone involved.

OPENING TOURS

The Purpose of Opening Tours

Opening a hot tour can jump-start your career and expose you to an entirely new audience. It's one of the most valuable things you can do for your career. Many times, openers will not make much per show. But, because you're playing in front of mostly new fans, the merch potential is infinite. As long as you work your merch game right and secure as many email sign-ups as possible, you will come out ahead.

Being an opener of a bigger tour has a lot to do with connections. Many headliners bring only their friends' bands as their openers. Many labels will pair smaller artists with larger ones on the label. Sometimes being the local opener for a touring band can get you on the road with them if they liked your set and you were a fun hang in the green room. There's no one way to get on a big tour. It's best to hit up the manager of the headlining band and ask. Most bands will have their manager's contact info listed on their website, LinkedIn or Facebook. Send them your draw numbers for every city on the tour and your EPK. Talk about how hard you'll work to help promote the tour. Make it clear you'll be easy to work with.

Buy-Ons

Some mid-level artists charge their openers a "buy-on" amount. Typically, it's a bulk amount of money up front to cover expenses for the bus and hotels. But the opener will make a performance fee for each show throughout the tour (of maybe $150), so in the end you may break even. Artists who charge openers a buy-on rate and provide nothing other than the opportunity to open (no space on the bus, no lodging, no food, no performance fee) are flat out unethical. But you will sell merch and make fans. Remember, the average dollar per head for venues 500–1,000 cap is $3.65 in merch sales. You'll have to crunch the numbers and decide if it's worth it for you.

Getting smart with backstage "experiences" and merch, you should be able to make every tour profitable.

HOW TO STAY SANE ON THE ROAD

I highly recommend setting aside time every morning to exercise. Going for a run before you leave for the long drive will not only give you a fun way to experience the city, but let off steam and prevent you from wanting to murder your bandmates.

> Tensions will be high, so keep your tour pranking
> to a minimal; also execute it in a tactful manner.
> Waking up on a scummy floor with only your trusty
> Spiderman duvet for comfort and the house owner's
> smelly dog licking your face is often a bad start to the
> day. In such a fragile state, getting shot at with a water
> pistol full of gravy might just push you over the edge.
>
> —LEWIS WILLIAMS, DRUMMER FOR PRESS TO MECO

THE BRIDGE
25 Things to Do Before You Leave for Tour

1) **Order Merch**
2) **Create the Merch Display** Big. Bright. Bold. Awesome.
3) **Create the Tour Poster** Hire a graphic design artist for this.
4) **Send Posters to Venues** Or have Bandposters do it for you.
5) **Send Promo Packages to Street Team** Posters, handbills still go a long way. Rally the troops!
6) **Write the Tour Press Release** More on how to do this in Chapter 15.
7) **Contact All Local Media** See Chapter 15.
8) **Set Up Digital Payments and Credit Cards** Square, PayPal, atVenu, Venmo, CashApp. Make it easy for people to pay you.
9) **Set Up Inventory Tracking Program** AtVenu, Merch Cat or Excel.
10) **Get Musician's Insurance** MusicPro Insurance insures US musicians, producers and recording engineers (like $250/year for $20,000 worth of gear). Or in the UK check out Insure4Music. Many other insurance companies do not cover nonclassical musicians. Think I'm joking? Try to file a claim with your renters/homeowners insurance plan. I learned this the hard way.
11) **Get a Security System for the Van** And if you're pulling a trailer, make sure to back it up against a wall every night so no one can break into it. And buy the

indestructible, uncuttable pad locks. You have to expect that people will try to break in to your trailer. Remove the possibility.

12) **Get the Tour Mobile**   Fifteen-passenger van, Sprinter, SUV, bus? Research what is best for your purposes.

13) **Tag the Gear**   It's like how your mom put your name inside your undies when you went away to sleepaway camp. Put your name on every piece of gear.

14) **Email List**   Set up a landing page that you can lock an iPad on, or a desktop computer that you set at the merch table, or print out enough sheets for the clipboard for the entire tour. Print out QR codes to display at the merch table around the venue for one tap signups.

15) **Text Message Sign-up**   Email is still king, but it's becoming more difficult to get people on your list even with great incentives. Try experimenting with a text message subscription service at your shows. You could have signage in the venue (or on stage) with a message like: "Text ROCK to 55444 before the end of our set to win a backstage pass and hang with us after the show in the green room."

16) **Full Tune-Up**   You don't want to break down 200 miles away from a service station in Podunksville, Utah, with zero cell service.

17) **Advance the First Week of Shows**   Email or call the talent buyers and confirm all details.

18) **Add Shows to Bandsintown, Songkick and Create Facebook Events**   Don't forget the ticket links.

19) **Increase Data Limit on Your Phone**   You'll be binging a lot of shows in the van.

20) **Pack a Cooler**   Stay healthy and save some cash on eating out. Swing by grocery stores and make some sandwiches.

21) **Packing List**
   - Air mattress
   - Pillow
   - Sleeping bag
   - Laundry bag
   - Toiletry bag
   - Flushable wipes
   - Toilet paper (just in case)
   - First-aid kit
   - Advil
   - Starbucks VIA packets (Coffee on the go! Gas station coffee? No, thank you.)
   - Tumbler
   - Car outlet converter
   - Power strips for van

- E-ZPass
- Trashbags
- Canteen
- Frisbee, football, soccer ball, dumbbells, jump rope
- Phone armband
- Running earbuds
- Fancy headphones
- Phone mount
- Tire jack
- Spare tire
- AAA card
- Duct tape
- Extra phone charger
- Nuts
- Protein bars
- PA system (to be able to set up and play anywhere if need be)
- King-size sheet if you're touring in an SUV (to cover your gear at night)
- Laptop
- Passport (if you're crossing borders)
- Visas/proper paperwork (if you're crossing borders)
- Tour binder
- Printer (for day sheets, set lists)
- Printer paper
- Cash for merch change
- Credit card swiper (bring 2 or 3 to be safe)
- Windshield washer fluid
- Sriracha (my comfort food)

22) **Plan Out Oil Changes**

23) **Secure a Tour Sponsor** More on this in Chapter 10.

24) **Get a Car Topper** If you're touring in an SUV or plain ol' car, I recommend getting a storage component for the top of your vehicle. Throw all of your merch in there. You'll definitely need the extra storage.

25) **Try Not to Tour with a Trailer** You'll save a tremendous amount of gas and you won't be as much of a target for thieves. Take out the back row of your 15 passenger van or fit all your gear in the back of a Sprinter van.

9.

HOW TO MAKE REAL MONEY PLAYING COLLEGES AND PERFORMING ARTS CENTERS

How can an unknown singer/songwriter make $1,800 or an unknown band make $2,500 for 60 minutes of original music? Or $10,000 for an obscure niche act? For some of you, you just hit the jackpot. As someone who has played over 100 college shows around the country, I can tell you firsthand how amazing (and simultaneously awful) this really is.

I'm going to first go into extreme detail about the college market first and then we'll get to the Performing Arts Center (PAC) market.

WHAT IS THE COLLEGE MARKET?

Playing colleges is unlike any other performance experience on the planet. Before the dollar signs start to blind your vision, you have to understand what the college market actually is. Nearly every university in the country has a campus activities committee, board and/or advisor. Some smaller schools just have one or two people in charge of setting up programming and booking entertainment, and the larger state schools may have an activities committee of 50 students. Most activities committees have subcommittees for music, comedy, homecoming, freshman orientation, Spring Jam, Big Concert, Welcome Week and so forth. These committees plan programming for their students around the year. This includes everything from a hypnotist for freshman orientation, a magician and a rock band for homecoming week, a singer/songwriter for coffee shop night, a comedian just because and a lecturer to mix in some brain juice substance. But they also program activities with moon bounces, sumo costumes, climbing walls, mechanical bulls, Guitar Hero tournaments, laser tag and cotton candy machines. Nearly every university has a budget for these kinds of programs. Most programming budgets range from $10,000 (for the tiny, community colleges) to $200,000+ (for big state and private schools) a year. A year. Wonder where all that money from tuition goes? Now you know.

The Campus Activities Board's (CAB) main job is to provide meaningful programming for the students. The activities have to be diverse enough to appeal to the entire student body. And the entertainers cannot offend anyone. There's a big difference between edgy and offensive. Colleges buy edgy, but very few buy offensive. Of course whether something is offensive is subjective, but when you're competing with a zillion other acts (not just musicians), you want the best possible odds.

Before you go any further, let me make this easy for you. If you are a hip-hop artist who swears a lot, a punk band or really any band that screams, a political folk act, or if you play music that may be considered offensive by anyone, skip to Chapter 10.

CABs, unlike college radio stations, will not book offensive entertainment. Whereas college radio gets off on pushing the envelope, CABs have to be absolutely certain the acts they bring to campus will not get the school sued.

WHO IS ON THE CAB?

The people in charge of booking entertainment are not music aficionados (snobs). They don't know the hippest indie band of the moment or the newest underground emcee to break out of Minneapolis. They know top 40. And they are on the board because they like organizing events (or are looking for a résumé builder). They don't typically know anything about the music industry and aren't interested in your Tom Waits cover. They've never heard of him. But these are some of the friendliest, sweetest, kindest and generally fun-loving people you will meet. And yes, remember, they are 17–22 years old. They don't have any real-life business experience. More on this in a bit.

After playing so many college shows and meeting so many CABs, I started to notice a trend. A type. It's so interesting how similar CABs are in every region of the country. I guess campus programming attracts a certain kind of person.

But let me repeat, the people on the CAB, in charge of the $200,000 annual budget, aren't looking for the next Jack White; they're looking for the next Taylor Swift. If you want to break into the college circuit, you have to understand this and market yourself as such.

MUSIC INDUSTRY VS. COLLEGE INDUSTRY

The college industry is not the music industry. There's only a small overlap. Understanding this is key to your success. You cannot approach college shows like you approach club shows. You cannot approach college booking like you approach club booking. You cannot approach advancing shows with colleges like you approach advancing shows with clubs. You cannot approach sleeping arrangements for college shows the same way you approach sleeping arrangements for club shows (unless you want to get arrested or sued by Daddy). These are completely different industries.

You should look to college shows for one purpose: to make money. These are typically not career-building opportunities—unless you're looking to be a career college musician. Because the money is so good, many musicians get stuck in the college circuit. It's hard to go from making $1,500 a show with all expenses paid to making $100 a show and a single drink ticket when you start touring clubs again.

Club Shows		College Shows
less up front, more long-term potential	$	more up front, less long-term potential
couch	LODGING	hotels
Subway	FOOD	Applebee's
lifelong	FANS	semester
venue works with your schedule	TOUR	you route to school's schedule
oftentimes own venue, older	BOOKERS	change every 1–2 years, age 17–22
expected to be done by artist	PROMO	done exclusively by school
run by professional	SOUND	run by student
career	PURPOSE	money

Club shows vs. college shows Venn diagram.

CAREER BUILDING VS. MONEY MAKING

It's counterintuitive, I know, to say that you can't build your career within the college circuit. Let me tell you a little story. My first NACA showcase (more on what NACA is in a minute) was in the spring of 2008 at the Northern Plains conference. I booked 50 dates on the spot. My entire

2008–2009 school year was filled up with colleges around the Northern Plains region (Midwestish). I promoted the bajeebers out of every show (via MySpace—that was hot at the time). And most shows were totally packed. I sold tons of merch. And the CABs were thrilled. I followed up a few of these shows with a club show a couple months later. Take Drake University in Des Moines, Iowa. I remember this show very well. There were about 200 students at the show, I sold a ton of merch, got a bunch of mailing list names, signed autographs, took photos, the works. The head of the CAB even came up to me with a burned CD (those were big in 2008) of a remix he did of one of my recordings. Man, I hit the jackpot. Or so I thought. I followed up the Drake show with a date at Vaudeville Mews in Des Moines (just a 10-minute drive from campus or a 15-minute bus ride) a couple months later. I emailed the list, promoted it to the students. Everything. The night of the show, 5 people showed up. Ouch.

What happened? I'll tell you (because I've analyzed this ad nauseam after so many failed follow-up club shows).

There's a huge difference for college students between a free event on campus for which all they have to do is fall out of bed, roll down the hallway and they're there and a show off-campus where they have to find someone with a car to drive them, get dressed, and pay money. Getting college students dressed or asking them to part with their money is nearly impossible.

When you play these campus-sponsored events, that's exactly what they are: events. They're not typically concerts. Sure, you look at them as concerts, but the students are constantly going to campus-sponsored programs like comedians, hypnotists, magicians and lecturers. You're just another visiting guest. They love you in the moment. May even buy your record and T-shirt. They'll give you a Follow on Instagram. But they've forgotten about you in two weeks' time. You're done. They've moved on.

Not to say that none of them become true fans, but if I had to guess, I'd estimate about 2% of each audience became lifelong fans who I saw at future club shows. But often these 2% were on the board that booked me.

The best way to approach your music career with college shows is to book the college dates first and route club shows around them. Promote the club dates. Not the college shows.

One of the best parts of the college market is that you don't have to promote. You get a guaranteed payment whether 500 students show up or 5. You still walk with a fat check. And, oftentimes, the school actually doesn't want you to promote because these are closed shows (only offered to students).

I learned very quickly that spending effort promoting these shows independently was a waste of my time. Sure, work with the school on coming up with creative promo tactics for them to use on campus, but don't feel you need to do anything other than have a conversation or two with the CAB.

THE "SHOWS"

As a singer/songwriter playing colleges, I've played every possible kind of venue on campus you can imagine, from on-site rock clubs, beautiful theaters and arenas opening for huge stars down to student unions, cafes, outdoor grassy malls, dorm lounges and cafeterias. Actually, cafeterias are probably the most common "show" I've played. And usually it's at 11 in the morning playing to hungover kids' backs as they down a cheeseburger while occasionally looking over their shoulder confused as to why this guy with the goofy hair is blasting a trumpet at them at 11 in the morning.

I used to worry a lot about the kind of show I was playing and urged the CAB to create the best possible experience for me and the students. Waste of time and energy. Now I just show up and roll with it. Want me to play in a hallway in the student union during welcome week while incoming freshmen and their parents walk past me with goofy smiles on their faces? Fine. Want me to set up next to the cotton candy machine, across from the moon bounce and kitty corner from the magician who is five times louder than me? OK. Want me to stand behind the pool table and next to the Ms. Pac-Man machine and plug into a sound system without any monitors with the only speakers built into the ceiling? Whatever. Sure. I'll take my $2,000 check and be on my way, thank you very much.

Remember, the purpose of college shows is to make money. Yes, you want to put on as entertaining a show as possible. And you want to be accommodating, easygoing and all-around fun to work with. But you must completely drop your ego if you want to get into the college circuit. Don't tell the CAB that you require a 16-by-16-foot stage if you're a solo act. If you're a 4-piece rock band, don't say you can't play your show without a 48-channel mixing board. Let's be honest—you could play with a 12-channel board if you absolutely needed to.

Now, this isn't to say that you shouldn't put any effort into the performance. Of course, bring your A game (always), but just know that you have to be flexible. You're going to have to perform in very uncomfortable situations with a damn smile on your face. Sure, help the CAB know what works best for your show, the size of the stage, the sound system, the performance space and environment, and how you think the room should be set up, but if they organize something completely different for you, you have two options: Tell them you refuse to perform unless your specifics are met to a T or do what you can to make it work, take the check and be on your way.

WHAT ACTS DO BEST IN THE COLLEGE CIRCUIT?

Male singer/songwriters tend to do very well and get lots of bookings. Pop/rock bands do well for big Spring Jam and homecoming kinds of events. That being said, CABs want to bring diverse talent to campus. Genre doesn't matter as much as performance. Can you put on a fun, interactive, entertaining performance? Is it "safe" for colleges?

Does it appeal to 18- to 22-year-olds? More specifically, do *you* appeal to 18- to 22-year-olds? This might be a hard pill to swallow, but many people "age out" of the college market. A good rule of thumb: If you're over 35, you're going to have a much harder time getting booked in the college market than your 20-something counterparts. Now, this being said, sure, there are plenty of examples of 40-, 50-, even 60-somethings succeeding in this market. But this is the exception that proves the rule.

If you have a fun, entertaining show but are older than 35, the performing arts center market is probably best for you. That audience skews older. So, skip to that section.

NACA AND APCA

Now that you understand what college shows are and have a better idea of whether you want to make a go at the circuit, you need to know exactly how to approach this. Believe me, if you make a go at this blind, you will waste a ton of money and get nowhere. I've seen it happen to far too many bands.

NACA (National Association for Campus Activities—pronounced *naca*, not *N.A.C.A*) and APCA (Association for the Promotion of Campus Activities) are the two biggest organizations in the United States for college booking, and they organize various conferences around the country throughout the year for colleges to scout out talent and diverse programming to set up for the coming year. NACA is the bigger of the two and has been around the longest. It is a nonprofit. APCA is for-profit. NACA typically draws higher-budget schools (four-year state and private schools). APCA caters more to the two-year community colleges. However, they're not exclusive. Many community colleges go to NACA and many four-year institutions attend APCA. And some go to both.

The colleges that attend these conferences will send members from the CAB to scout out talent to book for the coming school year. These CAB members are called "delegates" at the conference.

I've showcased at both many times. NACA is much larger. Typically thousands of students representing hundreds of universities attend both the national and regional conferences. APCA typically has hundreds of students representing fewer than a hundred schools attending. The conferences last two to five days depending on the region and the number of attendees.

They both operate fairly similarly though. They both have showcases and marketplaces.

SHOWCASES

At the conference, there are designated showcase times where every attendee piles into a ballroom for a couple hours to sample the showcasing talent. Each act gets exactly 10 minutes to show the audience what they can do. The conferences are incredibly strict about the time frame and will shut off the sound and lights if you go over. You get 10:00 on the dot. There's actually a clock on stage that counts down from 10:00 the moment the curtain opens.

There's typically a comedian emcee that introduces all the showcasing acts (the comedian has also been selected to showcase). And the acts range from jugglers, magicians, comedians, hypnotists, singer/songwriters, bands, DJs and, for lack of a better term, variety acts. I once saw two guys covered head to toe in skintight black body suits, wearing masks with programmed light pads all over their bodies. They didn't speak. They didn't sing. They didn't dance. They pressed PLAY and ran around the audience hyping up the crowd. For 10 minutes. They booked five shows.

Every attendee from every school gets handed a packet at the start of the conference. In the packet is every showcasing act with a photo, bio and cost.

If you get selected to showcase, you set a price that is not negotiated at the conference. The school either decides to bring you for the listed price, or not. There are, however, discounts that can be applied. More on these in a bit.

The main showcase categories are Spotlight High, Spotlight, Low, DJ, Speaker and Emcee. All the showcases take place in the main ballroom except the Sampler, Roving and Lecture.

The showcases are top-notch production events. They are run by professional sound, lighting and staging companies, and there is a stage manager and helping hands (usually students from the attending schools). The showcases are extremely impressive. They make you look like a star. Even though when you play the campus you may be set up in a corner with a sound system that only half works if you duct-tape the master volume knob just so, at NACA and APCA conferences, you perform on a giant stage, with a pro sound system and a sexy light show in front of hundreds or thousands of students. It's definitely an unforgettable and exciting experience.

How do you get a showcase? Keep reading.

BLOCK BOOKING

Both NACA and APCA offer block booking discount prices. Every act has the option to give discounts if nearby schools want to go in on booking the act during a set period of time. APCA offers 3 block booking tiers: 2 of 3, 3 of 5, and 5 of 7. NACA offers only 3 of 5 and 5 of 7. This means, that 3 nearby schools (typically within a few hours' drive of each other) come together to book an act within 5 days.

So, if your "Single Date" (SD) price is $1,200, your 3 of 5 could be $950 and your 5 of 7 price could be $800. This encourages schools to coordinate with other schools. They could save a lot of money. And it benefits you because instead of flying out and playing one school for $1,200, you can fly out, rent a car and bang out 5 schools and come home a week later with $4,000.

You can tack onto your price a lot of extras like travel (plane ticket, checked baggage fee, car rental), lodging, food, sound and lights. So, even though your rate is $1,200, you may walk with a $1,800 check which includes the cost of your expenses. Many times, though, colleges will have deals with local hotels or set you up in a guest house on campus. And more times than not, the CAB will take you out for dinner. That's one of the most exciting things for the CAB. Don't skip the dinner. This hang time is vital at winning over the CAB, gaining a great reputation and getting rebooked. More on this in a bit.

HOW TO GET A SHOWCASE

NACA is very selective about who can showcase. There is a panel of 8-12 students (judges) for each region and national conference that goes through every application, one by one, and votes on who gets to showcase. It's an extensive process and sometimes lasts for days. Each region has a different panel of judges. It's very possible to get selected for one conference and not others.

For APCA, however, anyone who registers for the conference pretty much automatically gets a showcase if there's room. First come, first served. So this breakdown on how to get a showcase is for NACA.

The Video

The application process is extensive and requires a lot of paperwork. NACA asks for press clippings, accolades, bio, photos, tech requirements. But the single most important part of the application is the video. If you have absolutely zero impressive accolades, no press, but an amazing video, your chances of getting a showcase far outweigh a seasoned act with a *Rolling Stone* 5-star album review, countless headlining tours, but a poorly made video.

Your video should be three minutes long (but they'll mostly only watch the first 90 seconds) and it needs to be live. It's not a requirement in the application, but I'm telling you, after speaking with the advisor of the NACA national showcase selection committee and grilling her on exactly how they chose their talent (backstage before my NACA national showcase), your video, first and foremost, needs to be live. Not a music video where you're "performing" (lip syncing) in a cool warehouse. Live. Live audio and live video. It doesn't, however, need to be from a live show. But it definitely helps to see the audience reaction.

Your video doesn't have to be just one song. And actually, it's recommended that it consist of clips of various songs. Well-known covers of pop songs work best. Classics are always good. Well-known classics that 17–22-year-old, non–music aficionados know. Like Michael Jackson or The Beatles hits. No deep cuts. You're not going to impress anyone with a cover that only hard-core fans know. The hits.

You absolutely should have at least one cover featured in your video. You can include originals, but you will increase your chances if you have well-known covers.

To put things in perspective, I got rejected at six conferences in a row (same year) before I got selected to showcase at NACA Nationals. But after every rejection I reworked my video. And I didn't even change up the footage, I just changed the order of the songs and the way it was edited.

The Selection Process

Each region operates slightly differently on how the selection process works, but for the most part it goes like this: The advisor hits PLAY on the video. At the 90-second mark, she pauses the video and takes a vote of the room: "everyone who wants to put this video through to round 2 raise your hand." If the video gets a majority of hands, it moves on to round 2. The committee will go through every submission video before moving on to round 2.

Round 2, the advisor will play the 90 seconds again and take another vote. At round 3, the members split off on their own with all submitted materials, including the video, and can spend as much time with everything (this is where they can watch all 5 minutes of your video, or even a second video if you submitted two). Each person comes back with their ranked list. And the committee makes a master ranked list.

There are what's called Spotlight High and Spotlight Low. At regional conferences Spotlight High acts have Single Date (SD) prices at $1,251 and higher. Spotlight Low acts are $1,250 and below. At nationals the threshold is $1,500.

When you submit your application, you indicate which showcase you're applying for.

Applying to Showcase

The only way you can actually apply to showcase at NACA is by going through a bunch of steps and jumping through many hoops. For one, you have to be a paid member of NACA to apply to showcase. But not just that—you have to purchase a booth at the conference (whether you get selected to showcase or not). There are delegate fees (per day), a showcase submission fee, a showcase fee (if you get selected), a conference fee, not to mention travel costs. When all is said and done, it will cost you about $2,000 per conference. Just the NACA annual membership costs $280 per region or $675 for a national membership, which enables you to submit and attend every region and the national conference.

APCA also has a myriad of fees. The showcase fee, for one, is much higher because everyone gets in.

GET READY FOR THE CONFERENCE

So, let's say you take the plunge, pay all the fees, and actually get selected to showcase at the conference. First and foremost, know that as a first-time attendee you are at an extreme disadvantage just by nature of it being your first time. All the established agencies not only know each other, they know the organizers, most CAB advisors and know how the process runs. It's not as simple as just showcasing, standing in your booth and waiting for people to come and secure dates. There are "co-op buying forms" with levels of interest that a single approved member of the CAB is able to fill out. There are co-op sessions where all the block booking is done in an art auction style. If you don't know how this process works, your head will spin right off.

So, I strongly advise you not to go into these conferences blind. Actually, I strongly advise you not to attend these festivals without an agent.

Agents cover all of the fees (except the showcase submission fee of about $100), have the connections and the knowhow.

Marketplace

Every day of the conference there are showcases and there are marketplaces. The marketplace is held in a huge convention center and is lined with booths upon booths of agencies, vendors, self-represented artists, and, really, anyone who has something to sell to colleges. If your showcase goes well, your booth will be swarmed with college kids wanting to meet you and take photos with you (and hopefully book you). Because, for this day, at the conference, you are famous. Everyone looks like a star on the showcase stage. At my last national showcase, an American Idol winner performed right after me. Acts large and small, known and unknown, perform on the same stage at the same conference. So, just because the students have never heard of you before now, if they liked what they saw, they'll want to meet you and get a photo with you to brag to all their friends back home about all the awesome musicians they met.

But more important, the marketplace is also where business is done. This is where you schmooze your ass off not only to get every student to fall in love with you, but actually to commit thousands of dollars to bring you to campus. This is where you'll get the interest forms, exchange business cards and potentially secure dates on campus. Oftentimes you'll get a handful of interest forms (if your showcase kicked a$$), tons of business cards and hopefully lock in a few dates.

Technically, business can only be done within the confines of the marketplace, but the networking and schmoozing extend through the entire time you're there. And, especially after your showcase, you will be recognized everywhere: in the hotel, at the restaurant, the cafe, everywhere. Remember, thousands of college kids have just descended on a very small area of this city. They're everywhere. So you want to make the most of it. I once ran into a group of kids at the Starbucks a block away from the convention center, sat down and shot the sh*t with them for fifteen minutes, got their business cards, sent one to my agent and was booked by night's end. I also attended a showcase (after mine), sat in the back next to a few kids from another school, talked them up and got them to book me at their school as well. That was $3,000 just from schmoozing.

And know that the cheaper your price, the more shows you will book. CABs have a budget, and if you charge $1,500 but a singer/songwriter who is not quite as good is only charging $1,000, they'll probably book the cheaper act.

Should You Attend NACA Without Getting a Showcase?

No. You will be attempting to drag people into your booth (without crossing your booth exit line—yes, that's a NACA rule). Even if you have a big TV screen with your high-quality video playing on repeat or you play your music on your iPhone and hand delegates headphones to sample, you're competing with all the other acts who they actually saw showcase. Your chances of getting booked without showcasing are very slim. So don't waste your money or time going to the conferences if you don't have a showcase. And really, don't go to the conference without an agent.

FINALIZING THE SALE

Even if you lock in a date at the marketplace, there's still a lot of work to do before you actually show up on campus. For one, every school requires an actual contract. They'll need one from you that contains the details of the performance and the fee, and you'll most likely need to sign the school's form contract as well. These are typically nonnegotiable.

I booked a handful of college shows on my own when I was between agents, and I calculated that there are about fifty emails from initial contact to actually showing up on campus. Multiply that by, say, fifty schools if you absolutely killed your showcase. And that's just the schools who book you. You probably also received hundreds of business cards from the conference. So there's the work of following up and convincing schools to book you postconference. You are able to negotiate more with price once the conference finishes, so this is a negotiating tactic you can use outside the confines of the conferences.

There's the routing of shows, scheduling the plane tickets and lodging (if the school doesn't provide this), so you're looking at hundreds if not thousands of hours of work.

This is why you want a college booking agent. Not only do they have all the connections and know how to maximize each conference appearance, they also typically have a staff that can handle all of the paperwork and play interference for you. They know how to talk to CABs. There are lots of bubbly emails with smiley faces and friendly encouragement. Very little of that, of course, happens during club booking. Whereas you can finalize a club date with a total of four emails, written all in lowercase letters and short fragmented sentences, if you write in lowercase letters to 19-year-old college students and are short with them, they'll think you're not only unprofessional, but mean. There is a completely different etiquette when dealing with CABs and club talent buyers. Remember that Venn diagram?

So get a college booking agent.

HOW TO GET A COLLEGE
BOOKING AGENT

Most college booking agents solely book colleges. And many represent college entertainers of every kind: musician, comedian, variety, and so forth.

Many can also provide the moon bounce and cotton candy machine. You don't hit up college booking agencies like you hit up club booking agents. College agents typically make 15%–20% of your earnings from colleges. Some take that percentage of net and some of gross. Net means, if you got a $2,000 check from the college, but it cost you $400 to fly to the show and $100 for your hotel, your agent would take 15%–20% of $1,500. Some agents will actually ask the college to cut the agent's check separately and send it to them directly. If they take it out of the gross, if the check is for $2,000, they take 15%–20% of $2,000.

College booking agents won't bring you on their roster simply if you're good. You have to have music that not only will get booked on campus, but get a NACA showcase. You have to be easy to work with. Most agency contracts contain stipulations stating that you won't sleep with any of the students, you won't drink or do drugs while on campus, you won't party with the students and you won't act like a d**k in general. You are a direct representation of the agency. If you mess up, the agency messed up. And this is why most colleges solely prefer to work with agencies. They know that agencies vet their talent. CAB's butts are on the line if it gets out that the musician they brought to campus not only hosted an underage drinking party in their hotel room, but also gave one of the students an STD. So, unless you showcase at NACA, there is virtually no hope of getting booked on college campuses by cold emailing and cold calling. Don't waste your time.

Get an agent.

Agencies only really want to bring on talent who can get showcases at NACA. Now that you know how to get a showcase (a killer 3-minute video), you should get this video together before submitting to agents. If you need examples of NACA submission videos, you can visit any college agency website, click on their music section and browse their artists. Most agencies will have their artists' videos right there on the site, and more times than not this will be the artist's NACA submission video.

Cross-reference the artists who got showcases with the videos that got picked.

How to see who got showcases? Visit Naca.org and the conferences that haven't happened yet announce Showcasing Acts a couple months before the conference.

So, once you have your video good to go, email the agent with an email like this:

Subject: NACA submission

Body: Hi Scott, I'm a Los Angeles–based singer/songwriter. I'm seeking college representation and specifically would like to submit to the upcoming NACA conferences with you. Let me know if we can discuss possibilities.

NACA submission video: youtube.com/myawesomevideo
My EPK: mywebsite.com/epk

Talk soon,
~Ari

When to Submit

Most conferences happen in the fall, but a couple happen in the spring. April and May are the best months to submit to agencies. The fall conferences start taking applications in June. If you don't find an agent until August, you have completely missed your fall NACA submissions window. However, you can still hit them up to submit to the spring semester conferences.

Don't hit up agencies in September or October, though. This is heavy conference season, and they are way too busy going to conferences, following up with schools and booking their acts from the interest generated at the conference. So April (at least two weeks after the conference finishes) and the month of May are best. Or all summer is fine, but know that you're missing the fall conference window. December-January is also a slower time when you will get more looks, but you're far away from any conference submission deadline.

THE TOP 10 MUSIC COLLEGE BOOKING AGENCIES

(in alphabetical order)

The Barry Agency
thebarryagency.com
info@thebarryagency.com
(763) 550-0513

Bass/Schuler Entertainment
bass-schuler.com
chris@bass-schuler.com
(773) 481-2600

Brave Enough Agency
braveenough.com
booking@braveenough.com
Mark Miller

The College Agency
thecollegeagency.com
booking@thecollegeagency.com
(651) 222-9669

Degy Entertainment (DMS)
degy.com
jeff@degy.com
(732) 818-9600

Developing Artist
developingartist.com
shawn@developingartist.com
617-497-8366

Diversity Talent Agency
diversitytalentagency.com
info@diversitytalentagency.com
(770) 210-5579

Houla Entertainment
houlaentertainment.com/
leemayer@houlaentertainment.com
(865) 385-5514

Neon
neon-entertainment.com
scott@neon-entertainment.com
(716) 836-6366

Sophie K Entertainment
sophiek.com
kate@sophiek.com
(212) 268-9583

WHAT TO DO ONCE YOU HAVE A SHOW

Whether or not you get an agent, once you have a show on campus, there are still things that you, the artist, need to do. You must advance every show. It's best to do this two weeks prior to the show to go over all details like load-in, sound-check times, dinner time, lodging (it will be listed on the contract), who is going to pick you up from the airport or if you need to rent a car, and who your day-of contact is with their phone number.

And remember, whenever you interact with anyone on CAB (or even the advisor, who most likely was on CAB when she was a student), be bubbly, friendly and include smiley faces in your emails. One time a CAB member got in touch with my tour manager and requested that I send over 300 CDs that they could use to promote my appearance. My tour manager explained (via email) that selling CDs is how I make my living and that we cannot send them 300 free CDs, however we would happily sell them 300 CDs for a very big discount of 50% off. I got a call from my agent a few days later saying that my TM made this girl cry. After that, my TM included lots of smiley faces and took a deep breath before every email interaction with college students. They're young. They're sensitive. Be gentle.

Fly Dates

Unless you showcase within the region you live in and route tours around your college dates, you'll likely fly to most shows.

President Obama signed into law the FAA Modernization and Reform Act of 2012, one section of which states that musicians are legally allowed to carry their instrument on the plane if at the time they board it fits in the overhead compartment. Most airlines don't give me a problem, but for some reason, United continues to insist that I gate-check my guitar, even after the infamous United Breaks Guitars viral video. What I do in that case is let them affix the gate-check tag to my guitar, but as I walk down the jetway, I rip it off and put it in my pocket. Then I board the plane, smile at the flight attendants, and pop that sucker into the overhead bin. (Just to be on the safe side, I always carry a copy of the section of the law that covers this. You can find it here: aristake.com/?post=87. So far, this has worked.)

And if you have to fly one of those tiny puddle jumpers, it won't fit up top. So, it's always advisable to get a case that can be gate-checked if absolutely necessary. I recommend the WolfPak Acoustic Guitar Poly-foam Case. Not only is it sturdy as hell, it's lightweight and has a back-pack strap, and lots of storage for strings, clippers, tuners and sheet music. I've flown with that sucker around the country with no problems.

I want to give a special shout-out to Southwest Airlines, as they have never once given me a problem flying with my guitar (even before the law went into place), and because of their no-fee flight change policy, I've been able to reroute my travel plans with no problems if I get a last-min-ute gig. They also allow two free checked bags, which I always utilize with all of my gear and merch. Southwest for the win!

GETTING REBOOKED

Just so you're not startled when this happens, most colleges will not book the same "event" two years in a row. You can imagine my horror after my first year of playing colleges—during which I booked fifty schools from my NACA showcase and nearly every show was packed and I made spe-cial moments and inside jokes with every CAB—when I didn't get asked back the following year by most of them. I thought I did such a good job promoting the shows, drawing such a big crowd, putting on such a good show and being all around a good hang that they'd have to bring me back. However, the CABs patted themselves on the back for putting on such a great event that brought lots of people. Because at the time I was working with an agent who went to only one regional conference, I had no other prospects and no plan B. I had gotten accustomed to the fat pay checks and lifestyle that reflected that. So it was back to the club hustle and PB&J dinners.

Moral of the story: Save, save, save. Even though you're rolling in it today, you may not be tomorrow.

BREAKING INTO COLLEGES

As you can see, it takes a lot of work to break into the college circuit. Lots of time and lots of money—even if you have an agent. Sure, your agent will cover all of the fees for NACA and APCA, but you still have to pay to get yourself to the conferences. You have to pay for hotel rooms at the conference. You have to pay for a rental car from the airport to the hotel. If you can't fly with your gear, you'll have to pay to rent gear at the conference. If you don't know how to shoot and edit high-quality video, you'll have to hire someone to do this. You could spend hundreds or even thousands of dollars long before you see your first check. Let's say you get three fall showcases and it costs an average of $400 per round-trip plane ticket, $100 a night for a hotel and $50 per rental car. You're looking at around $2,000 just to get to and from the conferences. Your first show won't typically be for 6 to 12 months. Or longer. Because schools book for the following school year.

So if you want to get into the college scene, make sure you are willing to stick with it for at least three years. Remember, I got rejected six times before I got a showcase. That was a full year of nothing but rejection. So if you really want to go for it, you have to stick with it. You won't start seeing results (checks) for a long, long time.

THE PERFORMING ARTS CENTER MARKET

Performing arts centers (PACs) are another hidden secret of the music industry. PACs are organizations that bring entertainment to their community or neighborhood. These include nonprofit groups without a venue that put on events at venues around town, theaters in town that book entertainment in-house, or even just summer concert series. There are around 1,400 PACs in the US, and each one books around 50 acts a year. Needless to say, there are a lot of opportunities for musical acts in this space.

The types of entertainment PACs bring in for the community range from touring Broadway musicals, plays, comedians and, of course, live music.

What Acts Do Best?

In the music space, the acts that do the best are ones with a clear concept. Something you could sum up in an elevator pitch that appeals to their (typically older) subscribers. That's the thing: The majority of the funding for PACs comes from annual paid subscribers. Sure, every show is open to the public and tickets are sold for every show, but the subscribers are the bread and butter.

So, the musical acts that do the best are: tribute bands (the Paul McCartney Experience, Motown Live), world music, lounge singers, and other easily marketable acts. Niche acts do very well here. That being said, I've seen some original songwriters with showstopping voices and performances also do very well in this market.

Compensation

Each PAC pays anywhere from $1,000–$15,000+ for unknown acts (of course they pay tens of thousands for the known acts). It is not uncommon for a 5-piece band to make $15,000 for one evening of music. And, like colleges, PACs pay for your expenses. However, they won't book your lodging or flights; you'll just calculate those costs and add them to your all-in rate. Meals, sound and lights are typically provided by the PAC.

Bigger acts with multiple members can demand a much higher rate—especially from PACs in big cities (they'll typically have much bigger budgets). Solo artists playing rural communities will be looking more at the low end of this range.

Block Booking and Residencies

Like the college market, PACs like to participate in block-booking rates. So, for instance, if your rate is $5,000 for a one-off show, it could be $3,500 if the PAC wants to team up with three to five neighboring towns' PACs for the same week.

Every PAC will require a contract, so you'll want to have yours at the ready with all details spelled out.

Outreach

Educational outreach is extremely important to most PACs. The PAC wants to know that you have educational programming for the community and can put on a workshop outside of your performance. This is because most PACs get grants from the government to supplement their budget, and these grants might require that the organization is providing educational community outreach.

Some outreach examples include songwriting workshops at a library, or performing a concert and talkback at the local high school, or talking about the history of the type of music you play. Anything that has an educational purpose to it can be considered outreach.

Conferences

Similar to NACA and APCA in the college market, the PAC market has various conferences all over the country. Some of the major conferences include:

> Association of the Performing Arts (APAP) in NYC
> Arts Northwest (ArtsNW)
> Canadian Association for the Performing Arts (CAPACOA)
> Folk Alliance International (FAI)
> GlobalFest
> International Performing Arts for Youth (IPAY)
> International Entertainment Buyers Association (IEBA)
> Montana Performing Arts Consortium (MPAC)
> Ohio Arts Professional Network (OAPN)
> North Carolina Presenters Consortium (NCPC)
> Western Arts Alliance (WAA)

The Showcases

There are many different kinds of showcases, depending on the conference. Some conferences like APAP and Folk Alliance have individually produced showcases, oftentimes sponsored by an organization or agency, and are put on in hotel rooms (yes, literally), conference rooms at the hotel or sometimes even at venues around town. And then there are more of the traditional showcases, like what we see at NACA or APCA, which are sponsored by the conference and put on in the convention center. Showcases are typically 12–15 minutes, or up to 30 minutes at Folk Alliance.

How to Showcase

Many conferences take showcase submissions through iwanttoshowcase. ca. However, some take submissions directly on their website. You will need a great 3-to-5-minute video. It should be live. Sizzle reels do best here.

But you can also host your own showcase or link up with a group hosting their own private showcase. You'll want to inquire with the conference if they support private showcases.

The Marketplace and Booking

At the conference, there is always a marketplace held in one of the big ballrooms or conference centers. This is where the buyers meet the sellers. It's important to know that most PACs book one to two years in advance. They book their entire seasons up before they announce the year. You want to have your availability for the next two years at the ready.

You'll also need your rates ready for one-off shows and block booking for three to five shows and five to nine shows (around the same time). You will need your outreach program fully laid out (it's best to have visual aids that help you explain it). And get that elevator pitch down.

After the conference, you'll get a block-booking report, which has the interest levels of different PACs.

Top Agents in the PAC Market

If you've played a few PACs already and showcased at a conference or two, you may be ready for an agent. Here are some good ones (in alphabetical order) you can hit up for possible representation:

AMAZ Entertainment

Canis Major Music

DCA Productions

EPIC Arts Management

FLi Artists

G. L. Berg Entertainment

Global Artists Collective

Harmony Artists

Indigenous Performance
　　Productions

Jean Schreiber Management

Jeff Turner Entertainment
　　Group

Knudsen Productions

Live Arts and Attractions

Liz Gregory Talent

Mariam Liebowitz Artist
　　Management

McCoy Artists Group

Myriad Artists

Patricia Alberti Performing
　　Artists Management

Producers, Inc.

Riot Artists

Skyline Artists Agency

The Source Management
　　Group

SRO Artists

ThinkTank Music Network

10.

SPONSORSHIPS AND INVESTMENTS

Guys like me are sitting out here just dying to have the right partners knock on our door.

—JAMES BOOK, MARKETING DIRECTOR, NINKASI BREWING CO.

WHAT ARE SPONSORSHIPS?

If you have built up a substantial fanbase, even just a local one, you should seek out sponsors. However, don't think of them as sponsors. They are partners.

The biggest misconception bands have about sponsorships is that the company will give the band a fat check and that's that. Why do you think they're giving you a check? It's not because they love your music and want to support you. That's why your Uncle Joe is writing you a check. Not why Budweiser is.

The reason any company wants to partner with you is because they see value in it. So you must offer value.

It's not about what they can do for you; it's what you can do for them.

The location of your fanbase will determine what kind of sponsors, ahem, partners, you should solicit. Are you drawing 500+ people to your shows in your hometown? Contact local breweries, car dealerships, pizza parlors, nail salons, sandwich shops, clothing stores—really, any local establishment who wants your fanbase to buy their product.

If you're an influencer and have a national or worldwide audience, you can think bigger. Who are your fans? Where do they live? What are their ages? You can find all of this info in your backend analytics.

If you're killing it on the national club circuit bringing 200–500+ people at every tour stop, with a 50-date tour, that's 10,000–25,000 focused eyeballs and eardrums on their product. These aren't 25,000 views on some banner ad, these are 25,000 engaged audience members willing to do whatever their favorite artist tells them to (and buy whatever he tells them to buy).

So, put together a list of companies who would be interested in marketing to your fan base.

A 2015 study done by AEG and Momentum Worldwide found that 93% of Millennials say they like brands that sponsor live events. And going to a music event that was sponsored made Millennials love that brand more, while those that stayed at home didn't have the same reactions.

The study also found:

- 89% like brands that sponsor a live music experience, compared to 63% among nonattendees.
- 89% perceive those brands as being more authentic, compared to 56% among nonattendees.
- 83% leave with a greater trust for brands that support a live music experience, compared to 53% among nonattendees.
- 80% purchase a product from a sponsoring brand after the experience, compared to 55% among nonattendees.
- 80% recommend brands that sponsor a live music experience to their networks, compared to 49% among nonattendees

If you're contacting a company to sponsor your local shows or tour, this is strong ammunition to use for your proposal.

HOW TO GET A SPONSORSHIP

The Proposal

Once you have your list of companies and contact information, you should put together a proposal packet to pitch the company. In the proposal you should have:

- **Your Band Logo Directly Next to the Company's Logo**
- **A Short Bio of Who You Are (If They Don't Know)**
  Include impressive accolades.
- **What You Are Asking For (Money, Gear, Van, T-shirts, Vinyl Printing)**
  Remember that a sponsorship doesn't just need to be for cash. Often, "trade" partnerships are the best kind. If you're working with a statewide car dealership, see if they will give you a van. You can wrap that van in the dealership's name, and if you tour around the state, they get a touring billboard with a sexy band inside which will be parked outside of every venue you play.
- **What You Can Provide for Them**
  It can be signage at all your shows. Mentions from the stage ("Bauhaus Brew Labs has been awesome to us and is helping us tour the country. Everyone go buy a Bauhaus beer. Our favorite is the Stargazer. Cheers!"). Subtle (or not so subtle) product placement in your videos. Shout-outs to them on all of your social media. A string of creative short-form videos featuring

their product. A jingle for their company to use in commercials, videos, their website. Interactive experiences at your shows (a photo booth with their logo tagged on every photo that gets uploaded to your socials and emailed to fans to post on their socials). Five Tweets a month mentioning the brand. Two Tik-Tok and Instagram Reels a month. Three total Instagram stories. An extended-write-up tour blog that creatively discusses the product posted on Facebook, Instagram and Twitter. The official music video for the next single prominently featuring the product at some point. Videos that will be posted to You-Tube, Facebook and Instagram. Get creative with what you can offer. The more you're able to offer, the more you can ask for.

■ **The Time Frame**

Is this for one local show? A tour? A year? Get specific.

■ **The Potential Reach**

10,000 YouTube subscribers. Average 50,000 monthly views. 50,000 TikTok followers, average of 5,000 views per video with max reaching 1.2 million views. 10,000 Facebook Likes. 20,000 Twitter followers. 350,000 Instagram followers. 10,000 average views per Reel, 8,000 average views per Story. 25,000 monthly Spotify listeners. 500 people attend every local show. Average of 200 college age kids per show at your upcoming 50-date college tour. Be realistic. But make this look impressive.

■ **What the Company Needs to Provide for You**

Make sure you include that they will need to provide the promo materials you promise: sign, beer to drink on stage, wrap for the van. If you promise to hang a sign onstage but don't specify that they actually need to provide the sign, they may expect you to create and print one, which may eat into much of the money they give you. It's good to have a sign onstage no matter what, so have them print a big banner with your name on it with a "brought to you by Company Name" below it. Not only does it get their name out there, people will see the company much more favorably because they are "bringing you," their favorite band.

▪ **Perks**

VIP access and seating for all shows. Tickets for all employees for all shows. Studio hang time.

▪ **Private Performance**

Offer to play a private show for the company (they must secure the venue). If you have your own sound and lighting, this can be easy and painless. Say this is a $5,000 value.

Don't attach this proposal to your initial email. Find the person at the company who is in charge of marketing. Get her email and phone number. Call her up and say "Hi, I'm Ari Herstand, manager of the band Roster McCabe. I have a partnership proposal I'd like to send you. The band loves Bauhaus beer and I think there are ways we can work together. Can I send over the proposal?" Let her give you her email. Then send the proposal the minute you get off the phone. If you don't hear back, reply from that same email three days later and confirm that she got it and if she'd like to discuss it more.

You should be realistic about the kinds of sponsors you can hit up. If you're a band playing to 200 people a night, you're not ready for Pepsi. However, a less well-known brand like Lagunitas might be interested. Especially if they're trying to break into the clubs you already have booked for your tour.

It's very possible for mid-level bands to obtain sponsors that can help cover expenses. You just have to be smart about it.

HOW TO GET AN INVESTMENT

You never know who's listening. I once helped a singer/songwriter playing a weekly 4-hour cover gig at the local watering hole secure a $100,000 investment from one of the regulars there. You don't need 1,000 fans to pay you $100 a year. You could just have one pay you $100,000. When someone approaches you for something like this, you should know how to go about securing this.

Typically, someone who has this kind of dough to invest in you isn't doing it to make money. They're doing it because they want to help you succeed. They aren't giving you a loan. It's an investment. A risky one at that. And they know this. So the proposal you put together should absolutely indicate that this person could make good money if you explode.

Set it up so that you don't have to pay back any money until your annual net income surpasses a set amount of, say, $30,000 per member (before salaries). Now, this is net income. After all expenses. So, if you have 4 band members, you will start to pay on the investment after your annual net income surpasses $120,000 (so each band member makes $30,000 minimum). This is quite modest and your investor will appreciate that. Your minimum annual income can increase by a small amount every year. So $30,000 minimum this year, $33,000 next year, $36,000 the year after and so forth. So, if your investment is for $100,000 with a term of 10 years, you have to make a minimum of $30,000 net income your first year to pay anything to the investor. If you make $25,000 (after expenses), you pay nothing. If you make $33,000, you pay a percentage of $3,000.

It's fair to pay 25% of your annual net income (above the base). So, in this example, if you made $33,000 net in your first year, you would pay $750 (25% of $3,000). If you also made $33,000 your second year (and $33,000 was your base your second year), you'd pay $750 your first year, but $0 your second year.

Your investors will want you to succeed, and they also will want to come along for the ride. So in addition to giving the investors a percentage of your earnings (above your base), give them perks like free tickets, VIP everything, shout outs and so forth.

This may sound pretty informal, but you're going to have to enter into a carefully drafted written agreement that sets out all these details and requires you to report to your investors periodically. It is important to understand that any investment arrangement implicates federal and state securities laws. You absolutely should not do any deal like this, no matter how little money is involved, without the help of a lawyer who knows this area of the law.

HOW TO WASTE AN INVESTMENT

Once you secure the dough, don't blow it on dumb purchases like vintage gear or expensive music videos. Approach your career with the income it is currently generating. Treat the investment as a true investment in your career. How can it best grow your audience? How can you use $100,000 to generate $150,000? A $4,000 guitar and $2,000 amp is not how. A $15,000 music video with no marketing behind it will go nowhere. The money would actually be best spent developing your own production studio where, instead of spending $5,000 per video, you spend $10,000 and purchase expensive cameras, lights, audio equipment, editing and recording software, and you become an expert on how to use it all (or have one of your band members learn this) and then pour the rest into marketing.

And remember, the 50/50 breakdown—50% of your budget goes to production; 50% goes to marketing. Whether you're working with $500 or $500,000, this is the ratio.

11.

HOW TO MASTER THE INTERNET

A person like Prince or a person like Michael Jackson could have
never survived in today's (social media driven) world.

—JAMIE FOXX

Chasing virality, that in itself can pigeonhole [artists] to be in a
position to have a shortened window of opportunity for them.
We would want to encourage them to think long-term and not be
hyper-focused on creating a viral moment. Really just be hyper-
focused on creating your craft.

—COREY SHERIDAN, SVP MUSIC, TIKTOK

TikTok is a very important piece of the marketing mix. It takes
the teams that are around the artist to then build a story and
find a way to take the trends and learnings that are happening on
TikTok to be able to translate on other platforms.

—DAVE MELHADO, HEAD OF MARKETING, UNITEDMASTERS

FROM 2005 TO 2008 A BAND'S ENTIRE ONLINE FOCUS WAS CONFINED TO
MySpace. The only thing musicians had to worry about was about
gaining friends, posting a "thanks for the add" on new friends' comments
section, organizing their top 8 list to give the appropriate shout-outs
without offending anyone by omission, and finding the proper theme

that accurately represented the project. There were entire MySpace marketing books on how to effectively grow an audience. It was an exciting time for musicians. For the first time in the history of the industry, the playing field was level. Every artist was on MySpace. The same MySpace. Major-label artists and 17-year-olds-living-with-their-parents artists had the same capabilities on MySpace. Mastery of the platform was dependent on how much time you spent on it—not how much money you had.

Unsigned artists were able to mimic major-label artists' MySpace accounts. And for a while, everyone did. Artists customized their profiles to match what the labels did. The idea was, "We have to make it look like we're a professional outfit and can compete with the big-timers."

Even though unsigned artists ran their own accounts, most made it look like an entire operation ran it. Artists put up an untouchable façade. They thought it gave them a mystique enjoyed by their favorite rock stars. However, what most artists didn't realize (until it was too late) was that fans craved access and authenticity. And artists who gave this to them were rewarded.

One of the biggest stars of MySpace was singer/songwriter Ron Pope. On the "unsigned" MySpace charts he was always in the top 3. His song "A Drop in the Ocean" went viral on the platform, gaining upward of 60 million plays. I happened to meet Ron right as he was gaining popularity on the platform. I was booking my first tour to New York City and searched for New York–based singer/songwriters on MySpace and saw he had a show at a small cafe in Greenwich Village during the time I was going to be in town. I asked to open the show and offered in return that I'd book him every day on a stage I was running at Summerfest in Wisconsin. Right around the date of our cafe show, his MySpace plays began to skyrocket. Hundreds of "A Drop in the Ocean" covers were popping up on YouTube from teens around the globe. I asked Ron what his trick was. Was he paying these kids to do this to make it look like he was big? He shrugged and said that there were no tricks. He just said that he made sure to reply to every message he got. And his bio was written in first person.

I was shocked. Dumbfounded. "But we independent artists should maintain mystique," I thought. But Ron proved that "shoulds" didn't exist in this new, open world. Artists that did it differently succeeded. Artists that did it like everyone else were ignored. Anonymous. Fans have always craved authenticity, but it was a rude awakening for most artists to realize how authentic they were really supposed to be. Open. Honest. Naked.

By the time most artists realized this, it was too late. People were leaving MySpace in droves and finding refuge on YouTube and Facebook. Different rules. Different game.

In 2011, just about a year after I moved to L.A., many of the people I knew were blowing up on YouTube. At the time, YouTube was still relatively young and "YouTubers" were quickly becoming a thing. Many of them lived in L.A. I found myself at this interesting intersection of new music, new media, new social, new recording techniques, new haircuts. The swoop was alive and well.

Anyway, I teamed up with a few friends who had blown up on YouTube to try the YouTuber thing. The first thing I learned was that they didn't just throw up videos from last night's show. Or just upload their new music video that they spent the past three months working on. They put up a new video. Every. Week. And it was high f'ing quality. Well, for 2011 standards.

I did a few collabs. Day one we chose a cover song to do (it was all about covers back then), hopped into a friend's recording studio (bedroom), camera ready, and tracked the song in about three to four hours. Filmed a bit of the session. The engineer/producer did a quick mix, and we were done. Day two we concepted the video, ran around town getting supplies, props, outfits, recruiting friends to be in it, and scouting locations. Day three we shot the video and began editing. Day four we finished editing the video and by this point had the final master of the song and distributed it to DSPs. Day five we added the finishing touches to the video and cued it up to YouTube to go live the next day.

Rinse and repeat. This was their life.

Some videos went viral. Some got tens of thousands of views. Some got just a few thousand.

After doing this for a few months, I realized I hated it. I thought, "If this is what a music career is, I want nothing to do with it."

For one, I wasn't proud of the recordings we made. They were, how do you say, fine. But I didn't really stand by them. The videos were cheesy, bubbly, fake. We were chasing trends and covering hit songs of the moment to catch the wave of what the masses were searching for in that moment.

The numbers were misleading. They were just that: numbers. Not fans. What's a million views if none of those people know who you are? Especially if you're not getting paid for those million views. Seriously, who cares? Your coworkers think you're cool for a week? You still gotta turn in your TPS reports on time. Cool points don't pay your bills.

I saw no end in this hamster wheel of content creation. I tapped out real quick. Others kept going for a couple years and eventually burned out too. And the select few who were able to actually launch long-lasting careers from YouTube were not participating in the chase as it was. They went their own way. Did their own thing. And built a fanbase. Albeit a bit slower. But it was deeper.

People who don't know anything about anything like to tell musicians all the time what they need to do.

In 1999, it was "You gotta get on the radio!"

In 2004, it was "You gotta get on iTunes."

In 2005, it was "You should go on *American Idol*!"

2007, "You gotta get on Myspace."

In 2012, "You gotta get on YouTube."

2013, "You should be on *The Voice*."

In 2014, "You gotta get on Vine."

2015, "Instagram!"

2016, "Snapchat!"

2017, "You gotta get on Spotify."

And in 2022, it was "You gotta get on TikTok."

Oh really, wise seatmate on the plane? That's *all* I need to do? Just get on *fill in the blank* and I'll have a successful music career? Damn, thank you soooo much for your wisdom. You just changed my life. *Ahem.*

If it was that easy, everyone would do it.

What your seatmate doesn't know is that behind that one musician who went viral and is now on the morning news, there are 100,000 who spent years trying to do what *you* said even though they hated the process, burned out, and just served you your coffee in Terminal B.

Burnout is real.

"Get on TikTok" is not a strategy. Just like "Get on YouTube" wasn't (and still isn't) a strategy.

Whatever you "get on," you have to enjoy the process.

You know how much 1 million views on a YouTube video pays? Around $3,000. And that's only if the video is monetized. And if most of the views came from the US. If it's a cover song, it's next to nothing for you. How often do you think people get 1 million views on YouTube? And of course, monetization is now only open to those with 1,000+ subscribers and 4,000 watch hours (!!) in the past year.

Want to know how much people get for 1 million views on TikTok? $0. What about 1 million views on Instagram? $0.

Why are you doing what you're doing? Do you even know?

If you chase a trend based on an offhand comment from a very confident seatmate on the plane, you're most likely going to fail.

And what is failure? Giving up. Why would you give up? By burning out.

Burnout is real.

There's a big difference from Lil Nas X making 100 memes to promote "Old Town Road" to you chasing every trend on TikTok. There's a difference between Justin Vibes posting TikTok videos of himself playing TV theme songs on the vibraphone and an artist doing the Skull Breaker, Unlock It, Face Wax, Corn Cob, and Cereal Challenge (yes, these were all real).

The difference? One is "on brand," and one is "off brand." One will inspire you to keep creating and engaging your growing fanbase. One will cause burnout very, very quickly.

If you're aspiring to be an Influencer (with a capital I), then yeah, chase all those damn trends. Your "brand" is trend. However, if you want to be a professional musician, you don't chase, you lead.

Sure, you can take inspiration from what's happening in pop culture, specifically on the social media apps of the moment. Artists throughout history have always made nods to pop culture. But don't chase. Lead.

How can you take a trend, and make it your own, on brand?

Today, artists don't have the luxury to solely exist on one social media platform. Fans are everywhere and expect artists to be as well. As new ones pop up and others evolve, artists have to constantly revise their strategies.

You rent your fans to social media platforms; you own your fans when you have their email addresses or phone numbers. And you own your website.

HOW TO BUILD A GREAT-LOOKING WEBSITE WITH NO WEB DESIGN EXPERIENCE

You absolutely need a dot.com website that you own. So much of the internet relies on verifying identities. If you don't have a website that you own, it will be that much more difficult to verify your existence and prove to the internet gods that you are who you say you are. Luckily, with template-based website creation services like Bandzoogle and Squarespace you don't have to deal with unreliable and expensive web developers anymore.

And now that you can track every visitor to your website (and then market directly to them via Facebook, Google, Instagram and TikTok ads), a website is now so much more than just a place to put official info. Every visit on your site is tracked. Every purchase is tracked. Bringing your fans to your website gets them into *your* ecosystem. Interacting with your fans solely on social platforms gives up the control and connection. You are at the wills and whims of the platform. They could flip a switch and you would lose all of your access.

WHAT SHOULD GO ON YOUR WEBSITE

- **Music**

  This may seem obvious, but I can't tell you how many musician websites I've visited that didn't have a way to actually play the music. A music player of some sort should be on your home page. Don't make a new visitor hunt around for it either. Within five seconds of visiting the site someone should be able to listen to your music if they want to. But, whatever you do, do not have it autoplay. There is nothing more annoying than visiting a site and being blasted with audio and having to frantically figure out how to turn it off.

- **Video**

  You should also have your best video front and center on your homepage. Do not have it autoplay either. Allow people to click play if they want to. If you don't have any high-quality video, get some. You should also have a video section on your site that features many more videos, but put your best or most recent video right there on the home page.

■ **Mailing List Sign-Up**

Make this prominent. Remember to give visitors incentives to sign up. And make sure there's an option to join the street team as well—it can be in your confirmation email.

■ **Show Dates**

If you want to have your concerts appear on the sidebar of Google when someone searches your band, you have to either embed a Bandsintown, Seated or Songkick widget on your site or use Bandzoogle's concert calendar or the GigPress plugin for Wordpress. It's no longer enough to just list your shows on your website; you have to make sure they get listed on Google as well. And you have to use a Google-approved show calendar and put it on your official website (just adding your shows to Bandsintown or Songkick is not enough).

■ **Photos**

Press outlets will want to quickly grab promo photos for their stories. Oftentimes they will grab something without asking you. So make it easy for them. Feature your best, highest-quality promo photos first. It's best to have the option to download high res-versions easily as well (for print). But you'll most likely be sending your EPK to the press outlets.

■ **Lyrics**

This is a biggie. So many artists forget to put their lyrics online. Don't make it difficult for your fans to find your lyrics. One of your tabs should be Lyrics.

■ **Bio**

Have both a short, promo bio that venues and press outlets can copy and paste, and your longer, personal bio. Reference how to write these in Chapter 4.

■ **Press**

Include impressive press quotes.

■ **Contact**

List email addresses to humans. Don't just have a contact form with a Submit button. No one knows where those go. And they're frustrating. List names and email addresses for everyone on your team. Or just the point person for your band at the very least. Names. Emails.

■ **Social Links**

■ **Purchase**

Make sure it's easy for fans to buy your merch and music or to become a subscriber. Bandzoogle and Squarespace have excellent embedded, on-site stores. Shopify is also a great store to embed to your website if you don't use Bandzoogle or Squarespace. And now that Shopify has the official integration with Spotify to offer merch on your Artist profile, you'll want to get a Shopify store setup no matter what.

■ **Extras**

The etiquette for official artist websites these days is: less is more. Don't embed your social feeds. Don't put anything on the website that clutters it up. It's one thing to include the social and streaming icons at the bottom for easy, one-click access; it's another to embed every embeddable feed on the internet, which makes you look unprofessional and detached.

- **EPK**

  This is actually a hidden page on your site that you send to industry people. See the Bridge from Chapter 7 on what your EPK should contain.

PLACES YOU NEED TO BE ONLINE

Google Knowledge Panel

You know when you search an artist, and their photos, social links, discography, bio and tour dates show up right there? That's Google pulling this information from various "trusted" sources around the web. It's called a Google Knowledge Panel. You don't have a ton of control over this; however, you can actually claim this Knowledge Panel when it starts to populate and then edit it at will. There's usually a prompt directly below an unclaimed Knowledge Panel with a link and instructions on how to claim it. Google will ask you to verify some information (like your Twitter, YouTube or official website). Having a Wikipedia page gives a ton of weight to your Google rankings (and display bio).

Wikipedia

You should get a Wikipedia page if you don't have one, as soon as possible. But, unfortunately, that's easier said than done. Wikipedia only includes pages for prominent figures. How do they determine if you're prominent enough? Press helps. Getting mentioned in other Wikipedia entries also helps. The more press references you have, the higher likelihood your page will stick. Review the guidelines for posting. Your entry must be neutral and factual (it cannot read like a bio). There are companies you can hire to create Wikipedia entries for you. It may be worth investing a little bit of money to hire someone to do this for you. Or, better yet, put a notice out to your fans. There's bound to be an active Wiki User among the bunch who would be willing to help you out for free tickets or a merch package in the mail.

CONSTANT CREATORS VS. I, ARTISTS

There's a spectrum of musicians who come of age in the New Music Business. At one end of the spectrum are the Constant Creators. And on the other end are the I, Artists (remember these, from Chapter 4?).

Many artists spend time behind the scenes conceptualizing and creating. And by the time they release their first single, everything is in its right place. Their Vision, Story and Aesthetic are on point. Locked in. Their socials fit their story, which fits their music, which fits their live show. Most often these artists are not teenagers/early twenty-somethings. It's hard to know yourself that early on. And it takes a lot of discipline to create the I, Artist world.

Whereas in the Old Music Business, the public only saw the Artists with a capital A (after the label, management and publicists polished the package to perfection). Most musicians these days begin on the other end of the spectrum, however. On the Constant Creator (CC) end. Traditionally, developing as a Constant Creator was in the form of playing a gazillion live shows in your local scene. It took hundreds of shows, in front of an audience, to figure yourself out. To settle into an I, Artist. And even that typically took some crafting and curating from an outside team. Today, Constant Creators develop, evolve and create online. Mostly on TikTok, Instagram, SoundCloud, YouTube, livestreaming apps and everywhere else. Instead of figuring themselves out on stage in a club, they are doing it from their bedroom in front of the internet.

There is a charm to witnessing an individual grow into an Artist. The first iteration of the Constant Creators were YouTubers. We saw this era explode at the turn of 2010 most prominently with music YouTubers like Madilyn Bailey, Alex Goot, Megan Nicole, Kina Grannis, David Choi, Boyce Avenue, Tiffany Alvord, Pomplamoose, Tyler Ward, Chester See, Taryn Southern, Daniela Andrade and Peter Hollens. These CCs posted videos regularly, oftentimes every week. Of course, most of these artists played covers, and for a little while, the videos got more and more elaborate to the point where these CCs were able to create full-fledged performance (or sometimes narrative) music videos every week. The style, tone and etiquette has shifted over the years, but this tradition has continued most prominently now on TikTok and Instagram. Most often, an audience falls in love with CCs as much for their music as for their personality.

As the social sites continue to evolve and settle into their lane, some CCs gravitate toward one and excel there. Others understand the etiquette, vibe and nuances of each platform and sprinkle their creations on the platform that makes the most sense. For instance, Jacob Collier put his full-length #IHarmU collaboration videos on YouTube (he asked his Patreon supporters to send in a short video of them singing or playing their "melody of the moment" and he remixed it in his own jazz-infused, harmonized sort of way). The main (YouTube) videos contained about fifteen to twenty of these video collaborations back-to-back-to-back. However, he uploaded each individual collaboration to Facebook for the most sharable experience. Which was a smart decision because some of the individual videos got more views than the official full-length ones (namely Herbie Hancock's and dodie's collaborations).

WHICH SOCIAL PLATFORMS TO IGNORE AND WHICH TO MASTER

The social media landscape continues to evolve and shift so rapidly that even from the first edition of this book to the second, so much had changed that I had to rethink the entire approach of how to guide you in this arena. And now with this third edition, it's become even more clear (there was literally just one mention of TikTok in the second edition). And in the first edition I talked about Vine—for 2 pages! Because technology evolves so rapidly and startups come and go seemingly overnight, by the time you're reading this the social media landscape may look drastically different than it does today. So, to explicitly tell you the platforms on which to focus your efforts would be flat-out irresponsible. Social media best practices evolve way too rapidly for a book like this to be able to keep up. So instead of telling you how to approach each platform, I'm going to explain how others have successfully approached each platform, with lessons learned. You should figure out if you are more strongly attracted to the Constant Creator lifestyle or to the I, Artist process. Every artist is different. You have to play to your strengths and humbly recognize your weaknesses. Some of the most successful TikTokers can't put on a live show to save their life. Similarly, some of the best live performers can't connect through the screen.

Growing on a platform (and in the music industry) is about the long game. So many musicians put all of their efforts into one video, and when it doesn't go viral, they give up. Growing a presence online is about defining your voice, building a connection with your audience, staying consistent and top of mind, and it's about collaboration. Lots of collaboration.

THE BIG 10

To help you figure out where to focus your efforts, make a list of 10 artists you admire: 5 traditional musicians and 5 Constant Creator musicians. Pick one local artist, one regionally touring artist, one indie-label (or no label) nationally touring artist, one major-label nationally touring artist and one worldwide superstar. The reason you want to follow so many CC musicians (you may not admire any now, I know) is because they are ahead of the curve when it comes to the internet and social media. They use social media in more creative ways than most traditional musicians. They have built their existence online and have a mastery of the internet in a way that most do not.

Research where each artist is most active and how they utilize every platform. This is not something you will be able to do in an afternoon. You'll want to follow them on every platform and note how they use it. Analyze how (and where) they post content. And how often. There is a different etiquette on every social platform. You can't just link them together. Every platform is a community, and if you act like an impostor, you will be ousted from the community (unfollowed). Learn to use each platform the way it is intended to be used. The only thing worse than not existing on a social platform is misusing it.

FOLLOWERS ARE NOT NECESSARILY FANS AND FANS ARE NOT NECESSARILY FOLLOWERS

People may follow you on Instagram because they think you're hot, but they may hate your music. They're not a fan, they're a follower. And your biggest fans may not even follow you on Instagram. Someone may have given you a follow on TikTok because of your take on a passing trend that they enjoyed and have never seen one of your videos in their feed since. Again, not a fan. Barely even a follower.

Some artists have hundreds of thousands of followers online, but can't get 15 people out to a show in their hometown.

Go where your fans are. Are they active on Instagram? TikTok? Facebook? The first few years of TikTok, it was used primarily by teens and early-twenty-somethings. If your audience was primarily 35 and older, it was a complete waste of time to focus your efforts on TikTok. Understanding who your fans are is crucial to figure out where you need to be.

How do you do this? Well, be everywhere at first and analyze the analytics and insights the platform provides.

PICK YOUR ONE

It's too tough to master every platform. So, if you want to be a CC, pick one that you go all in on. This doesn't mean ignore the others; it just means master one. Focus the majority of your efforts on increasing the engagement and growing your followers on the one.

YouTubers became YouTubers because they spent most of their time learning how to grow an engaged YouTube audience. Instagrammers became Instagrammers because they spent most of their time mastering Instagram. TikTokers became TikTokers . . . well, you get the point.

But make sure you pick the platform that makes the most sense to you. The only way to master a platform is to stay inspired by it. You can't force it. It will show. Fans can sniff BS a mile away.

And you should be your authentic self no matter how different you are. Yes, note how successful artists use the platform you choose, but use their method merely as inspiration. You have to set yourself apart. Find your niche. Define your voice.

Just like you define your sound in the studio, you have to define your voice online.

YOUTUBE

People fall in love with content, but they also fall in love
with personalities on YouTube. It's important to
make yourself accessible that way.
—DANIELA ANDRADE, 2M+ YOUTUBE SUBSCRIBERS

Whereas YouTube used to be the hottest online community for tweens, teens and twenty-somethings, it has evolved and grown up. It's still incredibly popular (obviously), with nearly 2 billion monthly users, but the way creators find success on the platform continues to evolve. "You-Tubers" aren't as prevalent as they once were. And many music YouTubers have fled the platform altogether or have refocused their efforts.

When YouTube first launched in 2006, the standard was to sit in front of your webcam with an acoustic guitar and sing through your crappy built-in computer mic. Terra Naomi became the first YouTube star doing just this and, of course, Justin Bieber followed shortly thereafter. But as high-quality audio and video recording became more affordable, the quality standards evolved. By 2011, if you didn't have a professional-looking (and -sounding) music video, you were ignored. The competition had stiffened. And YouTubers upped their game. Most YouTubers became completely self-sufficient, with home recording studios, DSLR video cameras and full lighting rigs. By being able to control every step of the production process, YouTubers were able to put out high-quality videos regularly. Most put out a video a week. It's astounding to visit some of the most successful YouTuber channels and see how much content they have created and released over the course of their careers. Whereas label artists typically put out ten songs every three years, YouTubers put out ten songs every three months. It became such a standard that, if you didn't put out high-quality content regularly, fans of YouTube moved on to a YouTuber who did.

QVCA

Alex Ikonn, cofounder of Luxy Hair, built his seven-figure business by creating a successful YouTube channel. He explains that the key success to YouTube and really, any Constant Creator platform, lies in four simple letters:

Q = Quality
V = Value
C = Consistency
A = Authenticity

If you don't have quality videos that provide value, and roll them out very consistently and authentically, you will not succeed in building a YouTube channel.

YouTube is less about the one viral hit and more about the connection with the audience. And that connection is earned and built over the course of hundreds of videos.

YouTube evolved to become teenagers' primary music-streaming service, TV network and movie studio (long before YouTube commissioned original TV shows, films and launched YouTube Music). So much so that a 2014 study commissioned by *Variety* revealed that the five most influential figures among Americans ages 13–18 were all YouTube stars, eclipsing mainstream celebrities like Jennifer Lawrence and Seth Rogen.

Like mastering an instrument, mastering YouTube takes lots of focus, practice and time. Lots of time. For one, YouTubers move extremely quickly. They don't fret over guitar tones or drum fills. It's all about the turnaround time. They know their audience will primarily be watching their videos on their phones, often without headphones. That's not to say YouTubers aren't perfectionists. They perfect what they've found their audience cares about most like vocals and visuals. You may scoff at their order of priorities, but while you're rolling your eyes, they're rolling on down to the bank. You can't argue with success. And successful YouTubers not only have millions upon millions of views, but hundreds of thousands (sometimes millions) of fans—fans who back them on Patreon, support their crowdfunding campaigns, purchase their merch and attend their shows if and when they go on tour.

If you want to be a YouTuber, it better inspire you, because it will take up most of your time. And you better have an alternative income source, because being a YouTuber doesn't pay much for a long time. There are YouTubers with 300,000 subscribers waiting tables.

> People grow and change and
> doing the same thing for six years is tiring.
> —EMMA BLACKERY, 1.3 MILLION SUBSCRIBERS

There's no one way to approach YouTube. You may think the only successful YouTubers are good-looking teenagers and twenty-somethings playing covers of pop songs. Sure, there are those, but the most successful YouTubers have paved their own way. And done things differently. And many are actually in their thirties.

When Scott Bradlee started his channel in 2009, people had been putting covers up on YouTube for years. Other YouTubers were bubbly and catered to a tween audience. Scott went a different way. He decided to post jazz renditions of pop songs. He went from merely recording solo jazz piano instrumentals from his bedroom to creating an ever-evolving and revolving collective of world-class musicians and dancers performing pop songs in period styles (with the outfits to match). He called it Postmodern Jukebox and his videos have been viewed over 1 billion times. Postmodern Jukebox now tours the world playing huge theaters. Scott built such a strong collective of various musicians that oftentimes he doesn't even go on the tours.

Peter Hollens started off singing in an a cappella group he founded at the University of Oregon. After college, Hollens built up a mobile studio business in which he traveled around the country recording, producing and mixing other a cappella groups. He didn't actually start his own You-Tube channel until 2011—pretty late to the YouTube game.

Peter Hollens was slowly building his channel posting solo a cappella renditions of classic and contemporary pop standards. He was at about 15,000 subscribers when the violin sensation Lindsey Stirling got in touch with Hollens to collaborate. Their rendition of "Skyrim" got over 38 million views and Peter's channel shot to 80,000 subscribers nearly overnight. He now has over a billion total views on YouTube, TikTok, Facebook and Instagram (2.6M+ YouTube subscribers) and makes over $8,000 per video from his patrons on Patreon. He has no desire to tour and lives a quiet life with his family in Oregon.

UK-based singer/songwriter dodie was one of the last music YouTu-bers to gain traction on the platform. Her social channels are under the name doddleoddle (and yes she stylizes her name in all lowercase letters). Like the YouTubers who came before her, she experimented with cover songs, makeup tutorials, quirky into-the-camera-type vlogs concerning everything from "How to Clean Your Room" to "i really like tea" and even "why do musicians 'quit youtube'? (will i?!?!?)."

Even though she started as a Constant Creator, she has grown into herself as an Artist with a capital A. She is one of the few YouTubers who have been able break off platform and get her fans to not only support her Patreon, but buy tickets and sell out her shows all over the world. A lot has to do with her songwriting. Anyone with a good voice can play covers, but to write songs that connect on a deep, spiritual level is what separates the creators with passive followers and those with (financially) supportive fans. Continuing in the footsteps of Ingrid Michaelson, she writes quirky songs that fit her personality perfectly. Whether her fans follow her vlogs, music videos, listen to her music on Spotify or see her live, it all feels like her, the Artist.

Now that YouTube has evolved into a film studio and full-fledged music-streaming service (rivaling Spotify and Apple Music), the landscape has shifted significantly. We're seeing fewer traditional music YouTubers of the kind we did in the early 2010s, but there are still creators popping up every day, gaining traction. YouTube ad revenues continue to pay peanuts, and the bar has been raised for who can qualify as an official "YouTube partner"—able to monetize their videos with ads and make money (at least 1,000 subscribers and 4,000 "watch hours" over the previous twelve months).

Many of the famous YouTubers of the early 2010s have burnt out, evolved, shifted focus or moved on completely. And the style of videos that perform best has shifted dramatically over the past decade.

Because YouTube is still the most popular music-streaming service in the world, and most people turn to YouTube first to check out music, you need high-quality content on YouTube no matter what. Whether you decide to develop a YouTube audience by following in the footsteps of the thousands of other successful YouTubers is up to you.

If you want to choose YouTube as your one, make sure you spend some time with YouTube's Creator Academy (creatoracademy.youtube.com). They have put together hours' worth of tutorials, with tips and tricks on how to master YouTube along with personal anecdotes and thoughts from some of the biggest YouTubers out there.

Believe it or not, over 155,000 channels have over 100,000 subscribers. With nearly 2 billion monthly users on YouTube, there's plenty of room for more creators. And you're not too late.

Excellence is never too late.

INSTAGRAM

People really respond to a genuine love of whatever it is you're
doing. People can tell if you're not genuine.
—EMILY C. BROWNING (@EMILYCBROWNING)

You can't hack the system. You can't cheat it. The algorithm is
there to put dope content to the top.
—SAM BLAKELOCK (@PICKUPMUSIC)

A relatively unknown 33-year-old singer/songwriter, Rachel Platten,
released her single "Fight Song" on February 19, 2015. She had about
35,000 Instagram followers at the time. The song was just bouncing
around adult radio (with a push from her label, Columbia), struggling
to gain traction. On June 6, though, that all changed. Rachel's manager, Ben Singer (also Andy Grammer's manager), contacted Taylor
Swift's manager to see if Taylor would be into meeting Rachel backstage
after Taylor's arena show in Pittsburgh. Hours later, Taylor Swift Instagrammed a 15-second video of the two rocking out backstage to "Fight
Song" with Rachel on guitar. Of course, Rachel was tagged, and Taylor
Swift's 50 million Instagram followers wondered a) what song this was,
and b) who was Rachel Platten? Within hours, Rachel's Instagram followers doubled. And by the next day she had well over 100,000 Instagram
followers. "Fight Song" reached #1 on the iTunes charts. And a month
later it cracked the top 10 *Billboard* Hot 100 and went on to be a worldwide hit. All from one Instagram video. And, of course, a great song.

Instagram has evolved from simply a photo-sharing app to one of
the most important apps for creating an Artist world and engaging an
audience. Subcommunities have now popped up within Instagram that
have single-handedly launched careers. @pickupmusic, @pickupjazz,

@brilliantmusicians, @musiciansshowcase, @talented_musicians, @chorus and @omgvoices were some of the first (and most powerful) accounts to feature the musicians of Instagram. PickUp has actually grown into a musicians' community, regularly hosting events around the world.

San Diego native Raelee Nikole (@raeleenikole) had been gigging around her hometown since she was seventeen. She'd had an Instagram account since the beginning of the platform (circa 2012) and posted to the platform like every other teenager. But it wasn't until late 2016 when she posted a video of herself playing guitar and singing Musiq Soulchild's "Just Friends" that everything changed. The @pickupjazz account featured her video, and followers came pouring in for Raelee. The next video she posted, playing the guitar part for John Mayer's "Paper Doll," John Mayer himself commented on the video. She attracted more and more attention as she posted more and more videos. Shawn Mendes followed her and even tweeted one of her songs (which subsequently hit Spotify's Viral 50 chart). Shawn introduced Raelee to his writing partner, Scott Harris, and soon Raelee was writing with some of the biggest songwriters in the world.

Also in 2016, New Zealand–based Emily C. Browning (@emily .c.browning) attended an Instagram clinic Sam Blakelock of @pickupjazz (also a New Zealand native) held. Emily, an incredibly talented guitarist/singer/songwriter, posted a cover song, tagged @pickupjazz, and soon she was featured as well. She began regularly posting songs on her account and got featured on not only the @pickupjazz account, but a few other popular music-focused accounts. About a year into the process, she looked at her Instagram analytics and realized she had a lot of followers in Los Angeles, so she booked a trip out to L.A., teamed up with a couple other L.A. musicians she had met on Instagram and sold out her very first show in the United States.

Sam Blakelock gave another Instagram masterclass in July 2018, which he livestreamed and added to the @pickupmusic IGTV channel.

He explained that the key to being a successful musician on Instagram relies on five key components:

1. **Quality Content**

    You can't fake your way to success on Instagram. The algorithm has gotten incredibly smart and highlights great content—regardless of the subject matter.

2. **Positive Community**

    Make sure you reply to some of your comments and interact with people in your DMs. But keep it positive. If people are trash-talking in your comments, don't stoop to their level or engage combatively. This ain't Facebook.

3. **Consistency**

    "You're not going to overpost if the content is high-quality and is varied," he says.

4. **Trial and Error**

    You don't want to merely be a follower on Instagram. You want to be a leader and experiment with ways to engage and grow your audience. Learn from other successful accounts, but come up with ways that showcase your personality and skills best.

5. **Collaboration**

    Find people who are doing what you want to do and collaborate with them.

Like YouTube, some of the most successful Instagrammers collaborate. It could be tagging the company who made a dress, tagging everyone in the photo, including friends in your Stories and showcasing their handles, mashing up other videos with your own, giving a shout-out to someone in the comments or making friends in the DMs. And you don't actually have to be in the same time zone as your collaborators. Just tag them and they may Regram and tag you back, as has been the case with the popular musician-feature accounts.

After Raelee Nikole posted a 20-second clip of her playing/singing her neosoul rendition of SZA's "The Weekend," New Zealand–based (something's in the water) @thejuneyboy took her video, sliced himself into it (cutting back and forth between her and him) and remixed her original audio, adding a beat and some lead guitar. This may not sound that impressive as remixes happen regularly now, especially since duetting like this is directly built into TikTok, but, remember that at the time, it took figuring out how to download her video (through hacks—as Instagram doesn't enable this), then dumping the audio into a DAW, mixing in his own creation, then syncing it back up to video (cutting in his own video). The remix video got over 150,000 views on her profile. Similarly, @p_larddd remixed Raelee's rendition of "Redbone." She Regrammed it with "Shoutout to 2017 for giving kids with bedrooms on opposite sides of the country a way to shed together!"

Multi-instrumentalist Elise Trouw (@elisetrouw) was incredibly active within the community when she first started on the platform. She regularly posted videos of herself singing, playing drums, bass, and guitar, and similarly got featured on popular musician-feature accounts (long before her looping videos on Facebook and YouTube went viral).

Again, it's not about one viral video; it's about staying active within the community, regularly releasing high-quality content, staying genuine (not forcing anything), trying (and failing) incessantly and keeping up with the trends of the times.

When Story Highlights were released, many musicians got creative and used the story bubbles at the top almost how a website toolbar functions: Music, Videos, Tour, Vlog, Merch, etc. Highlights with full linking capabilities per highlight. In the Tour Highlight, they could post a photo per date, linking directly to purchase tickets. The Videos Highlight could feature various video clips linking to the full video. Merch Highlight could feature merch items linking directly to each item on your website. Some just posted one image per Highlight (Spotify, YouTube, Apple Music, Tour, etc.) and linked directly to that. You get the idea.

When IGTV was released, people created content specifically for the medium. The 1975 made a custom (vertical) lyric video for their song "Give Yourself a Try," which played on the same aesthetic theme of their main music video but was specific for the platform. (They also made similar videos exclusive to Spotify for their 2018 releases.)

And now Instagram Reels functions similarly to TikTok, in that no matter how many followers you have, the algorithm may enable your Reel to go viral—or at least pick up a hell of a lot more traction than a post only seen by your followers.

Drummer Greyson Nekrutman found success initially on Instagram in early 2020 (and later on TikTok), racking up over 250,000 IG followers simply by posting videos of him drumming. Oftentimes recreating famous solos (like the solo from "Whiplash") or playing along to the recordings of complicated drum parts (like Frank Zappa, Dave Matthews Band, and Nekrutman's most frequent comparison, Buddy Rich). He was discovered on Instagram by the jazz fusion group Brand X, and they asked him to join them as their drummer on their nationwide US tour in 2021.

Many artists are now finding success on both TikTok and Instagram (Reels) by posting short-form content that goes viral quickly. These Constant Creators post the same videos on TikTok, Instagram Reels and YouTube Shorts. Some perform better on one platform or the other. But one thing's for sure, all like you to post frequently. Like, very frequently. And since no one can quite figure out the damn algorithm, the more videos you post, the more shots you have at getting one to catch. But these days, it's not about the one viral video. It's about building a following that connects and relates to you, the artist.

Bands often struggle with how to effectively use Instagram. As the platform evolves, former tips and tricks become obsolete or frowned upon. Keeping up with the trends is vital to being a welcome presence on the platform.

A good rule of thumb for keeping your Instagram feed engaging is to post photos and videos of you, and include your face in the majority of your posts. Your fans don't care what your salad looks like. That's not interesting. But you holding that same salad, in the green room, before you play a show? That's interesting. Following you on Instagram (and every platform), your fan should feel connected to you. Posting a video of just your hands playing guitar is not going to get anyone to identify with you the person. The artist. Seeing a photo of the empty club preshow isn't interesting. Seeing you in that same photo makes it a hundred times more interesting and gets your fans to connect with you on a deeper level. You make them feel like they are there with you. Anyone can post a photo of an empty club. How do they know you didn't just pull this from the internet? Because you're in it! Posting a photo of just your friend's face may be hilarious to the both of you, but none of your fans will get the joke. You just insulted everyone who doesn't know your friend. "Ha-ha, you don't get our inside joke!" The goal on Instagram is to get your audience to identify with you. Sure, post photos of your friends and include them in your Stories, but make sure you're in them as well. Go through your Instagram feed right now, and I bet you loads of money that the posts that have the most likes are ones you are in.

But be careful about the kinds of content you post. You want to attract the kinds of followers who will turn into supportive fans (of your music). If you just post photos of you in a swimsuit, you may get a lot of followers who like how you look in a swimsuit. You may think more followers is always better, but you'd be wrong. You'll soon notice that photos of you in swimsuits will continue to do great and videos of you playing music won't do so well. People are there for your body, not your music. And because most of your followers engage with your swimsuit photos, the algorithm will recognize what people respond to the most and will bury your music posts and feature your swimsuit posts. Similarly, if you post covers of popular songs you hate, you may get a bunch of followers who are fans of those songs, but when you start posting your original music, they may not like it and not engage—training the algorithm to bury the music that is most meaningful to you.

You don't merely want more followers. You want to build a highly engaged community of supporters who dig the authentic you. And will stick with you for life.

TIKTOK

TikTok is the home for music trends that permeate the industry, charts, and culture.

—OLE OLBERMAN, GLOBAL HEAD OF MUSIC, TIKTOK

If you're an artist who is creating content, and people are commenting at you, comment back. It's going to be pretty obvious if there's an artist account where the label is doing all the [TikTok] posting for them. This is definitely a platform where you can't get away with having an artist management team or label posting on their behalf. It needs to be authentic. It needs to be from the artist.

—KRISTEN BENDER, SVP OF DIGITAL STRATEGY, UNIVERSAL MUSIC GROUP

Boy has a lot changed since the previous edition of this book. When the second edition was released, TikTok was just getting going. It had just undergone a name change from Musical.ly, where it was merely a lip-syncing app.

Now? Well, TikTok is the most influential social media app for music since YouTube.

What makes TikTok the most interesting of all social media apps to date is not only the algorithm which propels videos to go viral from creators with very few followers, but also that songs can rapidly spread on the platform from artists of all sizes—even if the artist doesn't have an account. We're seeing songs from legacy acts like Fleetwood Mac, Reba McEntire, Bee Gees, Billy Joel, Earth Wind & Fire, Salt-N-Pepa, Destiny's Child, Jack Johnson, Simple Plan, Kate Bush and Run DMC get turned into viral memes, used by tens of thousands (and sometimes millions) of other TikTokers, which propels the song (back) to the top of the charts.

But we're also seeing this happen to indie artists with little to no backing. This happened to Ricky Montgomery in the summer of 2020, when two of his songs from his 2016 album went viral on the app—before he even had an account. Hundreds of thousands of people on TikTok used the songs in their own videos, and the songs—which had negligible streams prior to this—skyrocketed Ricky to hundreds of millions of streams. It helped him land a record deal with Warner Records where Ricky got to maintain ownership, with a 50/50 royalty split and massive advance. A previously unheard-of deal for a major label.

Similarly, Ritt Momney's cover of Corrine Bailey Rae's 2006 hit "Put Your Records On" spawned nearly 2 million videos (with collectively hundreds of millions of views) when makeup artist James Charles Duetted a video using the song to his 20+ million followers. Ritt Momney's song topped 400 million streams on Spotify and earned him a record deal from Columbia Records (with a 50/50 royalty split and massive advance as well).

Neither Ritt Momney nor Ricky Montgomery pushed the song on TikTok or had any involvement getting the song to go viral. It happened organically and translated into streams and fans for both artists.

Of course, major stars have had songs propelled on the platform, like

Megan Thee Stallion, Olivia Rodrigo, Doja Cat, Lil Nas X, Adele, and Saweetie. More times than not, these songs are catapulted by influencer agencies that pay TikTokers to use the song in videos. These campaigns often cost tens of thousands of dollars (or much more) to get these songs to go viral. But many times, a lot of money is spent with not much of a return. Nothing is guaranteed, and unfortunately there are far more cases of songs (which have major financial backing) flopping even with influencer agency support. The TikTok algorithm is a fickle beast.

But on the other end of the spectrum, we are seeing the Constant Creators in full force. These CCs are using the app to build a following while simultaneously promoting their music.

In 2020, when every artist was at home with a lot of time on their hands, many experimented (and succeeded) with TikTok.

The 21-year-old bassist Blu DeTiger had a full tour schedule playing with Caroline Polachek, FLETCHER and others. When the tours got canceled in early 2020, she took all of her free time to TikTok to experiment. She quickly found viral success by posting bass covers of Prince, Russ, Janet Jackson, and Megan Thee Stallion. She grew to over 1 million TikTok followers (with 17 million Likes) and 400,000 Instagram followers. She received press from *Rolling Stone* and *Billboard*, got an endorsement deal with Fender and signed to Capitol Records.

Another instrumentalist, guitarist Shalfi Edu, had been posting on Instagram since 2016 (18,500 followers) and on YouTube since 2018 (9,200 subscribers), but in under a year had amassed more followers, Likes and views on TikTok than the other two platforms combined. He regularly gets millions of views with hundreds of thousands of Likes and comments on his TikToks.

Mothica had been active on the app for months in 2020, creating mostly lifestyle videos, slowly building an audience. Then that June, she posted an 18-second video of herself listening to the masters she had just gotten back for her new song, "Vices." It was such a sweet, raw, vulnerable moment for a song that had relatable lyrics (captioned on the screen) pertaining to addiction, that the song exploded on the app. Mothica rushed to get it officially distributed to DSPs. The song went on to get over 20 million streams on Spotify. She has since grown her TikTok following to over 675,000 followers and 20 million Likes by posting regular videos and engaging with her audience in-app. She got multiple record deal offers and ended up striking a partnership with Rise Records/BMG, enabling her to start and own her own label.

The female-fronted vocal trio out of L.A. Trousdale saw rapid ascension on TikTok in 2021 by doing three-part harmony videos of trending songs (and originals) and using TikTok's features (like Duet, Stitch, replies, Who's Singing Challenge), and posting mini storytelling music videos to their own songs. This traction on TikTok converted into Spotify streams, where they passed 500,000 monthly listeners and 10 million streams in under a year. Independently.

The vibraphone player Justin Vibes, who had been a behind-the-scenes songwriter for artists like Eminem, Chris Brown, Tyga, and Kodak Black, along with performing with Capital Cities, took off on TikTok with videos of him just playing the vibes. Many of his standouts were of him covering TV theme songs, but he showcases much more of his artistry with his original songs and production work. After posting a video where he played the theme song to the Nickelodeon show *Gravity Falls*, he went to dinner. At the end of the dinner, he pulled out his phone and discovered that he had gained 90,000 followers—in 45 minutes! He has since grown to 8.5 million followers and has multiple brand deals.

Collaboration is much more seamless than ever before. You no longer need to be in the same city—or time zone—to collaborate. You don't really even need permission. With in-app features like Stitch and Duet, musicians from all over the world are collaborating in the most creative ways, oftentimes creating what could be considered multiple remixes or iterations of the same song—thousands of times over.

The jazz pop singer/songwriter Stacey Ryan posted herself playing piano and singing 60 seconds of a new song idea on November 11, 2021. Someone commented, "I would love to write a verse for this!" She responded to the comment with a new video of a basic demo recording of this song for her own Open Verse Challenge (a popular music trend on TikTok). She sang one line of the chorus, had a visual count-in on the screen, and then left it open for people to add their own verse via the Duet feature. 26,000 people added their own verse to this. One of those was the hip-hop artist Zai1k. The video of their duet was the one that actually went viral, with 40 million views and thousands of people asking them to make an official version and release it. The two of them (who had never met prior) decided to make a fully produced recording, and they officially released it just a couple months later. Their promo video for the new release (just a quick 15-second split-screen video of them mentioning that the song was out) got 6 million views. The song was released on January 16, 2022, independently and was instantly added to a bunch of official Spotify playlists and got over a million streams in the first week.

The multi-instrumentalist Zac Rose (@zacroseofficial) made a 30-second neo-soul instrumental loop and captioned it: "Someone sing something on thisssss 🗣️ #duet #sing #producer #piano #bass #beat #jazztok." Within 2 days, 1,400 people Duetted his video and essentially cowrote and coproduced original songs—without ever exchanging as much as a text. This is happening every day, with artists of every level, in every genre.

IS FACEBOOK STILL IMPORTANT?

Facebook has lost much of its prominence (in the US, at least) for the under-35 crowd. The kids have all but abandoned it for TikTok, Twitch, Snapchat and Instagram. I tried deleting it from my phone many times, but then realized a few of the sites that I initially signed up for via the Face-book Connect button required me to type in the security code (only found in the app). Foiled by the Zuck! Facebook made it clear pretty early on that it wasn't going to be a hub for music. And it never became so. Some artists, however, were able to grow from Facebook's seamless sharing capabilities.

Vulfpeck band leader Jack Stratton built a massive following by post-ing videos he knew would appeal to their fanbase (music nerds). Most of the videos were edited with the Vulf-filter (their custom filter), and every song used the Vulf-compressor (their custom compressor—which they sold as a plugin). They picked up steam in the mid-aughts by running in the opposite direction of the YouTubers. YouTubers perfected the inau-thentic sheen of bubbly, shiny cover videos. Shot well. Edited well. Bright and cheesy. Vulfpeck was the antithesis to all this. Their videos were intentionally shot poorly (usually one take with an iPhone) and edited with a grainy filter, but they sounded incredible. Oh, and they played mostly original music (very few covers). And the covers, when they did them, were not pop songs of the moment, but deep cuts that their fans would geek out on. Or simply instructional videos on "How to Properly Play 'Superstition' on the Clav."

Vulfpeck's videos got millions upon millions of views. Spawning video remixes, and (unauthorized, but very welcome) internet collabora-tions. They sold out tours all over the world, culminating with a Madison Square Garden sell-out just before Covid.

Vulfpeck didn't pander or chase. Vulfpeck paved their own way. They led. And their fan base followed. And so did an entire generation of bands.

As always, you should find what makes sense for you and your audi-ence. Experiment constantly. Trial and error is your best friend. Don't be precious about the "content" you post—as long as it's true to you, authen-tic and "on brand." How do you know if it's on brand? Well, refer back to the exercises in Chapter 4.

This all being said, there are still people on Facebook, of course. If your audience exists there, then connect with them there. There are sub-communities in Facebook Groups that could also be places for you to find and connect with your tribe.

FINDING YOUR FANS THROUGH ADVERTISING

Facebook, Instagram and TikTok advertising has become insanely powerful (and targeted). It's almost creepy how specific you can get with the kinds of people you want to target. Ads are no longer merely "Show this video to fans of the 1975." You can now upload your email list and not only target your email subscribers via ads, but you can create "lookalike" audiences targeting people who are similar to your fans. How do they do this? Your guess is as good as mine, but the marketing experts of the world say it's pretty damn effective. Digital advertising is extremely powerful (and necessary) for your music career. It doesn't actually cost that much to do. $5/day gets you going. Digital marketing now includes running ads via Meta and TikTok Ads managers, but also influencer campaigns. There are agencies and services out there that can assist in these pursuits, or if you have more time than money, you can learn to do all of this on your own.

TWITTER

Twitter was superhot around 2009–2012. Its growth has stalled, and it's definitely not used as actively by common folk as it once was. It's now mostly used by influencers, journalists and politicians. Now that Twitter is pushing video and photos, see how your Big 10 are using it effectively and model it.

But once again, Twitter is a community; if you're going to be a member of the community, be respectful and follow the etiquette. No linking to or from Facebook or Instagram. Tweet, heart, retweet, appropriately, and you'll do just fine.

James Blunt gained worldwide respect when he turned his Twitter feed into a snark fest, publicly responding to haters.

James Blunt @JamesBlunt
And no mortgage. RT @hettjones: James Blunt just has an
annoying face and a highly irritating voice.

Many artists are not on Twitter and don't feel a need to use it. That's completely fine. However, there is still a very active community on it and some very influential people using it.

One of the most prolific artist-tweeters in recent memory is Phoebe Bridgers. She has an extremely active fanbase on Twitter—with countless fan accounts and hashtagged conversations relating to her. Her fans pounce on all things Phoebe. And she regularly Retweets and responds to tweets about her.

In January 2021, Jensen McRae tweeted a 50-second video of herself playing a verse to a new song. Along with the video, she jokingly tweeted: "in 2023 Phoebe Bridgers is gonna drop her third album & the opening track will be about hooking up in the car while waiting in line to get vaccinated at dodger stadium and it's gonna make me cry. this is my preemptive cover of what I imagine it will sound like."

Bridgers Retweeted it with "oh my god." Other singer/songwriters proceeded to "finish" the song—adding a chorus, a bridge, more verses. This was collaboration on Twitter in real time. It got the attention of hit songwriter Justin Trantor, who tweeted Jensen that he was fanboying over her official work. At the time, Jensen had just a handful of followers on all platforms and just a few thousand streams. This little stunt set her up for writing sessions, publishing and record deals, tours—and millions of streams and views of her original work.

This worked so well for her because her music (and persona) is actually very similar to Bridgers's. She knew that by linking herself to Bridgers in this creative way, the Phoebe-tribe would seamlessly jump into her own music. It worked beautifully.

We've seen the power of the tweet from influential figures. A Justin Bieber tweet can single-handedly get a song to chart. And a Phoebe Bridgers tweet gets Spotify playlist editors (and the industry) to swoon.

Twitter has become niche like Snapchat. If you're going to use it, do it because you enjoy it. You can make it work for you, but you don't have to. It's there if it makes sense for you.

SNAPCHAT

Snapchat has gone through quite the evolution since its inception in 2011. It famously turned down a $3 billion Facebook acquisition offer and then lost a lot of market share when Instagram launched Stories. Snapchat still remains incredibly popular among the under-30 crowd, but it isn't widely used by the music industry. Snapchat has struggled to find its footing within the music community even after "the King of Snapchat" DJ Khaled exploded on the platform in early 2016 (well before his worldwide hits took over pop radio). He gained his loyal following by regularly posting inspirational catchphrases (and, of course, Snapping every mundane activity throughout his day). He has since amassed over 13.5 million subscribers (still far fewer than what he has on Instagram).

As of early 2022, Snapchat boasted over a half a billion monthly active users (about half of what TikTok had).

However, now that Snapchat has Spotlight, which is a direct replica of TikTok's core features, and has licensed music in-app, there is the possibility for growth and virality. Brands can now have public profiles with followers. And public subscriber and view counts. If you're already active on Snapchat, it may be worth experimenting with Spotlight and carving out your niche there.

LIVESTREAMING

Do you remember where you were when the world shut down and all concerts came to a screeching halt? I do. I was at home with a bunch of friends celebrating a TV sync appearance for Annabel Lee. Shortly after we caught her song on the show, we got frantic texts from friends telling us to turn on the livestream of the Mayor of Los Angeles. He proclaimed that all bars and venues would be shut down until further notice.

My friends Ashley Maietta, Andrew Leib and I sprang into action (thinking this was a temporary shutdown) and launched the UnCancelled Music Festival—which was a livestreamed concert series hosting over 350 artists from all over the world. Our goal was to help artists and music venues get through the live-music shutdown. Because we were one of the first livestreamed festivals and had pretty big names playing it—like Colbie Caillat, Waxahatchee, Snail Mail, Betty Who, Brian Fallon, Josh Radnor, Jukebox the Ghost, JP Saxe, Kevin Garrett, Beach Bunny, the Marias, Victoria Canal, among literally hundreds of others—we got a ton of press from *Rolling Stone*, *Billboard*, NPR, *Variety*, *Forbes* and *Deadline*. And raised over $100,000 for artists and music venues in 10 days.

A drop in the bucket. We didn't know it then, of course. We thought this should help these artists get through the next few weeks or so of this career-altering virus.

We hosted the festival on one of the only ticketed livestreaming platforms at the time, StageIt.

Since April 2020, as the music industry scrambled to salvage some of the $28 billion that live music generated in 2019, countless new livestreaming platforms have popped up. Bandsintown noted that over 21,000 musicians played over 75,000 livestream concerts in 2020. Some took to StageIt, while others hopped on the newer services like Veeps, Moment House, and Nugs. And of course, Zoom was a go-to platform for nearly everyone everywhere. When it was safe, many music venues offered livestreamed shows from inside their venues—fully outfitted with cameras and live-editing equipment on a ticketed livestream platform. Many others simply sold tickets via their website or Eventbrite and then sent out a private YouTube link.

Booking agent Marshall Betts told me in October 2020 on the *New Music Business* podcast that most artists pulled in about as much revenue from one ticketed livestream show as they would playing live in their biggest market. Not bad for not leaving the house.

But of course, the free social platforms, like Instagram, Facebook, Reddit, YouTube and TikTok, host the majority of livestreams. Most are not monetized at all; however, some artists figured out creative ways to make money off of these free livestreams. Dawn Beyer way back in 2017 actually made $100,000 (via a PayPal link in her bio) in one year off of her Facebook Live stream. Clare Means became one of the most-watched musicians on the (now-defunct) livestream app Periscope, where she initially livestreamed her street performances and made more than double what she made on the street. Clare conducted a twelve-hour marathon session, where she auctioned off guitars, artwork and other fun items. And she directed everyone to buy her album on iTunes. When the album was released, it hit #1 on the iTunes Singer/Songwriter charts.

Previously a platform primarily for video gamers to livestream themselves playing, Twitch arose as a destination for musicians during the pandemic—and now beyond. Twitch's primary focus isn't for ticketed streams; however, creators get support from their fans via in-platform tips ("bits"), subscriptions, and third-party platforms enabling more interactive monetization possibilities like song requests and custom tip jars.

The head of music at Twitch, Tracy Patrick Chan, told me on the *New Music Business* podcast in December 2020 that artists earning over $50,000 were doing so from just an average of 183 fans!

And that's the magic of livestreaming. In an age where everyone has become obsessed with macro numbers dealing in millions of streams and fractions of cents, livestreaming proves that you don't need virality or a massive audience to make a solid living from your fans.

The husband-and-wife duo aeseaes (pronounced "A C S" which stands for "A Couple Streams") play acoustic songs on Twitch. They have a very simple yet inviting setup. Utilizing OBS (broadcasting software), mics and a nice camera, their streams have extremely high audio and video quality. They don't have fire-blowing dragons or exploding gift boxes to keep their audience engaged (like many other Twitch streamers); they just play intimate acoustic songs (and they do have a camera on their sleeping cat most of the time which helps). Aeseaes have amassed over 175,000 followers on Twitch, with 2,500 subscribers (at $5/month), and make far more livestreaming than they ever did in successful national touring outfits. They've run two Kickstarter campaigns raising $70,000 collectively and have a Patreon with 350 ongoing supporters at $1–$5/month. They make healthy livings livestreaming on Twitch just from their fans' direct support via tips and subs.

Aeseaes debunks the myth that the way to succeed on Twitch is to be outgoing, flashy, bubbly and young. They are none of these.

Emily Henry, after taking the Ari's Take Academy Livestreaming for Musicians course, joined Twitch in early 2021. Within a month she had gained 1,000 followers, and her largest income stream quickly became livestreaming.

Ticketed Livestreams vs. Free Livestreams

There are two categories of livestreams: ticketed livestreams (TLs) and free livestreams (FLs). There are different intentions for each kind of livestream. If you have a sizeable, ticket-buying fanbase, TLs may be for you. Some TLs, like StageIt, also support tipping. Others support add-on purchases like merch or meet-and-greets. It's always a good idea to accept tips within the livestreaming platform—no matter how big of an artist you are. It's a fun way for fans to support you in real time. If you play their favorite song, interact with them in the chat box, sing them happy birthday or honor their request, they may tip you. They *want* to pay you. You should allow them to.

When Betty Who played the UnCancelled Music Festival, she sold 957 tickets and grossed about $6,100 in pay-what-you-can ticket sales. Without ever encouraging her fans to tip, they did so anyways (and of course she thanked them profusely—which inspired others to tip). And she made an additional $2,000 in tips. If tipping wasn't a possibility, there would have been $2,000 left on the table. Not bad for sitting at home for 45 minutes playing some music in front of her computer.

Always enable tipping and other monetization options for TLs if possible.

Free livestreams (FLs) are what most people on the internet think of when they think of livestreams. Twitch, Facebook, Instagram, TikTok, Reddit and YouTube are all FLs. Each platform has different monetization features. Some have robust features like Twitch, which essentially gamifies the stream. During the livestream, viewers can interact in a myriad of ways through the chat box, via Emotes, bits and other interactive features. Some are monetized, some aren't. And every Twitch creator has the ability to automate action animations based on viewer activity. Like when someone follows your channel, you could have Forrest Gump run across the screen (the Dapper Rapper actually does this)—although Twitch may get a takedown notice if a copyright owner claims that you infringed their character without permission. If your YouTube channel is monetized, you can accept tips directly within YouTube during your livestreams. And now TikTok and Instagram have in-app monetization capabilities for when you go live.

FLs are a great way to grow your fanbase while making money. And TLs are best if you have a dedicated fanbase.

THE BRIDGE

How This Band Made $250,000 Livestreaming from Home

Robert Brown, the founder and front man of the steampunk band Abney Park, remembers one week in March 2020 when every one of their upcoming concerts got canceled. The band had been gigging for two decades, supporting the four members and their families on live performances.

They sprang into action and booked their first livestream concert (ever). They sold tickets via Indiegogo—enabling them to sell tiered ticket packages. A $15 ticket got you a link to the livestream. A $25 ticket got you the livestream and a download to watch it later. A $35 ticket got you the livestream, download and mp3s from the show.

And a $100 ticket got you a ticket to the afterparty.

What was the afterparty? Well, it was just another concert, except in between each song, every member of the band took a shot of hard liquor.

This first show, after only being on sale for one week, made them $20,000.

Abney Park are not superstars. They are a hardworking band with a die-hard fanbase. Their social media numbers pale in comparison to the hottest newcomers of the moment, sitting at around 6,000 Instagram followers. "I haven't used Instagram in ages," Brown told me on the phone when I informed him that his link in bio wasn't working. They have around 70,000 monthly listeners on Spotify and 50,000 followers on Facebook.

Their ticket buyers, by and large, come from their email list of 10,000 dedicated fans. Because of the incredible success of the first livestream concert, they decided to keep them going. As they played more shows and made more money, they upgraded their gear.

Soon enough, they had 4 GoPros, an ATEM Mini video mixer, a DMX lighting rig that syncs up to MIDI. A "producer" (Brown's teenage daughter) to mix the video on the spot. And a big TV screen to see themselves and help them become better performers.

"Most independent bands don't know how to be on camera," Brown says. "The entire concert became a selfie concert. It taught us a level of professionalism. You don't have an audience, but you have to pretend you do."

Mind you, the cameras and video mixer cost them under $700.

They streamed the shows on YouTube Live. Yes, it's not the most protected way—the link could theoretically get shared for free—but it didn't seem that anyone wanted to hurt them in this way. And it definitely hasn't hurt their bottom line.

They average about $27,000 per show, and in just about a year and a half, from just 10 livestream concerts, they made over $250,000.

Yes, they've had their fair share of technical difficulties, but it wasn't anything they couldn't handle. Most of the issues came from bandwidth—the internet being too slow. Thirty minutes before the show, they unplug every device hooked up to the internet and turn off Wi-Fi from everything other than the laptop running the stream. And three days before the show, they do a full test stream. They meticulously check the mix ("Our guitarist runs the board," says Brown, "so we have to make sure the guitars aren't too loud") and the video. Once their check is over, they don't touch anything until they go live. Their producer is on hand to handle any issues that arise during the stream, such as an HDMI cable cutting out, or to adjust the mix when fans complain in the chat box about the guitars being too loud.

Indiegogo, while not typically used as a ticketing platform, has served them well. Indiegogo handles all customer support. They refund people who can't make the show. They handle broken-link issues. You name it. Yes, Indiegogo takes a 5% commission (on top of the ≈ 3% transaction fees), but it's worth it to the band when dealing with thousands of ticket buyers and potentially hundreds of customer support requests.

And although there are now more secure ways to livestream privately and sell tickets, Brown swears by this method.

The chat box becomes the central meetup for fans. Mid-show, the band will share memories of the last time they played the song or shenanigans that happened in previous livestream "afterparties"—inevitably getting more to buy-in to the $100 upsell.

Now that live music is back in full swing, Brown doesn't really see a need to hit the road ever again.

"It's pretty hard to say yes to a $5,000 show when I've been doing $30,000 shows," he told me.

Abney Park has no plans to ever stop doing these livestream concerts, and their fans don't seem to fatigue of them either.

"Will we go back to playing in-person shows?" Brown pondered eighteen months after the initial Covid quarantine began. "I would, because I want to get out of the house so bad."

How to Livestream Like a Pro

If you want to give livestreaming a go on an FL platform like Twitch, here are seven important things to focus on:

1. **Gear and Setup**

   Livestreaming etiquette has come a long way since 2015, when Periscope launched and the expectation was to merely interact with you via a chat box while you essentially Face-Timed. Now, the musicians making a living livestreaming are doing so because they have a high-quality setup. Most use some kind of software to enable graphic and text overlays, seamless multi-cam editing, video injections and third-party tipping capabilities. The most popular on the market are OBS, Streamlabs, StreamElements, and Wirecast. But there are many more. You want a camera better than the one built into your laptop. A simple Logitech HD webcam will do. And if you're singing, you definitely want a good mic.

2. **Accept Payments**

Even if the platform has built-in monetization capabilities, it's a good idea to have a virtual tip jar (VTJ). You can have a page on your website, like myband.com/tip-jar. On it, you should have links for your Venmo, Cash App and PayPal. You should also have a merch link there as well.

3. **Interact and Engage**

Livestreaming is very different from performing live in a club. Whereas in a club you seldom acknowledge the audience and don't necessarily comment on everything they do, on a livestream you should constantly be engaging with the chat box. The thing that makes it feel live and exciting for fans is knowing that you see them (well, their chats). And that they can communicate with you in real time. This is how you will make the majority of your money. You can reference the virtual tip jar (or subscriptions, gifts, emotes, whatever) or simply answer their questions or give them a shout out. This is what makes livestreams fun—interaction and engagement. On Twitch, people essentially pay to enhance their experience.

4. **Consistency**

You don't gain hundreds of fans by livestreaming once. There's no real virality in livestreaming like there is on other short-form video apps. It's all about consistency. If you want to be successful livestreaming, set a schedule for yourself. Maybe, Monday, Wednesday, Friday you livestream on Twitch, Sunday and Tuesday you livestream on Facebook and YouTube (via a multi-stream service like Streamlabs). And Saturdays you livestream on TikTok. Actually set these dates and times in your calendar and stick to the schedule. You'll be surprised how many of your fans will tune in regularly and interact with each other. A community will form in the chat box among your regulars.

5. **Go Long**

The most successful livestreamers broadcast for three to four hours at a time. The way that many livestream platforms work is that the longer you livestream, the more likely your stream will show up for other users on the platform.

6. **Pay Attention to Your Frame**

Every inch of your frame is important. Is your unmade bed behind you in the shot? People will notice it and comment on it. And boy, will that be distracting. Make sure you spend time setting up your set so that your frame represents you exactly how you would like to be represented. Some people have glittering lights, others have backdrops or use greenscreens. Whatever you do, make it interesting and representative of your brand.

7. **Be Unique**

Your livestreams should be a vibe. When people tune in, they should feel like they are entering your world. Everyone has some kind of schtick. Even if it doesn't seem like it. Some people take requests. Some rap artists will do freestyles based on the comments. Some artists give musical shoutouts when tips come in. Some run contests. Some on Twitch have automations cued up based on people's actions. Like, when someone subscribes to your channel, an animated zombie could run across the screen. Or when someone tips, Michael Jordan pops on the screen and dunks the ball. Come up with something fun that you can do during your streams that is unique to you.

THE METAVERSE

Long before Facebook changed its parent company's name to Meta, there had been virtual worlds forming online where people operate digital avatars to play games, attend events, meetup with others and go shopping. This virtual universe is referred to as "the metaverse." Initially, these virtual worlds were quite fragmented and primarily existed solely within video games like Fortnite, Minecraft and Roblox—collectively boasting nearly 200 million users.

The EDM artist Marshmello was the first artist to partner with Fortnite for an in-game concert experience, in 2019. But the floodgates opened after that, and all three of these games have hosted massive concerts with artists like Travis Scott, Lil Nas X, KoRn, and Ariana Grande. It was estimated that Travis Scott and Ariana Grande each earned $20 million for this one "performance." These were prerecorded performances of the artist's digital avatar within the game world, which players' avatars could attend live.

These concerts attract millions of players at a time whose virtual avatars attend the events. Some shows look and feel like a traditional concert—in an animated, virtual world. And others invent entirely new experiences—outside the traditional limitations of the game world (or physical restrictions like gravity: cue a digital Ariana Grande avatar flying through a multicolor, cylindrical highway alongside enormous dancing pink flowers).

Festivals even popped up inside these games, like Block by Blockwest (a take on South by Southwest) within Minecraft, which featured over forty artists, like Pussy Riot, Sir Sly, nothing,nowhere., and Grandson.

Each of these virtual concert experiences took place within preexisting video games, owned by a corporation.

Decentraland was one of the first 3D virtual worlds built using blockchain technology—not owned or operated by a corporation, but rather its userbase. What is blockchain technology? The full explanation is coming in Chapter 12 in the NFT section.

Decentraland hosted a music festival on October 21–24, 2021, called the Metaverse Festival, and featured over 80 artists, including Deadmau5, Nina Nesbitt, Paris Hilton, Alison Wonderland, 3Lau, and RAC—all performing as digital avatars. 50,000 virtual avatars attended. The festival was free to attend.

In addition to the performers (on different stages scattered around the virtual festival grounds), there were games, merch stands (to buy NFTs), a VIP lounge, chill-out zones and more. Because Decentraland is built on the blockchain, you don't buy stuff with a credit card like you normally would IRL or in a video game. You have to connect a digital wallet that can hold Decentraland's cryptocurrency and NFTs you acquire at the festival. What are NFTs? We're going into the full deep dive in Chapter 12.

If the web3 world interests you, it's definitely worth jumping into the metaverse and exploring. There are endless fan-engagement and monetization possibilities.

THE MUSIC-STREAMING PLATFORMS

Spotify, Apple Music, Tidal, Audius, Deezer, YouTube Music, Sound-Cloud and Pandora each have their own community of loyal users. SoundCloud is most popular among the electronic, DJ and hip-hop communities. Remixes by up-and-coming DJs have found a home on Sound-Cloud (as well as Beatport and Audius).

The Seattle-born electro duo ODESZA released their first single on SoundCloud in August of 2012. One half of the group, Harrison Mills, studied branding in college and applied what he learned to everything they released. Their SoundCloud channel was sleek from their first upload. The duo emailed their new track to popular users with similar tastes, and five days after the song was released on SoundCloud, it hit #1 on Hype Machine. And since 2012, 24 ODESZA tracks have hit #1 on Hype Machine. They have over 250 million SoundCloud plays and over a billion on Spotify. They now play festivals all over the world and sell out nearly every venue they book.

All this from smart networking on the underground music-streaming service.

Of course, SoundCloud was the home of "SoundCloud rap," which was a scene and sound in and of itself around 2017. Rappers like Lil Yachty, Doja Cat, Rico Nasty, 21 Savage, Lil Dicky, Juice WRLD, BROCKHAMPTON, 6ix9ine, and XXXTentacion blew up initially on SoundCloud and were part of this new wave. Of course, these artists went on to become superstars and most got snatched up by the majors. But they all started (and gained popularity) by uploading their songs directly to SoundCloud.

Similarly, around the same time, Billie Eilish went viral on Sound-Cloud with her song "Ocean Eyes," which propelled her entire career.

Nowadays, there is still a dedicated community on SoundCloud, but it doesn't feel like the breeding ground for discovery it once was. However, because of the timestamped commenting, it can feel a lot more social than the more mainstream streaming services. SoundCloud remains a place to put both your official releases along with demos, remixes and mixtapes. As DISCO, Dropbox, Box, and Drive have all but taken over the private song-streaming market, there are still quite a few people who share songs via SoundCloud. And many blogs still prefer to embed songs on their site via SoundCloud and Bandcamp.

Spotify and Apple Music require distributors to send them music. As the two largest music streaming platforms containing only official, artist- and label-distributed content (no UGC—user generated content), they also have various royalties baked into every stream that get paid out accordingly (more on this in Chapter 13).

Pandora started as just internet radio and also tightly curates its content. And of course, Amazon Music gained a massive user base driven by their Alexa-powered Echos. Amazon was late to the streaming game but, because of Echo's popularity, instantly became a huge player in the space. Amazon didn't initially ingest every song and, like Pandora, heavily curated their content. It's worth checking in with your distributor to see if your music is being sent to Amazon and how you can get it ingested if it's not already.

And now that China is finally paying for music, you absolutely want to make sure your music is on NetEase, QQ, KuGou, Kuwo, and Xiami. The Philadelphia-founded indie rock band Cheers Elephant had disbanded around 2017. A couple years later, their original (and final) manager, Andrew Leib, got an email from a promoter in China asking if they had any plans to tour China because they were so popular there. Andrew initially thought it must be a scam. But after doing more research and enlisting the support of the artist services company East Goes Global (which serves the China interests for artists like Will Smith, Halsey, Jessie J, the Weeknd and Shawn Mendes), Andrew realized that his former clients were, in fact, big in China, with hundreds of millions of streams and tens of thousands of engaged and active fans. They booked a seven-city tour, which nearly sold out shortly after going on sale (the tour was supposed to start in March 2020—*ahem*). You can hear Andrew tell the full story on the *New Music Business* podcast.

Because these are datacentric digital platforms, every stream is tracked and most can be pinpointed to a location. Analytics are available for most and it's important to analyze these stats and use them to focus marketing campaigns.

Spotify, Apple Music, Pandora, Amazon, Tidal, Deezer and YouTube have excellent insights which are visible in your "For Artists" account,

Apple Music for Artists account and YouTube Studio account. You also want to check with your distributor for analytics and other data points. Some have great transparency and provide helpful information.

As Spotify, Pandora, Facebook, Apple Music, Deezer, SoundCloud, YouTube, Tidal, Amazon and others dip into the concert ticket and merch game, an entirely new marketplace opens up for artists, enabling them to monetize their most engaged fans where they spend the most amount of time actually enjoying their favorite artists' content.

It's worth noting that SoundCloud now functions on fan-powered royalties. Instead of subscription costs getting dumped into a black box and then divvied up based on total stream numbers, SoundCloud pays out artists in a much more artist-friendly (and ethical) manner. If a user only listens to one artist all month and spends $10 that month on their subscription, then all 10 dollars would go to the artist (less SoundCloud fees). This is called the "user-centric payment" model. Whereas on virtually every other streaming service, that one user's $10 would get dumped into the black box of money and split among all streams on the platform.

The decentralized, blockchain-based streaming platform Audius has created an entirely new relationship with its user base. The service is built on the blockchain—a decentralized, immutable ledger technology—to create transparency for their artists. All decisions are voted on and made by their users. Artists earn tokens ($AUDIO) based on a myriad of factors— many of which the artist sets for their music. The artist could lock some songs behind a paywall or offer other exclusives to their most dedicated fans. Audius combines the fan-club offerings of Patreon and the transparency and monetization features of Bandcamp with the discoverability and streaming user experience of Spotify. And Audius gives far more data to its artists. On Spotify and Apple Music, you don't know who your most engaged fans are. You have no way to target them for exclusive, high-priced offers or to reward them for their fandom. On Audius, everything is open to the artist. And because a corporation doesn't own it (it's essentially owned by its user base), there are no greedy CEOs earning thousands of times more than their artists or opening high-rise NYC offices. Unlike Apple Music and Spotify, which pay out around 70% of their revenue, and Bandcamp (85%), 90% of all Audius tokens go to artists.

DON'T LOSE FOCUS

You're a musician. Not an aspiring internet star. I've been chastised on *Digital Music News* comment boards for giving advice because at the time my most popular YouTube video only had 40,000 views. I had to take a step back and reevaluate my entire existence. "Man, if I was really good, I'd have a gazillion YouTube views." But then I remembered that I just played a sold-out show to hundreds of people the night before and was actually making a living with my music, and let the dbag in the comments fall right off my back.

Everyone's metric of success is different. No one can define success but you. Don't fret over your social media numbers as much as the true connection you make with your fans. Fans support you financially. Followers want to be entertained for free. Which do you want to court?

12.

THE NEW ASKING ECONOMY: THE DIFFERENCE BETWEEN ASKING AND BEGGING

N 2009, I WAS CO-MANAGING ONE OF MY FAVORITE MINNEAPOLIS bands. I was actively touring, playing 100+ dates a year myself, so the day-to-day duties were mostly handled by my co-manager. The band had built up a loyal grass-roots following and were selling out venues in a five-state region. They were bringing 600 people to their local shows every couple months and were becoming known on the festival circuit. They were making just enough money to support the five band members' living expenses while on tour, but had virtually nothing left over to invest. They had the material for their next album, but we didn't know where we were going to come up with the funds. No matter how we crunched the numbers, no amount of gigging or merch sales was going to bring in the $10,000+ we needed to make the album.

Then one day, through creative googling, I stumbled upon this new site called Kickstarter. It had just launched a couple months prior, but a Brooklyn-based musician, Allison Weiss, had raised $7,700 from just 200 people through what this new startup called "crowdfunding." We thought, what the hell, it's worth a try. The band has a loyal fanbase that wants to support it. Could we replicate this other relatively unknown indie artist's success? We got Kickstarter to approve our project (by that point it was invite only) and on December 1, 2009, we asked the fans to help fund the new album. Sixty-five days later we raised $10,455 from 173 backers. We didn't really know what crowdfunding was, but we knew, whatever it was, it worked. It enabled the band to fund the new album.

Two years later, I decided to take the plunge for my album. Through a meticulously organized campaign (more on this in a bit), I raised $13,544 from 222 backers in 30 days.

It's funny to look back before Pono, Pebble, Coolest Cooler, Amanda Palmer, Zach Braff, Veronica Mars, Reading Rainbow and, er, potato salad broke records and thrust this scrappy startup into the mainstream. But not too long ago, asking people to pay for simply an idea was not just unheard of, but inconceivable.

Now crowdfunding is a commonly used practice utilized by hundreds of thousands of creators supported by millions of backers generating billions of dollars.

But for some reason, many artists still feel very uncomfortable with the entire concept of crowdfunding. Taking a fat check from a corporation who wants to own the rights to your creative properties (and your firstborn), no problem. Asking fans for financial support to create art in exchange for nothing more than, uh, art (and some fun rewards), big problem. Artists (incorrectly) referred to this as "begging" and many refused to even entertain the idea. While these artists struggled and starved, their less stubborn counterparts were forging ahead in this new asking economy, funding projects and building successful careers.

Luckily, the negative crowdfunding stigma has all but been removed from most artist communities and now if you don't crowdfund an album, eyebrows are raised. Oh, how the times have changed.

Since inception, over $270 million has been crowdfunded for 65,000 music projects on Kickstarter—not to mention musicians who have seen success on competitors like Indiegogo and the others.

CROWDFUNDING VS. FAN CLUBS

I think everyone is embarrassed about their low [YouTube] ad
revenue dollars because they read stories about people getting rich
off YouTube and they think "Ugh, I'm just not getting enough
views. I'm just not smart enough." And no one wants to speak out
and say "Yo this model sucks! It doesn't work for anybody!"

—JACK CONTE, COFOUNDER AND CEO OF PATREON

Crowdfunding is great for raising a bulk amount of funds for a big project, like an album. It's not so great at generating a livable income. Or
helping constant creators, putting out art, regularly, like YouTubers.
That's why Jack Conte, one-half of the band Pomplamoose (who rose to
fame on YouTube), created Patreon. Famous YouTubers were getting millions upon millions of views, but seeing a minuscule amount in ad revenue from YouTube. Jack knew he (and fellow YouTubers) had fans willing
to support them, they just didn't have an available mechanism to do so.
He was right. Creators on Patreon include musicians, bloggers, podcast-
ers, comedians, artists, comic book artists. Patrons of these creators either
pay per piece of content (like per song posted) or per month.

This ongoing patronage model, or Crowdfunding 2.0, can be looked
at as a fan club of sorts. Bandcamp enables similar style subscriptions as
Patreon. On Bandcamp, fans can support their favorite artists paying a
set amount per month or per year.

Even Beethoven depended heavily on the patronage of just a few
wealthy noblemen to make a living. At some point in the twentieth century, however, the music business became solely about selling small-priced
items (records) to lots of people. For some reason making $1 million from
100,000 people was better than making $1 million from 10 people. If
you can affect 10 people on such a deep level that they want to sup-

port you to this level, accept it. Appreciate it. Welcome it. Respect it. If Beethoven didn't have those few patrons who believed in him, he may have given up composing, become a piano teacher and deprived the world of some of the most beautiful music in the history of mankind.

Amanda Palmer, famously, broke the Kickstarter music record when she raised $1.2 million from nearly 25,000 backers in 2012. But that money was all spent on recording costs, packaging and shipping the rewards. She has since joined Patreon and is making over $35,000 per "thing," as she calls it.

Patreon calls it patronage. Bandcamp calls it subscription. Whatever you call it, you should look at it as a fan club. Make this space a fun, digital hangout for your biggest fans. You shouldn't just set it and leave it, you should give your fans a reason to be members—aside from their love of your music, of course. In addition to traditional fan club staples like discussion boards and access to advance tickets, give your fan club exclusive access to b-sides, demos, live streams from the studio or rehearsal studio. The beauty of the fan club (over an album-driven, one-time crowdfunding campaign) is that you don't have to worry about sending out (and paying for) physical goods. Fans are happy to support and happy to get solely digital exclusive content and behind-the-scenes access.

Crowdfunding 2.0 doesn't have to completely replace Crowdfunding 1.0. Many artists run traditional crowdfunding campaigns on Kickstarter or Indiegogo in addition to Patreon or Bandcamp fan clubs. Julia Nunes ran a $134,403 Kickstarter campaign and a $1,700/video Patreon simultaneously.

These are two completely different platforms for completely different purposes targeting different subsets of your fanbase. Pull out that Pyramid of Investment. More of your fans will back your album-focused crowdfunding campaign than join your subscription-based fan club. But some will join both.

It's all about how you frame it. Locking all of your music behind pay-walls, and forcing your fans to consume music in a way that no longer makes sense to them, alienates your fans and will turn them off. However, releasing all of your music for your fans to consume in a way that makes sense to them, while inviting them to support you for it (offering bonuses like exclusive, behind-the-scenes content and engagement) will overjoy and delight them.

Fans will pay you for music. Ask them. Don't make them.

Sure, the average pledge amount is $5 (per release/month) on Patreon, but that's not to say you can't court your rich fans and encourage them to support you for a high amount that makes sense to them.

WHAT ARE THE DIFFERENCES BETWEEN KICKSTARTER AND INDIEGOGO?

The most popular crowdfunding platforms for musicians are Kickstarter and Indiegogo. Creators on Kickstarter and Indiegogo set public, monetary goal amounts and in some cases only receive the funds if they reach the goal. Indiegogo allows "flexible funding" as well, which allows you to receive the funds no matter if you reach your goal or not, however I strongly advise against this model. For one, if you calculate that it will cost a minimum of $10,000 for the album production and $3,000 to fulfill (and ship) the reward packages (not to mention marketing costs), but only raise $5,000, you're still on the hook to fulfill all the promised packages of an album that you now cannot afford to create. And another downside of this flexible funding model is that if you set your campaign to last 30 days and 23 days in you've only reached 60% of your goal, you'll shrug and say "Oh well, too bad we couldn't reach our goal" and take the money you did make and do the best you can with it. Whereas if you ran a campaign where you would receive nothing if you didn't reach your goal and 23 days in were at 60%, you would make damn certain that you made up the 40% the final week.

I can speak to this firsthand. This was my exact situation. In my final week of my Kickstarter campaign I kicked it into high gear, sent out personal requests to fans, friends and family, added extra incentives and not only reached my goal, but surpassed it by 35%.

A major element that sets Indiegogo apart from Kickstarter is their "InDemand" preorder solution. Once your crowdfunding campaign finishes, the preorder begins. All of the work you put into rallying the troops around the crowdfunding campaign doesn't have to immediately shut down the moment the campaign finishes. All of the rewards, exclusives and packages stay live, but instead of backing the crowdfunding campaign, fans simply preorder the packages.

VINYL CROWDFUNDING

Vinyl is insanely expensive. To get around the up-front costs artists have to endure on their own, Qrates and Diggers Factory have created vinyl crowdfunding platforms. Your campaign is successful only if you reach the set goal number of vinyl orders. If that number is 100 and only 43 people order your record in the designated window of time, no one gets their vinyl (you don't have to pay anything out of pocket, and no one is charged). If over 100 people order, then everyone gets their record (and you still don't have to pay anything out of pocket). How much money you make is dependent on the goal you set. If you have a die-hard, vinyl-loving audience, it's worth trying out a campaign.

THE BRIDGE

16 Tips for Running a Successful Crowdfunding Campaign

1) **Rebrand** Like an album release, a crowdfunding launch is a full-fledged campaign and should be looked to as such. Everything online should be rebranded to reflect the campaign. Come up with a title that represents what the campaign is all about. Create a color scheme and design theme that you use everywhere that directly reflects the campaign. Do a new photo shoot that is released on launch day. Put together a to-do list of things you will do during the campaign to keep it fresh, and constantly release new content to energize your base.

2) **Create the Right Timeline** Don't make the time frame too long. Kickstarter has said the most successful projects are 30 days long. They say a longer time frame makes people lose interest, and when they check your project out initially, they don't feel a sense of urgency. You don't want this to drag on. If you do your job right, everyone who wants to pledge will know about it by the time the 30 days are up.

3) **Create Attractive Rewards That Make Sense for Your Fans** It doesn't matter how big your fanbase is, if you don't go about this right, you won't reach your goal. There are (unfortunately) tons of examples of musicians (and some have massive fanbases) with sloppy videos and unattractive rewards who never reach their goal. You can't just put up a crowdfunding campaign and expect the dollars to start flowing. Start planning out your rewards at least a month in advance of your launch. Bounce your ideas off of friends and fans and only use rewards that are exciting, enticing and things your fans would actually want.

Your backers aren't an elusive group of random nobodies from around the globe. They will most likely be people you know personally, have hung out with and are your biggest supporters. They have come to multiple concerts; they comment on your posts, Tweet you and follow your Instagram. You must tailor your rewards to them. These are your friends and fans, you know them best.

Make sure you have a minimum of 12 rewards. Create high dollar amounts even if you think there's no way anyone will give you that much. Someone might! Make it an option to be rewarded for a $1,000 pledge, a $5,000 pledge, $10,000 or more. Even though technically you can pledge any amount, most people don't know this and will only pledge amounts for which there are rewards.

Utilize your unique talents for the rewards. If one band member creates spray-painted T-shirts, then have that as one of the rewards. The reason it's going to be fun to be your backer and not a backer of all the other bands running simultaneous campaigns is that your backers get something that is unique to you and that they can't get anywhere else. You have to be more creative than "Get the album a month before it's released with your name in the liner notes." Sure, that can be one reward, but that should be the least interesting one.

4) **Celebrate the Launch** This is the biggest day of your year. You should spend the week leading up to the launch getting your fans excited for a big announcement. Release daily photos, videos and hints to what it could be. Start to become much more active on all your social sites and email list. Maybe you've been quiet for a while. Time to reengage! You should clear your schedule for launch day (and possibly a couple days after it). Take off work. Stay home with the band and do nothing but get the word out, all at once, about your campaign. Answer any questions people have immediately. Rally everyone online and get that momentum going. You will most likely raise one-third to one-half of your goal in the first week. This is an extremely important week.

5) **Create a Killer Video** This is the most important part of your entire campaign. The success rates for projects with and without videos are highly weighted on those with videos. Plan this out. Find someone with a good camera. Or use your phone, but make sure you get lights and create an interesting set. Don't film it in your bedroom with dirty laundry all over your bed. Wow your audience. This is the next phase of your career. Make your video represent this. Are you going to step up your studio game? Step up your video game. Write a creative script. Rehearse it. Use your creative talents to make this video unlike all the other ones out there. If you have any hope of penetrating the general Kickstarter/Indiegogo community, your video needs to stand out among the rest.

6) **Pick a Realistic Goal** If you have fewer than 100 email subscribers, you probably don't want to set your goal at $10,000. Remember you can always raise more money than the goal, but if you don't reach your goal, you get $0. So make sure you set a goal you will reach. You want to set it high enough so people will help you work for it and spread it around. Once the goal is reached, people seem less willing to help spread it because it doesn't seem as necessary. But make sure you set the goal high enough to be able to pay for what you are promising. Also remember that Kickstarter and Indiegogo will take about 8%–15% of everything you raise (including processing fees).

7) **Create Stretch Goals** Create incentives for people to continue backing even after you reach your goal. Create stretch goals like recording additional songs, music videos, longer tours and other benefits if you surpass your goal

at various levels. So if your goal is $10,000, create stretch goals at $15,000, $20,000 and $50,000.

8) **Make a Budget *Before* the Launch** I learned this the hard way. I promised vinyl, but I didn't do my research to see what the actual costs to create a vinyl package were before I launched my campaign. And I didn't realize that vinyl holds only about 22 minutes of music per side, and my album run time was probably going to far surpass 44 minutes, requiring a double LP, and double the cost. I had to spend about a third of my entire crowdfunding income just to create the vinyl package. You can imagine the horror and the feeling in my belly when I discovered this. You don't want to set the goal too high that you don't reach it, but you have to raise enough to actually deliver on what you are promising without going homeless. Don't underestimate the costs of sending out the packages to the backers either (shipping, supplies, ordering the T-shirts, CDs, vinyl, etc.). And remember the 50/50 rule: 50% of your budget is for production, 50% is for marketing. Plan accordingly.

9) **Don't Forget the Link** Every time you mention anything regarding your campaign, you must include the link. Don't assume people are going to track down the link or take the time to go to search for your project. They may have missed the past five posts about it where you included the link. If this is the only post/tweet they see and there's no link, they won't check it out. Maybe they've seen all the posts about it and have ignored it, and they see this post and are finally pushed enough to check it out and there's no link—you just lost a backer. You cannot post the link enough. Don't make people work to find your campaign. Link it. Every. Single. Time.

10) **Don't Lose Momentum** The slowest part of your campaign will be week 2 through a week before your last. The urgency isn't there like at the end and there isn't the initial excitement like at the beginning. So, to keep the dollars flowing you need to come up with reasons for people to pledge today. Right now. Contests help. Personal appeals help. And release fresh content often, like demos. And go live every day on all the platforms where you have a following. If you keep putting out videos and releasing new songs (for backers in the Updates section) then nonbackers will be inspired to get involved and become a part of the process.

11) **Maintain a "We're in This Together" Approach** In everything you do with the campaign, your angle should be that "we're in this together." Succeed or fail. And not just with the campaign. Make them believe they are part of the next phase of your career. This is the next phase of your career, and with their help you will reach the next level. Invite them to join you for this ride. You want them to feel like they are a part of the process. Invite them into the studio

(digitally), ask them for lyric help on lines you're struggling with (maybe vote on a line or two—I did this and it worked very well). Just remember to put in writing somewhere that they are not going to be joint copyright owners of the song. That may seem obvious, but better to sound a little anal than to get hit with a joint ownership claim by some crazy fan. Keep them engaged and treat them like they are a part of your team.

12) **Don't Beg** You can't look at the campaign like your backers are doing you favors. You must believe you deserve this. If you don't, why should they? Thank your backers profusely, but keep it exciting and uplifting. Positivity is key. Use phrases like "We just made it to our halfway point!"

13) **Embrace Your Passive Backers as Well** Understand that you will have active supporters who will comment on every update, but you will also have many passive backers who will pledge to support you and then unsubscribe from your emails and don't really care to hear about it again until they receive the package in the mail. You have to respect them too and invite those people to pledge. Get them to pledge by saying that they are preordering your album. Make it black and white. Sell them on why it's beneficial to them to pledge. They may not care to necessarily be "a part of the process," but they may just enjoy your music and are excited about a new album. They'll pledge to get a discount on it and to get it early. Come up with rewards for these people and target them in your outreach as well. Don't assume everyone who backs you will be following every word you say and are as excited about this project as you and your mom are.

14) **Run Contests** A crowdfunding campaign is already gamified in the sense that everyone is working together to help reach a financial goal. But take this a step further. Come up with multiple contests you can run over the course of the campaign that appeal to the various demographics of your fanbase. Jacob Collier, known for his jazz chops, vocal harmonies and videos where he plays all the parts, incentivized his Patreon backers to send in a short video of themselves singing or playing their "melody of the moment." He then remixed it (audio and video) in the way only he can. He got so many submissions from this campaign (and new Patreon backers), that he was still working on his #IHarmU project two years after it began. He released all of the videos publicly and some have been viewed hundreds of thousands of times. Huge artists like Herbie Hancock, Ben Folds, Jamie Cullum and dodie all sent in submissions.

15) **Get Annoying** This is the one time in your career that you have a right to get annoying through all your online mediums. Tweet about it all the time. Mention it in every Instagram, TikTok and Facebook post. Make everything you do about this campaign. This is the next phase of your journey, the biggest

thing in your life and your career at the moment. Pledge drives are annoying, yes (if you're an NPR junkie like me, you'll understand), but necessary. Remember, not all of your followers will see the launch post about it. They may not even see 80% of your posts about it, but then they'll get a glimpse at one post and may be intrigued, but then will forget about it. They need to be constantly reminded. Maybe they'll ignore it the first five times they see a post about it, but by the sixth post they'll check it out and maybe on the tenth post they'll actually pledge. Don't get discouraged because your mom says, "Maybe you're selling it a little too hard." She checks your page out every time she logs on. She is not a good sampling of all of your fans.

16) **Personalize, Personalize, Personalize** Write personal messages to friends, family, former coworkers and big fans who you may be friends with on Facebook, may have been to your shows, may want to support, but just haven't made the time. This personal appeal works wonders. Personalize the message. Spend a couple days doing this. Yeah it's time-consuming and annoying for you, but if you get $2,000 extra out of it for two days of hard work—well, that's better than any day job out there.

NFTS FOR MUSIC EXPLAINED IN MUSICIAN TERMS

I released an album in the spring of 2021. It was my first complete body of work (under my own name) in seven years. It meant a sh*t ton to me. It was a heavy, heavy thing to make. Not only because it was made during quarantine, but because it was how I processed my breakup from an eleven-year relationship. I wrote around forty songs during this process and settled on the final six for this offering. Which were then recorded (remotely) with my producer and the musicians who helped bring this thing to life.

I put out a few singles in advance of the album. The Spotify gods did not anoint these songs as playlist-worthy (they rarely do). The Spotify numbers were relatively abysmal weeks after release. I know that it's not about week one anymore. It's about week 51. Week 151.

But I digress.

The numbers on Spotify literally made me sick. Sick that I allowed them to define my self-worth. And the value of this work that so much of *me* went into.

But then, I got the messages. Most came through email (because that's where the majority of my audience lives). Some came through Instagram DMs. And some people paid well above the $5-minimum preorder Name Your Price on Bandcamp.

One person told me how they had just found out their wife of fifteen years was seeing another man. And now, in a daze, he'd been aimlessly wandering his neighborhood with my song on repeat while weeping; this music was bringing him solace and hope. I received more wonderful messages about the music than I could relay. One person told me that they'd listened to just one of the songs over twenty-five times, and it hit them so hard that they couldn't stop crying over it. But it was bringing them peace. And one person said this:

> I'm a fellow musician. Thank you for sending this along. It's beautiful and very poignant. I can relate to the loss and grief you express in this song but in a different way. As I was listening to it, I recalled leaving music for a period of time in order to enter into the 9-to-5 work world fulfilling the expectations of others. As you may imagine, there was a loss of identity and authenticity I experienced that I never really allowed myself to grieve over until very recently. Your song has become part of the process of letting go and recovering in order to move on to fulfill the work I came here to do as a musical creative. Thank you for that gift! I feel this is one of the most precious gifts musicians can give—the permission to fully feel through the emotions in order to allow the healing to follow.

These notes were encouraging and comforting. And they reminded me why I share the music I make. And how once it leaves me and falls into the world, it is no longer just mine, but can give meaning to others.

Do the Spotify numbers reveal this level of impact? Hell. No.

How do I know if one of these streams (which I got paid around $.0035 each for) changed someone's life, or if it came from someone who skipped it after 37 seconds on a playlist?

I don't.

Spotify streams do not measure impact. Spotify streams do not measure worth. Spotify streams do not measure anything other than streams on Spotify.

NFTs have the potential to bring some value back to music.

What Are NFTs?

NFT stands for "non-fungible token." WTF does "fungible" mean? When something is fungible, it means that it has a defined value. Like a dollar bill. A dollar bill equals $1. Or € 0.85. Or £ 0.73.

Bitcoin is fungible. BTC 1 equals like a gazillion dollars at this point.

So *non*-fungible simply means it doesn't have a set, defined value. Like Jimi Hendrix's Strat. Or the first pressing of *Dark Side of the Moon* on vinyl. Or Carter Beauford's drumsticks. Or the limited edition, numbered screen print I bought when Alabama Shakes played the Greek Theatre.

NFTs are the digital version of these unique collectibles.

NFTs are one of a kind—just like Jimi's Strat. Yes, there are many Fender Stratocaster guitars in the world. But there are only a few that Jimi Hendrix played. And those are worth a hell of a lot more than just the one off the wall at Guitar Center.

So, what's been happening here and why should you care?

In early 2021, it seems everyone and their mom was talking about NFTs. You couldn't get away from it. This niche, scarce, hard-to-understand digital good was parodied on *SNL*. It hit the mainstream. Why? Well, why do you think? There was *a ton* of money involved. Jaw-dropping numbers.

The electronic artist 3Lau made over $11 million selling his NFTs. Grimes's NFTs sold for $6 million. And Kings of Leon (as previously discussed) made over $2 million selling their new album (and other assets) as NFTs. Steve Aoki sold his NFT collection for $4.2 million. ODESZA made $2.1 million on their drops. VÉRITÉ made nearly $35,000 on 3-song NFTs. Trippie Redd made nearly $500,000 selling just over 1,000 "Trippie Headz" on a marketplace specifically created for this drop. Young & Sick made $865,000 on his drops.

And outside the music space there was, of course, the visual artist Beeple, who sold a digital piece of art for $69 million at auction. A screenshot of Jack Dorsey's first tweet sold for $2.9 million. And that weird rainbow cat meme sold for $600,000.

Between June 2020 and December 2021, there were over a million NFT sales in the music space, grossing nearly $80 million.

Let's just consider for a second the numbers of some of these artists. Because, of course, as an industry (and society, sigh), we're obsessed with numbers. Young & Sick only has 27,000 Instagram followers. He's both a visual and musical artist who made nearly a million dollars on his NFTs.

Also, it's worth noting that celebrity in the "real world" doesn't necessarily equate to NFT success. Shawn Mendes, with his 60 million Instagram followers, only made around $380,000 on his NFTs.

OK, so now you know that people are making money on NFTs. But why?

Very simply, an NFT can be any digital file: a jpeg, wav, mp4, mov, mp3, gif, whathaveyou. Most NFTs in the music space have been short visualizers—typically videos between 10 seconds and a minute.

These are limited edition items. Just like a screen print or an original pressing vinyl.

The question I know you're screaming at this point is "WHY WOULD ANYONE PAY MONEY FOR A DIGITAL IMAGE THEY CAN DOWNLOAD TO THEIR DESKTOP?"

Well, it's a status thing.

Why do people wear $50,000 Rolex watches? Or drive Bentleys? Or wear Yeezys? Or sport Nike? Or Yankee hats? Humans wear brands, typically, to showcase something about themselves. Why did someone buy a Hockney painting for $80 million when they could just hang a print up for $20?

It's the story behind the item! The status symbol.

NFTs are collectibles. Just like sports cards or band Ts.

And you aren't actually buying the jpeg. You're buying a certificate of authenticity stating that you're the rightful owner of this digitally scarce collectible. And now Twitter enables you to display authenticated NFTs as your avatar.

Some NFTs are tied to physical items. Like how Kings of Leon offered front-row tickets for life for one of their album NFTs. Whoever holds those tokens can redeem them. And they can't be scalped.

RAC tied his NFT to a cassette tape. 3LAU offered a physical sculpture alongside one of his NFTs, and he shipped it out to all thirty-three people who bought this NFT. He also included an experience: In one of his auctions, the top bidder could collaborate on an upcoming 3LAU track. (When/if the NFT gets resold, the seller does not need to send the physical item—that's not how NFTs work—this was just a perk for the original buyers).

In this sense, it's kind of like Patreon or Kickstarter packages. Artists include merch and experiences in those. However, these can't be resold, and the value doesn't change. The $100 Kickstarter package costs $100 and when the campaign is over, it's over.

And the best part is, the original artist makes a commission on every sale. If I go and sell an original pressing of Vulfpeck's *Thrill of the Arts* vinyl record (which I bought from the band for $20) to Amoeba Records for, say, $100, I just made an $80 profit and Vulfpeck made exactly $0 from that sale. When Amoeba sells this record to the customer for $200,

Amoeba makes a $100 profit and Vulfpeck also makes exactly $0 from that sale.

With NFTs, the original artist gets paid *on each transaction*.

When the artist puts up their NFT onto a marketplace, they can set whatever commission they'd like to earn on each sale: 10%, 25%, 50%. Whatever.

So, a fan could buy an NFT from me for, say, $1,000, and then flip it for a quick profit for, maybe, $1,500. If I set my commission at 25%, then I will have made $1,000 on the first sale AND $375 on the second sale. Let's say that second person holds on to my NFT, and I become super famous and the value of this NFT now skyrockets to $15,000. Well, I just made an additional $3,750. And so on and so on.

Not only does the artist get paid every time, it incentivizes fans to promote the artists for whom they own NFTs! If the artist becomes more popular, the NFTs will increase in value and that fan can decide to hold on to it for bragging rights or sell it and make themselves (and the original artist) some money.

Because NFTs are bought, sold and stored on the blockchain, each one can be transparently verified as to who the original artist is. And, on the blockchain, every transaction is noted. So, anyone can see who sold which NFT to whom.

There are plenty of brilliant art impersonators out there who could recreate a Picasso or Monet, and you and I wouldn't be able to tell the difference. And that's why the paintings that get sold at auction have all been verified by art experts. Diamonds are verified by experts. Hell, even Yeezys have to be verified before they can be resold on a secondary market.

Well, NFTs don't have to be verified by an expert because the blockchain is a public record for everyone to see. NFTs mostly started on the Ethereum blockchain (not to be confused with Bitcoin blockchain, which hosts, you guessed it, Bitcoin currency). Ethereum blockchain hosts the

Ether currency. And many NFT marketplaces require you to use Ether to buy your NFT.

There was a huge backlash in the artist community against the environmental impact of NFTs—specifically hosted on the Ethereum blockchain. One artist estimated that minting just one NFT would be the equivalent electricity usage of powering his studio for two years! Why? Well, so as not to go too deep into the technology and complex functionality of the blockchain, what you need to know is that the Ethereum blockchain used to operate on "proof of work." What this means is, for the blockchain to work, it needed many computers to solve complex equations. People got paid in Ether (Ethereum's cryptocurrency) to run their computers nonstop to solve these equations to help keep the blockchain running. They were called "miners." As Ethereum got bigger, it took more computers to run it, which meant more energy to run the computers. Anyone in the world could be a "miner." And many people ran multiple, high-powered computers nonstop (racking up thousands a month in energy bills). The blockchain is "decentralized," meaning, there is no one entity controlling it. No bank. No corporation. No one person. It's all of these computers, all over the world running it together—which takes a ton of energy (bad for the environment).

So, other NFT marketplaces popped up which host their NFTs on environmentally friendly blockchains. Crypto.com became one of the first—hosted on the crypto.org blockchain minting NFTs from the likes of Snoop Dogg and Janelle Kroll. And Quincy Jones Productions partnered with the NFT marketplace OneOf, where they hosted NFTs on the Tezos blockchain from Doja Cat, John Legend, Jacob Collier, Charlie Puth, Alesso and G-Eazy. The electricity used to mint an NFT on these blockchains? About the same as sending one tweet.

There are marketplaces out there where you can buy and sell NFTs. Some are curated and invite-only, some are open to anyone. Meaning, you could theoretically upload your piece of art today and list it tonight.

Some of these marketplaces allow limited edition sales (like 100 copies for $1,500 each). Some marketplaces are auction only (like one-of-one only, for whatever the highest bidder pays). Some marketplaces offer both.

The invite-only marketplaces have an entire community built into the platform. So, if one of these marketplaces puts up an NFT, that community will typically buy it.

Early on, selling NFTs was quite expensive. There can be a ton of fees associated with selling just one NFT. There's what's called "gas prices"—for the energy spent to put your NFT on the Ethereum blockchain. And then there are the fees the marketplaces charge. Some charge a commission fee (like 2.5% of the initial sale), others charge more or bake in flat fees.

Most require you to use Ether to purchase NFTs. So, you have to buy Ether with whatever your local currency is. Most steps of this process cost money. It can be a couple hundred bucks to sell just one NFT. However, many in the music-crypto space are finding ways to reduce the cost so it becomes accessible for any artist to mint an NFT.

Most of the people who bought NFTs early on were the early adopters of technology. The gamers. The blockchain aficionados. The crypto club. And most just speculated. Like investors. Hoping they could flip these and make a quick buck. Most average music fans don't have a crypto wallet. Or an NFT wallet. And initially it was super complicated to buy or sell NFTs. But what we do know now is, NFTs are the collectibles of the future. And more importantly, for the artist community, art will be given value once again.

Streaming has completely devalued music. NFTs bring some of that value back.

The person who cried with my song on repeat may spend $5,000 on an original version of the song or a visualizer. It's meaningful to them.

But probably not today. Because they've never heard of NFTs, let alone have any Ether currency.

But someday.

And when that day comes, when recorded music holds value once again, I will celebrate. With my newly minted album.

Fan Financing

Some artists these days are now inviting their fans to invest in their songs via the blockchain. Some are tying this process to NFTs, and others just have mechanisms set up where a fan can buy a piece of a song for a set royalty rate.

Lil Pump raised $500,000 from just 859 people who invested in his new song "Mona Lisa" feat. Soulja Boy. They invested anywhere from $100–$50,000 to share in future royalties. Nas sold 50% of his streaming royalties for his single "Rare" for $369,000 to investors. VÉRITÉ made $90,000 by offering 39% royalty share in her song "He's Not You" to investors. And Diplo made nearly $400,000 for offering just 20% of his streaming royalties to investors for his song "Don't Forget My Love."

So, unlike NFTs, where fans hope the artist will grow in popularity which will raise the value of their NFT (like how buying visual art has worked for centuries), with fan financing, the fan earns royalties ongoing based on the amount they invested (and what the song was valued at).

True fan financing.

So, you could value your song at, say, $200,000 and run a fan-financing campaign allowing your fans to invest in the song at whatever amount they'd like, capping the royalty share at 50%. Once $100,000 is reached, the campaign is over. So, one person could spend $100,000 and get 50% of all future royalties. Or 100 people could spend $1,000 each earning 5% of all future royalties. Or any other combination. And if these sales are done via tokens on the blockchain, they can easily be traded—just like stocks.

Royalty Exchange started as a marketplace for investors to purchase publishing or master royalties from established artists and songs. Set up almost like an eBay auction, there's a buy now price or the ability to make an offer. Right now, some of the publishing royalties for Harry Styles's debut album are going for the buy now price of $625,000. For clarity, you don't get the publishing copyright, just the ability to collect on all future publishing royalties (paid out by the songwriter's publisher, in this case BMG).

Royalty Exchange boasts $100 million raised from 1,200 deals.

And of course, Royalty Exchange has now jumped headfirst into the crypto and NFT market. Some of their auctions are transacted on the blockchain using Ether. And some come with an NFT. The manager of A Tribe Called Quest just auctioned off his share of the master royalties for the group's first five studio albums (and a commemorative NFT), with the ending bid settling at around ETH 40 (or the equivalent of $84,765).

13.

HOW TO GET ALL THE ROYALTIES YOU NEVER KNEW EXISTED (AND OTHER BUSINESS THINGS YOU NEED TO KNOW)

A 2015 BERKLEE COLLEGE OF MUSIC REPORT FOUND THAT ANYWHERE from 20% to 50% of music payments do not make it to their rightful owners. Kobalt calculated that there are over 900,000 royalty streams per song. How do you make sure you register your work properly and obtain all of the royalties that are rightfully owed to you? Keep reading.

As you study more about the music business, you'll see the distinction over and over again between "artist" and "songwriter." It's an important distinction to make because the royalties for "artists" and the royalties for "songwriters" are completely different.

The reason I'm putting quotes around "artists" and "songwriters" is because so many of us are both. And many of us use these terms interchangeably. And back in the day, when labels started signing artists who also wrote their own songs (which, at the time, was quite unique), they put in clauses in the contract to limit the royalties they'd (legally) have to pay out to their newly signed artists/songwriters. One of these clauses is the infamous controlled composition clause. The major labels have always tried to screw artists out of money. They look out for their own best interests and use artists' ignorance (and blind pursuit of fame) to manipulate and deceive. This is part of the reason why so many established artists and songwriters have jumped ship from their major labels (and major publishers) and headed over to independent entities.

To not get into too much history, and really just cut to the chase, before the digital age, royalties were difficult to track, but there were fewer platforms to consume music, so there were far fewer royalty streams to worry about.

With physical sales plummeting, people shifting from downloading to streaming, and the rise of digital radio, there are many more royalties out there, but they can be tracked much more easily. We're not quite there yet, but we're getting closer every day. For indie artists without a label or a publisher, you have to know what these royalties are and know where and how to get them.

So let's break them down.

TERMS YOU NEED TO UNDERSTAND

Artist

Artists record sound recordings. Rihanna is an artist. She did not write her song "Diamonds." So she is not the songwriter. Record labels represent artists. A band is an artist. A rapper is an artist. A singer is an artist. Typically whatever name is on the album is the artist.

Songwriter

Songwriters write the compositions. "Diamonds" was written by four songwriters: Sia Furler, Benjamin Levin, Mikkel S. Eriksen, and Tor Erik Hermansen. Publishing companies represent songwriters.

Sound Recording

Some call this the "master." It's the actual recording. The mastered track. Traditionally, labels (because they own the master) collect royalties for sound recordings. Sound recordings are not to be confused with compositions. Artists record sound recordings.

Composition

This is the song. Not the recording. Traditionally, publishing companies (because they own the composition and represent songwriters) collect royalties for compositions. Songwriters write compositions.

PRO

Performing Rights Organizations. In the United States, these are ASCAP, BMI, SESAC and Global Music Rights (GMR). In Canada this is SOCAN. In the UK it's PRS. Pretty much every country in the world has its own PRO and they work together to collect royalties from each other's territories. These organizations represent songwriters, not artists. These are organizations that collect performance royalties (not mechanical royalties—we'll get to those in a bit). PROs make money to pay their songwriters and publishers royalties by collecting money from thousands of venues and outlets (radio stations, streaming services, TV stations, department stores, bars, live venues, etc.) that have been required to purchase "blanket licenses" giving these outlets permission to play music in their establishment (or on the air). The PROs then pool all of this money and divide it among all of their songwriters and publishers based on the frequency and "weight" of each song's "public performance." The PROs then pay the publishing companies their 50% and the songwriters their 50%. PROs split "publishing" and "songwriter" royalties equally. 50/50.

This is not a deal you negotiate. This is just how they do it for everyone from Taylor Swift down to you and me. 50/50. Any songwriter in the US can sign up for ASCAP or BMI without being invited or having to apply. ASCAP and BMI are both not-for-profit organizations. SESAC and GMR are for-profit and you must be accepted. Find the PRO in your country and sign up. You do not need to sign up for more than one. You actually aren't allowed to in most instances.

ASCAP

American Society of Composers, Authors and Publishers represents 850,000 members (songwriters and publishers) and over 16 million compositions. ASCAP is owned and run by its songwriter and publisher members, with a board elected by, and from, its membership. They paid out over a billion dollars in 2021. They represent songwriters like Katy Perry, Dr. Dre, Marc Anthony, Chris Stapleton, Ne-Yo, Trisha Yearwood, Brandi Carlile, Lauryn Hill, Jimi Hendrix, Bill Withers, Carly Simon, Quincy Jones, Marvin Gaye, Stevie Wonder, Duke Ellington, annnnnd Ari Herstand.

BMI

Broadcast Music, Inc. represents over 1.2 million members (songwriters and publishers) and over 19 million compositions. They represent songwriters like Lil Nas X, Taylor Swift, Lil Wayne, Mariah Carey, John Legend, Lady Gaga, Eminem, (members of) Maroon 5, Michael Jackson, Linkin Park, Sam Cooke, Willie Nelson, Loretta Lynn, Dolly Parton, Fats Domino, Rihanna, John Williams and Danny Elfman.

SESAC

SESAC is not an acronym. Really. It represents over 30,000 members (songwriters and publishers) and over 400,000 compositions. They represent songwriters like Adele, Bob Dylan, Neil Diamond, Rush, Zac Brown, Hillary Scott of Lady Antebellum, the Avett Brothers, Shirley Caesar, Paul Shaffer and one-half of Thompson Square.

GMR

Global Music Rights (GMR) was founded in 2013 by industry legend Irving Azoff. Like SESAC, it's invite-only and for-profit. GMR pretty much exclusively represents superstars like Bruno Mars, Bruce Springsteen, Drake, Don Henley, Glenn Frey and Joe Walsh (the Eagles), John Mayer, John Lennon, Smokey Robinson, Jon Bon Jovi, Prince, Slash, Leon Bridges, Ari Levine and Pharrell. They pride themselves on getting the most amount of money for their very few clients. They have licensed over 33,000 songs with about 100 writers and 200 publishers on their roster.

You (as a songwriter) can only sign up for one PRO. You cannot be a member of ASCAP and BMI. You have to choose. Find out what the PROs are in your country and pick one and sign up.

THE BRIDGE
How to Collect 100% of Your Performance Royalties

If you are signing with ASCAP and you are your own publisher, then in order for ASCAP to pay you both the writer's share and the publisher's share of your royalties, you need to register with ASCAP both as a songwriter and as a publisher. To register as a publisher, you have to provide the name of your publishing company. You can just make up a name and use it as a d/b/a (mine is Proud

Honeybee Music). If you do that, make sure to tell ASCAP you are "doing business as" that name so they can write the checks appropriately. You can also sign up for direct deposit, which expedites this entire process. If you want to set up an actual company as your publishing company, you can set up an LLC or a corporation (speak to your accountant about which one makes sense for you) and set up a bank account for that company, and ASCAP will write your checks to that company or deposit your money directly to that bank account.

If you are an unaffiliated songwriter with BMI, you don't need to identify a publishing company. BMI will pay you 100% of the money, however, you may miss out on some of your international royalties.

But, if you sign up for an admin publishing company (like CD Baby Pro Publishing, Sentric, Songtrust or TuneCore Publishing), they will collect your publishing money from your PRO, take their commission (15%–25%), and pay you out the rest. This is a far easier option.

I recommend you make sure all of your songs are registered with a PRO and that you work with an admin publishing company. If you distribute through CD Baby, use CD Baby Pro Publishing. If you don't, use Songtrust, Sentric or TuneCore Publishing. If you haven't registered with a PRO yet, sign up for an admin publishing company first—they will then register your songs with a PRO (save some time and steps!).

Of course if you have a traditional publishing deal you don't have to worry about any of this as they will handle it all. But until then, get your house in order!

Digital Distribution Company

Some people call them digital aggregators. These companies are how you get your music into Spotify, Apple Music, TikTok, Instagram, NetEase, Amazon, YouTube Music, Deezer, Tidal and 80+ other digital stores and streaming services around the world. We covered this a bit in Chapter 4.

MLC

In 2018, the Music Modernization Act was signed into law in the US. One of the biggest things to come out of this was the Mechanical Licensing Collective (MLC). Prior to its official implementation in 2021, mechanical royalties in the US were collected by Harry Fox Agency (HFA) and Music Reports—with near complete exclusion of independent artists' ability to collect their mechanicals without an intermediary. Not only that, the DSPs (Spotify, Apple Music, etc.) notoriously could not figure out who to pay for mechanical royalties (which is why they kept getting sued). The MLC is now the only organization in the US able to issue blanket licenses to collect mechanical royalties. By law, every streaming service must pay all of their US mechanical royalties directly to the MLC, and the MLC will pay out publishers and songwriters (unless they've worked out special direct deals with publishers). Unlike the PROs, the MLC doesn't split up the money based on publisher and songwriter. They only pay one representative for each songwriter. So, if you don't have a publisher (or admin publisher) and are based in the US, then you'll want to sign up for the MLC (it's free) so you can get paid. The MLC has relationships with nearly every other Collective Management Organization (CMO) from around the world to pay out mechanical royalties. So, if you're currently with MCPS (in the UK), CMRRA (in Canada), SACM (in Mexico), SGAE (in Spain) or another CMO in your country, most likely, the MLC is paying your CMO, and you don't need to worry about registering with the MLC.

This all being said, the MLC doesn't actually collect *from* these other CMOs. So, if you're only signed up with the MLC, you're still missing out on your international mechanicals—something that a publisher (or admin publisher) will collect for you. What are mechanical royalties anyway? Read on.

Admin Publishing Companies

"Admin" stands for "administration." All publishing companies have an admin department. They also have a sync licensing department, an A&R department and many other departments. Admin publishing companies have started popping up over the past decade to help unrepped songwriters (like you and me) collect all the royalties out there from around the world.

Again, companies like Songtrust, Sentric, CD Baby and TuneCore are some admin publishing companies who will do this. These companies will accept anyone and everyone. If you have a bit more clout, you should look into more exclusive companies like Kobalt, PEN, Riptide and Secret Road. These companies operate like normal publishers, but work on an admin (commission only) basis. They do not retain ownership—like traditional publishing companies.

CMO

CMO stands for Collective Management Organization. These really only exist outside the US, as in the US, we have PROs for performance royalties and the MLC for mechanical royalties. CMOs license and collect *both* performance and mechanical royalties. So, essentially *all* your publishing royalties for streaming.

Sync Licensing

"Sync" stands for "synchronization." A sync license is needed to sync music to picture. TV shows, movies, commercials, video games, all need a sync license to legally put a song alongside their picture. Technically, so do YouTube, TikTok, Facebook and Instagram.

Only recently have YouTube, TikTok, Twitch, Facebook and Instagram officially struck deals with all the major (and most of the indie) publishers to officially allow cover videos on their platforms. That's why for a while, Twitch and Facebook were ripping down cover videos. Back in the day, believe it or not, YouTube did it too—per the publishers' request. But now that the platforms are licensed, publishers (and songwriters) can earn from cover videos on the platforms. YouTube was the first, with their Content ID technology, to be able to track and monetize songs uploaded by users on their platform. For verified partners, they will even split cover song earnings with the publishers and the creators of the videos. If you want to start earning from your Facebook videos, sign up for Facebook for Creators.

Sync Licensing Company/Agent

Sync licensing companies, sometimes referred to as sync agents, work to get your music placed in TV shows, movies, trailers, commercials and video games. More on these in the next chapter.

SoundExchange

A lot of people confuse SoundExchange with PROs because technically SoundExchange is a performing rights organization. But I'm not including them in the "PRO" classification out of clarity (and when most in the biz discuss PROs, they are just referring to the aforementioned ASCAP, BMI, SESAC, SOCAN). SoundExchange represents artists and labels whereas (the other) PROs represent songwriters and publishers.

SoundExchange is the only organization in America that collects performance royalties for "noninteractive" digital sound recordings (not compositions). "Noninteractive" means you can't choose your song. So, SiriusXM radio is noninteractive, whereas Apple Music and Spotify are "interactive." Beats 1 (within Apple Music) is digital radio (noninteractive). Part of Pandora is still noninteractive as well.

SoundExchange has agreements with twenty foreign collection agencies. When your music is played in their territory, they pay SoundExchange, and SoundExchange pays you.

Like the PROs, SoundExchange issues blanket licenses to digital radio (noninteractive) platforms (like SiriusXM) which gives these outlets the ability to play any song they represent. Like the PROs, the outlets pay an annual fee for the blanket license.

But, SoundExchange collects only digital royalties. The PROs collect digital, terrestrial (AM and FM radio) and live royalties.

The way the copyright law is currently written in the United States, AM/FM radio has to pay only composition performance royalties and *not* sound-recording royalties. Makes no sense. The US Copyright Office has recommended that this law be changed, but only Congress can do that, and the few times it has tried, the proposal was defeated, largely as the result of heavy lobbying by Big Radio.

So, again, SoundExchange = digital sound-recording royalties for noninteractive plays in the US.

And to complicate matters even more, not all digital radio services work with SoundExchange (but 2,500 do). Some opt out and they just negotiate rates directly with each label/distributor. But I need to make this super clear because there was some confusion from the previous edition. If you are not based in the US you do not need to register with SoundExchange. You can register with your local Neighbouring Rights Organization. And even if you are in the US, you can still register with a different country's Neighbouring Rights Organization, such as PPL in the UK, Re:Sound in Canada, AIE or AGDEI in Spain, VOIS in Russia, or ANDI in Mexico.

HOW TO SIGN UP FOR SOUNDEXCHANGE OR YOUR COUNTRY'S NEIGHBOURING RIGHTS ORGANIZATION

If you are a US-based artist, go to SoundExchange.com. If you are both the performer (artist) and the owner of the sound recording (meaning you don't have a record label), simply select "Both" on the second page of the registration when it asks you to select: Performer, Sound Recording Copyright Owner or Both. It's a long process and you have to submit a full catalog list. When I did this, I had to email in a complicated Excel doc with lots of info. Plan a weekend to do all of this. It's time-consuming, but worth it.

Fun fact: I encouraged Ari's Take reader and children's musician Andy Mason to sign up for SoundExchange, and the first check he got was for $14,000! Apparently, Pandora had his songs included on all the most popular children's music radio stations and he had no idea. Boom!

SoundExchange will hold your back royalties for three years, so register now if you haven't already. And if you have registered (maybe you did years ago), make sure you have also registered as the Sound Recording Copyright Owner. Because the "Both" option is very new, you may have missed it and are only receiving 45% of your total money. Why 45% and not 50%?

Session musicians can get some of this money too!

If you are a session musician, 5% of the total money earned for each song has been reserved for you. Contact the Intellectual Property Rights Distribution Fund (or "the Fund" for short) to get your money. More on this in just a moment.

SoundExchange's breakdown for payment: 45% to featured artist, 50% to the sound recording owner (label—or you if you self-released), and 5% to session musicians or, as they put it, "nonfeatured artists." Whether you have session musicians or not on your record, SoundExchange withholds 5% of all royalties from everyone for them.

If you live outside the United States, you do not need to sign up for SoundExchange. You should register with your country's neighbouring rights organization. What is that? Keep reading.

So, just to clarify, here is a breakdown for the royalties artists and labels earn (and how to get them):

INDEPENDENT/UNSIGNED MUSICIANS KEEP 95%

50% To
Copyright
Owner

45% Directly
to Featured
Artist

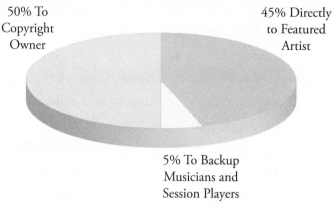

5% To Backup
Musicians and
Session Players

Breakdown of how SoundExchange royalties are split up.

Backup Musicians and Session Players

If you played on a record as a session musician, you are entitled to digital radio royalties! Visit the Fund (https://www.afmsagaftrafund.org) to see if there is any money waiting for you. You do not, let me repeat, you do *not* need to be a member of any union to get your money. Even though SAG-AFTRA and the AFM manage the Fund, every session musician is entitled to 5% of all digital radio royalties in the US. The Fund has a list of over 50,000 performers who are entitled to money but have not claimed their money. So, if you played on a record as a backup artist and have not been paid by the Fund, there's probably money waiting for you here. Go claim it!

And I know I'm going to get asked this question, so I'll just answer it: "What if I played on a record, have not been paid by the Fund, and my name is not one of the 50,000 listed. Am I still owed money?" Good question! This most likely means that the label or artist who hired you to play on their record did not send in the credit information to the Fund (most artists don't know to do this). So, you may need to spend some time with a representative at the Fund to get this sorted out (and get them to contact the master owner of the record you played on for credit info). But it's really only worth it to do this if you're certain the recording you played on has earned some serious dough. If it's in heavy rotation on SiriusXM or iHeart Radio or has millions of streams on Pandora, then it's most likely worth it. If the recording has mere thousands of streams on Pandora and has never been spun on the others, it ain't worth it. Save your time and your sanity.

Neighbouring Rights

In nearly every country outside the United States, there's what's called "neighbouring rights." Yeah, if this was an American thing, it would be spelled "neighboring," but it's not. It's European and beyond. Neighbouring rights are similar to what SoundExchange administers and collects (sound recording performance royalties for artists and labels); however, they also collect royalties from music played on terrestrial radio, television, in bars, jukeboxes and everywhere else in the physical world. In the UK, the organization that does this is PPL. In Canada this is Re:Sound. In Spain, it's AIE or AGDEI. In Russia, this is VOIS. And in Mexico, it's ANDI. Just search "neighbouring rights (Your Country)" to find how to collect your royalties in your country. Once again, if you live outside the US, you do *not* need to register with SoundExchange. Register with your country's neighbouring rights organization to collect sound recording performance royalties. Nearly every neighbouring rights organization works with SoundExchange to collect US royalties.

ARTIST ROYALTIES

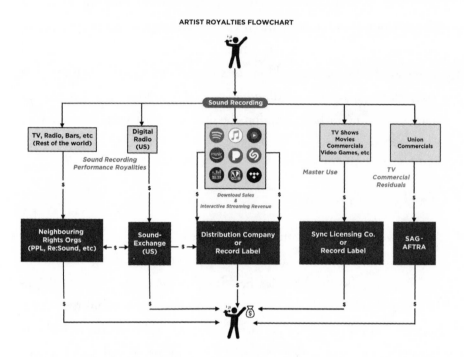

Sound Recording Performance Royalties

In the United States, these are just from noninteractive digital streaming services, also known as digital radio. Outside the US, these are from radio (digital and terrestrial), TV, jukeboxes, bars, cafes, shops, nightclubs, gyms, universities, and anywhere there is a "public performance" of a recording.

How to Get Paid: SoundExchange in the US, PPL in the UK, Re:Sound in Canada, or your country's neighbouring rights organization.

Download Sales

These result from someone downloading your music on iTunes, Amazon, etc.

How to Get Paid: Your distribution company

But, remember, if a fan downloads your music on Bandcamp, you get a check directly from Bandcamp because Bandcamp is a self-managed (as in you manage it yourself) store.

Interactive Streaming Revenue

There are lots of different kinds of streaming revenue. But interactive (meaning you choose the song) streaming revenue (like from Spotify, Apple Music, Deezer, Tidal) goes to the artist/label. When these services claim they pay out 70% of all revenue, the 70% is for both the artist/label revenue and the songwriter royalties (mechanical and performance royalties). Streaming revenue to artists is way more than the royalties paid to songwriters.

How to Get Paid: Your distribution company

Social Media Sound Recording Revenue

Technically there are a bunch of "assets" (streams of revenue) for each video on the social platforms like YouTube, Facebook, Instagram and TikTok. To make it simple, we'll just get into how you can earn money. First, for the sound recording (we'll get into the composition in the next section). You can make money off of any video that uses your sound recording (whether you uploaded the video or not) if your page is enabled for monetization. Either videos you upload or fan-made videos with your sound recordings can generate ad revenue that you can collect if you are a verified partner. Every platform calculates revenue differently. On YouTube, it's counted per ad view (not video view). On TikTok it's calculated based on the number of users who use your song in their video. Believe it or not, you'll get more money if 1,000 users use your song in their videos and they each get just a couple views versus one person using your song in their video getting 50 million views. YouTube splits the ad revenue 45%/55% in your favor. Twitch splits all revenue 50/50. Facebook, Instagram and TikTok have not publicly revealed how they split the money up.

How to Get Paid: Most digital distribution companies have this option via an opt-in check box. If your distributor doesn't handle this, you can work directly with YouTube to become a verified partner or sign up for an independent revenue collection company. But it's easiest if you keep everything under one roof.

Master Use License

Any TV show, movie, commercial, trailer or video game requires both a master use license (from the artist/label) for use of the sound recording and a sync license (from the songwriter/publisher) for use of the composition. These days, most music supervisors (the people who place the music) will just pay you (an indie artist) a bulk amount for both the master use license and the sync license (because most indie artists wrote and recorded the song).

But if you're repped by a label and a publisher, the supe (that's short for music supervisor) will go to your label and pay for a master use license and then to your publisher and pay for a sync license. Usually it's the same amount, but not always.

How to Get Paid: Directly from the TV studio, ad agency (for a commercial), production company (for a movie or trailer) or game company.

It's best to work with a sync licensing agent for this. More on this in the next chapter.

TV Commercial Residuals

If your music (with vocals) gets on a SAG-AFTRA union commercial you can also earn these royalties. And these definitely add up. I was in a Bud Light commercial (as an actor), and in SAG-AFTRA residuals, I got about $10,000 *a month* for the duration it was on the air. That was for hanging out at a (fake) barbecue holding a can of Lime-A-Rita and laughing on cue a lot. If one of your recordings with vocals gets into a union commercial, you might make something like that. Many commercials run about six months—that could be $60,000 just in SAG-AFTRA residuals. When getting a song synced on a commercial, make sure you always ask if it is a SAG-AFTRA commercial so you can call up SAG-AFTRA and get these royalties.

How to get paid: SAG-AFTRA

If, however, SAG-AFTRA doesn't have your mailing address, they won't know who to pay. Contact SAG-AFTRA directly and give them your info when you have a recording played on a TV commercial. Worth mentioning, you do not need to be a SAG-AFTRA member to get paid.

SONGWRITER ROYALTIES

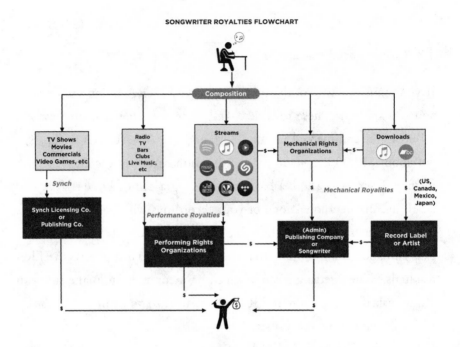

SONGWRITER ROYALTIES FLOWCHART

Composition Performance Royalties

These come from plays on the radio (AM/FM or digital), interactive and noninteractive streaming services (Spotify, Apple Music, Deezer, Pandora, YouTube Music, Amazon), live at a concert (yes, even your own and livestreamed counts like on Twitch), in restaurants, bars, department stores, coffee shops, TV. Literally any public place that has music (live or recorded) needs a license from a PRO to be able to legally play music in their establishment. For some reason, American movie theaters are exempt from needing a public performance license for the music used in the films, and no one gets paid residuals when songs are played in the films. Music played in movie theater lobbies and bathrooms is different and can be licensed (and earned on). When a movie is played on TV, the songs in that movie earn royalties. When that same movie is played in a movie theater, those songs do not earn royalties. Makes no sense. It's just the way it is.

However, royalties are generated for movie theaters outside the US And for an international smash, it could add up to be some serious cheddar. I've heard of amounts in the hundreds of thousands of dollars. Not yen. Dollars, baby!

Of course if a coffee shop has the AM/FM radio playing, and if you're with ASCAP, you (most likely) won't get paid when your song is played there, because ASCAP most likely won't be conducting a survey of that radio station at that exact moment, but if the shop has Pandora or SiriusXM on (or other piped-in Muzak services), this is tracked and you will (eventually) get paid on the plays. The system is currently being worked out and not everything is tracked yet, but eventually, say, in a few years, it will be. ASCAP uses a "sampling" method, where they employ an electronic monitoring system, MediaMonitors/MediaBase, for sample performance data from commercial, public, satellite and college radio. The sample data is then loaded into ASCAP's Audio Performance Management system where it is (mostly) electronically matched to the works in the ASCAP database. ASCAP states that they supplement this data with station logs and other technology vendors and methods that capture ads, promos and themes, and background music.

BMI also uses sampling. They say they use "performance monitoring data, continuously collected on a large percentage of all licensed commercial radio stations, to determine payable performances." They also use their "proprietary pattern-recognition technology." They call it a "census" and claim it's "statistically reliable and highly accurate."

My song was played as bridge music on NPR's *All Things Considered* (for 13 million people). I won't be getting paid for this (unless ASCAP happened to be running a sample of NPR at that exact moment).

TIP: Most PROs (like ASCAP, BMI, SOCAN, PRS, etc.) have a program where you can import your setlist and venue information to secure payment of your live performance royalties (for performing your originals in a club, theater, grocery store, arena, Twitch, YouTube, wherever). This can actually be a pretty good chunk of change. In the UK, for instance, PRS calculates this as £10 per show for nonticketed gigs (like cafes and pubs) or at least 4% of box office sales for ticketed venues (any size from clubs to arenas). The 4% is then divided among all of the songs performed at that venue that year split between headliners (80%) and openers (20%). I recently heard that an opener of a big arena tour in Europe playing just four songs a night was making about £9,000 (about $11,000) per night in performance royalties! So it's superimportant that you register your setlists with your PRO. Some admin publishing companies (like Sentric) will register your setlists with the PROs in the regions you tour—but you must ask about this. Many PROs, however, require the artist to input their setlists directly. ASCAP also runs a separate survey of the 300 top-grossing tours of each year, according to Pollstar. This includes both headliners and openers' set lists.

How to Get Paid: Your PRO

Mechanical Royalties

Mechanical royalties are earned when a song is streamed, downloaded or purchased (like a CD or vinyl). In America, the rate is set by the US government. And in 2018, the rate increased (for the first time in many, many years)!

Worth noting, in the United States, Canada and Mexico mechanical royalties get passed on to the label/distributor from download stores; however, nearly everywhere else in the world, mechanicals get collected by local collections agencies before the money gets to your distributor. So if you don't have an admin publishing company, you won't get any of your international mechanical royalties. Most international collection agencies will hold on to this money (for about three years) until a publisher comes and claims it. You technically could try to do this by calling up collection agencies in every country, but I just recommend going with an admin pub company—they already have all the relationships built (and they only take about 15%–25%; it's worth it).

How to Get Paid: Admin publishing company, the MLC or your local CMO.

Sync License

Like the master use license, any TV show, movie, commercial or video game requires a synchronization (sync for short) license to put the composition alongside their picture.

How to Get Paid: Directly from the TV studio, ad agency (for a commercial), production company (for a movie or trailer), or game company. It's best to work with a sync agent for this.

HOW TO RELEASE COVER SONGS (LEGALLY)

If you want to release a cover song as a download (remember, song, not video), you have to get a mechanical license. US law states that once the song has been publicly released, anyone can cover it, without permission from the copyright owner, as long as they get a compulsory mechanical license for the song. Sounds scary and complicated, but it's actually quite simple. Your digital distribution company may handle this for you. But if they don't, you have to get a license via HFA's Songfile, Easy Song Licensing or another service that will handle getting you a compulsory mechanical license.

RIGHT OF FIRST USE

A protection you have under US copyright law prohibits anyone from releasing a song you wrote without your permission if it has not been publicly released. So, if you write a song, no one can release it before you do without your permission.

HOW TO COPYRIGHT YOUR MUSIC AND WHY YOU SHOULD

Remember when Marvin Gaye's kids sued Pharrell and Robin Thicke because "Blurred Lines" kind of sounded like "Got to Give It Up"? Utterly laughable. Except when they actually won and were awarded $5 million. Legal debates will rage on for years over the validity of this verdict, but regardless, one thing we can learn from this is to always copyright your songs. Had Marvin Gaye not registered the copyright of his song back in 1977, his kids would have never been able to even bring this suit nearly forty years later. So copyright your songs—you know, for your kids' retirement plan. Just go to Copyright.gov and follow the prompts. Again, make sure you do this correctly. One tiny mistake could void your registration. It's always best to consult an attorney.

TRADEMARKING YOUR BAND NAME

Before you choose a band name, you want to make absolutely certain no one else is using that name. A simple Google and Facebook search will give you some indication, but it's always best to consult a trademark lawyer to be absolutely certain you can use the name you settle on. Once you land on a band name that no one else has, you should apply to register the trademark to be safe. Once you start using the name, you can use ™ on the name if you so choose, but to get a national registration and use the ®, you have to apply to the US Patent and Trademark Office. To make sure you do this properly, as it's quite complicated, you should hire a trademark attorney to help you with this.

14.

HOW TO GET MUSIC PLACED IN FILM AND TELEVISION

CREDIT ALEXANDRA PATSAVAS WITH WHAT SHE DID WITH *THE O.C.* back in 2003. She started the musical revolution in television by giving unknown indie artists featured placements on the show. *The O.C.* became known just as much for the soundtrack as for the girl-on-girl action. It paved the way for other music-heavy shows like *Scrubs*, *Grey's Anatomy* and *One Tree Hill* known for breaking artists in the early aughts.

Now shows, ad agencies and movie producers pride themselves on including the hottest undiscovered talent.

Alabama Shakes' song "Sound and Color" started charting on the *Billboard* Hot 100 the week Apple released a new commercial featuring the song (even though the song had been out for seven months).

The idea of "selling out" just doesn't exist anymore in the placement world. It's cool to get songs in ads. It's a career milestone. And it brings hot new artists into the homes of millions who may have otherwise never heard them. Many artists have in fact gotten their big breaks from being placed in commercials first.

But aside from "the big break," which is happening less and less these days, licensing has proven to be a serious revenue stream for independent artists. As someone who has gotten over fifty songs placed in film and TV, I've seen firsthand what sync pays (and does not pay). Some artists are so successful in the sync world that they are able to support their family on just sync income.

If pursuing sync is your main focus, you need to plan this out long before you write your first song, let alone record it. The fact of the matter is, not every song or every genre works for sync. If your chorus is all about Sarah, but the main character of the show is named Issa, they aren't going to use your song, no matter how perfect it may be musically. And because TV moves so quickly, they aren't going to ask you to go replace "Sarah" with "Issa." It either works or it doesn't. For the most part.

A good rule of thumb: *The more universal your songs are, the better chance you have at getting placements.* Lyrics are huge in the placement world. Sure, many times the spot will just use the instrumental version of the song, but often they want the option to use the full version, with vocals. If the lyrics don't work, the song doesn't work.

And production style is also huge.

I'm going to break down what each category is looking for and what it pays. Just to clarify, this is for sync licensing of songs already recorded, not for composers creating scores specifically for the project. That's a completely different process for a completely different book.

MOVIE TRAILERS

Movie trailers call for a certain kind of production. They typically want epic. A song that has turning points. Because they only have about two and a half minutes to sell a two-hour film, they need to show how many dramatic twists and turns the film has. Similarly, the best movie trailer songs have dramatic twists and turns as well. Florence and the Machine got a major bump because her song "Dog Days Are Over" was used in a big movie trailer. This is a perfect example of a song that's epic and also contains multiple dramatic turning points.

Movie trailers for huge studio films pay upward of $100,000 (or more) for a single placement. I'll wait while you pick your jaw up from the floor.

COMMERCIALS

Commercials also demand a very specific production style. And also pay very, very well. Anywhere from $1,000 (for internet only use) to $550,000 (or more, for a huge national campaign) for a single placement. No exaggeration. I've seen the briefs. The wonderful thing about commercials is that if the song works, it works. Whether you are a chart-topping superstar or a recently formed band and this is your first song, if your song gets selected, you get the money. Unlike TV and movie studios, ad agencies will pay top dollar for a song that works regardless of the party that reps the artist.

For a while, nearly every song in every commercial had whistles, handclaps and/or gang vocals yelling "Hey." And nearly every ad agency brief for a time called for songs that were either "edgy like the Black Keys or Fitz and the Tantrums" or sweet and sunshiney, like the Lumineers and Ingrid Michaelson.

Take, for instance, Imagine Dragons' "On Top of the World," the Lumineers' "Ho Hey," Mozella's "Life Is Endless," Kathryn Ostenberg's "Be Young," American Authors' "Best Day of My Life," Locksley's "The Whip," the Highfields' "I Like It," Fitz and the Tantrums' "The Walker," Edward Sharp and the Magnetic Zeros' "Home" and Philip Phillips's "Home." All of these songs have been placed on commercials and/or TV shows (in some cases quite a few times). At first glance you wouldn't put these songs in the same category, but listen to them back-to-back and you'll see the common production themes. They all contain either handclaps, whistles and/or gang vocals. Their lyrics are universal. And they fall into one of the two production camps. But production styles of course change with the times. No one is looking for this sound anymore. Fast forward a few years after this, and every brief seemed to call for songs that sounded like Sofi Tukker or Run the Jewels.

And ad agencies will typically not use sad songs. They're trying to sell their product, not depress their audience. So if your album has only down-tempo ballads, kiss your chances for commercial placements goodbye. They mostly want fun, upbeat, high-energy, exciting, epic, happy songs.

Just as every song on top 40 radio sounds the same (thanks, Max Martin), most songs on commercials these days sound the same. There's a formula. And if you follow it, you can make a ton of moola.

Although the production styles ad agencies request evolve as contemporary music evolves, the lyrics used pretty much stay the same. Most ad briefs want lyrics that call for themes about "home," "together," "friendship," "freedom," "let's go," "sunshine," "feels great," "enjoying life," "new beginning," "things are gonna be great," "feels so good," "change," "tonight's the night," "light" and "time." Pay attention the next time you're watching commercials and note how many songs actually contain these lyrics.

To find the current production trends being used in commercials, just camp yourself out in front of network TV during prime time and crank up the commercials. Or, better yet, browse commercials and discover the songs used on splendAd.com and TuneFind.com.

If you want to write songs for commercials, you need to master the current production standards and write songs with the most used lyrical themes. If you do, any licensing company on the planet will beg to work with you.

MOVIES

There's a bit more flexibility in the kind of music movies place because they are so narrative; however, using universal themes definitely helps. Movie placements for huge studio films pay very well. The sky is the limit. But $100,000 is not uncommon for an end title placement. Indie films, of course, pay much less because they're typically working on shoe-string budgets. Most will pay just a few thousand dollars, if anything. And if the movie hits television (or theaters outside the US) you'll earn royalties from your PRO.

TV SHOWS

TV shows don't pay nearly as well as the rest of the bunch. They usually pay anywhere from nothing (for reality shows on cable) up to about $15,000 for a Netflix or a prime time network show, featured placement. These rates are for indie artists. Major labels and publishers demand much more. This is one main reason why TV shows actually prefer to place songs by independent artists. It's also a huge point of pride if they help break the artist off of the placement.

VIDEO GAMES

Like TV shows, video games don't typically pay nearly as much. Oftentimes they'll pay a "buyout" rate of $2,000 to $30,000 or so. But sometimes they'll pay per game sale. Royalties are around 10 cents a sale.

IF IT WORKS, IT WORKS

The beauty of sync licensing is that the only thing that matters is if the song works with the spot. It doesn't matter what the band looks like, how many Facebook Likes they have, how many they can draw to their shows, or how many Spotify plays they've gotten. If the song works, it works.

MUSIC SUPERVISORS

Music supervisors (or supes, as they're referred to) are the actual people who take the cues from the producers and director when the "picture is locked" and underscore the picture with songs.

How to Contact Music Supervisors

Well, I advise against contacting music supervisors directly, as most don't take music from people they don't know. They get too many pitches from too many people. Supes may get pitched hundreds of songs a week. They don't have time to listen to everything. And if they don't know you, your email will most likely go straight to the trash.

That being said, independent, unrepped artists have had success pitching supes on their own in the past (including me). To increase your chances, start with supes at new shows. They're going to be scrambling for music. If it's an established show, do your homework. Every show has a style of music they place. Many shows will have websites devoted to just the music. Some shows even have Spotify playlists of all songs placed. Above all, do not, I repeat, do not hit up a supe without knowing exactly what kind of music she is looking for.

So, if you're absolutely certain that your music will fit the project, you can try to cold-email.

THE BRIDGE

8 Things Every Music Supervisor Wants in a Pitch

1) **No Attachments** Do not clutter up their inbox with attachments of mp3s. Only include links to where they can stream or listen to the song.

2) **DISCO Links** Most supes prefer to receive DISCO links for songs. These links allow supes to stream, add to their playlists or download the song. DISCO has become such an industry standard in the sync world, that your chances of getting considered drastically increase if you send a DISCO link instead of Box, Dropbox or, horrors, an mp3 attachment.

3) **Tagged Mp3s or AIFFs** Many times, supes will have a bunch of songs they are trying out for a certain spot. Once they land on the song they want to use, they will need to "clear" it. That means to get the rights to use the song. But they will probably have forgotten where the song came from. But if you added your contact info to the metadata, they can find you easily. So, first, create a 320kbps mp3 or AIFF from your original WAV file. In the comments, include contact email, phone number and "one stop" if you actually own all of the rights to your song. But, again, if you send them a DISCO link, it will all be included right there and you don't need to worry about any of this.

4) **"One Stop"** A "one stop" is usually a sync agent, artist or manager who has the ability to license all the rights in a recording—the musical composition copyright and the sound recording copyright, which are separate copyrights—at once. If you wrote 100% of the song and own 100% of the master, then you have the ability to license the recording fully and can list "one stop" in your pitch. If that is not the case (like if you have cowriters), then, in addition to getting permission from you, the music supervisor must clear the song with whoever co-owns or controls the publishing or master recording rights. Supes like placing music that is easy to clear. That's why they love working with sync licensing agents. Most sync agents (a.k.a. sync licensing companies) are one-stop shops for the music they represent. Instead of having to go to all the publishers of all the songwriters and negotiate a sync license fee and then going to the label and negotiate a master use license, they'd like to just talk to one person and negotiate an "all-in" fee for the use. So, if you wrote and released the song yourself, without a label, or if you cowrote the song with an unrepped songwriter and you got permission from her to be able to place the song without her direct consent and you recorded the song with (or purchased Beats from) a producer who gave you full permission to place the song without further consent, then you can say you are a one stop. If, on the other hand, you cowrote the song with someone else, and your cowriter hasn't assigned her

rights to you or given you permission to license out the song on your own, or if you and your cowriter jointly own the rights but you've agreed between you that each of you needs the other one's consent to license it out, then you are not a one stop, because the supe will need the cowriter's consent—and if your cowriter is signed to a publishing house, the supe will need the publisher's consent also. (Be careful: even if your cowriter gives you permission to license out the rights on behalf of both of you, if she is signed to a publishing company, she may not realize that she doesn't have the right to do that.) Obviously, there are a lot of ways this can play out, but at a minimum, it's good to get every collaborator on a song to agree in writing that you have full permission to license out that song.

5) **Subject Line: Sounds like _____ (artist you sound like).** Supes don't have time to open every email, let alone listen to every song. But, if they know what they're going to get when they open your email, you have a much better chance of getting a listen. So title your subject line who you sound like: "Sounds like Run the Jewels." If they need a song that sounds like that, you'll definitely get a listen—even if they don't know you.

6) **Only Mastered Tracks** Do not send demos. They only want high-quality, mastered songs.

7) **You Must Have Instrumentals** Often they will want to use only a few lyrics of your song, or none at all. They will typically want the instrumental sent over in addition to the main master. So, before you give your mixing engineer the final check, make sure you get instrumentals for every song. It's also good to get stems (vocal only, drum only, etc.). These can be helpful for remixes as well.

8) **Work with a Sync Agent** This all being said, most supes prefer to work with people they know and trust. Find a sync agent to rep you.

SYNC LICENSING COMPANIES AND AGENTS

Sync licensing companies, oftentimes referred to as sync agents, typically only represent artists who are also the sole songwriters. Sync agents are one-stop shops for music supervisors. They want to make it as easy as possible for the ad agency or TV show to use the song. Licensing companies can clear the songs immediately for the music supervisors.

So if you cowrite with anyone, first make sure they are not signed to a publishing company (if they are, it makes things very difficult and will almost certainly prevent a sync agent from working with you—or repping that song). And make sure you get in writing (email is fine) that you have full rights to the song to license without getting permission from your cowriters.

WORD TO THE WISE: Never pay a sync agent money up front to go pitch you. If they believe in your music, they will pitch you and work solely on commission. Commissions are typically between 25% and 50% of the up-front fee. Some will take a commission of your backend PRO royalties and some will not.

37 of the Biggest and Most Reputable Sync Licensing Companies Out There

411 Music Group	Mutiny Recordings
A&G Sync	Pick & Mix Music
Aperture Music	Position Music
Artists First	PrimalScream Music
ASX Music	Pure Sync
Bank Robber Music	Pusher
Bleed 101 Music	Resin8 Music
Blue Buddha Entertainment	Secret Road
Concord	Shelly Bay Music
Crucial Music	Silo: Music
Dawn Patrol Music	Silver Side Productions
DMP Sync	The Stable
Friendly Fire Licensing	Sugaroo!
Greater Goods Co.	Syncalicious Music
Hidden Track Music	Terrorbird
HyperExtension	Think Music, Inc.
Lip Sync Music	Whizbang
Lyric House	Zync Music
The Musicbed	

However, there are literally hundreds more. The above licensing companies mostly won't take submissions directly from artists (they're too big). It's best to get someone they trust to refer you (like another artist on their roster, a manager or lawyer).

MUSIC LIBRARIES

Also, there are music library and licensing companies that specialize in issuing relatively inexpensive sync licenses for wedding photographers, corporations (for in-house training videos) and indie filmmakers. This can help you bring in some extra dough. These kinds of companies are definitely worth looking into. They don't work to get you the $200,000 Verizon commercial spot; they're soliciting wedding photographers to pay $60 to license your song in their video, or even a $4,000 GMC new features video embedded into their website. These can add up. There are a bunch of these music library companies out there. Most companies are quite selective about what songs they bring on (to keep their quality up). But they all take applications from unknowns. If the quality is there (and it fits their format—they're probably not going to take death metal or hard-core rap for a wedding video licensing business), you're golden. Most music libraries are non-exclusive, meaning you can work with a bunch of them. And many music libraries have a hands-on sync agent arm. There's a lot more overlap when it comes to this space now than there was even a few years ago.

24 Reputable Music Libraries to Look Into

5 Alarm Music	Artlist
Alibi Music Library	Audiosocket
Altitude Music	BMG Production Music

Bruton Music

Cavendish Music

EMI/APM music library

Extreme Music Library

FirstCom

Immediate Music

Jingle Punks

Killer Tracks

Parigo

Pennybank Tunes

Selectracks

Songtradr

Triple Scoop Music

Universal Music Library

VideoHelper

Warner Chappell Production
   Music

West One Music Group

X-Ray Dog

WHAT DO "NONEXCLUSIVE" AND "EXCLUSIVE" MEAN?

If a sync licensing company reps you nonexclusively, it means that you can also get pitched and repped by other companies (or pitch yourself). Often, nonexclusive sync licensing companies will "retitle" your songs, meaning actually change the titles of your songs and reregister them with the PRO. So that they only get paid on the placements they actually secure.

It's worth noting that very few sync licensing companies are working on nonexclusive bases anymore because many ad agencies, music supervisors and TV networks refuse retitled songs. Many create cue sheets from sonic recognition software, and if conflicting rights holders come up, no one will know who to pay. The nonexclusive practice primarily still exists only with music libraries.

If pursuing sync licensing is one of your top priorities, search "sync licensing Ari's Take," and you'll find a ton more articles and resources on the topic to get you going strong.

15.

BUMP EVERYONE ELSE
OFF THE COVER

Watch The Weeknd survive a car crash in the
video for a new song, "The Hills."
—*PITCHFORK*

You don't want to just send a blanket email out to 1,200 people
that isn't personalized. You want to make sure you're reaching out
to the right people and not spamming them.
—NINA LEE, THE ORIEL

Have something to say and then find an interesting way to say it.
—KEVIN BRONSON, BUZZBANDS.LA

Whether you're an up-and-coming singer-songwriter or a heritage
act, you still need a partner to help shape your angles, your
strategy and present the narrative that you want to tell.
—REBECCA SHAPIRO, SHORE FIRE MEDIA

'VE TALKED A LOT ABOUT THE IMPORTANCE OF "YOUR STORY" IN THIS
book. You'll soon realize why it's so important for you to have a story.
Everyone wants press. It makes you feel important. Special. Vali-

dated. But does it really do much for your career? It can, but only if you approach it right.

Of course everyone wants a 5-star album review in *Rolling Stone* or an 8.7 in *Pitchfork*, but you have to be realistic about your press pursuits. If you have never received press, there is a very slim chance that you will get a review in a popular blog or nationally distributed magazine. Your best chance for media coverage is your hometown papers, magazines, smaller, more specialized blogs, and local publications in cities you're touring to.

The difference between *Rolling Stone*'s music editorial staff and the *La Crosse Tribune* music editorial "staff" (person) is that one of them has a backlog of tens of thousands of albums waiting to be reviewed and the other is in constant need of material. Can you guess which is which?

The reason it's, dare I say, easy to get press when you're on tour is because local publications are always looking for material, especially the daily papers. Even blogs with a local focus need material. *Rolling Stone*, *Pitchfork*, *Complex*, *Consequence of Sound*, *Stereogum* and the bunch get inundated with more music than they have bandwidth for.

There is a different way to approach local, national, digital, trade and print outlets. You always want to keep in the back of your mind when reaching out to any outlet: "What can I do for them? Why does my story deserve coverage?"

Sometimes just being a touring band playing a reputable venue in their town is enough to get a few paragraphs. Other times you'll need an interesting story that sets you apart from every other band playing a show in town that night.

Don't expect album reviews. They are boring to read by the majority of the public. Very few publications even write them anymore. Yes, I know you'd like every publication to talk about how this new album of yours will be generation-defining, but the local newspaper is trying to bring the most interesting story to its readers. And right now it's that you are going to put on a great show in their town. Notes about your most recent album can be included in your press release—especially if you're on a tour supporting it—but they don't need to be more than a couple sentences.

Before you start this process, ask yourself why you want press. And what kind do you want?

Press doesn't move the needle like it did in 2012, when virtually everyone was reading music blogs. Now that blog traffic has plummeted, fewer people are turning to publications to decide what to listen to. The value proposition has shifted. Music journalists are no longer the dominant tastemakers. Social media influencers are. Spotify playlist editors are. And frankly, the TikTok algorithm is. Whereas ten years ago getting a great write-up in *Consequence of Sound* or trending on Hype Machine would equal hundreds of thousands of streams and getting hit up by managers and record labels, now, if you get either or both, you'll be lucky if your fans even notice. It doesn't make an impact. Well, not in an instantly noticeable way.

More on blogs in a minute.

THREE MAIN KINDS OF PRESS/ MEDIA ATTENTION

1) Local
2) Trade
3) National

HOW AND WHY YOU SHOULD GET
LOCAL PRESS

Local press includes the local newspapers, magazines, news stations and radio stations. Even though most local outlets will have an online presence as well, with blogs and Facebook pages, the majority of their readership is local, so the majority of the things they discuss are local. So, when you pitch local media outlets, you must have a local focus. Are you a local band? OK, what are you promoting? A local show? A new album? A music video? Whatever you're pitching must be hyperlocal. Hometown press outlets take great pride in their city. So customize the press release to celebrate the local scene.

If you're a touring band approaching local media, it will most likely either be because you have a tour stop in town or because one of your members has some strong tie to the city.

Don't just seek press to get press. Make sure there's a coordinated effort to maximize your features around one important event: big show of some kind, new release (new means less than a month old) or career-defining moment like a record label signing, van crash, band breakup, viral song, tour announcement. It must be pressworthy. A local four-band bill on a Wednesday night is not pressworthy.

HOW AND WHY YOU SHOULD GET
TRADE PRESS

Trade press includes instrument, genre or craft-focused publications like *Guitar Player, Guitar World, Acoustic Guitar, Modern Drummer, Bass Player, American Songwriter, Billboard, Digital Music News, Pollstar, Hypebot, Music Connection Magazine, DownBeat, Electronic Musician, EQ, Live Sound International* and *Professional Sound*. They each have a specific focus. *DownBeat* primarily covers jazz. *Modern Drummer* obviously covers drums, drummers and everything drumming. If you want to get a feature in one of these publications you have to know the focus. You have to customize your pitch for the publication. If your drummer is doing something extremely innovative and is being recognized in the field for it, that's press-release-worthy for *Modern Drummer*. Just because your song has drums in it is not reason enough to contact *Modern Drummer*. Don't just send your music video to *Digital Music News*. DMN covers the business of music. DMN will not write about your innovative music video like *Stereogum* might. But if you had to sue your label to let them release your video, that is something that DMN would write about.

Know each publication's angle and focus.

Why should you get trade press? Honestly, it's nearly the same reason to get blog coverage: the pull quote and bragging rights. And once people discover you from social media or a playlist, they will start to google you, and ideally these articles show up. It gives you validation. Authority. And it gives the fan (and playlist editors) confidence that you are an artist worth paying attention to and investing in—because others are! Once again, there is very little discovery happening from press—in a measurable way—these days.

HOW TO GET NATIONAL MEDIA AND WHY YOU SHOULD

National press includes national blogs (not run by a local newspaper/radio/TV station), NPR, CNN, *The Tonight Show*, *Ellen*, *SNL*, *Rolling Stone* and *Spin*. Obviously the national outlets like *Rolling Stone*, *Ellen* and *The Tonight Show* are very tough to crack if you have very little happening for you on a national scale. And NPR and CNN are only going to cover very interesting, unique stories that their audiences would appreciate. A cool music video won't cut it. A viral music video seen by 100 million people may.

National blogs are a different story though.

Like the trade publications, every blog has a focus. Some are specific to hip-hop and electronic. If you're a sensitive singer/songwriter, it's a waste of time to contact those blogs no matter how brilliant you are. They aren't going to write about you.

You have to understand that the financial incentives for music journalism have changed. Traditionally, journalists wrote high-quality articles because it would get the publication high-paying subscribers. If the quality stayed high and kept the subscribers happy, everyone got paid. Now, very few people are subscribing to blogs (some have found homes on Patreon or Substack). But by and large, blogging is a passion project that doesn't really pay. Music writers are not getting paid by publications anymore. Most publications either pay their writers a pittance or nothing at all. And *Rolling Stone* actually had the gall to *charge* "tastemakers" to write for them (under the guise that they were paying for a membership to their "Culture Council"—which of course gave them the ability to publish whatever they wanted to Rollingstone.com).

Most publications are hurting. Ads don't pay enough to support a well-paid writing staff. Writers know that artists are willing to pay. SubmitHub (and the others) know that artists are willing to pay. So, the money is now flowing in different directions. Most music writers are making their money from submission platforms (and, believe it or not, artists, labels and publicists directly). Everyone needs to eat. And if the publication can't afford to pay, someone's got to; otherwise, the publication will go under.

So, if you want to get write-ups on blogs, know all this going into it. There are still a few blogs out there that are doing it because they love it—not to make money. And if you find those, great!

HOW TO FIND THE BLOGS TO CONTACT

Most of the top music blogs are included on the blog aggregator site Hype Machine (hypem.com).

If contacting blogs is part of your release campaign strategy, I highly recommend you spend some time getting to know Hype Machine. On the site, search for artists who are similar to you. You'll know if your style of music gets written about by the blogs they aggregate. For some reason, music bloggers love indie, experimental, electronic and hip-hop. They don't care very much for poppy singer/songwriters or right-down-the-center pop/rock bands. Knowing this going in will save you a lot of time and stress.

SubmitHub, created by Jason Grishkoff of Indie Shuffle, has over 150 blogs listed that you can submit to for a fee. Bloggers, playlist editors, Influencers, and others get paid to listen to your song and give you feedback (and/or write a review or consider you for other opportunities). Many blogs are only accepting submissions through services like this (or from publicists/managers/labels). You can read my review of SubmitHub on ArisTake.com.

But once again, it ain't 2012. Blogs don't have the power like they once did. Yes, Spotify playlist editors have said they like to see that an artist is getting press—it gives them confidence in putting you on a playlist because others in the industry are talking about you. And the Spotify algorithm actually crawls the web for your name to see what blogs are writing about you—pulling out keywords to help with its Fans Also Like and other internal sorting mechanisms. So, press *can* help. Absolutely. But does it guarantee success? Absolutely not. Is it worth hiring a $3,000/month publicist to get you blog coverage? That's for you and your bank account (or label) to decide. Is it worth paying the writer or publication for guaranteed inclusion (because, yes, this is happening)? That's for your ethical gut check to decide. Is it worth it to spend money on submission platforms? Maybe. For the googleability if you don't have any press. You want *some* kind of internet presence other than just your own website and socials. Also, to get a Wikipedia page that won't get removed, you need *a lot* of press. So this definitely can be part of the strategy.

THE BLOG SHEETS

Make a shared Google spreadsheet of all the bloggers who have written about artists similar to you from Hype Machine, plus any other blogger you know of that writes about your kind of music. Invite your band members, fellow bands in your scene with similar sounds, and music tastemakers in your friend group who regularly read blogs to contribute to the Blog Sheets. Make eight columns: Blog, Website, Writers (include all the writers at the publication who cover your style of music), Location, Email, Twitter, Instagram, Recent Article(s), Submission Requirements.

Bloggers like writing about songs and music videos. Very few review full albums. Do your research and find a writer's email address at the blog. Try not to just submit through the general contact form. Send this person an email. Start it off with their name. A compliment about one of their most recent articles can't hurt either (shows you took the time to get to know them).

Below is what an email to a writer can look like. Want to make sure you get your email opened? Reference one of this writer's previous articles on an artist who is similar to you.

Subject: Your article on [recent artist they wrote about]

Body: Hey Jon, I really loved your article on JP Saxe. How you described the juxtaposition of the fluid guitars and his broken voice on "Same Room" was pure poetry. I especially loved the line, "Saxe feels more than most see and exudes love when most reflect loss." Hit me hard, man. Well done.

I want to pass along YiiP's new song (out November 5th), "Next Door." It's in the same vein as JP, and I think you'd really dig it.

Produced by Justin Glasco (Andrew Bird, Annabel Lee), "Next Door" evokes nostalgia and pain with ethereal drums and lush string arrangements performed masterfully by the L.A. Youth Symphony orchestra (YiiP grew up with them). With delicate atmospheres, textured percussion and an underlying feeling of comfort, YiiP invites the listener into the autobiographical sounds of transformative heartbreak.

Two Story Melody said YiiP is "diving in where Jeff Buckley left off." You can read their review here.

Listen to "Next Door" here. (private DISCO link)

Press release and bio here. (Link to Google Doc)

Photos here.

Thanks for listening!
~Ari

Make sure your socials and website are up to snuff, with images and branding that is consistent with your entire project. You don't need an endless list of accolades. Just enough to reel them in. Keep it succinct. To the point. Complimentary. Not desperate. Not needy. Let the music speak for itself. Unlike nearly every other pursuit in this industry, for bloggers (and supes) it really is all about the music. You can also include a link to your bio or EPK so they can easily get more info about you. It should be a page on your website, so once they land on it they can easily browse your site with a couple clicks. And if you don't get a response, make sure to follow up!

It may be worthwhile to hire a publicist if you have the funds and believe you're ready for one. Go reread the section on publicists in Chapter 2.

HOW TO WRITE A PRESS RELEASE AND WHY YOU SHOULD

The traditional media world operates very differently from the indie music blog world. Many times they will respond better to someone not in the band than to the band itself. It may be worth breaking out your alias for this kind of press pursuit.

They will want and appreciate a press release.

A press release is a one-page, objective (more or less) fact sheet illuminating the who, what, where, why and when of your event.

Contact Information

Make sure it is very clear who the reviewer should contact.

Title

Every press release should have a title. If you're doing a mass blast, put the title in the subject line of your initial email. Titles should be to the point, but exciting enough for a reviewer to look deeper. "Touring Band to Play Birmingham" is boring. "Red Pills Bring Their Fire/Rock Show to Birmingham" is better. "This Band Lights Stuff on Fire on a Birmingham Stage" will definitely get a read. Like "Watch The Weeknd survive a car crash in this video for a new song."

Old-school publicists may disagree with the sensationalist approach of the title, but we've entered into a new era of press. Upworthy and BuzzFeed are masters at click baiting and are trumping nearly every traditional news outlet's digital traffic.

Reprinting Word for Word

Many times a publication will reprint your press release word for word. So make it readable and enticing. I'd say about 20% of my local press coverage has been a publication (online or in print) literally reprinting my press release about my visit to town. These sometimes will get added to the digital edition's calendar or "Upcoming Events" or "What to Do This Weekend" section. Oftentimes, the music reviewer runs out of time and needs to fill content. So your press release gets reprinted.

It Must Be an Event

There's no use sending a press release to let a reviewer know that you have a three-month-old album out. And, uh, how about a review? No. The only way you're going to get press is if you're pitching an event. A show. A release. The birth of your baby (if you're a celebrity). A charity event. A dance-off. The release of a music video. Something newsworthy.

First Paragraph

Who, what, where, why, when, how much. The facts. This needs to be first so the reviewer (or reader) can easily find this information and immediately know what this event is.

Second Paragraph

This is where you list the background of your band, your interesting story (the hook) and accolades. What makes your band unique? Include only the background info that's most interesting—one or two sentences. Include your most impressive accolades: who you have toured with, opened for; TV shows/movies your songs have been placed in; quotes from celebrities about your band; awards/contests you've won; festivals you've played. Be careful not to make it seem too braggy. If this press release is sent by you, the reviewer will know you wrote it. Keep it objective(ish).

You can use adjectives, but no superlatives.

Third Paragraph

Information about the event. Why should they cover this event? What makes it special? If this is a general tour press release, you can discuss the tour here (50-date US tour with stops at local children's hospitals in 20 cities). If you have any other press, discuss and link it here.

Last Sentences

Other interesting information. This is your final effort to showcase to the reviewer why she should cover your event or band and to the reader why he should come out to your show, watch your music video, listen to your album.

The Bio

At the very bottom put the promotional bio of the artist along with social media links. The bio shouldn't be longer than a paragraph. These are loose paragraph guidelines, but this is the order.

Never Attach It to an Email

When you contact a local reviewer via email, the subject line should be your title. You should write a brief personalized introductory paragraph, link to the album on Bandcamp or a private streaming link, link to your EPK and explain that you've linked to the press release and promo photo below.

It can be something like this:

> Hi, Kim, Minneapolis-based, The Red Pills, are stopping through Denver on October 3rd as part of our 50 date US tour. Our new song, "I Hope I Never Know," was just featured on Ted Lasso last week and Lizzo once called us "pancake butter"—true story! Let me know if you'd like to set up an interview with the band for a piece in the Denver Post. I've included a link to our album, new music video and the press release below.
>
> Thanks!
>
> EPK, press release and promo photos: http://myband.com/epk
>
> —Ari Herstand (The Red Pills manager/guitarist)

No Response Does Not Mean No Coverage

I can't tell you how many times I have reached out to press outlets with an email very similar to the one above when I have never received a response, but I got either a full preview of my show in the paper/blog or they copy/pasted my press release.

Always check the publication in print and online when you tour through the city. Sometimes their print edition will list show previews which do not make the digital version, and vice versa.

"For Immediate Release"

You see this statement in many press releases sent out by companies announcing things like a new iPhone or whatnot. However, when you're contacting music reviewers weeks before your show, you don't want them to print a show preview in the weekly newspaper a month before your show. So list at the top of the release when you'd like it printed/posted:

"For release the week of October 2nd."

Lead Time

For local press, contact them about four weeks before your show. Many times the music reviewers will have stuff cued up a couple weeks in advance of printing, but sometimes they are scrambling looking for content for this week. Sometimes (depending on how organized they are) they'll ask you to get back to them a few days before they go to print (or post the blog). If you're too early (two months), they'll ignore it because it's not pressing, but if you're too late (less than a week), you may have missed your window and that edition may be already set.

If you don't get a response, follow up a week later. Giving yourself a four-week window allows for follow-ups. Giving yourself one week does not.

Publication Research

Before contacting the reviewer, make sure you do a bit of research on the publication. Make sure they actually cover arts and entertainment. Find out how often (weekly, daily, monthly). And, of course, make sure you get the contact email and name of the music or community events reviewer.

THE CRITICS

The critic who doesn't like your work is correct. He doesn't like
your work. This cannot be argued with.

—SETH GODIN

Critics have been giving me a hard time since day one. Critics
say I can't sing. I croak. Sound like a frog. Why don't critics say
that same thing about Tom Waits? Critics say my voice is shot.
That I have no voice. Why don't they say those things about
Leonard Cohen? Why do I get special treatment? Critics say
I can't carry a tune and I talk my way through a song.
Really? I've never heard that said about Lou Reed.
Why does he get to go scot-free?

—BOB DYLAN

You know you're doing something right when you get criticized. The only
thing worse than bad publicity is no publicity. I was once trashed three
times in the span of five months by the same publication. Did it hurt?
You're damn right it did. But, you know what? Hearing Dylan talk about
his critics kind of gives me solace. As it should you. If you do your job
right, you will be criticized. Wear it as a badge of honor.

16.

SO, YOU DON'T WANT TO
BE A MUSICIAN?

So MUCH OF THIS BOOK HAS REVOLVED AROUND THE WORLD OF recording and performing artists. Of course, being an artist myself, this is my perspective. And in this crazy New Music Business we're living in, artists initially have to figure out how to navigate the confusing industry on their own.

However, lots of *nonartists* have read this book as well, to better understand the nuances of the industry and what it takes.

As I have interviewed hundreds of music industry personnel—on both the *New Music Business* podcast and privately in preparation for this book and for Ari's Take articles—I have been constantly amazed by just how many professions there are in the New Music Business other than merely recording artist and performing musician.

So, let's discuss some of them, shall we?

100+ JOBS IN THE MUSIC INDUSTRY OTHER THAN RECORDING ARTIST

1. A&R

A&R stands for "artist and repertoire." This is a term that gets thrown around far too frequently, and very few actually understand what A&R

is or does. An A&R person traditionally worked at a record label signing and managing talent and matching artists with the right songs. The A&R rep is usually the artist's point person at the label (or publishing company). These days, A&R study data and cultural trends as much as they listen to music or attend shows.

2. Accompanist

Employed by high schools for choir classes or contracted for musical theater productions at all levels. From elementary school productions, to community theater, up to Broadway—and everything in between—accompanists (nearly always pianists) are needed. And accompanists aren't just for musical theater, but also needed for soloists auditioning for university or performing in competitions or for official events.

3. Arranger

Arrangers work all across the music industry. More traditional arranger roles deal with string and horn arranging for records. But these days you have arrangers at video game companies, working alongside composers for film, TV and musical theater, and for cover bands (like the ones thriving online). Sometimes they will work with transcribers.

4. Artist Development

Now that most labels don't develop artists anymore, companies (and individuals) have popped up who focus on just this. Black Box and godmode are two great examples. But even some hands-on distributors help with this. It can be everything from creative direction, social media management, songwriting support and matching, demoing, recording, you name it. These companies help turn talented artists from a lowercase *a* to an uppercase Artist.

5. Artist Manager

The artist manager handles the business. As discussed in Chapter 2, they work directly with artists and touch every aspect of their career. Most work freelance on commission, however, some are employed by big artist-management companies. There are various levels of artist managers, like day-to-day managers who work under the primary artist manager. Most big-time managers will have day-to-day managers and assistants working under them.

6. Assistant

This takes many forms: personal, executive, virtual. Personal assistants are typically for the stars. Picking up dry cleaning, booking travel, that sort of thing. Executive assistants are more for, well, executives in the industry—scheduling meetings, answering calls, handling the day to day. Virtual assistants are becoming much more commonplace. They handle lots of the busy work that can be taught quickly and cheaply.

7. Attorney

Music attorneys are in high demand at every level, from helping indie artists negotiate contracts with producers and managers to being on staff at record labels, publishing companies and booking agencies. Obviously, a law degree is required for this role.

8. Audio Software

There are quite a few companies employing quite a few people responsible for all of the various sounds used in productions these days. Some of the bigger employers include Native Instruments, Splice, Ableton, and Avid.

9. Backline and Instrument Rental

Artists who fly to shows and don't travel with their gear need to rent gear locally. There are companies that serve these needs. Especially in L.A. and NYC, where this happens frequently.

10. Backline/Instrument Tech

You know the person who hands the guitarist her guitar in between songs? That's the guitar tech. Many drummers have their own drum tech. These techs set up and tune the instruments every night for the musicians and make sure that all the gear is in tip-top shape.

11. Booking Agent

As discussed in Chapter 2, booking agents book shows and tours for artists. The ones who represent superstars may also book paid engagements and negotiate brand deals. Booking agents work on commission, and in some states the commission is capped. Some booking agents work freelance, however many are employed by agencies.

12. Box Office and Ticketing Manager

These people are employed by music venues and handle all of the ticketing and box office operations. They work hand in hand with the venue manager, promoter, talent buyer, agent, manager, and artist handling guest list and VIP along with all ticketing operations.

13. Business Manager/Accountant

This is the person who manages the finances for the artist. The business manager usually sets up the payment systems and pays the people who need to get paid and collects the money from the places money needs to be collected. Business managers crunch all the numbers, create good profit-and-loss and projection reports, and make recommendations on smart ways to invest. Some business managers are also accountants who can handle taxes, but many just work with licensed accountants in the state where the artist is based. Many business managers are paid hourly, however, some work on monthly contracts or commission.

14. Catalog Manager

Often employed at publishing companies or record labels, they manage the metadata of every song in the catalog. Who are all the writers on the song? Who are their publishers? What is everyone's contact information?

15. Caterer/Private Chef

Some artists are lucky enough to have a private chef on tour with them. If you're an incredible chef, love a band and wouldn't mind hitting the road with them, why not offer your services? Dave Matthews Band's former private chef, Mitch Rutman, was also a fantastic guitarist whom the band invited on stage to jam with them occasionally. Not a bad gig!

16. Community Manager

We now see this most commonly with livestreamers. Musicians who livestream multiple hours a day can't always moderate the comments in real time or manage the community so that fans feel engaged and connected (and inspired to empty their pocketbooks in a friendly way). A livestreaming producer might also dip into the role of community manager, or they may focus primarily on the technical aspects of the stream. As Discord has grown, many livestreamers (and artists in general) are hosting their fan communities there. It's helpful to have a familiar face in addition to the artist who can keep the community engaged and connected.

17. Composer

There are composers needed in many facets of entertainment, from feature films to video games, production libraries to orchestras.

18. Copyist

Copyists typically work for composers and take their notes or MIDI files and transcribe them into sheet music that musicians can read. This is usually an entry-level job for an aspiring composer. However, some copyists may be hired by sheet music companies as the final step of the process after the transcriber creates the basic notation.

19. Copywriter

Artists and publicists need bios and press releases written. If you're a great writer, you could offer your services directly to these clients or even on platforms like Fiverr and Upwork.

20. Creative Director

Some bigger management and indie labels have creative-director departments. And some marketing agencies have evolved into creative-development companies. This can be everything from creating the artist's vision boards, overall aesthetic and vibe to full album roll-out campaigns touching every aspect of the promotional strategy, like photo shoots, album art design, music videos, social videos, color scheme, and stage and tour design. If you want more info on these roles, listen to the episodes on the *New Music Business* podcast with Jessica Severn (Scooter Braun's former creative director), and the episode with Livia Tortella and Brian Popowitz of Black Box.

21. Crowdfunding Manager

For the artists who have big Patreon, Kickstarter or other crowdfunding operations, a crowdfunding manager keeps it all together. The community will often get to know the crowdfunding manager because they will frequently interact. This person handles fulfillment responsibilities and makes sure everything stays on track.

22. Dance Choreographer

For pop and hip-hop music videos and big tours, dance choreographers may be brought into the enterprise. Sometimes, the choreographer will be one of the dancers on stage or in the video, and other times they just work with the dancers.

23. Data Analyst/Data Scientist

Now that so much in the industry relies on data, most labels and DSPs employ data analysts. A&R departments often have data analysts. And there are data-science companies, like Chartmetric, popping up every day that take all the available data and filter it into revealing trends and indicators.

24. Digital Service Provider

Otherwise known as DSP. This is the catchall term to include all streaming services, like Spotify, Apple Music and the rest. As you can imagine, there are a ton of jobs at these companies—sexy ones like playlist curator, and less sexy ones like metadata manager.

25. Digital Specialist

We touched on this in Chapter 2. This is the catchall term that includes (basic) web design and development (they can update your Bandzoogle website), marketing (running the social media ads, handling influencer marketing campaigns), SEO, and social media management.

26. Distribution and Label Services

There are now countless distributors out there, from the hands-off companies servicing DIY musicians to the "label services" distributors working with a roster of select artists. Many "label services" distributors these days look very similar to labels and have similar departments and roles, like marketing, promotion, radio, project management, A&R and accounting.

27. DJ

We're not talking Marshmello here. More of the wedding-circuit type. But also on the radio—those still exist believe it or not. Get a DJ mixing board and put your great music taste to work! To find freelance opportunities, check out the Bash, GigSalad, and Thumbtack.

28. Driver

For big tours, there will be a dedicated bus driver with a special license.

29. Equipment Sales

Matt from Sweetwater is a superstar in this world. If I could only figure out how to save all the trees he's single-handedly chopped down from all the pamphlets that have arrived in my mailbox. Guitar Center, Sam Ash, Sweetwater and the many other local music stores have plenty of job opportunities for musicians and music lovers.

30. Festival Grounds Personnel

There are so many jobs that go into putting on a festival. And job titles often intersect and interchange. What's in a title anyway? Here are just a few that fall under this umbrella: art department (visual design), artist relations and hospitality, food and beverage, campground activities and management, catering, media, merch, stage production, site operations, sponsorship liaisons, administrations (HR, management, etc.), marketing, vendor management, VIP management, medical staff, public safety and security, cleanup crew, guest services, box office and credentials, traffic and parking, ADA access, dispatch, site lighting, and drivers.

31. Food and Beverage Director (F&B)

At festivals and venues, there will be an F&B director to keep the operations running smoothly.

32. Freelance Musician/Hired Gun/Session Musician/ Player

Whatever you call it, if you are a master at your instrument, you can get hired by artists, band leaders, music directors, and producers for recording sessions, gigs and tours. Most of these musicians work freelance, however, some are employed full-time by (very wealthy) artists. A lot of this work will be in the music hubs like L.A., Nashville, London and NYC. However, there are, of course, hired guns in every city—you'll just have a much harder time making a living outside of a music hub. If you have a home recording setup you can offer remote recording services. Check out platforms like SoundBetter and AirGigs to advertise your services.

33. Front-of-House Engineer (FOH)

This is the most important person for every concert. The FOH controls whether the sound in the house will sound good or bad. Plain and simple. Most venues have FOHs on rotation who run sound for select shows. Even if the artist brings their own FOH, the house FOH works alongside the artist's FOH for the evening, making sure they have everything they need. Some FOHs are hired by the artist for tours, and some are hired by venues and festivals. Oftentimes for smaller tours, FOHs double as the tour manager.

34. Grant Writer

Many countries support the arts in tremendous ways—namely financial. The US, not so much. But other countries, like Canada, have many government-funded grants that musicians of all levels can apply for to support their careers. Typically, this is an arduous process that requires an experienced grant writer to know how to secure these funds.

35. Graphic Designer

Whether it's concert posters, web design, social media posts, or logo and brand design, graphic designers are in high demand. Sometimes they are employed by record labels or design houses, but most work freelance. Many find work on Upwork, Fiverr, 99designs, Toptal and Thumbtack.

36. Influencer

TikTok busted open the door for influencers to promote music. We've come a long way since the Fyre Festival days where Instagram influencers (i.e., models) promoted a festival that didn't exist. Now influencers can make tens of thousand dollars for one post! Influencers usually have an influencer agent or manager who helps them secure deals with brands and labels (or artists directly).

37. Influencer Agent

Influencer agents work with influencers to secure them deals with brands and record labels (or artists) who pay the influencer to promote their product or song. Like booking agents, influencer agents typically work on commission. There are many influencer agencies out there, and I profiled a couple of these people on the *New Music Business* podcast. Listen to the interviews with Austin Georgas of Flighthouse and Griffin Haddrill of VRTCL.

38. Jingle Writer

This may be an outdated job title, but these people still exist. They may call themselves composers, songwriters, producers, arrangers. Whatever you call them, they typically get hired by ad agencies (or even businesses directly) to write songs for their ad campaigns.

39. Label Services

This is the catchall term now that many hands-on distributors use for all of the services they offer. Under this umbrella you typically see playlist pitching, influencer marketing, music video creation, and social media management. Some label services companies include Create Music Group, Vyida, AWAL, Stem, INgrooves, Believe, and the Orchard.

40. Livestreaming Producer/Engineer

Now that livestreaming is big business and many artists are regularly putting on livestreaming shows, there are livestreaming producers and engineers to assist. There are full-fledged livestreaming production companies with studios, full gear, and full staffs of camera operators, audio engineers, OBS operators and directors. From giant music festivals down to bedroom artists, livestreaming producers and engineers are in high demand.

41. Marketing Manager

This person traditionally worked at record labels in the, you guessed it, marketing department. Now that so many artists are independent, there are marketing managers who work on the artist's or manager's team or even at marketing agencies. This person specializes in all marketing components for an artist, but is most active these days running social media ads and negotiating influencer campaigns. Marketers typically get paid per campaign or per month, unless they are employed by a marketing agency.

42. Mastering Engineer

This is the final person to touch a record. Most mastering engineers started as recording and mixing engineers. Some mastering engineers are employed at mastering companies like Sterling Sound in NYC or Bernie Grundman Mastering in L.A. Mastering engineers have a very specific and hard-to-understand skillset, but can dictate the overall vibe of a record. Learn more about mastering engineers in Chapter 2.

43. Mental Health Professional

I don't need to tell you that people working in music struggle with mental health more than many other professions. More and more organizations are incorporating ongoing mental health services within the organization, and all music professionals should prioritize good mental health practices. If you are a mental health professional, consider focusing your efforts on music professionals—we could use your services! And check out Backline for more mental health services geared specifically for music professionals.

44. Merch Manager

Merch managers handle all merch operations for artists or venues. For most midsize to large tours, the artist will bring their own merch manager who will set up the merch every night, train the local sellers, keep track of the inventory, run the point of sale (POS) systems, keep cash on hand for change, make deposits, keep all of the payment-processing systems in order, count the money in and out each night and make sure there is enough inventory on hand (and preemptively order more so it's never sold out). Merch managers usually wear multiple hats for smaller tours—most frequently doubling as the tour manager or driver.

45. Mindset Coach

I know, I know, you're thinking Ari's gone all Hollywood on us now. But I promise you this is a real thing and it's really important. Mindset coaches deal with creativity, business strategies, mental health, you name it. Not a licensed therapist (however, that job is also super important), but your accountability and mindset advocate and partner. The best ones out there keep you on track, focused and inspired.

46. Mixing Engineer

As noted in Chapter 2, this can be one of the most important people to touch a record. Most mixing engineers are paid a flat rate per song, however, some superstar mixing engineers earn points on the backend. Most mixing engineers work freelance.

47. Monitor Engineer

For bigger venues and festivals there will be both the front-of-house engineer (FOH) and monitor engineer. The monitor engineer usually works under the FOH and production manager. This is the person at the monitor board running the, you guessed it, monitor mix for the band. Most monitor engineers are hired by venues, however, some artists on big tours will bring their own.

48. Music Contractor

Music contractors are typically in the orchestral space with a roster of musicians they can contract out for recording projects and concerts. If a band wants to enhance their late night TV or festival appearance with a string quartet, they could hire a music contractor to find them the players. Or if an artist needs a full orchestra for their record, they can similarly hire a music contractor to help fulfill their needs. Composers often hire music contractors to help them make recordings and demos of their compositions.

49. Music Director (MD)

The music director is the person (typically in the band) who hires the musicians, runs rehearsals and, for bigger artists, is generally in charge of the band. MDs may get hired to put a band together for a one-off TV appearance or a full tour. MDs typically start off as side(wo)men and work their way up into the trusted circle.

50. Music Journalist

If you're a great writer, there are a handful of outlets out there that will hire you for your skills (and ability to pump out articles, fast). If you run your own music blog, you can make some money on submissions from submission platforms.

51. Music Supervisor

As discussed in Chapter 14, music supervisors are the people who work on contract for TV shows, movies, ad agencies, and video game companies and are responsible for choosing (and clearing the rights for) the music used. Music supervisors work with publishers, labels, sync agents, managers, and artists to secure the music they need for the project they are working on. If you're interested in becoming a music supervisor, listen to the episodes on the *New Music Business* podcast featuring Jen Malone (*Euphoria*, *Atlanta*), Brian Vickers (Disney), Madonna Wade-

Reed (Reign, Batwoman), and Lindsay Wolfington (*One Tree Hill*, *To All the Boys*). And follow the Guild of Music Supervisors on Instagram.

52. Music Teacher

We've come a long way since the local piano teacher in your neighborhood. With so many instructional institutes out there, from traditional music schools to online learning like Fender Play, if you want to educate and empower musicians, there is a place for you. Some traditional institutions (like high schools) require you to have a degree, however, there are plenty of opportunities to teach even if you don't have a degree.

53. Music Therapist

This is one of the very few careers in music that has majors at most major universities. Music therapists often work in hospitals, rehab centers, nursing homes, correctional facilities, halfway homes, schools and private practice. A music therapy degree is typically needed to get hired in this field.

54. Music University Professional

This comes in all forms, from professor to career developer to administration to, well, ever been to college? It takes a lot of people to make universities run. If you have a passion for music (and music business) education, check out all of the job opportunities at music schools.

55. Musical Instrument Research and Development

When instrument companies are developing new products, they enlist professional musicians to test them out and give feedback. If you want to be contracted for this work, contact the R&D teams at your favorite company.

56. Musician Contractor

There are people out there who act somewhat as agents for musicians. This is most prominent in the orchestral world. These types of contractors work alongside composers, film producers, event managers and music producers.

57. NFT Consultant

As NFTs start to take off, artists, managers, labels and everyone else are hiring NFT consultants to help them set up their NFT drops and manage the campaigns. If you're a master in the crypto space, you could offer your services for a hefty fee.

58. Orchestra Conductor

Sometimes the orchestra conductor is the star of the orchestra, like the L.A. Phil, but orchestras often bring in guest conductors. Some conductors are contracted to conduct their own works, and some are contracted for their experience, talent and prestige.

59. Orchestra Staff

Most major cities have a pretty substantial local orchestra. And most smaller cities have at least a community orchestra or part-time orchestra of some kind. It takes all sorts of people to make the orchestra run. Inquire with your local orchestra (or even performing arts center) to see what openings there are.

60. Orchestral Musician

There are thousands of orchestras all over the world, from the local community orchestra all the way up to the London Symphony Orchestra. If you play an orchestral instrument, there are plenty of jobs available that aren't necessarily confined to playing in an orchestra. Like playing in the pit orchestra of a musical and doing session work on pop records.

61. Photographer

Photographers are needed at every step of the artist's journey. There are tour photographers—who sometimes double as social media and content managers—and also photographers who specialize in promo and album shoots and who typically work out of a photo studio.

62. Playback Engineer

Many hip-hop and pop acts bring a playback engineer on the road with them to trigger the tracks during the show if they don't have a musician to handle this. Laura Escudé was Kanye's and Ariana Grande's, and she discussed this job on the *New Music Business* podcast.

63. Playlist Editor

Believe it or not, many people are making a living as playlist editors. Some playlisters are employed by streaming services like Spotify, but most are self-employed and get paid by submission services where artists pay to submit their music for consideration. Many playlisters get paid per submission they review. Some playlisters also make money directly from artists and labels to include music in their playlists—even though this is technically against Spotify's terms of use.

64. Playlist Promoter

The Spotify playlists are tough to crack, and Spotify has put up an iron-clad wall around them; however, every label and many label services distributors have playlist promoters to pitch their records to playlists at all the DSPs. There are also third-party playlist promoters who have built up a network of playlists who get hired by labels and artists to pitch their music to user-generated playlists. However, now that most user-generated playlisters make their livings from submission services that pay them for consideration and placement, there are fewer independent playlist promoters out there.

65. Producer

Yes, the title producer is used in almost every creative profession out there. In the music industry, the producer helps bring records to life. We went deep into this in Chapter 3. Nowadays, producers not only work with artists, but create sample packs, plugins and wear many other hats. Many producers have day rates, song rates, and get cut into backend royalties. Most producers freelance; however, some are on staff at sync licensing companies, record labels and publishing companies.

66. Producer Manager

Like an artist manager, a producer manager handles the business for producers. Typically, they will seek out clients and negotiate deals. Producer managers work on commission. Most work freelance, however, some are employed by big artist-management companies.

67. Product/Label Manager

Most product managers work at labels and distributors, however, many are increasingly getting hired by nonlabel artists to run their release campaigns. If you're interested to hear more about this job, listen to my interview with Lauv's label manager, Emma MacDonald, on the *New Music Business* podcast.

68. Production/Lighting Designer (LD)

Midsize to large music venues will most likely have an LD in addition to an FOH on staff. Sometimes, the FOH will also run lights. Most touring acts, once they hit theaters and above, typically bring their own LD. And especially when acts start touring with full production, the LD/production designer is a critical component of the show.

69. Production Manager/Building Operations

Most big venues, festivals and events have production managers who handle the on-the-ground operations to make sure the event runs smoothly. They work with all of the technicians, engineers and stage manager and stagehands. For smaller events, this person may wear many hats: set up the sound system, build the stage, make sure the bathrooms are stocked and cleaned, and make sure the venue is generally in order. For larger venues, this person manages the staff of people who handle all the roles.

70. Promoter/Talent Buyer/Booker

Even though promoters and talent buyers theoretically should be (and sometimes are) two completely separate roles, more times than not they are the same person or work at the same company. This is the person that books the talent for venues. They work directly with agents, managers and artists to work out all of the details about the show: compensation, lineup, ticket price, showtime, etc. Some also work to promote the show or tour (however this is increasingly rare). Some bigger promotion companies, like Live Nation, AEG, Bowery Presents, Nederlander Concerts, Jam Productions, First Avenue Productions, and Goldenvoice, run festivals, set up big tours and own or run venues. Every promotion company has in-house talent buyers, typically focusing on the venue they are assigned to.

71. Publishing Company

Like a record label, publishing companies have a myriad of personnel, from A&R to licensing, royalty collection, and business affairs. Publishing companies sometimes employ producers and composers to work with their songwriters and create music for sync.

72. Radio DJ

On-air radio DJs aren't the cultural tastemakers anymore like in the heyday of Delilah, Casey Kasem and Big Boy, but there are still many influential radio DJs out there. Some work at nationally syndicated stations representing large markets, but the most prominent are the local radio DJs. Many NPR affiliate stations employ their DJs on a very-part-time basis, and payment can be quite low, but perks can be high.

73. Radio Promoter

Every major label still has a radio promotions department (or outsources to their parent company's radio promotions dept). Songs that get added

to commercial radio rotation are typically chosen because a radio promoter from the label (or hired by the label or artist) worked that record.
Radio promoters are a dying breed these days since most of the power is
in streaming, but this job still exists.

74. Record Label

As discussed in Chapter 2, there are many different kinds of record labels,
from the Big 3 majors—Sony, Universal, Warner (and their many subsidiaries)—to independents and artist-run or -owned labels. The big labels
have in-house A&R, marketing, distribution, account managers, DSP
relations, radio, publicity, accounting, finance and all the other departments that companies have, whereas some of the smaller labels outsource
many of these duties to third-party companies. And there are managers,
VPs and other fancy job titles at every level.

75. Recording Engineer

The person who sets up the mics, handles the outboard gear and runs the
DAW. Some recording engineers work in major recording studios (the
few that are left), but most work as both recording engineer and producer
and wear all the hats to create a record from start to finish. Recording
engineers are experts when it comes to recording gear (analog and digital)
and are the producer's right hand. Recording engineers typically work
freelance, however, some are employed by recording studios or record
labels. And the lucky few are put on salary by superstar artists.

76. Rights Clearance Professional

The unsung heroes working with music supervisors or at film and TV
production companies are the rights and clearance professionals who

spend their days tracking down all the parties involved who need to give clearance for a song to be used in a show.

77. Rights Organizations

There are over 100 rights organizations around the world that handle licensing and payment for various rights, including performance, mechanical, neighbouring, master use, sync and so on. Many well-known PROs, like ASCAP, BMI, PRS, SOCAN and GEMA, employ hundreds. In the US, the MLC is now a huge employer of music professionals since launching in 2021, and SoundExchange similarly has many roles for people interested in working in this field.

78. Road Manager

On bigger tours, the tour manager and road manager roles are split. These can be called different things, and various tours will have various titles.

79. Roadie

This is essentially the catchall term for touring personnel. Sometimes, not everyone has a title, and the act just needs more hands to handle all of the various jobs of the road, like load in/load out, stage setup and teardown, merch setup, driver—you get the drift.

80. Royalty Investment Manager

Some people like to invest in stocks. Some like to invest in crypto. Some like to invest in music. Some like to invest in all of it. There are now marketplaces where investors can purchase copyrights or shares of royalties.

And of course, they will need someone to help them with this (in addition to a lawyer).

81. Royalty Manager/Administrator

This role is typically at a publishing company or record label, however, some artists hire outside help to make sure they're collecting all of their royalty streams. As more artists stay independent and have to manage the many royalty streams out there for them, they enlist the help of royalty managers.

82. Runner

The runner at a venue or a recording studio is the person on hand who will run out if anything is needed. Because things are always needed. Batteries, duct tape, coffee, lunch, blunt papers. Whatever's needed, it's the runner's job to go get it. Fast.

83. Security

Many people get their foot in the door at venues by working security or checking IDs at the door. You meet everyone as the security guard at a music venue. This could be a great way to make connections.

84. Social Media Manager

Most social media managers are employed at record labels or management companies, but some are hired directly by artists. These people advise and guide the artist's team on how best to run their various social media platforms. Some are very hands on, working out posting schedules and timelines, setting up photo and video shoots, editing the content and doing the actual posting with proper captions and hashtags, and responding to comments and DMs. Most social media managers work on a campaign or monthly basis.

85. Songwriter

There is no music industry without the song. We may only think about songwriters as those profiled on *And the Writer Is . . .* , who write songs they're looking to get cut by pop stars to turn them into massive hits, but there are working-class songwriters as well, who write custom songs for birthdays and special occasions. If you're interested in this, you can check out platforms like Songlorious and Songfinch.

86. Sound Designer Developer and Reviewer

When companies make new plugins or other kinds of software or hardware, they need people to review, test, consult and tweak. Some companies employ people to do this. Others pay people to test their products behind the scenes and offer feedback. And some pay influencers to review products on their social channels.

87. Sports Entertainment Booker

You know the national-anthem singers and the (non–Super Bowl) half-time performers at your local sports games? That's a job!

88. Stage Labor

Stage techs, stagehands, stage riggers, there's a bunch of different roles that go into the stage at (typically) a large venue. The bigger the venue, the more hands. The more roles. The more titles. The International Alliance of Theatrical Stage Employees (IATSE) union represents most of these workers. If you're interested in working at a large venue and being a stagehand, inquire more with IATSE about opportunities in your area.

89. Studio Manager

Yes, believe it or not, there are some excellent recording studios still standing. You know, the big, traditional ones with the 48-channel Neve consoles. Especially in L.A., Nashville, NYC and London there are plenty of studios that employ full personnel—including someone to manage all of the operations, like booking sessions, hiring the cleaning crews and keeping the gear working and serviced.

90. Stylist, Hair and Makeup Artist

Sure, these roles are often broken up. There are many excellent makeup artists who don't do hair and many hair stylists who don't really touch outfit styling. But many do it all. If you got the eye, you got the eye. And most musicians and indie labels don't typically have budgets to line-item these three roles. If you can handle the Big 3, you're going to get hired. If you can throw in creative direction, you'll be unstoppable.

91. Sync Licensing Company/Sync Agent

As discussed in Chapter 14, sync agents work with music supervisors and ad agencies to get music placed in film, TV series, video games, commercials and other visual media. Many sync agents work for sync licensing companies; however, many others are freelance. Depending on how large the sync licensing company is, there may be A&R (who scout, sign and nurture talent), accountants crunching the numbers, staff songwriter and producers.

92. Tour Manager

This is the person that handles the day-to-day operations of the tour. They are on the road with the artist in the van or bus (sometimes driving it) and make sure everyone shows up on time (and at the right location). The TM works with the venue staff to make sure the show runs smoothly and handles payment at the end of the night. The TM communicates with the artist manager regularly and often handles VIP, meet and greets, and sometimes pulls double duty as the front-of-house engineer (FOH) or merch manager. They are usually hired by the artist on short-term contracts for the duration of the tour. For more information, see Chapter 8.

93. Transcriber

Transcribers typically create sheet music from recordings. Sometimes the transcriber works alongside an arranger to create sheet music for jazz ensembles, school bands, orchestras and cover bands.

94. Union Professional

There are many unions that touch the music industry. In the US, these include: AFM, SAG-AFTRA, IATSE, Actor's Equity. Often the staff are hired from the union's members.

95. Video Game Composer, Arranger, Sound Design

As one of the largest industries in entertainment, video game companies employ a lot of people. Sound design is, of course, extremely important in video games. There are many roles at video game companies for composers, arrangers, producers and sound designers.

96. Video Production (for venues and festivals)

Any venue that is big enough for screens needs a video crew to make that happen. From the camera operators to the live editors/directors, to the livestreaming operations.

97. Video Production Company

Video production companies handle all of the responsibilities of creating music videos, promo videos, behind-the-scenes (BTS) videos or any other kind of video. Most companies specialize in a particular type of video and have directors, DPs, editors and everyone else on staff (or in their network) needed to make a video.

98. Videographer

These are the people who do the shooting, editing, directing, animating, aftereffects, set design, and all that it takes to create a video. Whether it's a TikTok video or a full-fledged music video. This role is one of the most important jobs in the industry today. If you can master as many of these roles as possible, you'll get hired early on by every musician on a tight budget needing videos done well, fast, cheap (well, we know you pick two, but you get the idea). Yes, the majors and superstars get a budget to line-item every little role when creating a gigantic music video, but I ain't got a budget for a grip.

99. Vocal Coach

Not quite a music teacher, these people usually work with the stars (or future stars) to make sure their pipes stay healthy and strong.

100. Web Developer

Even though there are many simple website-design services out there, like Bandzoogle, WordPress and Squarespace, many artists and companies require more involved web development that takes a skilled developer.

17.
OUTRO

CONGRATULATIONS! YOU MADE IT THROUGH. IF YOU REALLY made it to the end and read every word, then you must be actually serious enough to pursue a full-time, professional, money-making music career. I applaud you. Yeah, it's tough. Yeah, it's hard. But is anything in life that's worth pursuing easy? I truly hope this book has brought you a few steps closer to becoming a successful music professional. And if you already are I hope this brings you ten steps closer to world domination.

I wrote this book because I don't want to see any more talented bands break up or any more talented musicians quit what they love because they can't support themselves doing it. If you work hard enough, you can and will have a very successful career doing what you love. Don't let anyone tell you that music is not a viable career path. Hand them this book and tell them to shut the . . . front door.

Hopefully we will get to meet out there on the road someday, share a bill or two, jam together, cowrite, or just high-five. I'm into it all. We're all in this together. You and me. Us and them.

Let's define what this new music industry can look like.

And, so far, it's looking pretty darn amazing.

Much love,
Ari

MUSIC PUBLICATIONS YOU SHOULD BE READING

(in alphabetical order)
Ari's Take (aristake.com)
Bandzoogle Blog (bandzoogle.com/blog)
Billboard (billboard.com)
CD Baby's DIY Musician (diymusician.cdbaby.com)
Digital Music News (digitalmusicnews.com)
Hypebot (hypebot.com)
Indie on the Move (indieonthemove.com/blog)
Music 3.0 (Music3point0.com)
Music Business Worldwide (musicbusinessworldwide.com)
Music Connection Magazine (musicconnection.com)
The Unsigned Guide blog (members.theunsignedguide.com/news)
Water and Music (waterandmusic.com)

MUSIC PODCASTS YOU SHOULD BE LISTENING TO

(in alphabetical order)
Anatomy of an Artist by VÉRITÉ
And the Writer Is . . . with Ross Golan
Broken Record with Rick Rubin, Malcolm Gladwell, Bruce Headlam
    and Justin Richmond
DIY Musician by CD Baby
The Music Business Worldwide Podcast
The Music Industry Blueprint Podcast by Rick Barker
New Music Business with Ari Herstand

Song Exploder by Hrishikesh Hirway
Switched on Pop with Charlie Harding and Nate Sloan
The Third Story with Leo Sidran

MY CURRENT RANT ABOUT THE MUSIC INDUSTRY

How and Why the Royalty Structure Needs to Change Once and for All

We've set up a system where talented people who have so much to offer have no way to survive in this industry.

—EMILY WARREN, HIT SONGWRITER, DUA LIPA, THE CHAINSMOKERS, SHAKIRA

Enough is enough. I feel we are nearing a tipping point of equity in the music industry. It was about 100 years coming, but we're getting closer every day.

In March of 2021, a group of hit songwriters representing billions of streams and countless Grammys signed a petition where they exclaimed that they would no longer give up writing credit to artists who had no hand in writing the song. "The Pact," as they called it, stated, "If we take the song out of the music industry, there is no music industry."

Why this came to a head is because professional songwriters had been increasingly forced by artist managers to give up a piece of the publishing so their artist could have a cowriting credit. This is not a new practice. It was famously attempted by Elvis's manager, the Colonel, in 1974, with Dolly Parton's song "I Will Always Love You." The Colonel demanded 50% of the publishing. His argument was essentially, "You're nothing. Your song is nothing without a star to bring it to the masses."

Ms. Parton turned them down. And of course, Whitney Houston cut the song decades later and turned it into a hit.

More recently this has become such a common practice that most of the hit songs you're hearing on the radio were not written by the artist who's performing the song—even if the credits say so. The artist (well, their manager, typically) bullies the songwriter into giving up a portion of the publishing to the artist. If the songwriter refuses, the manager says the artist won't cut the song.

The way the economics of music currently work for professional song-writers (those who write songs every day to get cuts with artists who will hopefully turn that song into a hit) is that the songwriters typically don't make any money unless that song is a bona fide *radio* hit.

Isn't radio dead you ask? Well, oddly enough, radio is the last remaining revenue stream that compensates songwriters well. In the US, the only royalties generated from terrestrial (AM/FM) radio are performance royalties—100% of those go to publishers and songwriters. Whereas with streaming, only around 20% or so go to the publishers and songwriters.

Pop songwriters are essentially playing the lottery. And they know that unless their song gets chosen by an artist as a single and succeeds at radio, the songwriter may not eat this year. There are songwriters with millions upon millions of streams on their songs who are driving for Lyft.

You may be thinking right now that this is an issue with the streaming services not paying enough. This is only part of the discussion. And not the real issue.

The real issue lies with the major record labels.

The major labels are at the top of this totem pole. They strong-arm their artists into horrendous deals where the artist is only making around 18% *after recoupment*. So, artists need to find other sources of revenue. Sure, they can make money on touring, merch, sponsorships and the myriad ways that artists can monetize their fan base these days. But if they're not making passive income from their recordings (because they haven't recouped the cost of their label advance), the artists are attempting to make some passive revenue from these recordings in other ways. Publishing can be a way. Even if it's not ethical.

This can be compared to actors in movies asking for a piece of the screenwriting credit merely because they acted in the film and helped promote it. Of course, that's absurd and never happens. But in music, this happens all the time.

But back to the real issue here.

The National Music Publishers Association (NMPA—the organization representing the major publishing companies), spearheaded by David Israelite, over the past decade has waged war on Big Tech (like Spotify, Amazon, Facebook, Google, etc.), attempting to make them the enemy of the music industry. Whereas in reality, streaming is the sole reason that the music industry is massively profitable again and gaining revenue year over year. The RIAA (the organization representing the major labels) sometimes comes out against Big Tech and joins the NMPA, but for the most part the major labels are happy with the system as it is—it gets them paid handsomely and they don't want people looking too far under the hood—for what they will find does not make the major labels look very good.

What they will find is that the major labels are making the majority of the recording revenue to be had. By far.

The royalty breakdown needs to change.

There should be a 50/50 split for all revenue streams across the board.

In sync, this already happens most of the time. A sync license typically pays 50% of the money directly to the publisher (and songwriter) and 50% of the money directly to the label (and artist) for an up-front fee. This is how it should work across the board—for every other royalty stream.

The labels will say, "But hey, we don't make any money from radio!" You're right, that should change too! Instead of 100% of the radio royalties (in America) going to the publishers, let's split that 50/50 as well.

Everything split 50/50.

Streaming revenue should not be split as it is, where nearly 80% of all the money goes to the labels and only 20% to the publishers. When there are multiple songwriters (and publishers) that need to split up that 20%, it works out to be not much at all.

Every revenue stream: 50/50. Master/composition. Label/publisher. Artist/songwriter.

But every label contract should also be 50/50. No longer should major labels be able to coerce their artists into immoral deals, which in turn force the artist to bully the songwriters into immoral deals.

It needs to start at the top. That's the major labels.

Fortunately, in the past few years as the independent music community has continued to gain market share with DIY, self-released artists realizing they need labels less and less, the majors are starting to cave. More and more majors are offering 50/50 licensing deals. And because of the Pact, artists (and their managers) are no longer demanding publishing on songs they didn't write.

If the royalties were split up more equitably, more songwriters and artists would take risks. There would be a musical renaissance in pop. The reason all pop songs sound the same is because the songwriters are following a formula, desperate to get a radio hit. Because these days, that's the only way they get paid.

It takes artists and songwriters of every level to stand up for themselves. Artists should no longer accept any deal that is less than a 50/50 split. And songwriters should no longer give up credit to artists who didn't have a hand in writing the song.

Because without the songwriter there is no music industry. And without the Artist there is no record industry.

It starts with you.

HOW I HELPED CHANGE A LAW FOR MUSICIANS

■

On September 18, 2019, Assembly Bill 5 (AB5) was signed into law by Governor Gavin Newsom in the state of California. This law essentially made it illegal to hire people as independent contractors. Instead, if you wanted to hire someone from California, you had to classify them as a W-2 "employee"—with all the red tape and additional costs that come along with that.

What did this mean for musicians? Well, if you wanted to hire a bass player to play your gig for $100, you would have to put that bassist on payroll, pay unemployment taxes, provide benefits, follow labor laws, get workers compensation insurance, deduct taxes, work with a payroll company, and W-2 that bassist, as they would now legally be designated your employee. FOR ONE GIG. Want to hire a violinist to play one song on your record for $150? She's now your employee. FOR ONE GIG.

Venues couldn't just cut solo artists a check anymore. You play a 45-minute set at the Echo and make $800? Well, you're now technically an employee of the Echo; they must deduct taxes and put you (and the hundreds of artists who play their venue each year) on payroll. FOR ONE GIG.

Accountants estimated that it would cost band leaders (who hire musicians) an additional 20% to comply with this law. Not to mention the exorbitant fees to incorporate in California, set up payroll, withhold taxes, get all the proper insurance. As a band leader who might hire 40 musicians in a single year for one-off shows and recordings, my accountant estimated it could cost me an additional $6,000 to comply with this new law.

You can see how this isn't workable for the music industry. This law was about to single-handedly crash the California music economy.

The following organizations attempted to get the music industry exempt from AB5 before it was signed into law: the Recording Industry Association of America (RIAA), the organization representing the major labels; American Association of Independent Music (A2IM), the org representing the indie labels; and a new org that popped up around this time called Music Artist Coalition (MAC) founded by industry stalwarts like Irving Azoff and Coran Capshaw along with superstar artists like Anderson .Paak, Dave Matthews, Don Henley and Maren Morris.

But they couldn't.

Why? Because the American Federation of Musicians (AFM), the musicians union, blocked it. See, in California, unions have a lot of sway with the politicians. Even though the AFM represents a tiny fraction of working musicians (mostly just orchestra musicians and those who play on major-label records), they had major sway with the author of this bill to make sure that the music industry was *not* exempt (even though around thirty-five other industries were—like manicurists, telemarketers, lawyers, vets, PIs and repo men).

But most California music professionals didn't hear about this law until *after* it was signed by the governor—myself included.

I learned about this law in November 2019 when I attended a couple musician friends' house where they hosted a sort of teach-in with their lawyer, who explained to the room full of musicians how detrimental this law was going to be for us when it was implemented in about a month.

I went home from that meeting and wrote an article on Ari's Take titled "California's Music Economy Is About to Crash," where I relayed everything I had just learned (with a bit of my color commentary and choice words for the AFM and Assemblywoman Lorena Gonzalez, who wrote the bill).

That article went viral. Hundreds of thousands of views within a couple days. People were now in uproar. Within days, I was tweeting with the author of the bill, Assemblywoman Gonzalez, and had thousands of California musicians emailing their representatives and the governor.

A Change.org petition was also created by fellow activist-musicians Alicia Spillias and Adrianne Duncan, which in the end got 185,000 signatures from California music industry professionals who were against the law.

Some of us from the teach-in, including the attorney, Ned Menoyo, Alicia and Adrianne formed an impromptu org called Independent Music Professionals United (IMPU), which included Elmo Lovano, Danica Pinner, Nick Campbell, Karen Garrity and Katisse Buckingham. And we began our campaign.

We met with legislators up and down the state. I remember our meeting with Senate Majority Leader Robert Hertzberg vividly. We all went around and explained to him how detrimental this law was going to be for us. After he listened to our pleas and stories, he said something to the extent of, "Wow we really f'd you guys here, huh. This is really bad for you." We all concurred and asked him if he could amend it for us. He said no. We were dumbfounded. Here we were sitting in the senate majority leader of California's office, who now understood this law would be unbelievably detrimental for the music industry; we had a petition signed by (at the time) tens of thousands of California musicians, and he wouldn't do anything? We asked him what would it take to get this done. He said that the only thing that moves his colleagues in the senate and the assembly is bad press. He listed off some news outlets that they all read and pay attention to. I took extensive notes.

From left to right: Nick Campbell, Danica Pinner, Karen Garrity, Ned Menoyo, Robert Hertzberg, Ari Herstand, Elmo Lovano, Peter Petro, Katisse Buckingham, Adrianne Duncan

So, we began our public-pressure campaign. Adrianne and I drove down to Assemblywoman Gonzalez's home district in San Diego and appeared on her local news stations—twice! Within minutes after one of our live appearances, she was angrily tweeting at me that I had misrepresented her.

I did interview after interview with all the publications Senator Hertzberg mentioned—and many more around the country.

Much of this was happening after the start of the year when the law went into effect. Within weeks, we started seeing its effects. People stopped hiring California musicians and began taking that work out of state. Venues stopped having music altogether. Community arts organizations that hosted small opera and musical productions began shutting down and canceling upcoming performances. Artists, bandleaders and singer/songwriters stopped hiring backup bands for their gigs. Composers stopped contracting musicians to record demos for their new works. Contracting agencies, which hired arrangers, musicians, librarians, orchestrators, recording studios and recording engineers, had to shut down. Artists stopped hiring recording engineers, producers and musicians to make their albums. And schools laid off accompanists for their choirs and musicals—which forced the schools to shut down the upcoming performances.

These are documented cases that I received of what actually happened in the first few months of 2020 after the law went into effect.

So, we got louder. Did more press. Tweeted at politicians more actively and took more meetings.

Finally, the governor's office took notice and put pressure on Assemblywoman Gonzalez to write a new bill exempting music professionals.

But that was only the beginning. The assemblywoman said that we had to get everyone in the music industry to agree on language for the bill.

She meant all of the organizations that had a dog in this fight and had the organizational infrastructure to cause her headaches. Namely, this was the RIAA, A2IM and the unions. Yes, the AFM, but also all the other unions that represent stagehands, musical theater personnel, screen actors, radio DJs, and so on.

So, I, along with members of IMPU and Jordan Bromley, the attorney representing MAC, the RIAA and A2IM, went to battle with the AFM. See, the AFM was happy with this law as it stood. They thought that if every musician had to be W-2'd for every gig, then they would join the union (only "employees" working union jobs can technically join the union). The AFM had no incentive to change this law and exempt us. But they came to the table with us because of the pressure we put on the politicians—which in turn they put on them to get an agreement done.

I'll never forget one day we spent at the AFM offices in Burbank with the president of the AFM Local 47, John Acosta, and all the other local reps across the state on the phone, hashing out the language. We had a deadline of 5 P.M. to submit language to Assemblywoman Gonzalez. We worked our butts off to meet this deadline. But in the end, Acosta sent Gonzalez the AFM's language without any of our edits. He essentially told us that this was "placeholder" language for now, as the bill needed to go through the legislative process for the next couple weeks, but that we could spend the next few days finalizing the "real" language which would appear in the bill.

Well, I bet you can guess what happened next. That night, Assemblywoman Lorena Gonzalez started tweeting this language, explaining that the music industry had agreed!

I was at a Jamestown Revival show at the Fonda in Hollywood when my phone started blowing up. I got out of my seat and ran to the back patio where I took matters into my own hands. I sent an assertive email to the assemblywoman and Acosta threatening to engage our 185,000 petition signatories if she didn't delete her tweets. I then started publicly tweeting at the assemblywoman correcting her tweets. This went deep into the night (I missed the entire show).

It all culminated at 2:40am when Assemblywoman Gonzalez deleted all of her tweets with the incorrect language.

In the end, it came down to me on the phone with John Acosta literally going line by line hashing out language. My side had agreed to let me negotiate on behalf of music, and the unions had agreed to let John negotiate on theirs. After all this, I was literally writing language that ended up in the final law. Crazy.

The "cleanup bill," AB2257, was signed by Governor Newsom and became law on September 4, 2020.

AB2257 exempts the vast majority of music industry professionals from AB5. We weren't, unfortunately, able to get *all* music industry professionals exempt (thank the AFM).

WHO IS EXEMPT FROM AB5 NOW?

With respect to the recording process:
- Musicians, vocalists and other recording artists
- Composers, songwriters, lyricists
- Managers of recording artists
- Musical engineers
- Sound mixers
- Record producers
- Others involved in the creating, marketing, promoting or distributing of the sound recording or musical composition

And all musical groups performing live except:
- The main featured act headlining at a concert venue with more than 1,500 attendees or
- Musical groups performing at a large festival with more than 18,000 attendees per day.

Note, it's the headliner, not the openers. So, if you headline the Fonda in L.A. (1,250 cap) or the Fillmore in San Francisco (1,315 cap) and sell it out, you're fine. If you headline the Wiltern and sell it out (1,850 cap), you'd be required to W-2 your hired guns. If you only sell 1,400 tickets to the Wiltern, you're also fine. Now, most bands who headline the Wiltern are on tour and are at a level where they could afford to W-2 their members.

Also, it's worth noting that any music attorney will tell you that if you go on tour, "the Borello test" (the criteria established in a previous California court decision that determine whether you have to classify someone as an independent contractor or employee) requires that you W-2 your touring entourage, because they are "under your control"—you have to get on the bus at this time, show up at this time, etc., etc. So, nothing is really changing here. If you previously classified your touring entourage as contractors (1099), you were doing it wrong.

Musicians we were not able to get an exemption to include:
- A musical group regularly performing in a theme park setting
- A musician performing in a symphony orchestra
- A musician performing in a musical theater production
- A musician performing at the same venue more than once a week, but only *if* that musician is not "marketing or promoting a sound recording or musical composition." Which means, if you're playing at a venue multiple times a week, put up one song online (original or not). Because the purpose of this gig could be to promote that song. If so, you can hire your band as contractors, and the venue can hire you as a contractor.

Again, we tried. Fought hard for the rest. I know there are small community orchestras out there that cannot afford to W-2 every single member. The AFM, however, assured me that they work with many community orchestras, and if you run an orchestra, I encourage you to write to the AFM and ask them how they can help you stay afloat. The AFM genuinely did not seem to want any community orchestra to go under. So, contact them!

As far as musical theater productions go, we fought to get this removed, but the unions would not budge. It was a "deal breaker" for them, so we could either blow up the entire negotiation or give in to these concessions in the spirit of compromise and the greater good.

In the end, we fought on behalf of the music industry.

We couldn't fight the theater industry's fight as well. Or other industries for that matter.

It's funny, as a songwriter and author, I never thought that one of the most impactful things I'd have a hand in writing would be a law for the state of California.

I never expected to get into politics. And I honestly don't have much desire to continue. But I'm proud of our work. And I will always advocate for independent music professionals. That fight is worth it to me.

From left to right: Alicia Spillias, Raquel Rodriguez, Elmo Lovano, Ari Herstand, Lorena Gonzalez, Danica Pinner, Nick Campbell

SOME WORDS OF CAUTION (AND OTHER STUFF YOU REALLY NEED TO READ)

■

The advice I give in this book is based on my experience. As I said up front, "results may vary." I can't promise you that if you do what I've done in any particular situation, you'll get the same results that I did. For example, my product recommendations come from my own experience or from artists I trust. But you should always do your own research.

As I also said at the beginning, I'm not a lawyer, and I can't give legal advice. In parts of the book, I describe or suggest doing things that seem simple but can cause legal problems if not done right. A lawsuit can kill you financially even if you end up winning, and saving money by doing without legal advice up front is almost never a good idea. I've tried to point out situations where you need an attorney throughout the book, but here is a short list of the kinds of things that should scream "ask a lawyer":

■ *Anything in writing that puts you on the hook to someone else or puts someone else on the hook to you.* Whether or not it's a formal contract, if it obligates you or someone else to pay money or perform services, it should be written or reviewed by an experienced lawyer. The same goes for any agreement that gives you rights in something, whether it's a share of revenue or a copyright. Some examples are agreements about rights and responsibilities of band members; the details of a gig; an arrangement with a publicist, photographer, band manager or tour manager; use of a song or recording on TV; the formation of a corporation or partnership; sponsorship or investment deals; and even the terms and conditions of online services.

■ *Anything relating to ownership of copyright in a song or in anything else that someone creates for you.* Just paying someone for something—a logo, a poster—does not mean you own it.

■ *Copyright registration.* I've mentioned a few times in the book that you can register several songs for copyright at once, for one fee, instead of paying separately for each song. There are different ways to do this, but it's trickier than it looks, and doing it wrong can cause you problems later on. Talk to a copyright lawyer or follow the Copyright Office's guidelines very, very carefully.

■ *Licenses and permissions to use other people's content.* Don't pull stuff off the internet, whether it's a photo, a graphic or a few bars of a recording. Get a permission agreement that specifically covers what you want to do, and make sure it comes from the person or company that owns or controls the rights.

■ *Choosing and registering a band/artist name (trademark).* You can get sued for using someone else's band name or something very close to it. A trademark attorney can help you find out if the name you want is available (it's rarely enough just to do a Google and Facebook search, or even to search the US Trademark Office database) and can guide you through the process if you want to apply for a federal trademark registration in the US Trademark Office.

■ *Forming a company.* There are different kinds of companies. An LLC is not the same as a corporation, and neither of those may be right for your financial or tax situation. Also, if you are forming a company with someone else, you'll probably want your operating or shareholders' agreement to include an exit strategy, among other protections for you, so that you don't end up spending thousands of dollars later trying to arrive at a fair split. There is no one-size-fits-all form for these agreements, despite the websites that offer them.

■ *Raising money.* Any time you are going to raise money that will have to be paid back someday, talk to a securities lawyer or a music lawyer who is experienced in this kind of deal and knows federal and state securities laws. You really don't want problems in this area.

■ *Collecting email addresses and other personal information on your site.* In the privacy world that we all read about every day, names, email addresses, credit cards and other kinds of information about your fans are "personally identifying information." If you collect any of that kind of information on your site, you'll need a privacy policy that tells users on what basis you are collecting their info (this goes back to what I said earlier about getting consent), what you do with the info, who has access to it, and how people can delete or change it. On top of that, if you are collecting personally identifying information of people in the European Union, you have to comply with the GDPR. Here, too, one size does not fit all (and you can't rely on your eblast provider's policy). Your best bet is a lawyer that specializes in this kind of thing.

■ *Sending out eblasts.* Emails that promote your upcoming gigs or sell merch to US recipients are subject to federal law and have to meet certain legal requirements. In Canada, you can't send this kind of email at all unless the recipient has "opted in" to receive it from you.

■ *Running sweepstakes, contests and other promotions.* Contests, sweepstakes and other kinds of promotions have to comply with very specific rules and requirements that vary from state to state. Plus, social media sites have their own rules about running promotions. Talk to a lawyer who knows this area of the law to be that sure you're covered and that your promotion is not technically a lottery, which is illegal in all fifty states. Also, if you use influencers to promote your performances or recordings in exchange for free tickets or merch or anything else, they should clearly and conspicuously disclose in their posts that they received those things.

This is not a 100% complete list of every legal issue that may come up in the course of your music career. In an ideal world, you should have a lawyer—or a stable of different kinds of lawyers—peering over your shoulder all the time to make sure you don't get yourself in trouble. But if you can't have that—and most of us can't afford it—you have some idea of what to look for as you go along.

GLOSSARY

3 OF 5 A discount given to colleges at NACA and APCA conferences if 3 schools within a close geographic location book an act within 5 days.

360 DEAL Labels take a percentage of nearly every aspect of an artist's income including merch, touring, sponsorships and sales.

5 OF 7 A discount given to colleges at NACA and APCA conferences if 5 schools within a close geographic location book an act to give performances at the schools within 7 days.

THE 50/50 RULE You should spend half of your time and money on the music (the art) and half of your time and money on the business.

ADVANCE (NOUN) A lump sum a record label, distributor, funding org or publisher pays a new signee up front which is recouped (paid back) from royalties earned.

ADVANCE (VERB) Getting in touch with the show's point person in advance of the show to go over details.

AGENT Also referred to as booking agent. This is the person that books your shows and tours.

ALBUM A collection of songs released at the same time. Traditionally albums were packaged on vinyl records (LPs), cassettes or CDs, contained at least 6 songs and were approximately 35 to 70 minutes long. "Album" and "record" are sometimes used interchangeably.

AMAZON PRIME MUSIC A subscriber-based, music-streaming service.

APAP Association of Performing Arts Professionals. The conference hosted in New York for entertainers, staff and associates of performing arts centers.

APCA Association for the Promotion of Campus Activities. The second-largest college entertainment conference.

APPLE MUSIC One of the world's largest subscriber-based music-streaming services.

A&R Artist and Repertoire. Typically the scouts at a record label or publishing company. The artist's point person at the company. Helps guide the production process.

ARI'S TAKE The most important music business education company on the planet.

ARTIST Sometimes referred to as recording artist. This is the person or act that records the songs and performs the shows. Sometimes the artist is also the songwriter, but the terms mean different things legally (and for purposes of royalty payments).

ASCAP American Society of Composers, Authors and Publishers. An American not-for-profit performing rights organization (PRO) representing songwriters, composers and publishers.

BACKLINE Typically the drum set, guitar amp, bass amp and sometimes keyboard. Sometimes this is provided by a venue or festival.

BANDCAMP Artist-managed download store, merch store and subscription service.

BANDZOOGLE Recommended website building platform.

BANTER The talking an artist does in the mic, on stage, in between songs.

BFM Best Friend Manager.

BLOCK BOOKING A deal given to buyers at conferences in the college and performing arts center markets if the buyers can route their show with other neighboring organizations.

BLOCKCHAIN Digital, decentralized public ledger that exists across a network, recording transactions. It powers the technology for and hosts cryptocurrencies and NFTs.

THE BIG 3 The three parent companies of all major labels in the world: Sony, Warner Music Group (WMG) and Universal Music Group (UMG). All major labels fall under one of The Big 3.

BMI Broadcast Music, Inc. An American not-for-profit performing rights organization (PRO) representing songwriters, composers and publishers.

BOOKER The person who books music at a venue. Sometimes "booker" and "talent buyer" are used interchangeably.

BRASSROOTS DISTRICT The greatest band in the world.

BUSKING Street performing.

CAB Campus Activities Board. The group that books entertainment for their college.

CMO Collective management organization. Organizations representing songwriters and publishers that license and collect both mechanical and performance royalties.

COMPOSITION The music and lyrics. "Composition" and "song" are sometimes used interchangeably. Songwriters write compositions.

CONSOLE A mixing board that can be used in live settings or in the studio. Every input is run through the console before the signal reaches the speakers or the DAW (or tape). "Console" and "board" can be used interchangeably.

COVER A song performed or recorded by an artist that was previously released (and made popular) by a different artist.

CROWDFUNDING Raising a bulk amount of funds from your fans for a singular project (like an album). Kickstarter, Indiegogo, and GoFundMe are the most popular music crowdfunding services.

CROWDFUNDING 2.0   The new fan club. Having fans contribute funds on an ongoing basis. A subscription or patronage service. Patreon and Bandcamp are leading this front.

CRYPTOCURRENCY   Decentralized, digital currency using blockchain technology. Some popular cryptocurrencies include Bitcoin and Ether.

DAW   Digital audio workstation is a recording program like Pro Tools, Logic, Cubase, FL Studio, Reason and Ableton Live.

DAY SHEET   The sheet that outlines all details about the day while on tour (travel, lodging, venue, times).

DEEZER   A subscriber-based music-streaming service.

DISTRIBUTION COMPANIES   The companies that send releases from labels (and artists) to stores and streaming services.

DIY   Do It Yourself. Musicians who run their careers without the help of a manager, agent, label or publicist.

DP   Director of photography. Camera person.

DSP   Digital Service Provider. This is the catchall term for streaming services like Spotify, Apple Music, YouTube Music, Amazon Music, etc.

THE ELEVATOR PITCH   The one-sentence description of your sound as compared to other artists. You should be able to say this aloud at any moment without stumbling.

ENGINEER   Also referred to as the recording engineer. This is the person that operates the DAW (like Logic or Pro Tools), sets up all mics and knows how everything in the studio works. There are also mixing and mastering engineers.

EP   Stands for extended play and originated from an extended-play single. It's a compilation of 4 to 6 songs released at the same time on any format (vinyl, CD, cassette or digital download/stream).

EPK   Electronic Press Kit, in its current form, is a (hidden) web page containing all relevant information intended for industry people.

FACEBOOK   The social network your grandma is on.

FL Free livestream.

FM Family Manager.

FOH Front of house engineer. Sound guy. The person who mixes the live performance.

GATEKEEPER The person in charge of the decisions that aid artists' success. These can be bookers, radio DJs, bloggers, playlisters and music editors.

GLOBAL MUSIC RIGHTS A US for-profit performing rights organization (PRO) started by Irving Azoff in 2013 that collects performance royalties for songwriters, composers and publishers.

HEADLINER The main act most people at the concert came to see. Typically the headliner is listed at the top of the bill and plays last.

HIRED GUN Freelance musician for the stage or studio typically hired by singer/songwriters, band leaders and music directors.

INFLUENCER Individuals paid to promote products, events, songs, causes or companies on their social media.

INSTAGRAM The social network your best friend is on.

INTERACTIVE You can choose the song you'd like to listen to. Interactive streaming services include Apple Music and Spotify.

KUGOU China-based streaming service owned by Tencent.

KUWO China-based streaming service owned by Tencent.

LOAD-IN The time designated at the venue for the band to bring their gear inside.

LOGIC Apple-made digital audio workstation (DAW). One of the most popular DAWs used by recording studios worldwide.

LP Stands for long play. It's a 33⅓ vinyl record which holds about 22 minutes per side. Sometimes "albums," "records" and "LPs" are used interchangeably.

MANAGER This is the person in charge of your career. The manager helps craft the vision and direction of your career, and the manager is the buffer between you and everyone else. Also referred to as Artist Manager.

MASTER (NOUN)   The final recording. Sometimes the word "master" is used to differentiate between the song (composition) and the sound recording. "Master" and "sound recording" are sometimes used interchangeably.

MASTER (VERB)   The process of putting the finishing touches on a fully mixed recording. This is the final step of the recording process. Mastering makes the highs glisten and the lows thump. Mastering also makes sure the volume of every track is at about the same level and places the amount of space between songs (also called sequencing).

MASTERING ENGINEER   The person who puts the finishing touches on a record. This person "masters" the record.

MCPS   The UK's mechanical rights organization, collecting royalties from interactive streams (and sales) for songwriters and publishers.

MD   Music director. The person who is hired to lead the band during rehearsals. The MD is typically in the band as well.

MECHANICAL ROYALTY   Songwriter royalty generated from sales of CDs, downloads on digital music retail sites, and interactive streams.

MERCH   Short for merchandise. Any branded item an artist sells, typically at concerts or online.

MIX (NOUN)   The unfinished version of a recording.

MIX (VERB)   The act of making all of the tracks in a recording (or live performance) sound good.

MIXING ENGINEER   The person who mixes the recording.

MLC   Mechanical Licensing Collective. The mechanical rights organization in the US created by the Music Modernization Act. This is the sole organization in the US able to issue blanket licenses, and all DSPs are required to pay all of their statutory mechanical royalties to the MLC. The MLC then pays out this money to publishers (and songwriters).

NACA   National Association of Campus Activities. The largest college entertainment conference in America.

NETEASE Chinese music streaming (and video game) service.

NFT Non-fungible token. Scarce digital collectibles sold and traded on the blockchain.

NONINTERACTIVE You cannot choose the song you'd like to listen to.

NSAI Nashville Songwriters Association International.

ONE-OFF One show, not during a tour.

ONE SHEET A single page (typically in PDF form) containing all relevant information intended for industry people.

OPENER Sometimes referred to as the opening act. This artist plays before the headliner at a concert.

P.A. The sound system.

PAC Performing arts center.

PANDORA A US-based streaming service. Originally, the largest digital radio service.

PATREON Crowdfunding 2.0 patronage site.

PAY-TO-PLAY When a promoter or venue charges a band to perform. Or when a promoter or venue requires bands to purchase tickets in advance of a show to resell.

PER DIEM (PD) Literally means "per day." The amount of money given to members on tour for food and other daily expenses.

THE PERFECT 30 The test every gig should pass before being accepted. Compensation = 10, Career Building = 10, Enjoyment = 10. Don't take gigs that equal less than 15.

PERFORMANCE ROYALTY Songwriter royalty generated from any public performance of a composition.

PINTEREST The social network your girlfriend is on.

PPL The UK's not-for-profit neighbouring rights organization collecting sound recording performance royalties for artists and labels.

PRO Performing rights organization. Organizations of this kind represent songwriters and publishers. In America, these are ASCAP, BMI, SESAC and Global Music Rights. In Canada, this is SOCAN. In the UK. it's PRS. Nearly every country in the world has their own PROs.

PRODUCER The person who helps create your record. Typically this person crafts the sound, vision and overall vibe of the record.

PROMOTER The person who is the liaison between the venue and the booking agent. The promoter works out deals with the venue and pays the artist or agent. "Booker," "talent buyer" and "promoter" can be interchangeable.

PRO TOOLS Avid-made digital audio workstation (DAW).

PRS The UK's not-for-profit performing rights organization (PRO) collecting performance royalties for songwriters, composers and publishers.

PUBLISHING COMPANY Also called a publisher. An organization that represents songwriters and compositions.

QQ Chinese music streaming service owned by Tencent.

RECORD (NOUN) Can mean a single recording (like the Grammy classification) or more commonly it is another term for album.

RECORD (VERB) The process of capturing music for a recording. "Record" and "track" are sometimes used interchangeably.

RECORD LABEL Sometimes just referred to as a label. An organization that represents artists and sound recordings.

THE RULE OF 7 Fans need to be hit at least 7 times before they will take action.

SAG-AFTRA Screen Actors Guild and American Federation of Television and Radio Artists. The union that represents screen actors.

SEQUENCING Done during the mastering process. The act of placing the amount of space between tracks on an album.

SESAC An American for-profit performing rights organization (PRO) representing songwriters, composers and publishers.

SETTLE UP To count and collect the money from the point person at the venue (or the promoter) at the end of the night.

SINGLE One song released outside of (or as part of) an album (typically in advance of the album release). Traditionally, this was the song promoted to radio a couple months before the album was released.

SNAPCHAT The social network that won't come back to bite you in the a** from future employers.

SOCAN Society of Composers, Authors and Music Publishers of Canada. A not-for-profit performing rights organization (PRO) representing songwriters, composers and publishers.

SONY MUSIC One of the Big 3 major labels. Many major labels fall under Sony's umbrella.

SONGWRITER This is the person that writes the words and music for the artist to record and perform. Sometimes the songwriter is also the artist, but these terms are differentiated for legal clarity (and royalty payments).

SOUND CHECK The time on stage at a venue the band and live sound engineers and stage crew spend testing all of the gear to make sure everything works and to get a feel for the venue. This typically happens before the doors open to the public.

SOUNDCLOUD Artist-managed music-streaming platform and social network heavily favored by DJs, hip-hop and electronic artists.

SOUNDEXCHANGE US sound recording performing rights organization. Collects royalties for artists and labels from digital, noninteractive streaming services.

SOUND RECORDING The actual audio recording (not to be confused with the composition). "Sound recording" and "master" are sometimes used interchangeably.

SPOTIFY One of the world's largest interactive, subscriber-based music-streaming services.

SQUARESPACE Recommended website building platform.

STREET TEAM Fans that help promote artists' music and concerts. Typically, they put posters up and pass flyers out around town in advance of the show.

SYNC LICENSING "Sync" stands for synchronization. The process of getting music placed in TV shows, commercials, video games, trailers and films.

SYNC LICENSING COMPANY A company that works to get songs placed on TV shows, commercials, trailers, video games and films. Sometimes referred to as "song plugger" or sync agent.

SUPE Short for music supervisor.

TALENT BUYER The person who books talent at a venue or festival. Sometimes "talent buyer" and "booker" are used interchangeably.

TIKTOK The social network your niece is on (and that you're most likely to blow up on).

TL Ticketed livestream

TM Tour manager. The person who goes on tour with the band and handles all of the business on the road like advancing shows, settling up, managing meet and greets, training the merch seller, etc. The TM is the liaison between the band and everyone else while on the road.

TRACK (NOUN) Can refer to a single recording on an album or a single recording element in the mix. Every mix is made up of multiple tracks.

TRACK (VERB) To record. "Record" (verb) and "track" are sometimes used interchangeably.

TWITTER The social network your dad is on.

UGC User-generated content. This is content uploaded by average users (who do not own the rights to the content). This is how "unauthorized" content gets uploaded to YouTube, Facebook, Instagram, TikTok and SoundCloud.

UMG Universal Music Group. One of the Big 3 major labels. Many major labels fall under UMG's umbrella.

VENUE Any establishment that hosts music.

VTJ Virtual tip jar

WCM Well-Connected Manager. See pages 52–53 for full description.

WECHAT China's most popular social network, messaging and payment platform.

WMG Warner Music Group. One of the Big 3 major labels. Many major labels fall under WMG's umbrella.

YOU PICK TWO Fast, good, cheap. You can only have two of these.

YOUTUBE The social network where you can find the shaky, iPhone-shot video of your concert from five years ago with the drunk dude yelling "Free Bird" incessantly.

ACKNOWLEDGMENTS

■

If you had told me eight years ago that I would be an author of a book, I would have called you crazy. "I'm a musician, not an author," I'd protest. But here we are. And I couldn't have completed this thing without the love and support of some incredible people.

First off, my wife, Sarah. The love of my life. My quarantine buddy. She inspires me every day through her art, music and humor. She keeps me grounded and keeps me dreaming and is the most talented and inspiring artist I have ever come across. I was a fan before a friend, a friend before a partner, and a partner before a husband. I honestly don't know how I would have gotten through these past few years if it weren't for her (and her art). They say that art can change the world, well, hers has sure changed mine. This book is dedicated (and my life devoted) to her.

Philip Marino was a rock-star editor. Thank you for believing in this thing and being my cheerleader.

David Dunton, I never knew agents could be so real. No offense to my other agents out here in Hollyweird. The sweater you wore on that cold New York November day when we met sealed the deal. Never toss that thing.

Thank you, Andrew Leib, for emailing me out of the blue saying that because we're both music people from Wisconsin living in L.A. we had to meet. You have been a great friend, supporter and advisor. This book wouldn't be what it is without you.

Micah Herstand, my brother. My friend. The smarter son. Your constant support has truly been so encouraging and meaningful. When the world ignored a song I put out, just hearing your heartfelt praise was enough to keep me going. Thank you for using your web genius to create my websites and for accepting hearty hugs and cheap whiskey as payment.

Gadi Rouache, my brother from another mother. I'll never forget looking out at the festival in Rochester, Minnesota, over a thousand bobbing heads to see you singing along in the back. Since we were twelve, you have been there for me. Thank you for pulling an all-nighter designing Ari's Take and for accepting high-fives and beer for payment. You're one of the most talented people I've ever met, and I'm honored to call you my close friend.

Thank you, Marc Behar and Jeff Sbisa, for allowing me to stay in your beautiful guesthouse in New Orleans as my respite from the craziness of L.A. to focus on this book. What a magical city.

Thank you to the District Donuts in New Orleans for allowing me to write this book ten hours a day for a month straight in your inspiring establishment. Your staff couldn't have been more welcoming and your chais couldn't have been tastier.

Thank you, Mom and Dad, for raising me right. You taught me to care about people other than myself. And that's really why I started Ari's Take in the first place. And why I wrote this book.

These people and groups have given me tremendous support and guidance over the years and I wouldn't be where I am without you. Thank you (in alphabetical order):

Jerome Behar	Susan Goldberg
Gabriel Douglas	The Hotel Cafe
Lisa Felix	Will Hutchinson

Daniel Lifshitz

Los Angeles music community

Jesse MacLeod

Paul Marino

Roster McCabe

Minneapolis music community

David Olson

Drew Preiner

Saurabh Saluja

Derek Sivers

David Steffen

Varsity Theater

Marilyn Victor

Dan Wilson

And these tremendous people were incredible references for this book's research. Thank you!

Sarah Abelson

Kris Ahrend

Dr. Joseph Akins

Andrea and Mark from Makar

Jonathan Azu

Baby G

Stephen Bach

Jacomo Bairos

Jean-Paul Barjon

Dan Barracuda

Nick Bearden

Stephanie Belcher

Felicia Bennett

Jessica Berg

Marshall Betts

Harmeet Bhatia

Amanda Blide

Rob Bondurant

Ciph Boogie

Mikayla Braun

Kevin Breuner

Winslow Bright

Jordan Bromley

Robert Brown

Emily C. Browning

Matt Burke

Kelsey "VÉRITÉ" Byrne

Annie Calder

Victoria Canal

Antonio "Tony" Carr

JC Cassis

Rogét Chahayed

Tracy Patrick Chan

Clarence Charron

Ryan Chisholm

Khloe Churko

Jack Conte

Dave Cool

Joe Conyers III

Chris Crawford

Quinn D'Andrea

Tommy Darker

Natalya Davies

Dennis Llewellyn Day

Dani Deahl

Caroline Dezelle

Kim Dickens

Michi DiGiulio/Megawave

Gaetano DiNardi

Chris Douridas

Drew Dugan

Tommy Economou

Ifiok Effanga

Eleni

Talya Elitzer

McKenzie "Mothica" Ellis

Phillip Englehart

Laura Escudé

Eva & The Perrin Fontanas

Mikey Evans

Théo Fédronic

Maxwell Felsheim

Katie Ferrara

Fiokee

Flighthouse

Bruce Flohr

Liz Fohl

Carlo Fox

Jessica Friedman

Bina Fronda

Taishi Fukuyama

Champian Fulton

Madame Gandhi

Kevin Garrett

Karen Garrity

Nick Gatfield

Austin Georgas

Hilary Gleason

Steve Gordon

Andy Grammer

Nathan Graves

Devin Gray

Dana Greaves

Georgia Greene

Robin Greenstein

Lynn Grossman

Harold Alejandro Guerrero
Echavarria

Griffin Haddrill

Julia Hannan

Imogen Heap

Roberto Hermosillo

Marco "Jhny Wzdm" Herrera

Peter Hollens

Danika Holmes

Bruce Houghton

Cherie Hu

Sam Hyken

Gina Iaquinta

ISY

Austin James

Garrett James

Arielle Jasmine

Justin Johnston

Lauren Jones

TJ "Lucidious" Julia

Seth Kallen

Philip Kaplan

Peter Kastaris

Emily Kinney

Artëm Kovalëv

Jordan Kurland

Saturn Lane

Acantha Lang

Dina LaPolt

Val Larsen

Kyle "Circa" Lemaire

Shay Leonia

Joe LePore

Tyson Leslie

Lisa Lester

Andrew Levin

Peter Levinson

Jared Lindbloom

Zack Lodmer

Steve Logan

Emma MacDonald

Ashley Maietta

Jen Malone

Dan Mangan

Axel Mansoor

Nicholas Marks

Kristen Mathe

Tushar Mathur

Adele McAlea

Daniel McCarthy

David McTiernan

Clare Means

Yael Meyer

Jonny Meyers

Jenn Miller

Ricky Montgomery

Kayla "Kaymo" Morgan

Jesse Morris

Christian Nielsen

Raelee Nikole

Ari Nisman

James Numbere

Randy Ojeda

Niraj Pandya

Jun Park

Ashley Patrick

Ed Patrick

Carol Peck

Arnold Pinkhasov

Andria Piperni

Ron Pope

Brian Popowitz

David Potter

DJ Axis Powers

Jenny Powers

Jeff Price

Carey Rayburn

EB Rebel

Jack Rennie

Liz Reznichek

Galina Rin—Death Ingloria

Ross Robey

Rick Rocker

Etan Rosenbloom

Lenni Rosenblum

Gerry Rosenthal

Danny Ross

Greg Ruby

Bill Rusin

Jack Rutter

Jacque Ryal from RYAL

Jen Ryall

A. Sarr

Bryce Savage

Anwar Sawyer

Lauren Scales

Kenny Schick

Dane Schmidt

Maxton Schulte

Stacy Schwartz

Hunter Scott

Jessica Severn

all the members in Shinobi Ninja

James Shotwell

Kid Shreddi

Jennifer Silva

Marty Silverstone

Duke Sims

Ali Spagnola

Andrew Spalter

Sean Stevens

Liam Sullivan

Ryan Sullivan

Effi Summers

DJ Swivel

Benoni Tagoe

Sam Tall

Terminator Dave

Justin "Vibes" Thomas

Suzanne Torrison

Livia Tortella

Allyson Toy

Natalie Tsaldarakis

Brian Vickers

Militia Vox

Madonna Wade-Reed

Eleni Webster

Murray Webster

Adam Weiner

Chris West

Jordan West

Dan Whateley

Fred Wiemer

Alexandre Williams

Kashlee Williams

Sarah M. Williams

Vo Williams

Ben Willis

Lindsay Wolfington

Cory Wong

Calista Wu

Allie X

Yuna

Zaytoven

Jaime Zeluck Hindlin

Austin Zhang

INDEX

■

Page numbers in *italics* refer to illustrations, charts, and graphs.

ABOUT THE AUTHOR

ARI HERSTAND is the CEO and founder of the music business education and artist advocacy company Ari's Take. Started in 2012 as a blog, Ari's Take has become the go-to resource for independent musicians on how to run a successful music career in the new music business. In 2018, he opened the online school Ari's Take Academy (ATA), which brings in experts in the field to teach courses on running successful careers in the new music business. ATA currently has over 5,000 students enrolled.

Herstand is also the host of the Webby Award–winning podcast *The New Music Business*, where he interviews innovators and experts in the music industry. An independent musician who has played over 1,000 shows around the country, he has performed on *The Ellen DeGeneres Show*, has had his music featured in countless TV shows, commercials and films, and has charted in the top 10 on iTunes. He currently leads the immersive funk/soul concert experience Brassroots District.

Herstand has written for many of the top musician trade magazines and websites, including *Music Connection Magazine*, *American Songwriter*, *Digital Music News*, *Playback Magazine*, CD Baby, Tunecore, Roland, Discmakers, ASCAP, Hypebot and others. He has been a featured speaker at SXSW, BBC One's Amplify, NAMM, ASCAP Music Experience, SF and NOLA MusicTech, CD Baby's DIY Musician Conference and in music business classrooms worldwide.